Proceedings of the 2nd Advances in Business Research International Conference

Fauziah Noordin · Abdul Kadir Othman
Erne Suzila Kassim
Editors

Proceedings of the 2nd Advances in Business Research International Conference

ABRIC2016

Springer

Editors
Fauziah Noordin
Universiti Teknologi MARA
Shah Alam
Malaysia

Erne Suzila Kassim
Universiti Teknologi MARA
Shah Alam
Malaysia

Abdul Kadir Othman
Universiti Teknologi MARA
Shah Alam
Malaysia

ISBN 978-981-10-6052-6 ISBN 978-981-10-6053-3 (eBook)
https://doi.org/10.1007/978-981-10-6053-3

Library of Congress Control Number: 2017949147

Printed on acid-free paper

This Springer imprint is published by Springer Nature
The registered company is Springer Nature Singapore Pte Ltd.
The registered company address is: 152 Beach Road, #21-01/04 Gateway East, Singapore 189721, Singapore

This book is dedicated to wonderful readers who want to advance the existing knowledge to the next level through the network of experts.

Prof. Dr. Fauziah Noordin
Dr. Abdul Kadir Othman
Dr. Erne Suzila Kassim

Foreword

"Advancing knowledge, connecting the world" is the right theme to illustrate the importance of knowledge advancement in improving our life. Our today's civilization cannot be achieved without the advancement of knowledge. Another aspect highlighted in the theme is pertaining to connecting the world. It means that knowledge advancement is facilitated when people across the globe are collaborating with each other to create new knowledge. Everyone knows that working in isolation brings little benefit to the people as compared to working in teams where the team can experience outstanding outcome through synergistic effect. Sometimes the desired outcome is difficult to be achieved because of the assimilation process, as one of the reasons. This book is a novel effort to compile the works that were presented in the 2nd Advances in Business Research International Conference, which was successfully held in Langkawi Island, Malaysia, on 16 and 17 November 2016.

The book contains articles written by prolific researchers and authors from various parts of the world, which were organized into four different themes: Economics and Finance, Marketing and Communication, Management and Information Technology in Business. Each theme highlights the latest development in terms of theories, models and practices relevant to specific fields. Each article was well-written, making it easy for the readers to understand the whole write-up, without compromising the quality of a good research article. Readers might ask this question: Why does the book contain different fields of studies together? The answer is simple. Having different fields of studies in one book facilitates the advancement of knowledge to a greater height. Connecting these different fields of studies is expected to generate greater ideas that can be manipulated for the betterment of the human civilization.

This book reflects the great effort put forward by various parties, including authors from various fields of studies, the event organizers, the paper committee and not forgetting the publisher in making sure that the book is timely. The book is considered as a must have reference for the academics, research students and industry players or managers, which serves as a guideline in their effort to make significant contribution in their respective fields. Since new knowledge must be founded on the existing knowledge, this book serves this perspective very well as it provides the basis for other researchers, academics and managers to continue their quest for excellence.

Dr. Abdul Kadir Bin Othman
Universiti Teknologi MARA, Shah Alam, Malaysia

Preface

With the intention to create the network of academics and practitioners (industry players or the managers) for the purpose of sharing knowledge, ideas and best practices, this book has become the main agenda of the conference. From the 2nd Advances in Business Research International Conference that was organized on 16 and 17 November 2016, several articles were chosen to be included in this book based on the quality and the novel contribution in their respective fields of studies. Since conference proceedings are limited in their circulation, having this book published is expected to increase the readership so that the sharing of knowledge can be optimized.

Since the articles in this book address the contemporary issues, theories and models in business and other related fields, disseminating this knowledge to the interested parties is a must. Some people including the academics, students and practitioners are in doubts in identifying the right theories, models and practices to be applied in their work because they cannot find the resources required to assist them. By having this book, academics, research students and practitioners are able to get the latest knowledge so that they can use it to obtain the optimum benefits in their effort to contribute to the betterment of life in their respective fields.

Shah Alam, Malaysia

Fauziah Noordin
Abdul Kadir Othman
Erne Suzila Kassim

Preface

Acknowledgements

This book is the outcome of hard work of many individuals who want to ensure the advancement of knowledge through networks of experts. I would like thank ABRIC 2016 Chairperson, Prof. Dr. Fauziah Noordin, for her leadership that inspires us to move forward. A special thank to Deputy Chairperson 1, Dr. Abdul Kadir Othman, and Deputy Chairperson 2, Dr. Erne Suzila Kasim, for the enduring spirit and effort to keep the planned activities can be achieved on time. I would like to acknowledge the great contribution of each individual below, and this book is not possible without them: Secretary 1, Dr. Idaya Husna Mohd; Secretary 2, Mrs. Rodiah Sharif; Treasurer, Dr. Norlida Jaafar; Promotion Committee, Mr. Mohd Khirzanbadzli A. Rahman, Dr. Norol Hamiza Zamzuri and Mrs. Sarinah Sabar; Website Committee, Mrs. Nur Atiqah Rochin Demong and Mr. Muhamad Naim Husain; Review Committee, Dr. Veera Pandiyan, Mrs. Zarina Abdul Munir, Mrs. Zuraidah Ismail, Mrs. Nur Afizah Muhamad Arifin and Mrs. Nor Azian Abdul Rahman; Journal Committee (ABRIJ), Mrs. Lailatul Faizah Abu Hasan, Mrs. Ainunnazlee Mohd Ali, Mr. Mohammad Zaim Mohd Salleh and Mrs. Emi Normalina Omar; Logistics Committee, Mr. Mohamad Naqiuddin Md Mansor, Mrs. Mumtaz Ahmad, Mr. Mohd Khalid Mohd Abas and Mrs. Mariam Khiri; Accommodation/Registration Committee, Dr. Maimunah Mohd Shah, Dr. Mohd Zulkifli Abdullah, Mrs. Noor Hayati Sarman and Mrs. Ruhayah Juraimi; Colloquium Committee, Dr. Shereen Noranee, Assoc. Prof. Dr. Normala Daud, Assoc. Prof. Dr. Noorlaila Haji Yunus and Mrs. Norlela Mohd Yasin; Event Committee, Mr. Muhammad Hafizi Zamri, Mrs. Kadulliah Ghazali and Mrs. Nor Sara Nadia Muhamad Yunus; Sponsorship Committee, Dr. Nazura Mohd Sayuti, Mr. Irwan Ibrahim and Mr. Afizan Amer; Technical Committee, Mr. Muhammad Faizal Jaafar, Mr. Muhamad Naim Husain and Mr. Syed Suharizad Said Radzwan; Special Commitment, Assoc. Prof. Dr. Md. Mamum Habib, Editor in Chief, International Journal of Supply Chain Management; and Administration, Mrs. Sutinah Kassim.

We would like to express our highest gratitude and appreciation to all contributors of the articles; this book will not be possible without your contribution.

Thank you.

Prof. Dr. Fauziah Noordin
Dr. Abdul Kadir Othman
Dr. Erne Suzila Kassim

Contents

Abbreviations

ADF	Augmented Dickey-Fuller
AQ	Accrual Quality
BFR	Base Financing Rate
BLR	Base Lending Rate
BMKC	Bursa Malaysia Knowledge Centre
BR	Base Rate
CNY	Chinese Renminbi
CPI	Consumer Price Index
CR	Cash Ratio
DEA	Data Envelopment Analysis
DLNFS	Difference Natural Logarithm of Firm Size
DLNIP	Difference Natural Logarithm of Inverse Price
DTPB	Decomposed Theory of Planned Behaviour
EE	Emotional Exhaustion
EMH	Efficient Market Hypothesis
EO	Entrepreneurial Orientation
EOT	Entrepreneurial Orientation Theory
EPU	Economic Planning Unit
EUR	Euro
e-WOM	Electronic Word of Mouth
FAQ	Frequently Asked Questions
FBMKLCI	FTSE Bursa Malaysia Klci
FTSE-BMKLCI	FTSE Bursa Malaysia Composite Index
GDP	Gross Domestic Product
GMM	Generalized Method of Moments
HKSE	Hong Kong Stock Exchange
HPHRPs	High-Performance Human Resource Practices
HPI	Housing Price Index
HPWPs	High Performance Work Practices
HRM	Human Resource Management

IC	Intellectual Capital
ICT	Information and Communication Technology
IEO	Individual Entrepreneurial Orientation
IM	Internal Marketing
IMF	International Monetary Fund
IMI	Investable Market Index
IT	Information Technology
ITL	Intention to Leave
ITU	International Telecommunication Union
JIQ	Job Involvement Questionnaire
JPY	Japanese Yen
KLIBOR	Kuala Lumpur Interbank Offered Rate
KL-PBR RI	Kl-Purpose-Build Office Rental Index
KM	Knowledge Management
LHDN	Lembaga Hasil Dalam Negeri
LMX	Leader Membership Exchange
LNRLS	Natural Logarithm Relative Spread
LNTR	Natural Logarithm Turnover
LNTV	Natural Logarithm Trading Volume
MFIs	Microfinance Institutions
MHP	Myhealth Portal
MOSTI	Ministry of Science, Technology and Innovation
MSCI	Morgan Stanley Capital International
MTDC	Malaysian Technology Development Centre
NAD	National Audit Department
NGOs	Non-Government Organizations
OCB	Organizational Citizenship Behaviour
OLS	Ordinary Least Square Method
OPR	Overnight Policy Rate
PLS-SEM	Partial Least Squares Structural Equation Modeling
PP	And Philip-Perron
QoL	Quality of Life
R&D	Research and Development
RMP	Royal Malaysian Police
S&P 500	Standard and Poor 500
SAARC	South Asian Association for Regional Cooperation
SET	Social Exchange Theory
SMEs	Small and Medium Enterprises
SSE	Shanghai Stock Exchange
TAM	Technology Acceptance Model
TASI	Tadawul All-Share Index
TE	Technical Efficiency
TFP	Total Factor Productivity
TPB	Theory of Planned Behaviour
TRA	Theory of Reasoned Action

TSE	Tokyo Stock Exchange
TV	Trading Volume
UiTM	Universiti Teknologi Mara
US	United States
USD	US Dollar
VAR-GARCH	Vector Autoregressive—Generalized Autoregressive Conditional Heteroscedasticity
WBHIS	Web-Based Health Information Service

Chapter 1
Internal Marketing and Employees' Performance: Relating Marketing Strategies in Human Resource Efforts

Hurul Ain Zainal Abidin, Rosmimah Mohd Roslin and Norlida Kamaluddin

Abstract Internal marketing (IM) as one of the key concepts in the marketing discipline has often been seen as duplicating many of the core understanding of human resource management (HRM). This is predominantly so as the focus of IM is the internal customer of the organization or more precisely the employees. While IM recognizes the importance of treating the internal customers very much like external customers, how this is actually executed within the organizational context is not often conceptualized firmly. This paper establishes the similarities of IM executions with specific HRM practices and relates how these are integrated to influence employee performance. Unlike many previous studies that linked IM with organizational performance or customer satisfaction, this paper proposes to assess the link between IM practices and employees' performance where the focus is essentially on employees' behaviour in terms of their satisfaction in the work place.

Keywords Internal marketing · Employee performance
Human resource management

1.1 Introduction

Marketing efforts carried out by many corporations whose main aim is to garner as much financial gains as possible rarely focus on the internal market as the core customer base. Internal market is essentially the employees of organizations whose involvement in the marketing efforts for satisfying external customers is deemed

H.A. Zainal Abidin (✉) · R. Mohd Roslin
Universiti Teknologi MARA (UiTM), Shah Alam, Malaysia
e-mail: ain_hurul@otmail.com

R. Mohd Roslin
e-mail: rosmimah@salam.uitm.edu.my

N. Kamaluddin
Universiti Teknologi MARA (UiTM), 40450 Shah Alam, Malaysia
e-mail: norlidak@salam.uitm.edu.my

F. Noordin et al. (eds.), *Proceedings of the 2nd Advances in Business Research International Conference*, https://doi.org/10.1007/978-981-10-6053-3_1

crucial for the successful performance of the company (Davoudi and Kaur 2012). However, in recognizing the employees as the internal market, the principle of managing the internal market in the same way as the external markets is often arguable as there are those who do not see how both markets could be handled in similar ways. But it is the employees who are the ones reaching to the external customers and therefore ensuring that the internal market is satisfied in order to satisfy the external market is indeed plausible. It has been established by Gounaris (2008) that internal marketing (IM) efforts are apparent on two major premises. First, the notion that employees' needs must be satisfied before tackling customers' needs is pertinent in addressing IM. This inherently implies that the rules executed in the external market must be used similarly in IM. Berry (1981) establishes that from a managerial perspective, the implementation of IM involves accepting the idea that the internal and external markets of an organization are similar and therefore can be treated in the same manner. Indeed, IM should be addressed as a set of both internal and external exchange relationships where the aim is essentially to benefit the organization in terms of its overall performance (Lings 2010). Yet, employees' performance in relation to the execution of IM efforts by the firms has not been directly linked in earlier studies that look at performances, both at the organizational level and at the individual employee level.

In human resource management (HRM), positive employee performance is a critical aim that managers seek when planning their HR initiatives. Employee performance is a widely used term to imply the wholesomeness of employees' intent towards achieving and completing their tasks or in carrying out tasks that go beyond what is required. HRM stresses that employees' well being and satisfaction in the workplace are important to enhance job performance. This, however, is still widely debated as studies on HRM implementations are often cross-sectional, contrasting and lacking in conclusive evidences (Guest 2011). It is, however, postulated that HR initiatives are aimed at satisfying the internal market to the extent that they will be able to reach out to the customers more effectively. Satisfied employees deliver better services (Schmit and Allscheid 1995) which affects customer confidence positively and contributes to achieving customer loyalty. Thus, for firms that understand the importance of focusing on their IM efforts, the marketing strategies that ensue will definitely have the employees' well being in mind. These firms understand that employees' performance is derived from superior IM efforts which are then translated to the execution of superior customer services by the employees. The association between IM and employees' performance is the context of this conceptual paper in contrast to existing studies where the relationship between IM and customer satisfaction is often the key focus (Aburoub et al. 2011). The implementation of IM efforts entails the systematic execution of internal processes, with the help of marketing management and HRM tools, in order to impose marketing as an internal way of thinking through a consistent orientation that has both customers and personnel in mind (Bruhn 2001).

It has also been established that people is the key factor towards developing the competitive edge for organizations (Caldwell et al. 2015). It is indeed people in the organizations that make the difference and therefore warrant a specific focus as a means of strategizing. As such the direct link between employees' performance with IM efforts is a sensible association. Such an association establishes that management would be able to detect whether the IM steps taken by the organization is fruitful in encouraging better performance or whether there are other factors that would affect performance such as individual employee factors including personality, value and motivation (King and Grace 2012). Knowledge in this area would give management an upper hand not only to balance between the various available IM efforts to get the maximum effect on performance, but at the same time give indications where the concentration of efforts should be in order to maintain optimal performance.

1.2 Literature Review

1.2.1 Internal Marketing

It has been suggested by Cahill (1995) that IM is the philosophy of treating employees as customers and is the strategy of shaping jobs as products that fit human needs. As a process, IM focuses on attracting, developing, motivating and retaining qualified employees through job-related initiatives that make them happy (Aburoub et al. 2011). IM is clarified by Berry and Parasuraman (1991) in terms of viewing employees as internal customers, viewing jobs as internal products, and endeavouring to offer internal products that satisfy the needs and wants of these internal customers while addressing the objectives of the organization (p. 272). On the other hand, Nikbin et al. (2010) defined it as the measure to get all parties involved in providing services to create memorable and enjoyable encounters with customers. Thus, the linkage between the employees and the external customers is clear when specifying the conduct of IM. It is with this understanding in mind that the tools in HR development should be integrated with the marketing initiatives meant for the internal customers of the organizations.

Bateson (1989), in defining IM, indicates the similarities between the process of IM and the marketing exchange process in the examination of the relationship between employee and job. IM is described as '…viewing employees as internal customers, viewing jobs as internal products, and then endeavouring to offer internal products that satisfy the needs and wants of the internal customers while addressing the objectives of the organisation' (p.300). This definition attests to the importance of management to adhere to a firm and effective HRM that will enable the employees to carry out their jobs efficiently while understanding the importance of servicing the customers effectively. A satisfied employee is likely to reflect such satisfaction in the conduct of his/her job, and therefore when management regards the employees to be as important as the external customers, it is likely that satisfaction will be attained by both the internal and external customers.

It is clear that such a proliferation of definitions proves the growing interest among marketers to get employees to adopt the marketing concept of customer orientation and to become part of the organizations' team in the execution of marketing strategies (Joseph 1996). One of the consequences of IM is to increase the organizational commitment of employees, and this should translate to how they perform in their jobs. This in turn leads to increased job satisfaction, job performance and essentially lower turnover of staff. However, Gibson et al. (2003) indicated that these factors are rarely instrumental in bringing about high job attitudes and do not focus on the job itself. They commonly focus on the characteristics of the context in which the job is done. These include working conditions, interpersonal relationships, supervision, company policies, and administration of these policies, effects on the employees' personal life, job security and salary. Job satisfaction, like any other attitude, generally develops over a period of time, as an employee gains more and more information about his organization. However, it is dynamic as the level can decline even more rapidly than it increased.

The importance of IM as a concept has been the focus of many past studies that linked IM initiatives and various benefits that IM brings to the organization including brand/organizational commitment (Burmann and Zeplin 2005, King and Grace 2008 and Nikbin et al. 2010), brand loyalty (Papasolomou-Doukakis and Vrontis 2006), job satisfaction (Nikbin et al. 2010) and brand performance (Punjaisri et al. 2009) as well as gaining support towards brand strategy and implementation (M'zungu et al. 2010). Thus, the possibility of exploring and establishing a relationship between IM and employees' performance is postulated as more views have surfaced in declaring the importance of studying its implications on specific performance.

1.2.2 Employee Performance

Employee performance is interpreted as employees' willingness and devotion to present service quality as well as the desire to perform beyond what is required (Kandampully 2002 and Clark et al. 2009). Previous studies have highlighted the importance of the role played by employees because experience encountered during employee–customer interactions has long-lasting effects (Gull and Ashraf 2012). One of the elements that is used to measure organizational performance is employees' performance through the level of their productivity (Wong and Wong 2007). This includes the quality, quantity, knowledge or creativity of individual towards accomplishing tasks assigned to them. Aguinis (2009), however, asserted that employees' performance does not include the results of an employee's behaviour, but only the behaviours themselves. Performance is about behaviour or what employees do, not about what employees produce or the outcomes of their work. In essence, how employees behave in the work setting is of more relevance to the notion of employees' performance rather than that of productivity. Perceived employees' performance represents the general belief of the employee about his behaviour, and although this may not be directly linked to the organizational performance, contributions to the success of the organization may still exist through the interplay of the employees' behaviours that emanate positive vibes to the organizational environment and ultimately to the external customers with whom they may interact with.

HR initiatives are often described in terms of the various means of handling the organizational workforce or the internal market. It has been proposed by Carlson et al. (2006) that HRM practices that affect performance can be addressed by focusing on the establishment of competitive compensation level, training and development, performance appraisal, recruitment package, and maintaining morale. On the mode of IM, researchers have listed various types of IM methods. King and Grace (2008), for example, stressed on the importance of training, exposure to customer- and market-related information and the existence of conducive work environment. Punjaisari et al. (2009) examines the role of training and employee orientation, the importance of briefings and group meetings and the need for internal communication. In addition, awarding system, supervisor support, empathy, appraisal system and empowerment are also deemed as critical (Shekary et al. 2012), while communication, education and information are cited as the key elements by Quester and Kelly (1999). On another note, established literature also stresses the importance of motivating and developing, educating or training employees (Cahill 1995; Grönroos (1990); Rafiq and Ahmed 1993) as well as attracting, hiring and retaining employees (Berry and Parasuraman 1991). The overlapping of methods described in HRM and IM suggests that both have similar intentions and while the focus on the work force is similar, the intention that these will lead ultimately to some means of customer satisfaction is what binds both disciplines. According to Dunne and Barnes (2000) and Varey (2001), considering human resources as internal customers would be most relevant through the contributions of both the marketing and human resources functions as it reflects the common roots of each discipline in the theory of psychology. The important role of IM is to nurture and develop effective human resources, which imply both IM and HRM are closely related to each other. Bansal et al. (2001) also assert that some relevant aspects of HRM practices in achieving employees' commitment, job satisfaction and trust are related to the success of IM. As such, it makes sense to relate HR practices as means of executing IM initiatives.

1.3 Research Framework

1.3.1 Conceptualizing the HR and IM Framework

It is already established that HRM and IM have overlapping directions and elements and as such could well be linked in a framework that further evaluates the relevance of specific dimensions. For the purpose of conceptualizing the framework, a list of suggested IM efforts established by Jou et al. (2008) is used as the elements to be tested. They are empathy and consideration (paying attention to employees' personal needs), benchmarking (what competitors offer for their employees), job quality and rewarding (the financial and emotional values associated with the employees' job), upward communication (the opportunity for employees to communicate their dissatisfaction or suggestions to their managers), information sharing (venues for managers to convey organizational messages, missions and values to their subordinates) and promotional activities (where the company engages in promotional or public relation activities).

With employees' performance being addressed from the HR perspective (Carlson et al. 2006), the framework conceptualizes the relationship between IM initiatives and performance of the employees in terms of the behaviours displayed as a result of the IM efforts. It is indeed interesting to see how such behaviours may be interpreted when marketing and HR principles are used as the basis to derive the dimensions. Although the IM dimensions appear to be predominantly, HR principles but the fact that it is the employees who are regarded as the internal market provides a novel premise to how the dimensions are conceptualized. Indeed, the employees are now seen as the customer and the marketing principle of addressing customers' needs dominates the establishment of the dimensions. Focusing on the employees as the customers is what sets IM different from the HR perspectives. HR principles look at employees from an organizational angle, while IM dictates that the focus and the orientation of the employees should now be from the stance of the customers. Internal customers may have specific wants and needs that require a differing view of addressing them. The proposed framework is depicted in Fig. 1.1 where the relationship between IM efforts and employees' performance is postulated.

Based on the conceptual framework, the following hypotheses are proposed:

H1: IM efforts influenced employees' performance

H1a: Empathy and consideration displayed by management affect the performance of employees.
H1b: Benchmarking efforts in the assessment of employees affect their performance.
H1c: Job quality influences employees' performance.
H1d: Upward communication by top management affects the performance of employees.
H1e: Information sharing by top management affects the performance of employees.
H1f: Promotional activities involving employees influence their performance.

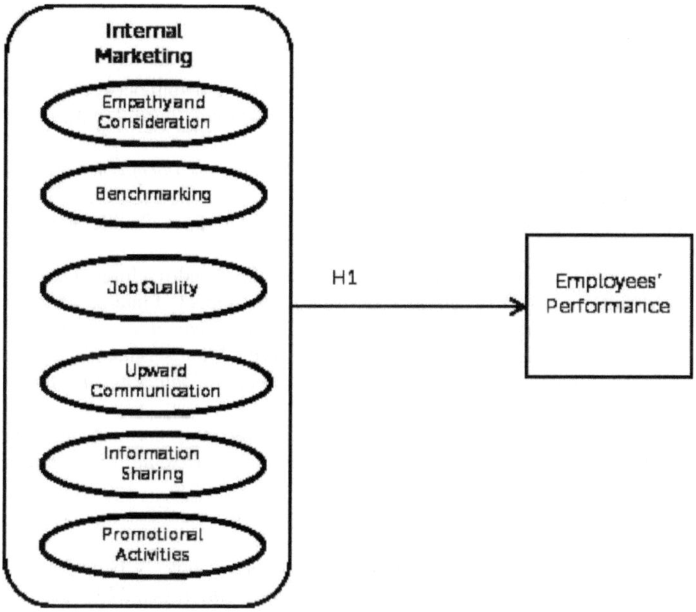

Fig. 1.1 Proposed conceptual framework

1.4 Conclusion

1.4.1 Research Direction

The proposed study may well set the premise for a more robust evaluation of IM and HRM as these are integrated in a more meaningful manner through selected dimensions relevant in both marketing and HR disciplines. It has been established that IM orientation focuses on ways to improve job characteristics such that employee satisfaction increases. The implied assumption from this is that satisfied employees will perform their jobs better and thereby indirectly impact customer satisfaction (Berry 1981). This then paves the way for a more structured study that addresses the specific elements that looks at both HRM and IM. Indeed, job satisfaction as one key HR element does not receive clear support in its relationship with IM orientation (Salem 2013). Thus, it is therefore befitting to extend the present literature on both IM and HRM by encompassing the relevant dimensions and integrating them in a research setting that would allow for a clear understanding of both these disciplines.

References

Aburoub, S. A. S., Hersh, A. M., & Aladwan, K. (2011). Relationship between internal marketing and service quality with customers' satisfaction. *International Journal of Marketing Studies, 3* (2), May, 107–118.

Ahmed, P., & Rafiq, M. (2002). *Internal Marketing: Tools and Concepts for Customer-Focused Management*. Chicago: Taylor & Francis.

Aguinis, H. (2009). *Performance Management* (2nd ed.). Upper Saddle River: NJ, Pearson Education Inc.

Bateson, J. E. G. (1989). Managing Services Marketing: Text and readings, Dryden.

Bansal, H. S., Mendelson, M. B., & Sharma, B. (2001). The Impact of internal marketing activities on external marketing outcomes. *Journal of Quality Management, 6,* 61–76.

Berry, L. L. (1981). The employee as a customer. *Journal of Retail Banking., 3*(2), 33–44.

Berry, L. L., & Parasuraman, A. (1991). *Marketing Services: Competing through Quality*. New York: The Free Press.

Bouranta, N., Chitiris, L., & Paravantis, J. (2009). The relationship between internal and external service quality. *International Journal of Contemporary Hospitality Management, 21*(3), 275–293.

Bruhn, M. (2001). *Orienting toward clients – the base for a successful business*. Bucharest: Economic Publishing.

Burmann, C., & Zeplin, S. (2005). Building brand commitment: A behavioural approach to internal brand management. *Journal of Brand Management, 12*(4), 279–300.

Cahill, D. (1995). The managerial implications of the learning organization: A new tool for internal marketing. *Journal of Services Marketing, 9*(4), 43–51.

Caldwell, C., Licona, B., & Floyd, L. A. (2015). Internal marketing to achieve competitive advantage. *International Business and Management, 10*(1), 1–8.

Carlson, D. S., Kacmar, M. K., Wayne, J. H., & Grzywacz, J. G. (2006). Measuring the positive side of the work-family interface: Development and validation of a work-family enrichment scale. *Journal of Vocational Behavior, 68*(1), 131–164.

Clark, R. A., Hartline, M. D., & Jones, K. C. (2009). The effect of leadership style on hotel employees' commitment to service quality. *Cornell Hospitality Quarterly, 50,* 209–231.

Davoudi, S. M. M., & Kaur, R. (2012). The link between marketing and human resource management, *Journal of Economics and Management, 1*(2), May, 59–72.

Dunne, P. A., & Barnes, J. G. (2000). Internal marketing – A relationships and value creation view. In R. J. Varey & B. R. Lewis (Eds.), *Internal Marketing: Directions for Management*. London: Routledge.

Gibson, J. L., Ivancevich, J. M., Donnelly, J. H., & Konopaske, R. (2003). *Organizations: Behavior, structure, processes* (11th ed.). McGraw Hill-Irwin: IL.

Gounaris, S. (2008). The notion of internal market orientation and employee job satisfaction: Some preliminary evidence, *Journal of Services Marketing, 22*(1), 68–90.

Gull, S., & Ashraf, S. M. (2012). Impact of Internal Branding on Service Employees' Quality Commitment – Study on Education Sector of Pakistan. *International Journal of Business and Social Science, 3*(14), 302–311.

Grönroos, C. (1990). Relationship Approach to the Marketing Function in Service Contexts: The Marketing and Organizational Behavior Interface. *Journal of Business Research, 20*(1), 3–12.

Guest, D. E. (2011). Human resource management and performance: still searching for some answers. *Journal of Human Resource Management, 21*(1), 3–13.

Hashim, R. A., & Mahmood, R. (2011). Comparing commitment to service quality among academic staffs' in private and public Malaysian universities. *Journal of International Management Studies, 6*(1), 1–8.

Jou, J. Y. H., Chou, C. K., & Fu, F. L. (2008). Development of an instrument to measure internal marketing concept. *The Journal of Applied Management and Entrepreneurship, 13*(3), 66–79.

Joseph, W. B. (1996). Internal marketing builds service quality. *Marketing Review., 16*(3), 54–59.

Kandampully, J. (2002). *Service Management the New Paradigm in Hospitality.* Australia: Pearson Education.

King, C., & Grace, D. (2012). Examining the Antecedents of Positive Employee Brand-Related Attitudes and Behaviours. *European Journal of Marketing, 46*(3/4), 469–488.

King, C., & Grace, D. (2008). Internal Branding: Exploring the Employees' Perspective. *Journal of Brand Management, 15*(5), 358–372.

Liao, J.F. (2009). The effects of Internal Marketing on Customer Orientation in the Banking Industry. ProQuest Dissertations and Theses.

Lings, I. N. (2010). Internal Market Orientation and Market-oriented Behaviours. *Journal of Service Management, 21*(3), 321–343.

M'Zungu, S. D. M., Merrilees, B., & Miller, D. (2010). Brand management to protect brand equity: A conceptual model. *Journal of Brand Management, 17*(8), 605–617.

Nikbin, D., Saad, N. N., & Ismail, I. (2010). The Relationship between Internal Marketing and Implementation of Strategic Orientations in Malaysian Service Industry. *International Journal of Business and Management Science, 3*(1), 17–37.

Papasolomou, I., & Vrontis, D. (2006). Building corporate branding through internal marketing: the case of the UK retail bank industry. *Journal of Product & Brand Management, 15*(1), 37–47.

Punjaisri, K., Evanschitzky, H., & Wilson, A. (2009). Internal branding: an enabler of employees' brand-supporting behaviours. *Journal of Service Management, 20*(2), 209–226.

Quester, P. G., & Kelly, A. (1999). Internal Practices in the Australian Financial Sector: An Exploratory Study. *Journal of Applied Management Studies, 8*(2), 217–229.

Ramseook-Munhurrun, P., & Nundlal, P. (2013). Service Quality Measurement for Secondary School Setting. *Quality Assurance in Education, 21*(4), 387–401.

Salem, K. M. O. (2013). The relationship between internal marketing orientation and employee job satisfaction in public sector. *International Journal of Learning and Development, 3*(5), 111–120.

Schmit, M. J., & Allscheid, S. P. (1995). Employee attitudes and customer satisfaction: making theoretical and empirical connections. *Personnel Psychology, 48,* 521–532.

Varey, R. J. (2001). Internal marketing communication. In: Marketing communication, Taylor & Francis Ltd., Abingdon.

Wong, W. P., & Wong, K. Y. (2007). Supply chain performance measurement system using DEA modelling. *Industrial Management and Data Systems, 107*(3), 361–381.

Chapter 2
Individual Entrepreneurial Orientation and Talent Retention of Engineers: A Pilot Survey

Idris Osman, Fauziah Noordin and Normala Daud

Abstract Solving a crucial shortage of engineers in the internal labour market and a turnover cost are the major concerns to reassess a strong determination of engineers' behavioural expectations towards current employment. A recent retention problem occurred when organisations rarely highlighted engineers as intrapreneurs. Consequently, engineers' entrepreneurial behaviours are slowly undebated and limited action has been taken to assess individual entrepreneurial orientation (IEO) to predict years that remain among talented engineers. Therefore, the objective of this study is to assess the items used for IEO in predicting retention outcome (intention to stay) among Malaysian engineers in manufacturing companies. This study adopted IEO and talent retention (intention to stay) items and a survey that recruited 110 engineers based on convenience sampling technique. Participants were recruited from various manufacturing companies located in Malaysia. Strong evidence was found that innovativeness (*0.766*), proactiveness (*0.793*), risk-taking (*0.830*) and autonomy (*0.884*) items were reliable (*>0.70*) for predicting the engineers' intention to stay (*0.879*). Developing engineers with IEO behaviours and organisations can closely monitor the mobility of engineers to other jobs. The links between IEO and talent retention interpret a better solution to meet engineers' career orientations and positive behavioural intentions.

Keywords Individual entrepreneurial orientation · Talent retention · Engineers Intrapreneurs

I. Osman (✉) · F. Noordin · N. Daud
Faculty of Business and Management, Universiti Teknologi MARA (UiTM), 40450 Shah Alam, Selangor, Malaysia
e-mail: idrisphd2015@gmail.com

F. Noordin
e-mail: fauziah716@salam.uitm.edu.my

N. Daud
e-mail: normala648@salam.uitm.edu.my

F. Noordin et al. (eds.), *Proceedings of the 2nd Advances in Business Research International Conference*, https://doi.org/10.1007/978-981-10-6053-3_2

2.1 Introduction

Matching an entrepreneurial orientation (EO) to engineers' behaviours is a strategic process in transforming talents into organisational core assets. Still, talents remain crucial when organisations realise that talent substances become more valuable, unique and hardest to imitate (Govaerts et al. 2011; Tansley 2011). Engineering talents move flexibly, and a talented engineer brings his or her talents in a new organisation if there is no reciprocity recognition that exists between engineers and current employers. Getting engineers to stay depends on desirable attitudes and behaviours from the initial staffing process to assess engineers' capacity to perform tasks. Ideally, staffing system requires exceptional organisational strategy (e.g. develop talent) to explore the engineers' self-determination, an expansion of how engineers' determine his or her engineering career path orientations. Engineers' behavioural intentions will fully develop from his or her discretions to determine the destination to which talents must be capitalised. The appropriate ways of many talented engineers which are frequently discussed are how his or her entrepreneurial behaviours influence positive behavioural intentions towards current employments.

Unless attention is paid to EO, talented engineers who leave voluntarily and a turnover cost may become challenging issues. An engineer who is viewed as a talented individual of the organisation has possibly vetted his current employers to create a special engineering environment to support entrepreneurial behaviours. Theoretically, developing internal entrepreneurial environment is linked to the entrepreneurial orientation theory (EOT), which consents organisational business strategies to commit with the basis of entrepreneurial processes, practices and decision-making activities (Covin and Slevin 1986; Lumpkin and Dess 1996; Rauch et al. 2009). The business strategy entails innovativeness, proactiveness, risk-taking, autonomy and competitive aggressiveness behaviours to perform, as all these behaviours are associated with individual entrepreneurial traits, attitudes and behaviours (Bolton and Lane 2012; Covin and Slevin 1989; Lumpkin et al. 1996). Research suggests focusing on a matching EO as individual behaviours affect organisational readiness to produce innovativeness and competitiveness (Wu 2009). As expectations are a cause to change an individual's behavioural intention, individual entrepreneurial orientation (IEO) is evaluated and developed to improve engineers' attitudes and behaviours towards the successful internal entrepreneurial activities of an organisation.

IEO has been a secondary issue for many organisations in predicting years that remain among talented engineers. From the organisational level, EO has been positively connected to organisational performance. Consequently, dependency on IEO behaviours to predict engineers' retention has slowly condensed. Previous gaps earlier identified rare highlighted engineers as intrapreneurs, a person who is actively involved in entrepreneurial activities within an organisational area. Less exposure of IEO into actual implementation affects the engineers' core passions on engineering orientations, such as technical knowledge, solving technical problems and innovating activities. Once these elements are gone, engineers' will probably turn his or her weak interests to support innovativeness, creativity and capability to become an intrapreneur. Organisations, however, have limited options to pursue competitive business strategies without a link between IEO and intrapreneurs' behaviours to respond to uncertainties in the business environment and challenges. Thus, the main objective of this pilot study is to measure the IEO major dimensions (e.g. innovativeness, proactiveness, risk-taking and autonomy) in predicting the engineers' intention to stay with the same employment.

2.2 Literature Review

The underlying theory to emphasise entrepreneurial behaviours of an individual who is likely to remain in the job can be generated from the EO theory (EOT). Though none of the specific studies confirmed direct effect of EOT to an individual's outcome (e.g. retention), the process of successful EO must consider intrapreneurial behaviours of the organisational members who use creativity, innovativeness, capability and competency to perform tasks and to solve problems. EOT generates core elements, namely innovativeness, proactiveness, autonomy, risk-taking and competitive aggressiveness (Covin et al. 1989; Lumpkin et al. 1996). Several researchers who have examined the dominant elements of EOT found that innovativeness, proactiveness and risk-taking are important substances for organisational performance (Antoncic and Hisrich 2001; Covin et al. 1989; Entebang et al. 2010; Jia, Wang and Yu 2014; Kropp et al. 2006). Only a few available empirical studies on IEO have addressed the needs of an individual's (e.g. students, farmers) perception on EO towards entrepreneurial intentions and individual performance (Bolton et al. 2012; Dingilian 2015; Wu 2009).

Returning to what core elements affect engineers to perform entrepreneurially, this present study relates to the engineers' pure behaviours, traits and attitudes. As an intrapreneur, an engineer represents a person who has innovating ideas, has strategies for technology development and develops thoughts and freedom to be more creative and original (Alavi et al. 2012; Igbaria and Siegel 1992; Kharbanda et al. 1990; McDonnell and O'Neill 2009; Menzel et al. 2007; Williamson et al. 2013). Attention is also given to the engineers' creativity in solving technical and non-technical problems and the ability to think conceptually, and the ability to adapt changes and deal with circumstances (Champbell et al. 2012; Kaewsri and Tongthong 2013; Kennedy and Daim 2010). Lastly, an engineer desires autonomy in his or her works to experience interesting and challenging tasks. Often, these entrepreneurial behaviours, namely innovativeness, proactiveness, risk-taking and autonomy, are all supported by research findings to optimise the engineers' behavioural positive impact on retention (e.g. intention to stay) outcomes.

2.2.1 IEO and Talent Retention of Engineers

One possibility of engineers' leaving their current employers is their unawareness of the evaluation of entrepreneurial behavioural intentions to be used in his or her daily task performance. The measurement used to assess IEO is necessary to expect the extent of individual behavioural patterns to react within an organisation. Prior research findings on IEO have argued that elements of EO are potentially applied for predicting positive individual performance and behavioural intentions. Retention, for example, is closely linked to how an individual's behaviour affects his or her behavioural intentions. This link is called talent retention, a process to encourage positive behavioural intentions of talented individuals to remain in the same employment (Gangrade et al. 2014; Sahi and Mahajan 2014). A classic thought of behavioural intentions (e.g. intention to stay or leave) involves the individual's psychological, cognitive and behavioural aspects (Takase 2010). These aspects are interrelated with one another, beginning from fulfilling the psychological needs to reflect to cognitive needs and producing an actual decision, either to stay or to leave.

How far can IEO items be predicted for an engineer's intention to stay? The development of IEO items was conceptually defined at an individual level as a pre-determinant to measure entrepreneurs from different directions. Kollmann et al. (2007) developed several propositions from a cross-cultural framework to assess an IEO from the areas of cultural environment, political and legal environment, macroeconomic environment and micro environment. They argued that EO constructs probably need to be emphasised and can be transferred to the individual level. Bolton et al. (2012) clearly determined three core elements of IEO, and ten items of the five-point Likert scales *(innovativeness—four items; proactiveness—three items; and risk-taking—three items*) were identified and developed. Based on 1,100 samples, only these three main items were considered consistent, innovative (α—*0.80*); proactive (α—*0.765*); and risk-taking (α—*0.767*). Unfortunately, items for autonomy *(α—0.208)* and competitive aggressiveness *(α—0.585)* were not considered due to low consistency. The significant implication of this study revealed that IEO constructs are relevant for measuring an individual's entrepreneurial behaviour and frequently measuring autonomy and competitive aggressiveness items that will increase the factor loadings. Vast implication from this study has extended to the interest from other researchers to study IEO from different perspectives. Recently, Dingilian (2015) adopted ten items of Bolton et al. (2012) IEO to measure farmers' and faculty members' entrepreneurial behaviours, and the results of consistency of innovativeness, proactiveness and risk-taking items were similarly ranged between 0.70 and 0.75.

Talent retention. The separation between core talents and positive behavioural intentions will probably affect the engineers' attitudinal aspect, since this behavioural pattern is complex to measure. Igbaria and Siegel (1992) found that several retention factors are related to the engineers' decision to stay; for example, task characteristics (e.g. task challenging) and intention to leave are negatively related

($r = -0.39; -0.37; p = <0.001$). Engineers' turnover can be controlled by assigning interesting task and providing feedback, and encouraging the engineers' creativity and originality. Such efforts can be found in the studies of Abdull Rahman (2012) and George (2015) which highlighted the engineers' and professionals' motivation to remain. Abdull Rahman (2012) measured 226 engineers' intention to stay with the seven items on the seven-point Likert scale ($\alpha = 0.72; SD = 0.60$). Seven statements are used to measure the engineers' intention to stay which included "*I will remain with this organisation indefinitely*" and "*I plan to stay here a long time*". On the other hand, George (2015) focused on retention factors (e.g. autonomy, creativity) of professional workers, and a strong association was found between these factors and the intention to remain ($\alpha = 0.82; M = 3.22; SD = 0.54$). These separate studies measured retention items as dependent variables to predict the actual individual engineer's intention to remain.

2.3 Methodology

The data were collected from the manufacturing companies in Malaysia. A total of 110 engineers were recruited based on convenience sampling method. A self-administered survey was distributed to engineers who are registered under the Board of Engineers Malaysia (BEM). The participants were anonymous and voluntary, and the participation was assured that all responses would be confidential. The human resource (HR) representatives from the manufacturing companies were contacted to seek an approval before distributing the survey instruments. The participants consisted of graduate engineers (87.9%), and a majority of the participants were Malays (84.8%), males (67.4%) and ages ranged between 25 and 29 years (44.7%). In regard to the highest academic qualification, 76.5% of the participants obtained a Bachelors Degree, 12.1% a Masters Degree and 9.1% a Diploma. The largest number of participants was employed for 2–5 years (37.1%), and 39.4% of the participants held the same position for a period of 2–5 years. Majority of the participants are working in Selangor (50%), whilst 34.1% of the participants are currently attached with petroleum/chemical industries and 28.0% for the electrical and electronics industries.

2.3.1 Measures

This pilot study contains two main constructs, namely IEO (innovativeness, proactiveness, risk-taking and autonomy) and talent retention (intention to stay). The scales for measuring the four dimensions of IEO were derived from the previous literatures on EO (Bolton et al. 2012; Covin et al. 1989; Lumpkin et al. 1996; Wu 2009). This study adopted the ten-item innovativeness, seven-item proactiveness, nine-item risk-taking and eight-item autonomy scales of the IEO. All items used for measuring these dimensions were based on a seven-point Likert scale with 1 representing strongly disagree and 7 representing strongly agree. Cronbach's α of innovativeness scale was 0.766, proactiveness (0.793), risk-taking (0.830) and autonomy (0.884), indicating that the instruments were reliable *(>0.70)*. To measure talent retention, this study formulated the six-item scales from Govaerts et al. (2011). The sample items included "*If I wanted to do another job or function, I would firstly, look at the possibilities within this company*" and "*If it were up to me, I will definitely be working for this company for the next five years*". Cronbach's α of this scale was 0.879. The participants' responses were analysed on a seven-point Likert scale, ranging from 1 (*strongly disagree*) to 7 (*strongly agree*).

2.4 Results

This study was employed the SPSS 22.0 to assess the mean, standard deviation, factor loading and the reliability of the items. The scores from the 110 engineers are presented in Table 2.1. On a seven-item Likert scale, mean values for IEO dimensions and talent retention were ranged from 4.7 to 5.3 (*innovativeness—4.918, SD ± 0.5; proactiveness—5.195, SD ± 0.6; risk-taking—4.796, SD ± 0.7; autonomy—5.327, SD ± 0.6; intention to stay—5.227, SD ± 0.8*), respectively.

Table 2.2 presents the factor loadings for IEO and talent retention. An exploratory factor analysis (EFA) was conducted for each IEO and talent retention item. From the 40 items, only 39 were considered for the analysis. The item loading ranged from 0.40 to 0.70 (innovativeness), 0.5 to 0.70 (proactiveness), 0.40 to 0.70 (risk-taking), 0.50 to 0.80 (autonomy) and 0.70 to 0.80 (intention to stay). Factor loadings below 0.40 were not included for analysis; thus, the remaining items that were higher than 0.32 were considered as appropriate variables (Tabachinick and Fidell 1996). Only one item was removed from the analysis (*A12* = *−0.224*), as this item was lower than 0.32. The values of Cronbach's alpha were greater than 0.70, indicating that all items used had high internal consistency. Table 2.2 shows the Cronbach's alpha values for IEO and talent retention variables. The Cronbach's

Table 2.1 Means and standard deviations for IEO and talent retention

Variables	*N*	Mean*	Std. Dev
IEO			
(a) Innovativeness	*110*	4.918	0.5870
(b) Proactiveness	*110*	5.195	0.6109
(c) Risk-taking	*110*	4.796	0.7023
(d) Autonomy	*110*	5.327	0.6961
Talent retention			
(a) Intention to stay	*110*	5.227	0.8145

**Responses to each are made on a seven-point scale, ranging from 1 (strongly disagree) to 7 (strongly agree)*

Table 2.2 Results of the factor loadings and Cronbach's alpha of the IEO and talent retention (*N-110*)

Constructs/Sources	No. of items	Items	Factor loading	Cronbach's alpha
IEO				
(a) Innovativeness (INNO)	Ten items	*INNO1*	0.468	*0.766*
		INNO2	−0.224	
		INNO3	0.680	
		INNO4	0.596	
		INNO5	0.817	
		INNO6	0.677	
		INNO7	0.769	
		INNO8	0.620	
		INNO9	0.693	
		INNO10	0.662	
(b) Proactiveness (PROAC)	Seven items	*PROAC1*	0.616	*0.793*
		PROAC2	0.846	
		PROAC3	0.712	
		PROAC4	0.602	
		PROAC5	0.550	
		PROAC6	0.640	
		PROAC7	0.723	
(c)Risk-taking (RISK)	Nine items	*RISK1*	0.405	*0.830*
		RISK2	0.703	
		RISK3	0.681	
		RISK4	0.678	
		RISK5	0.800	
		RISK6	0.797	
		RISK7	0.709	
		RISK8	0.686	
		RISK9	0.488	
(d) Autonomy (AUTO)	Eight items	*AUTO1*	0.667	*0.884*
		AUTO2	0.739	
		AUTO3	0.777	
		AUTO4	0.679	
		AUTO5	0.775	
		AUTO6	0.773	
		AUTO7	0.736	
		AUTO8	0.805	
Talent retention				
(a) Intention to stay (ITS)	Six items	*ITS1*	0.771	*0.879*
		ITS2	0.673	
		ITS3	0.870	
		ITS4	0.828	
		ITS5	0.779	
		ITS6	0.815	

alpha values of IEO dimensions were above 0.7 (innovativeness—0.766; proactiveness—0.793; risk-taking—0.830; and autonomy—0.884), whilst talent retention (intention to stay) was 0.879.

2.5 Discussion

The purpose of this study was to assess the IEO items for predicting retention (intention to stay) among engineers in manufacturing organisations. The main results described that the IEO items were reliable *(>0.70*) and beneficial for determining the engineers' positive behavioural intention towards their current employment. This study postulates that IEO and engineers' behaviours are interconnected, the more entrepreneurial activities demonstrate within engineering-related tasks, and the higher will the intention to stay be. An employer needs more intrapreneurs to build an innovative environment, a freedom to generate ideas and thoughts, and producing exceptional characteristics for being talented intrapreneurs. As an agent of change, an engineer exposes his or her self to deal with uncertain situations and risks, the major contributions of analysing technical-related problems and transforming those into challenging and interesting tasks. Two-way relationships between engineers and employers about flexibility and innovation are the core elements of reciprocity that must exit within the organisational area. The recognition of engineers as intrapreneurs and considering principles of EO (e.g. innovativeness, autonomy) will integrate inflow talents and lock internal talent mobility.

IEO and talent retention focus on recognising the engineers' entrepreneurial behaviours that will be considered if they remain in the same employment, along with a positive behavioural intention. The present results will help in determining positive behavioural intentions (e.g. intention to stay) for engineers to fully utilise entrepreneurial activities and act as intrapreneurs within the organisational area. It is further assumed that these entrepreneurial behaviours are known as catalysts for talented engineers to spend and transfer his or her talents throughout the entire employment. This study responds to core determinate behaviours of entrepreneurial orientation by determining how intrapreneurial behaviours can predict the engineers' intention to stay. The development of IEO on engineers' positive behavioural intention contributes to the body of knowledge of the link between innovativeness, proactiveness, risk-taking and autonomy and retention. When engineers leave their current employer, he or she has already developed the knowledge, skills, experience and expertise, and will transfer those elements in the new organisations. This is a crucial phase of the talents mobility, in which the engineering path orientations are created and new behavioural expectations will be developed.

Detailed discussions of the process to encourage engineering talents remain the same jobs that are confronted with several contemporary issues. First, the upward mobility of engineers is related to technology forces which deny labour as a main source. Second is the shortage of engineering talents in the internal labour market, and third is tasks challenging for acquiring superior technical knowledge. In a sense, it is clearly possible that exploring retention strategies did mean organisations really focus on an individual engineer's behavioural expectations. The efforts to study the engineers' retention have contributed to encouraging the engineers' positive behavioural action. Also, unspecific retention factors have unlocked wider gaps for future researchers to match engineers with behavioural-related intentions. In some areas, IEO supports individual entrepreneurial intentions and actions towards implementing entrepreneurial behaviours that have been proposed by several authors. For example, Kollmann et al. (2007) conceptualised IEO and the cultural environment, political, micro- and macroeconomy that potentially affects entrepreneurial behaviours of employees within the organisation. Claims of IEO eventually require higher individual intentions to develop entrepreneurial intention and recognise opportunity recognition (Wu 2009). Enforcing IEO is an initial step to develop entrepreneurial intentions, and the unidimensionality constructs (e.g. innovativeness, proactiveness, risk-taking and autonomy) permit students, business practitioners and employees to act as entrepreneurs within an organisation (Bolton et al. 2012; Kollmann et al. 2007; Wu 2009).

2.6 Conclusion

The links between engineers and IEO provide a coordination to prepare engineers as intrapreneurs within organisational area. The purpose of matching engineers with IEO is desired behaviours; at the optimum, an intrapreneur's greater performance will enjoy performing challenging tasks and a freedom to be a creative employee (Igbaria et al. 1999). The dual engineers–intrapreneurs behaviour creates potential advantages for engineers to think conceptually as an agent of change and commonly determine career orientations (Kharbanda et al. 1990; Menzel et al. 2007). The best conclusion is that opportunity for clear entrepreneurial paths has caused less mobility of engineers looking to other jobs (Tremblay et al. 2002). Of course, to ensure that engineers remain in the same employment includes establishing engineers with technical and EO, including the management of career orientations that will possibly increase engineers' perception of his or her creativeness towards generating innovative ideas. This process, however, requires organisational structures to promote innovative ideas, define a strategic focus to foster innovative efforts, knowing where and how innovative ideas will be used, optimise organisational resources to support innovative ideas and provide a platform of competitive environment for increasing engineers' job satisfaction and retention (Kharbanda et al. 1990).

Retention (e.g. intention to stay) is an ultimate outcome that has been established in the way of core engineers' behaviours to act as an intrapreneur. Primary characteristics of engineers as intrapreneurs involve innovativeness, proactiveness, risk-taking and autonomy behaviour. Innovativeness will influence the engineers' willingness to develop innovate ideas and transform them into tasks and development of products. Mature engineers are attracted by proactive behaviour, the initiative to improve current circumstances that will involve challenges to adapt the present changes. Expert engineers can be produced by allowing them to take risks, willingness of engineers' to tolerate uncertainties and mistakes subject to handling engineering-related problems. Lastly, engineers are very demanding in generating ideas; as a result, autonomy increases the engineers' power to make decisions towards jobs and he or she has freedom to control task-related matters (Dess and Lumpkin 2005; Lumpkin et al. 1996). Engineers with specialised engineering skills have clearly determined his or her career targets, and the same time, to improve the ability to balance acceptable risks, controlling situations, innovating ideas and proactively seeking opportunities.

A talent retention study becomes, in essence, a channel to guide researchers, policy makers and employers to assess talented individuals' behavioural expectations towards employment. The assessment on engineer's characteristics and behaviours is emphasised to ensure that the entrepreneurial spirit is continuously developed. One major implication of this study extends the use of IEO in predicting the engineers' retention decision. IEO must be exercised in controlling and decreasing the amount of voluntarily turnover among talented engineers. Yet, there is less research carried out in IEO and talent retention, so this study is necessary to understand the engineers' entrepreneurial behaviour expectations. In summary, solutions to the retention problems of engineers require a continuous organisational assessment towards the engineers' employment expectations. Behaviour, too, is the crucial developmental process to match the engineers with EO, and specific action must be taken to consider the new competitive retention strategies that will shape all engineers' positive behavioural intentions.

References

Abdull Rahman, R. H. (2012). Malaysian firms' role in retaining engineers. *The Economic and Labour Relations Review, 23*(4), 57–78.

Alavi, S. B., Moteabbed, S., & Arasti, M. R. (2012). A qualitative investigation of career orientations of a sample of Iranian software engineers. *Scientia Iranica, 19*(3), 662–673.

Antoncic, B., & Hisrich, R. D. (2001). Intrapreneurship: construct refinement and cross-cultural validation.*Journal of Business Venturing*, *16*, 495–527.

Bolton, D. L., & Lane, M. D. (2012). Individual entrepreneurial orientation: Development of a measurement instrument. *Education and Training, 54*(2/3), 219–233.

Campbell, R. I., Gluesing, J., & Perelli, S. (2012). Mindfulness and product failure management: An engineering epistemology. *International Journal Of Quality & Reliability Management, 29*(6), 642–665.

Covin, J. G., & Slevin, D. P. (1986). The development and testing of an organizational-level entrepreneurship scale. In R. Ronstadt, et al. (Ed.), *Frontiers of entrepreneurship research*, Babson College, Wellesley, MA, 628−639.

Covin, J. G., & Slevin, D. P. (1989). Strategic management of small firms in hostile and benign environments. *Strategic Management Journal*, *10*, 75–87.

Dess, G. G., & Lumpkin, G. T. (2005). The role of entrepreneurial orientation in stimulating effective corporate entrepreneurship. *Academy of Management Executive*, *19*(1), 147-56.

Dingilian, G. (2015). *Exploring group differences in individual entrepreneurial orientation between farmers with distinct agricultural conservation practices*. Unpublished Doctoral Dissertation, Northcentral University, ProQuest Dissertations Publishing.

Entebang, H., Harrison, R. T., & Run, E. C. (2010). Entrepreneurial orientation of public enterprises in Malaysia. *Business Strategy Series, 11*(2), 75–77.

Gangrade, D., Dubey, S., & Chouhan, O. (2014). Talent retention: Winning competitive edge (a study in academic sector). *Envision a Monthly Referred Journal of Management and IT, 1*(1).

George, C. (2015). Retaining professional workers: What makes them stay? *Employee Relations, 37*(1), 102–121.

Govaerts, N., Kyndt, E., Dochy, F., & Baert, H. (2011). Influence of learning and working climate on the retention of talented employees. *Journal of Workplace Learning, 23*(1), 35–55.

Igbaria, M., & Siegel, S. R. (1992). An examination of the antecedents of turnover propensity of engineers: An integrated model. *Journal of Engineering and Technology Management, 9*, 101–126.

Igbaria, M., Kassicieh, S. K., & Silver, M. (1999). Career orientations and career success among research, and development and engineering professionals. *Journal of Engineering Technology Management, 16,* 29–54.

Jia, J., Wang, G., & Yu, X. Z. X. (2014). Exploring the relationship between entrepreneurial orientation and corporate performance. *Nankai Business Review International*, *5*(3), 326–344.

Kaewsri, N., & Tongthong, T. (2013). Professional development of female engineers in the Thai construction industry. *Procedia-Social and Behavioral Sciences, 88*, 291–298.

Kennedy, E., & Daim, T. U. (2010). A strategy to assist management in workforce engagement and employee retention in the high tech engineering environment. *Evaluation and Program Planning, 33,* 468–476.

Kharbanda, O. P., & Stallworthy, E. A. (1990). Management for Engineers. *International Journal of Operations and Production Management, 10*(6), 2–91.

Kollman, T., Christofor, J., & Kuckertz, A. (2007). Explaining individual entrepreneurial orientation: conceptualisation of a cross-cultural research framework. *International Journal of Entrepreneurship and Small Business, 4*(3), 325–340.

Kropp, F., Lindsay, N. J., & Shoham, A. (2006). Entrepreneurial, market, and learning orientations and international entrepreneurial business venture performance in South African firms. *International Marketing Review, 23*(5), 504–523.

Lumpkin, G. T., & Dess, G. G. (1996). Clarifying the entrepreneurial orientation construct and linking it to performance. *Academy of Management Review, 21*(1), 135–172.

McDonnell, L., & O'Neill, D. (2009). Developing tomorrow's engineers: A case study in instrument engineering. *Education and Training, 51*(3), 210–214.

Menzel, H. C., Aaltio, I., & Ulijn, J. M. (2007). On the way to creativity: Engineers as intrapreneurs in organizations. *Technovation, 27,* 732–743.

Rauch, A., Wiklund, J., Lumpkin, G. T., & Frese, M. (2009). Entrepreneurship orientation and business performance: An assessment of past research and suggestions for the future. *Entrepreneurship Theory & Practice, 33*(3), 518–528.

Sahi, G. K., & Mahajan, R. (2014). Employees' organisational commitment and its impact on their actual turnover behaviour through behavioural intentions. *Asia Pacific Journal of Marketing and Logistics*, *26*(4), 621–646.

Tabachinick, B., & Fidell, L. (1996). *Using Multivariate statistics* (3rd ed.). New York: HarpCollins College Publishers.

Takase, M. (2010). A concept analysis of turnover intention: Implications for nursing management. *Collegian, 17*, 3–12.

Tansley, C. (2011). What do we mean by the term "talent" in talent management? *Industrial and Commercial Training, 43*(5), 266–274.

Tremblay, M., Wils, T., & Proulx, C. (2002). Determinants of career path preferences among Canadian engineers. *Journal of Engineering Technology Management, 19,* 1–23.

Williamson, J. M., Lounsbury, J. W., & Han, L. D. (2013). Key personality traits of engineers for innovation and technology development. *Journal of Engineering Technology Management, 30,* 157–168.

Wu, J. (2009). Entrepreneurial Orientation, Entrepreneurial intent and new venture vreation: Test of a framework in a Chinese context. Unpublished Doctoral Thesis. Virginia Polytechnic Institute and State University.

Chapter 3
Entrepreneurial Orientation of Technology-Based SMEs in Malaysia

Azlin Shafinaz Arshad and Amran Rasli

Abstract Many researches all over the world have been studying entrepreneurial orientation in the past. Despite the vast amount of studies conducted, many of these studies adopt Covin and Slevin (1991) dimensions and focus on Small and Medium Enterprises (SMEs). The purpose of this study is to identify the critical dimensions of entrepreneurial orientation and determine the level of entrepreneurial orientation in technology-based SMEs in Malaysia. This study uses survey questionnaire on 150 respondents who are the owners or top managers of technology-based SMEs. Factor, reliability, descriptive, and inferential analyses were subsequently conducted. The factor analysis confirmed five dimensions of entrepreneurial orientation, i.e., innovativeness, proactiveness, risk-taking, competitive aggressiveness, and autonomy, which are consistent with earlier studies. The descriptive and inferential analyses indicate that all the dimensions of entrepreneurial orientation are apparent within technology-based SMEs, and the levels are generally high. Interestingly, innovativeness is the most prevalent among other dimensions for technology-based SMEs. The originality of this paper lies on being among the first few to examine the entrepreneurial orientation using Lumpkin and Dess (1996) dimensions within the context of technology-based SMEs in Malaysia.

Keywords Entrepreneurial orientation · SMEs · Technology-based SMEs

A.S. Arshad (✉)
Malaysian Academy of SME & Entrepreneurship Development (MASMED), Universiti Teknologi MARA, Shah Alam, Malaysia
e-mail: azlinshafinaz@salam.uitm.edu.my

A.S. Arshad
Faculty of Business and Management, Universiti Teknologi MARA, Puncak Alam, Malaysia

A. Rasli
Faculty of Management, Universiti Teknologi Malaysia, Johor Bahru, Malaysia
e-mail: m-amran@utm.my

F. Noordin et al. (eds.), *Proceedings of the 2nd Advances in Business Research International Conference*, https://doi.org/10.1007/978-981-10-6053-3_3

3.1 Introduction

The complexity of doing business transactions has seen the importance of entrepreneurial orientation to be demonstrated by firms to ensure the success of a business. Entrepreneurial orientation—innovative, proactive, and willing to take risk—is essential as the business environment today is getting even more complex, dynamic, and competitive. Lumpkin and Dess (1996) emphasized that entrepreneurial orientation reflects a strategic organizational posture that describes the specific processes, practices, and activities that allow firms to build values by engaging in entrepreneurial endeavors. Despite the vast amount of entrepreneurial orientation studies conducted, many of these studies adopt Covin and Slevin (1991) dimensions and focus on Small and Medium Enterprises (SMEs). Few studies have focused on technology-based SMEs (Arshad et al. 2014; Yoo 2001).

Chen et al. (2011) described the importance of entrepreneurial orientation to the growth of a company as well as to the growth of the economy of a country. Some scholars agreed that entrepreneurial orientation is a significant contributor to a firm's success and contributes to a healthier business performance (Mohammed Anis et al. 2016; Mahmood and Hanafi 2013; Zainol and Ayadurai 2011). Khan et al. (2015), Rodrigues and Raposo (2011) and Rodrigues (2005) provided evidences that firms with higher entrepreneurial orientation tend to have superior performance. As such, firms need to be entrepreneurial in order to survive and successfully compete, especially within fast-changing industries (Teece 2007), what more in technology-based small and medium enterprises which is impacted by rapidly evolving technological platforms (Rasli et al. 2014). The five dimensions of entrepreneurial orientation which was proposed by Lumpkin and Dess (1996) are adopted in this study as presented in Table 3.1.

Table 3.1 Entrepreneurial orientation dimensions

Dimensions	Descriptions
Innovativeness	A willingness to introduce innovation and novelty through experimentation and creative processes aimed at developing new products and services, as well as new processes
Proactiveness	A forward-looking perspective characteristic of a marketplace leader that has the foresight to seize opportunities in anticipation of future demand
Risk-taking	Making decisions and taking action without certain knowledge of probable outcomes; some undertakings may also involve making substantial resource commitments in the process of venturing forward
Competitive aggressiveness	An intense effort to outperform industry rivals. It is characterized by a combative posture or an aggressive response aimed at improving position or overcoming a threat in a competitive marketplace
Autonomy	Independent action by an individual or team aimed at bringing forth a business concept or vision and carrying it through to completion

Source Lumpkin and Dess 1996

The present study is important as it aims to identify the critical dimensions of entrepreneurial orientation and to determine the level of entrepreneurial orientation in technology-based SMEs in Malaysia. This chapter consists of four parts in which the first section provides an overview of entrepreneurial orientation followed by research methodology, results, and finally, discussion and conclusion were presented.

3.2 Methodology

A quantitative method using survey questionnaire is adopted in this study. Since the database for technology-based SMEs is not readily available, the authors have approached Malaysian Technology Development Centre (MTDC), an integrated venture capital company, for assistance as MTDC has been entrusted by the Malaysian Government in overseeing the development of technology-based firms in Malaysia since 1992 (Low et al. 2012). Arshad (2016) definition of technology-based SMEs where technology-based SMEs are defined as SMEs that follow the general admission policies, comply with the clusters listed by the Ministry of Science, Technology and Innovation (MOSTI) and involved in commercialization of research and development (R&D) activities, and acquisition of foreign technologies is adopted in this study.

The dimensions proposed by Lumpkin and Dess (2001) and Lumpkin and Dess (1996), i.e., innovativeness, proactiveness, risk-taking, competitive aggressiveness, and autonomy is used in this study to measure entrepreneurial orientation. The application of five entrepreneurial orientation dimensions with 18 items utilized by Lumpkin et al. (2009) in their study indicated that the content was adequate to measure the five-dimensional entrepreneurial orientation construct.

The questionnaires were distributed to 150 technology-based firms using simple random sampling method. However, only 86 responses fall within the scope of SMEs and were deemed to be usable for subsequent analyses. The respondents are owners or top managers as they have the knowledge and expertise with regard to the establishment, operation, and direction of the firm (Che Senik 2010). Data obtained were analyzed using SPSS statistical program using factor, reliability, descriptive, and inferential analysis. The single mean t-test is performed to further strengthen the descriptive analysis and determine whether a set or sets of scores are from the same population (Bordens and Abbott 2005; Carver and Nash 2012). In this case, the mean for entrepreneurial orientation is 3 which is the midpoint of the 5-point scale used for measurement (Arshad 2016; Bodie et al. 2011). Test results with p-values <0.05 will indicate that the null hypotheses should be rejected. The proposed hypothesis is as follows:

$$H_O : \mu < 3$$

Table 3.2 Factor analysis and Cronbach's alpha for entrepreneurial orientation

Entrepreneurial orientation items	Factor				
	1	2	3	4	5
Favors experimentation and original approaches to problem solving	0.828				
Strongly emphasis on R&D, technological leadership, and innovations	0.824				
Prefers to adapt to processes and methods of production and techniques that others have developed and proven	0.800				
Have marketed many new lines of products or services	0.759				
Prefers working autonomously with no reliance on teamwork and guidance from others		0.848			
Pursues business opportunities without obtaining approval from others		0.832			
Ensures the management team plays a major role in identifying and selecting the entrepreneurial opportunities to pursue new markets		0.780			
Believes best results occur when individuals and teams provide primary impetus for pursuing business opportunities		0.640			
Believes that owing to the nature of environment, it is best to explore the environment boldly with wide-ranging acts necessary to achieve firm objectives			0.799		
Prefers to study thoroughly before deploying resources to solve a problem			0.789		
Adopts cautions "wait and see" approach to minimize the probability of making costly mistakes in uncertainty situations			0.775		
Makes no special effort to take away businesses/markets from the competitors				0.783	
Most likely to respond to actions initiated by competitors				0.763	
Uses unconventional strategies to challenge competitors				0.712	
Introduce new products/services, administrative techniques, and operating technologies					0.818
Typically seeks to avoid competition clashes, preferring a live and let live posture					0.746
Strong tendency to be ahead of competition in introducing novel ideas and practices[a]					
Kaiser-Meyer-Olkin (KMO)	0.824				
Eigenvalue	3.177	2.879	2.221	2.141	1.726
Cumulative variance explained (%)	17.652	33.647	45.984	57.878	67.465
Cronbach's alpha (dimension)	0.881	0.854	0.759	0.744	0.631
Overall Cronbach's alpha	0.877				

[a]Loadings below 0.6

Table 3.3 Results of descriptive and inferential analysis

Constructs	Test value = 3		
	Mean	t	P-value
Innovativeness	4.241	23.479	0.000*
Proactiveness	4.180	29.813	0.000*
Risk-taking	4.101	25.759	0.000*
Competitive aggressiveness	4.016	18.335	0.000*
Autonomy	4.227	24.416	0.000*
Entrepreneurial orientation	4.161	33.077	0.000*

*Significance at 0.05

3.3 Results

The first test conducted was factor analyses in which items with factor loading below 0.6 were removed as suggested by Hair et al. (2009). Subsequently, reliability tests based on Cronbach's alpha of not less than 0.6 was applied to ensure reliability of the instrument (Loewenthal 2004; Sekaran 2003).

Factor analysis results for entrepreneurial orientation were loaded into five factors which appear to be consistent with theorized dimensions suggested by Lumpkin and Dess (1996) even with removal of one item. These dimensions are innovativeness, proactiveness, risk-taking, competitive aggressiveness, and autonomy. KMO value of 0.824 indicates the adequacy of sampling, and the data is significant in factor analysis. The five factors cumulatively explain 67.47% of the variance. The reliability tests conducted on EO and its five dimensions were above the recommended value. The results of the analyses are presented in Table 3.2.

The results for the dimensions of entrepreneurial orientation were significant at 0.05 where the highest mean is innovativeness (M = 4.241), while the lowest mean is competitive aggressiveness (M = 4.016). This study found that of the five dimensions of entrepreneurial orientation, innovativeness is perceived to be the most important factor for technology-based SMEs in Malaysia due to the highest mean of 4.241 (refer Table 3.3). When all the constructs are measured as a single value, significant result was demonstrated at 0.05, and the mean values were all above 4.0 (overall entrepreneurial orientation = 4.161) which indicate these results were slightly higher than the population mean of 3. Therefore, the proposed research hypotheses are supported (refer Table 3.3).

3.4 Discussion and Conclusion

The purpose of this study is to identify the critical dimensions of entrepreneurial orientation and to determine the level of entrepreneurial orientation in technology-based SMEs in Malaysia. To conclude, the findings show that the factor analysis conducted confirms the dimensions demonstrated by technology-based SMEs in this study are consistent as with Lumpkin and Dess (1996). The multi-dimensionality of entrepreneurial orientation dimensions of innovativeness, proactiveness, risk-taking, competitive aggressiveness, and autonomy verify the findings of Lumpkin and Dess (1996). Thus, it can be explained that the findings of this study validate further the results of the previous studies where entrepreneurial orientation dimensions can vary independently in many situations (Hansen et al. 2011; Kusumawardhani 2013; Nonyane-Mathebula 2010; Lee et al. 2011). The researcher believes that it is essential to identify the critical dimensions of entrepreneurial orientation as it allows the researcher to place questions with a similar concept in the same category while combining several questions into a more important concept. Hence, it removes questions that are redundant or unnecessary.

The level of entrepreneurial orientation dimension is considerably high where the mean values are all above 4. This indicates technology-based SMEs are entrepreneurial oriented, and they take entrepreneurial orientation seriously as one of the driving factors for them to succeed. A higher level of entrepreneurial orientation allows firms to identify and seize opportunities in a way that differentiates them from non-entrepreneurial firms (Covin et al. 2006). Rauch et al. (2009) highlighted businesses in high-tech industries gain more benefits from pursuing an entrepreneurial orientation; which supports the findings of this study. To add further, Kreiser et al. (2002) explained an entrepreneurial business would exhibit high levels of each dimension of entrepreneurial orientation. This study proves that each entrepreneurial orientation dimension is significantly high where the mean values are all above 4 (see Table 3.3). This indicates that technology-based SMEs in Malaysia perceive that entrepreneurial orientation dimension is essential for them to be successful. As explained by Covin and Slevin (1991), firms which have higher levels of entrepreneurial orientation have the ability to recognize and grasp opportunities differently in comparison to non-entrepreneurial firms. Richard et al. (2004) described entrepreneurial orientation dimensions vary independently, and firms may demonstrate relatively high levels of some and at the same time relatively low levels of others. This finding of this study is in line with Richard et al. (2004).

References

Arshad, A. S. (2016). *Leadership styles, entrepreneurial orientation and business performance of technology-based small medium enterprises in Malaysia.* Doctor of Philosophy (Management), Universiti Teknologi Malaysia (UTM), Malaysia.

Arshad, A. S., Rasli, A., Arshad, A. A. & Mohd Zain, Z. (2014). The impact of entrepreneurial orientation on business performance: A study of technology-based SMEs in Malaysia. *Procedia—Social and Behavioral Sciences, 130*, 46–53.

Bodie, G., Fitch-Hauser, M., & Powers, W. (2011). *Teaching social skills in instructional design: Concepts, methodologies, tools and applications* (3 Vol., pp. 1689–1713). Hershey, PA: Information Resources Management Association.

Bordens, K. S., & Abbott, B. B. (2005). *Research design and methods* (6th ed.). New York: Mc Graw Hill, Inc.

Carver, R. H., & Nash, J. G. (2012). *Doing data analysis with SPSS version 18.0.* United State: Brooks/Cole Cengage Learning.

Che Senik, Z. (2010). *Models, processes and factors influencing internationalization: The case of Malaysian SMEs*. Doctor of Philosophy, Murdoch University, Perth, Australia.
Chen, G., Du, H., & Chen, Y. (2011). Research on entrepreneurial orientation and entrepreneurial behavior: An empirical study. In *IEEE International Conference on Management and Service Science* (MASS), 2011 (pp. 1–3).
Covin, J. G., & Slevin, D. P. (1991). A conceptual model of entrepreneurship as firm behavior. *Entrepreneurship Theory and Practice, 16,* 7–25.
Covin, J. G., Green, K. M., & Slevin, D. P. (2006). Strategic process effects on the entrepreneurial orientation-sales growth rate relationship. *Entrepreneurship Theory and Practice, 30*(1), 57–81.
Hair, J. F., Black, W. C., Babin, B. J., & Anderson, R. E. (2009). *Multivariate data analysis*. Upper Saddle River, NJ: Prentice Hall.
Hansen, J. D., Deitz, G. D., Tokman, M., Marino, L. D., & Weaver, K. M. (2011). Cross-national invariance of the entrepreneurial orientation scale. *Journal of Business Venturing, 26*(1), 61–78.
Hassim, A. A., Nizam, A., Talib, A., & Bakar, A. R. A. (2011). The effects of entrepreneurial orientation on firm organisational innovation and market orientation towards firm business performance. *International Proceedings of Economics Development & Research, 10,* 280–284.
Khan, N. U., Qureshi, M. I., Rasli, A., & Ahmad, A. (2015). The impact of multiple organizational climates on performance of public sector organizations: Evidences from Pakistan. *International Journal of Economics and Financial Issues, 5,* 270–276.
Kreiser, P. M., Marino, L. D., & Weaver, K. M. (2002). Assessing the psychometric properties of the EO scale: A multicountry analysis. *Entrepreneurship Theory and Practice, 26*(4), 71–94.
Kusumawardhani, A. (2013). *The role of EO in firm performance: A study of Indonesian SMEs in the furniture industry in Central Java.* Doctor of Philosophy, Sydney Business School University of Wollongong.
Lee, S., Lim, S. B., & Pathak, R. (2011). Culture and entrepreneurial orientation: A multi-country study. *International Entrepreneurship and Management Journal, 7*(1), 1–15.
Loewenthal, K. M. (2004). *An introduction to psychological tests and scales* (2nd ed.). Hove, UL: Psychology Press.
Low, H. H., Rasli, A., & Senin, A. A. (2012). Knowledge determinant in university commercialization: A case study of Malaysia Public University. *Elsevier Procedia—Social and Behavioral Sciences, 40,* 251–257.
Lumpkin, G. T., & Dess, G. G. (1996). Clarify the EO construct and linking it to performance. *Academy of Management Review, 2*(1), 135–172.
Lumpkin, G. T., & Dess, G. G. (2001). Linking two dimensions of entrepreneurial orientation to firm performance: The moderating role of environment and industry life cycle. *Journal Business Venturing, 16*(5), 429–451.
Lumpkin, G. T., Cogliser, C. C., & Schneider, D. R. (2009). Understanding and measuring autonomy: An entrepreneurial orientation perspective. *Entrepreneurship Theory and Practice, 33,* 47–69.
Mahmood, R., & Hanafi, N. (2013). Entrepreneurial orientation and business performance of women-owned small and medium enterprises in Malaysia: Competitive advantage as a mediator. *International Journal of Business and Social Science, 4*(1), 82–90.
Mohammed Anis, S. N., Rasli, A. M., & Hashim, N. A. (2016). Through the looking glass: Enhancing Public University Librarians' entrepreneurial competencies in facing the impact of globalization (Conceptual Paper). *International Review of Management and Marketing, 6*(4), 70–79.
Nonyane-Mathebula, B. T. (2010). *Engineers as entrepreneurs: Entrepreneurial orientation of engineers in South Africa.* Masters of Business Administration, Gordon Institute of Business Science, University of Pretoria, South Africa.
Rasli, A., Norhalim, N., Tan, O. K. & Nik Mustaffa, N. Z. (2014). The interplay of value creation and managerial competencies: Evidence from small technology-based firms in Malaysia. Recent trends in social and behaviour sciences. In *Proceedings of the 2nd International*

Congress on Interdisciplinary Behavior and Social Sciences 2013 (ICIBSoS 2013) (pp. 567–571). Published by CRC/Balkema Taylor and Francis.

Rauch, A., Wiklund, J., Lumpkin, G. T., & Frese, M. (2009). Entrepreneurial orientation and business performance: An assessment of past research and suggestions for the future. *Entrepreneurship Theory and Practice, 33*(3), 761–787.

Richard, O. C., Barnett, T., Dwyer, S., & Chadwick, K. (2004). Cultural diversity in management, firm performance and the moderating role of entrepreneurial orientation dimensions. *Academy of Management Journal, 32*(4), 745–772.

Rodrigues, R. G. (2005). *Market orientation, entrepreneurial orientation and performance in Portuguese manufacturing SMEs: Exploring the relationship between marketing and entrepreneurship.* Unpublished Doctoral thesis, University of Beira Interior, Covilhã, Portugal.

Rodrigues, R. G., & Raposo, M. (2011). Entrepreneurial orientation, human resources information management and firm performance in SMEs. *Canadian Journal of Administrative Sciences, 28* (2), 143–153.

Sáez-Martínez, F. J., Díaz-García, C., & González-Moreno, A. (2014). Environmental orientation as a determinant of innovation performance in Young SMEs. *International Journal Environment Research, 8*(3), 635–642.

Sekaran, U. (2003). *Research methods for business: A skill building approach* (4th ed.). New York, NY: Wiley.

Subrahmanya, M. H., Mathirajan, M. & Krishnaswamy, K. N. (2010). *Importance of technological innovation for SME growth: Evidence from India.* Working Paper/World Institute for Development Economics Research.

Teece, D. J. (2007). Explicating dynamic capabilities: The nature and microfoundations of (sustainable) enterprise performance. *Strategic Management Journal, 28*(13), 1319–1350.

Yoo, S. J. (2001). Entrepreneurial orientation, environmental scanning intensity, and firm performance in technology-based SMEs. *Frontiers to Entrepreneur Research.*

Zainol, F. A., & Ayadurai, S. (2011). Entrepreneurial orientation and firm performance: The role of personality traits in Malay family firms in Malaysia. *International Journal of Business and Social Science, 2*(1), 59–72.

Chapter 4
Financial Literacy of Entrepreneurs in the Small and Medium Enterprises

Husniyati Ali, Emi Normalina Omar, Hanisah Abu Nasir and Muhamad Rahimi Osman

Abstract The success of any small and medium enterprises (SME) has been associated with the ability of the entrepreneurs to be financially literate in managing the financial matters. The task of entrepreneurs does not only focuses on purchasing, allocating, and distributing the resources efficiently, but to be able to understand the running of the business in terms of possessing the knowledge on accounting, costing, and budgeting. Those entrepreneurs who are financially literate normally are able to sustain in the market, regardless of economic condition. A total of 100 respondents from SME have been chosen in this study. The study has revealed that the entrepreneurs are really give time and energy to know and possess the skills in financial matters. Among the variables chosen, budget control seems to be the main factor that entrepreneurs wanted to be expert at since a correct budget will determine the survival of the firm.

Keywords Financial literacy · Small and medium enterprises · Budget control
Skill

H. Ali (✉) · E.N. Omar · H.A. Nasir
Faculty of Business Management, Kampus Puncak Alam, Universiti Teknologi MARA, Shah Alam, Malaysia
e-mail: husni833@salam.uitm.edu.my

E.N. Omar
e-mail: emi128@salam.uitm.edu.my

H.A. Nasir
e-mail: nisajacksonaww@gmail.com

M.R. Osman
Academy of Contemporary of Islamic Studies, Kampus Shah Alam, Universiti Teknologi MARA, Shah Alam, Malaysia
e-mail: mrahimi313@salam.uitm.edu.my

F. Noordin et al. (eds.), *Proceedings of the 2nd Advances in Business Research International Conference*, https://doi.org/10.1007/978-981-10-6053-3_4

4.1 Introduction

Entrepreneurs play an important and significant role in ensuring the businesses are making profit and efficiently administered. They are the one who directly involved in purchasing, allocating and distributing the resources, effectively and efficiently, in order to maximize the profit. It is important to point out that the entrepreneurs should possess and understand the basic financial skill, such as knowledge on accounting, costing, budgeting, in order for them to prosper and success in the businesses and able to compete and survive in the market. Jindrichovska (2013) has highlighted that there are those who start a business but have not involved themselves in managing the financial matters. They have no sufficient knowledge in documentation such as recording transactions, preparation, and analysis of financial statements. They normally rely on their accountants to run their financial transactions. In other words, the entrepreneurs should be financially literate in managing their financial activities and able to manage all aspects of businesses, hence enabling them to overcome any obstacles that they may face. Overall, the general objective of this study is to know to what extent do the entrepreneurs are financially literate. Specifically, this study tries to show the relationship between financial literacy with budget control, skill and knowledge and managing the cash flow.

4.2 Literature Review

Various studies have shown that there are positive impacts of financial literacy on the firm's performance. Moore (2003) and Perry and Morris (2005) were in the view that those entrepreneurs who are financially literate do better at budgeting, saving money, and controlling spending, while Campbell (2006) and Lusardi and Tufano (2009) relate those who are financially literate has the ability to handle mortgage and other debt.

For a start-up business, preparing a budget is very essential and crucial for them and it is a great responsibility that the entrepreneur must shouldered up to ensure the business is on the track and has a future and able to sustain in the market regardless of the economic conditions. Epstein (2014) viewed that budgeting is necessary and it allows to control the cash flow and make provisions for larger costs, as well as giving a clue and guidelines when the time is right to invest in the idea further as well as to expand it. A budget usually includes the revenues, costs, and the profits or cash flow so that it can figure out whether it has any money left over for capital improvements or capital expenses. In addition, Cornwall (2012) said that budget is not seem like simple process; it can thoroughly impact on the culture of an entrepreneurial firm. Meanwhile, Pilkington and Crowther (2007) has opined that the effectiveness of the budgeting process can be considered to be connected to the level of environmental uncertainty and to organizational behavior. Environmental uncertainty is significant in new areas of business, which applies to small firms and micro organizations, particularly those in e-commerce. Furthermore, Qi (2010) said that the budgeting underlines predicting and quantifying the future in financial terms and predicting the future needs for finance. Therefore, budgeting is situated between the disciplines of finance and planning. The other studies which were similar to Yang Qi were conducted by Akande et al. (Oluwaseun 2014) that budgetary control is for the purpose of translating policies, coordinating activities, as well as to ensure financial controls could achieve the possible results.

Other works have further demonstrated the link between skill and knowledge and the success of business. Generally, skill refers to a specific ability or competency in executing a task or responsibility, would come from knowledge, information, practice, and natural inclination in an individual (Ahmad et al. 1999). Many studies have emphasized on the importance of having good skill and knowledge as to sustain the firm in the market. Even a firm is said to be at advantage if the manager possesses certain skill in managing the firm. A research conducted by Zahiruddin et al. (2011) in the services sector indicates that the management skills possessed by the entrepreneurs have indeed contributed toward the success of this sector in Malaysia. The entrepreneurs have shown that there is a relationship between high entrepreneurial success with high business operating skills, skills to obtain market share that suits the size and capability, and skill to offer more special services. Normally, the skill and knowledge can be acquired from the experience and observation. In addition, a research carried out by Jusoh et al. (2011) proposes that the entrepreneur needs to qualify and adorn themselves with a new skill and restructure priorities in applying high technology and entrepreneurial culture that is dynamic. It implies that one needs to be a knowledge-based economy as to complement them to be a better entrepreneur. The findings were in line with the national vision of "K-Economy Master Plan" that outlines the development of human resources through increased knowledge and to guide the generation of knowledge workers to increase the national output. Gross domestic product (GDP) growth will be driven by knowledge-based industries in all sectors, especially manufacturing and services sectors.

Managing the cash flow is also important for the entrepreneurs as pointed out by Scott (2007) that a firm's success is measured by its capacity to generate sufficient cash flow from operations to pay its obligations, enhance its credit rating, and maximize shareholder value. Mitchell (2014) shared the same view with Scott by stressing the importance of keeping the cash flow in check and to avoid from late payment. By managing cash flow, the entrepreneurs would be able to be aware of any potential issues that they may face as Lall et al. pointed out that cash flow management is essential for every business and it would ensure increasing profitability, future planning, and sustainability.

4.3 Research Methodology

This study has used a convenience sampling method in selecting respondents, who were the SMEs entrepreneurs. The self-administered questionnaires were used for the data collection. The researchers have also explained the objectives of the study, and respondents were guaranteed of confidentiality. In total, 100 respondents took part in the survey. The questionnaires used in this study consisted of three sections. The first section sought to collect demographic information such as respondent's age, gender, marital status, ethnicity, and the type and ownership of business. In the second and third section, data for the independent and dependent variables were collected, respectively. The wording of the items for all variables was adapted to accommodate the context of the present study. The possible outcomes from the tested variables will determine its significance of the relationship. All the items in the questionnaire were assessed based on a 5-point Likert scale with 5 being strongly agree to 1 being strongly disagree. Besides descriptive statistics, Pearson correlation was also employed to establish the relationship between the variables. Cronbach's alpha was also tested for reliability and validity, by using the SPSS Version 21.

4.4 Findings

Data on the respondents' profile are presented in Table 4.1.

The analyses continued with the evaluation of Cronbach's alpha to determine reliability of the instrument and that the variables are consistently understood by the respondents. Table 4.2 provides the Cronbach's alpha of the variables used in the study.

Table 4.2 shows the result of the reliability statistics. The reliability test coefficient for dependent variable (Financial Literacy) is 0.621, while those for the independent variables are to be 0.837 for budget control, 0.708 for skill and knowledge, and 0.794 for managing cash flow. Generally, reliability coefficient which falls more than 0.80 is considered good (Sekaran 2010). The testing of the hypotheses proceeded and Tables 4.3, 4.4 and 4.5 describe the coefficient and regression analysis (Table 4.6).

Table 4.1 Demographic profile

Variable	Frequency	%
Age		
20 to 25 years old	26	26
26 to 30 years old	30	30
31 to 35 years old	22	22
35 and above	22	22
Gender		
Male	49	49
Female	51	51
Marital status		
Single	56	56
Married	44	44
Ethnicity		
Malay	55	55
Chinese	23	23
Indian	17	17
Others	5	5
Type of business/sector		
Manufacturing	16	16
Trading	31	31
Service	48	48
Others	5	5
Form of the ownership of the business		
Private enterprise	89	89
Limited company	6	6
Joint stock company	4	4
Others	1	1
Business established		
Less than 2 years	49	49
2–5 years	31	31
6-10 years	14	14
More than 10 years	6	6
Business annual sales		
Less than RM1 million	94	94
RM2 million to RM5 million	5	5
More than RM5 million	1	1

Table 4.2 Croncbach's alpha

Variable	Cronbach's alpha coefficient	No of items
Financial literacy	0.621	9
Budget control	0.837	8
Skill and knowledge	0.708	7
Managing cash flow	0.794	10

Table 4.3 Pearson correlation analysis

		DV	IV1	IV2	IV3
Financial literacy	Pearson Correlation	1	0.294**	0.305**	0.411**
	Sig. (2-tailed)		0.003	0.002	0.000
Budget control	Pearson Correlation	0.294**	1	0.410**	0.397**
	Sig. (2-tailed)	0.003		0.000	0.000
Skills and knowledge	Pearson Correlation	0.305**	0.410**	1	0.435**
	Sig. (2-tailed)	0.002	0.000		0.000
Managing cash flow	Pearson Correlation	0.411**	0.397**	0.435**	1
	Sig. (2-tailed)	0.000	0.000	0.000	

Table 4.4 Regression analysis

Model	R	R square	Adjusted R square	Std. Error of the estimate
1	0.447[a]	0.200[b]	0.175	0.43628

[a]Predictors: (Constant), Budget Control, Skills and Knowledge, Managing Cash Flow
[b]R square shows the relationship between independent and dependent variables. The R square of .200 indicates that only 20% of the variation in financial management among SME entrepreneurs in Klang Valley can be explained by budget control, skills and knowledge and managing cash flow. The remaining 80% can be explained by the other variables

Table 4.5 Coefficient

Model		Unstandardized coefficients		Standardized coefficients	t	Sig.
		B	Std. Error	Beta		
1	(Constant)	1.016	0.493		2.062	0.042
	IV1	0.147	0.126	0.121	1.170	0.245
	IV2	0.213	0.187	0.121	1.144	0.256
	IV3	0.327	0.111	0.310	2.945	0.004

a. Dependent Variable: Financial Literacy

Table 4.6 Summary of Descriptive Statistics for Independent and Dependent Variables

Variable	N	Mean	Standard Deviation
Financial literacy	100	3.9900	0.62757
Budget control	100	4.1100	0.73711
Skills and knowledge	100	4.0300	0.65836
Managing cash flow	100	4.0500	0.72995

4.5 Discussion and Conclusion

Many entrepreneurs in this world today have given great effort and concern to be financially literate, because of its impact on the performance and reputation of the businesses itself. Financial literate usually exerts large positive impacts on the performance of entrepreneurs, in terms of income, savings and the availability of planned, emergency and retirement funds, and is related to lower levels of debt. There are various kinds of education and knowledge on financial matters that need to be known by the entrepreneurs. This study only focuses on the ability of the entrepreneurs to do budget controls, skills and knowledge and managing the cash flow. What can be gathered from this basic analysis is that the independent variable of budget control has the highest mean which is 4.1100. This explained that the respondent is mostly agreed or strongly agree that budget control is the most important factors that affecting financial management among SME entrepreneurs in Klang Valley. In the correlation, the R^2 produced between independent variable (budget control, skills and knowledge and managing cash flow) with dependent variable (financial literacy) is 0.200. The 0.200 indicate that 20% of the variation in financial literacy among SME entrepreneurs in Klang Valley can be explained by budget control, skills and knowledge and managing cash flow. The remaining 80% of the financial literacy among SME entrepreneurs in Klang Valley could not be explained by the regression model or perhaps can be explained by the other variables.

In reliability analysis, among these three independent variables, the first independent variable which is budget control indicates the highest alpha coefficient range among others independent variables, which shows that it has a good strength of financial literate among entrepreneurs. It indicates that the Cronbach's Alpha for this variable is 0.837. Therefore, the internal consistency reliability of the measure used in this study is considered as a good. In correlation coefficient analysis, budget control and skills and knowledge both less than 0.01 which shows that there is significant relationship between dependent and independent variables.

This study presents a general indication for advancing the knowledge of entrepreneurs in financial matters. It is very important and significant for them to be financially literate as the economy today is open and becoming more challenging and robust.

References

Ahmad, A. M., Ahmad, F., Din, G., Razak, H. A., & Noor, N. A. M. (1999). *Pengantar pengurusan*. Sintok: Universiti Utara Malaysia.

Akande, O., & Oluwaseun, Y. (2014). Influence of budgeting system on Entrepreneurial Business performance: Perspective of Small business Owner in Lagos state Nigeria. *Journal of Business and Management, 16*(6), 58–64. www.iosrjournals.org.

Campbell, J. Y. (2006). Household Finance. *NBER Working Paper No. 12149*. Cambridge, MA: National Bureau of Economic Research.

Cornwall, J. R. (2012). Budgeting for entrepreneurs. Retrieved from http://www.csmonitor.com/Business/The-Entrepreneurial-Mind/2012/1112/Budgeting-for-entrepreneurs.

Epstein, G. (2014). How to budget for start-up success. Retrieved from http://www.entrepreneurmag.co.za/advice/starting-a-business/launch/how-to-budget-for-start-up-success/.

Jindrichovska, I. (2013). *Financial Management in SME*, European Research Studies, *16*(4).

Jusoh, R., Ziyae, B., Asimiran, S., & Kadir, S. A. (2011). Entrepreneur training needs analysis: implications on the entrepreneurial skills needed for successful entrepreneurs. *The International Business & Economics Research Journal, 10*(1), 143–148.

Lusardi, A., & Tufano, P. (2009). *Debt literacy, financial experiences, and overindebtedness*. Dartmouth Working Paper

Mitchell, L. (2014). *A small business entrepreneur's guide to brilliant cash flow management*. Retrieved from http://www.businesszone.co.uk/topic/finances/entrepreneurs-guide-brilliant-cashflow-management/58406.

Moore, D. (2003). Survey of Financial Literacy in Washington State: Knowledge. *Behavior, Attitudes, and Experiences*. Technical Report n. 03–39, Social and Economic Sciences Research Center, Washington State University.

Perry, V. G., & Morris, M. D. (2005). Who is in control? The role of self-perception, knowledge and income in explaining consumer financial behavior. *Journal of Consumer Affairs, 39*(2), 299–313. http://dx.doi.org/10.1111/j.1745-6606.2005.00016.x.

Pilkington, M., & Crowther, D. (2007). *Budgeting and control*. Financial Management. [Online] Available at http://www.cimaglobal.com/financialmanagement.

Qi, Y. (2010). *The Impact of Budgeting Process on Performance in Small and Medium-Sized Firms In China*, 1–9.

Scott, S. (2007). The importance of cash flow analysis for small businesses. *Commercial Lending Review, 37–40*, 48.

Sekaran, U., & Bougie, R. (2010) *Research methods for business: A skill-building approach* (5th ed.) United Kingdom: John Wiley.

Zahiruddin, A. Y., Fatt, C. K, Abdullah S. O, Ishak A. R, & Jumaat, M. (2011). Management skills and entrepreneurial success of small and medium enterprises (SMEs) in the services sector. *African Journal of Business Management* 5.26 (Oct 28, 2011): 10410–10418.

Chapter 5
Customers' Intention to Repurchase Halal Personal Care Products: The Moderating Role of Religiosity

Sulaiman Bin Nawawi, Rosmimah Bt. Mohd. Roslin and Norlida Bt. Abdul Hamid

Abstract **Purpose**—The purpose of this paper is to examine the factors that may influence the customers' intention to purchase halal personal care products using decomposed theory of planned behaviour (DTPB). In addition, it also aims to identify the relevant factor that may moderate the relationship between the TPB constructs and the dependent variable. **Design/methodology/approach**—A comprehensive review of customers' purchase intention on halal products is undertaken with a particular focus on halal personal care products. **Findings**—The review found that the intention to purchase halal personal care products was influenced by attitude, subjective norm, and perceived behavioural control. In addition, it was found that determinants such as knowledge, safety and health concern, media exposure, interpersonal influences, self-efficacy, and resource-facilitating conditions have a significant positive impact on attitude, subjective norm, and perceived behavioural control. On top of that, it was further discovered that religiosity moderates the relationship between the TPB constructs and the dependent variable. **Originality/value**—None of the purchase intention studies on halal personal care product has utilized decomposed theory of planned behaviour (DTPB) as the theoretical framework of their research. In addition, this is the first study utilizing this particular model in examining the moderating effect of religiosity on the relationship between the TPB constructs and the dependent variable in the context of halal personal care products.

Keywords Halal personal care products · Attitude · Subjective norm · Perceived behavioural control

S.B. Nawawi (✉) · R.Bt. Mohd.Roslin · N.Bt. Abdul Hamid
Universiti Teknologi MARA, Shah Alam, Malaysia
e-mail: abangleman12345@gmail.com

R.Bt. Mohd.Roslin
e-mail: rosmimah@salam.uitm.edu.my

N.Bt. Abdul Hamid
e-mail: norlida054@salam.uitm.edu.my

F. Noordin et al. (eds.), *Proceedings of the 2nd Advances in Business Research International Conference*, https://doi.org/10.1007/978-981-10-6053-3_5

5.1 Introduction

Halal personal care products industry has turned out to be one of the most tremendous and fastest growing industry (GIFR 2015). For instance, in 2013 alone, Muslim customers consumed US$46 billion on halal cosmetic and personal care products which is 6.78% of the global expenditure, and this figure is predicted to increase to US$73 billion by 2019, making up over 8.2% of global expenditure (*State of Global Islamic Economy Report* 2014). In the same year, top countries with halal cosmetics and personal care products customers were United Arab Emirates ($4.9 billion), Turkey ($4.4 billion), and Indonesia ($3.4 billion) (GIFR 2015). This growing halal personal care products industry is deemed by analysts as the next in line for growth after the profitable halal food and Islamic financial services (Rahim et al. 2015).

In the local scene, halal personal care products contribute 10–20% of the local personal care products market (GIFR 2015). As of third quarter of 2015, Malaysia's export value for halal personal care products stood at RM1.7 billion, reflecting 5.5% of the total halal exports which is valued at RM31.1 billion (MITI 2015). In addition, Malaysia's halal personal care products industry recorded sales of approximately RM3 billion in 2013 with the growth rate of 13% annually (Rahman et al. 2015).

However, in a world that is becoming more spiritually conscious, the acceptance and awareness level of halal cosmetics and personal care products is still low within the Muslim community (Hunter 2012). For instance, in the Middle East, a survey conducted by KasehDia Consulting (2012) showed that customers' awareness towards halal personal care products in Saudi Arabia and United Arab Emirates (UAE) was relatively low in comparison with their counterparts in Europe and Asia. Another report by WHF (2011) also revealed that the customers' level of awareness towards halal personal care products in these two countries was comparatively low at 18–30% as compared to halal meat and meat-based products and halal food which was estimated at 94–98% and 40–64%, respectively. According to KasehDia Consulting, this scenario happened due to the customers' misconceptions that the halal concept is only meant for meat and food-related products and that it has nothing to do with non-food products segments such as personal care products (Hajipour et al. 2015).

In the local front, a research by KasehDia Consulting (2012) also found that the customers' acceptance and awareness towards halal personal care products in Malaysia was comparatively low. For instance, both Muslim and non-Muslims in Malaysia are familiar and aware with the concept of halal foods products, but the term halal personal care products are relatively new even for Muslim consumers (Rahim et al. 2013). Additionally, not all Muslims look for the halal certifications when they purchase personal care products (Teng and Wan Jamaliah 2013) and majority of them will purchase these products without the halal certifications when there were no alternatives (Hunter 2012).

Another report by HDC (2014) further revealed that Muslim customers' response towards conventional and imported brands is, however, still overwhelmingly encouraging. In other words, Muslim customers in Malaysia are still prioritizing conventional and imported brands whose halal status and safety issues are questionable and doubtful (Mokhtar et al. 2012). According to EuroMonitor's Trade Sources and National Statistics 2012, only 0.5% of the Muslim customers in Malaysia are using Safi, the leading halal local brand for cosmetics and personal care products (Ramlee 2013). The brand carries a comprehensive range of personal care products aimed at catering and meeting the needs of both Muslim men and women (Hashim and Musa 2014). It seems that the local halal personal care products have yet to become a "household brand" for Muslim customers in Malaysia (Mohd Hashim and Musa 2013).

Therefore, it is essential to explore and identify what are the factors that may actually influence the customers' behavioural intention to purchase halal personal care products. Currently, an abundance of halal personal care products are widely available in the market. These include Qu Puteh, D'Herbs, Southern Lion, Wipro Unza, Zaitun, Johnson and Johnson, Shurah, Safi Rania, Mukmin, Syahirah, TanaMerra, SimplySiti, Clara International, Forest' Secret, and Alliance Cosmetics, to name a few (MITI 2015). Hence, it is questionable as to why Muslims' purchasing behaviour nowadays is still not inclined towards this halal personal care products whose ingredients have been proven to be halal and safe. This raises the issue of examining what factors that may actually affect their behavioural intention to purchase these halal products.

5.2 Intention-Behaviour Theories in Halal-Related Studies

A great deal of research has been conducted to determine factors that may influence the customers' behavioural intention towards halal products. Due to a lack of grounded theory in the marketing field, researchers have turned to models that have been established in other areas as a foundation for their research. For example, in the case of predicting an individual's intention to purchase halal-related products, marketing researchers have borrowed intention-behaviour theories from social psychology such as the theory reasoned action (Fishbein and Ajzen 1975) and the theory of planned behaviour (Ajzen 1991) as the theoretical foundation for their studies.

Theory of reasoned action (TRA) looks at beliefs within the individual to predict adoption behaviour (Morris and Dillon 1997). The TRA hypothesizes that both attitude and subjective norm will influence intention, which in turn influences behaviour (Ajzen and Fishbein 1980). Basically, intention indicates the probability of a person acting in a certain way (Fishbein and Ajzen 1975). TRA has been rigorously used to predict the customers' behavioural intention to select an extensive variety of products and services such as organic food purchasing behaviour (Sparks and Shepherd 1992), eco-friendly products buying intention (Kalafatis et al. 1999), and online purchasing behaviour (Bhattacherjee 2000; Khalifa and Limayem 2003).

However, the applicability of TRA was found inadequate in predicting the customers' behaviour to choose something at his own free-will (Ajzen and Fishbein 1980; Ajzen and Madden 1986). In other words, the theory did not take into consideration the conditions where an individual has full or complete control against their own behaviour (Ajzen 1991). To overcome this, Ajzen (1991) has introduced the perceived behavioural control into the model, and this new model was later known as the theory of planned behaviour (TPB). Hence, the theory assumes three independent determinants of intention: attitude towards behaviour, subjective norm, and perceived behavioural control (Ajzen 1991).

TPB has been extensively used to predict the customers' behavioural intention to select an extensive variety of products and services such as food choice and healthy eating behaviour (Chan and Tsang 2011; Jas 1988), technology adoption behaviour (Aboelmaged 2009; Gentry and Calantone 2002), Internet purchasing behaviour (George 2002; Gopi and Ramayah 2007), entrepreneurial behaviour (Engle et al. 2010; Iakovleva et al. 2011), and even behavioural misconduct (Bailey 2006).

Although these two theories are considered as a universal model in customer behaviour research, both models have been criticized for not proposing operational antecedents or determinants of behavioural attitudes, subjective norm, and to some extent, behavioural control (Taylor and Todd 1995a). To meet this criticism, Taylor and Todd (1995a) had extended the original theory of planned behaviour (TPB) into specific antecedents or determinants. This new theory was later known as the decomposed theory of planned behaviour (DTPB).

The DTPB has been applied in various information system researches (Bhattacherjee 2000; Shih and Fang 2004; Taylor and Todd 1995a, b; Zolait and Sulaiman 2009) and Islamic financial service, i.e. family takaful scheme (Husin and Rahman 2013; Husin et al. 2016), but has yet to be employed in research of other natures including halal personal care products. Even though DTPB was specifically tailored to understand the adoption of information technology (IT), antecedents such as interpersonal influences (i.e. friends', family members', and colleagues' influences), self-efficacy (i.e. self-confidence), and resource-facilitating conditions (i.e. time, money, and information) can still be applied in research of other natures (Husin and Rahman 2013), including halal personal care products.

5.3 Development of Research Framework and Hypotheses

The main structure of the framework is adopted from DTPB by Taylor and Todd (1995a), a powerful research model in the information system settings. Although DTPB is specifically tailored to understand the adoption of information technology (IT), antecedents such as interpersonal referents (i.e. friends, family members, and colleagues), self-efficacy (i.e. self-confidence), and resource-facilitating conditions (i.e. time, money, and information) can still be applied in research of other natures (Husin and Rahman 2013; Husin et al. 2016) including halal personal care products. DTPB framework describes that behavioural intention to purchase halal personal care products is determined by the individual's attitude, subjective norm, and perceived behavioural control (Taylor and Todd 1995a).

Originally, DTPB identified three latent dimensions of a person's attitude which are perceived usefulness, perceived ease of use, and compatibility. However, since the nature of this study is to understand the consumer behaviour in the context of halal personal care products, adapting all the three determinants of attitudes, namely perceived usefulness, ease of use, and compatibility is inappropriate. Therefore, the proposed determinants of attitudes which are knowledge, safety and health concern, and media exposure are more relevant in the context of this study. In fact, proposing these determinants seems justified because it is reasonably rationale to anticipate that individuals who are knowledgeable about halal products, concerned about safety and health, and highly exposed to halal products will perceive that they have the positive attitude towards the products.

In addition, the original DTPB also decomposed the subjective norm into two latent antecedents, namely "peer influence" and "superior influence" (Taylor and Todd 1995a). Taylor and Todd's (1995a) initiative to decompose the subjective norm into peer influence and superior influence seems justified in an organizational settings because it is rationale to presume that one's purchase behaviour is most likely influenced by their peers and superiors in the workplace. However, since the nature of the study is more focused on marketing approaches, the authors propose that the two determinants in the original DTPB were to be replaced with the element of "word-of-mouth referents" or better known as "interpersonal referents". These interpersonal referents include friends' influence, family members' influence, and colleagues' influence (Husin and Rahman 2013; Khalid and John 2008; Limayem et al. 2000; Parthasarathy and Bhattacherjee 1998). The logic here is that one may believe that his interpersonal referents such as friends and family members may encourage him to purchase halal cosmetics and personal care products or else he may believe that his colleagues in the workplace would also encourage him to purchase the products.

Furthermore, the original DTPB also identified three latent determinants of perceived behavioural control which are self-efficacy, resource-facilitating condition and technology-facilitating condition (Taylor and Todd 1995a). Again, due to different nature of the study, only two of the determinants namely self-efficacy (self-confidence) and resource-facilitating condition are adopted in the study. The technology-facilitating condition was deemed inappropriate since the main purpose of the study is to predict the behavioural intention towards halal consumer products and it has nothing to do with technology. In the context of this study, it is reasonably rationale to presume that individuals who have high self-confidence (i.e. self-efficacy) towards halal personal care products will perceive that they have the ability (i.e. high perceived behavioural control) to purchase and use them. Similarly, it seems justified to anticipate that individuals who believe that they have the resources such as time, money, and information (i.e. high resource-facilitating conditions) will perceive that they have the ability (i.e. high perceived behavioural controls) to purchase halal personal care products.

In this study, the authors also identify one controlling variable that is believed to moderate the relationship between the TPB constructs and the dependent variable. The main reasons to consider this moderating variable is to enhance the predictive nature of DTPB and facilitate its application in the context of halal personal care products. Additionally, the authors believe that factors that may influence the intention to purchase halal personal care products are likely to vary among customers. Therefore, in the context of halal personal care products, an additional explanatory factor is needed beyond attitude, subjective norm, and perceived behavioural control.

5.3.1 Research Framework

Figure 5.1.

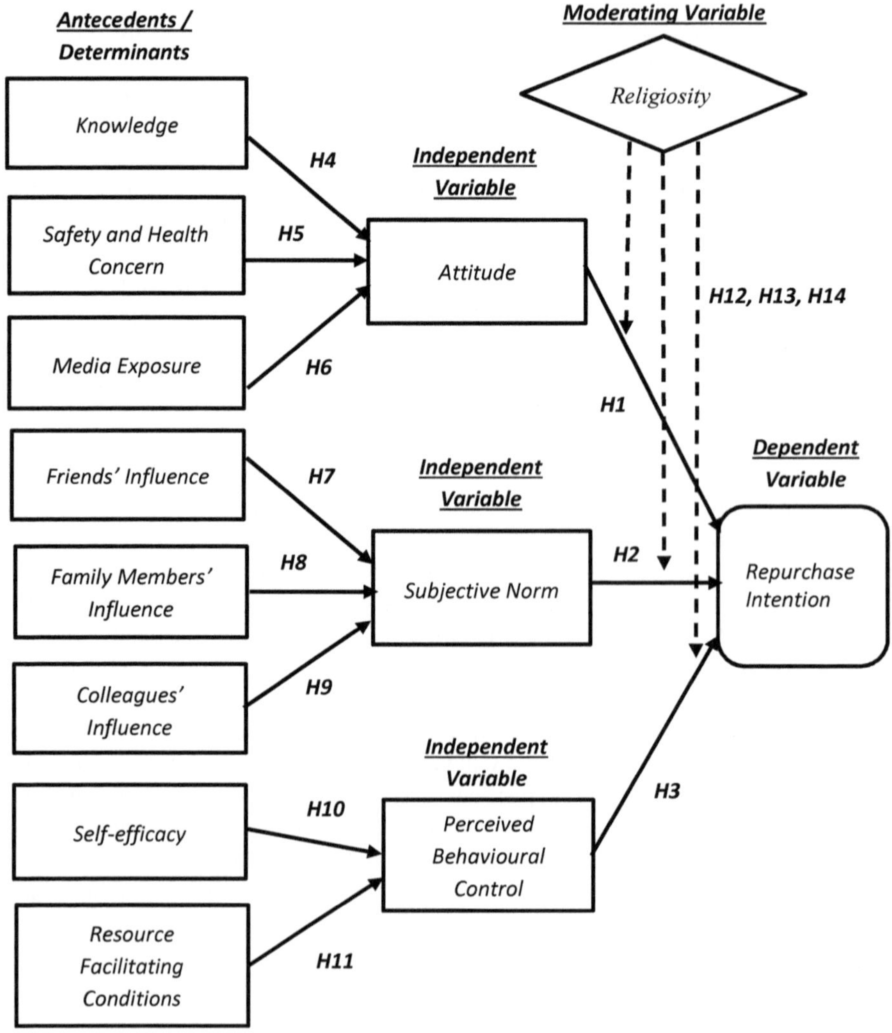

Fig. 5.1 Research Framework: Ajzen (1991), Taylor and Todd (1995a)

5.3.2 Hypotheses

There are fourteen hypotheses in this study, and each of them will be discussed in the following section.

5.3.2.1 Attitude

The effect of attitude on the intention to purchase and consume halal product has been theorized and validated by numerous studies (e.g. Lada et al. 2009; Rahman et al. 2015). For example, a study by Rahman et al. (2015) on the effect of knowledge and religiosity on customers' attitude towards halal cosmetic and halal food revealed that there was a significant positive relationship between attitude and behavioural intention. Meanwhile, using TRA, Lada et al. (2009) found that attitude towards halal products positively affected a customer's intention to purchase them. Hence, the first hypothesis is proposed as follows:

Hypothesis 1: There is a positive relationship between attitude and intention to purchase halal personal care products.

5.3.2.2 Subjective Norm

Numerous studies have documented the significant relationship between subjective norm and behavioural intention towards halal products (e.g. Haque et al. 2015; Hashim and Musa 2014). Explained in more details, based on theory of planned behaviour (TPB), Hashim and Musa (2014) revealed that subjective norm has a positive effect on young adult urban Muslim women towards halal cosmetics. Consistent with the above studies, Haque et al. (2015) also revealed the significant effect of subjective norm on the non-Muslim customers' intention to purchase halal food products in Malaysia. Therefore, the subsequent hypothesis is proposed as follows:

Hypothesis 2: There is a positive relationship between subjective norm and intention to purchase halal personal care products.

5.3.2.3 Perceived Behavioural Control

The relationship between perceived behavioural control and behavioural intention has received supports from several empirical studies related to halal products (e.g. Alam and Sayuti 2011; Khan and Azam 2016). For example, in a study applying theory of reasoned actions (TRA) to predict halal food purchasing behaviour in Malaysia, Alam and Sayuti (2011) found that perceived behavioural control was a significant determinant of behavioural intention. Meanwhile, Khan and Azam (2016) also found that there was a significant positive relationship between perceived behavioural control and customers' purchase intention towards halal-certified products in India. These lead the authors to the next hypothesis:

Hypothesis 3: There is a positive relationship between perceived behavioural control and intention to purchase halal personal care products.

5.3.2.4 Knowledge

The link between knowledge and attitude has been supported by numerous studies related to halal products (e.g. Abdul Aziz and Chok 2013; Ayyub 2015). To elaborate, Abdul Aziz and Chok's (2013) study on halal purchase intention among non-Muslims in Malaysia revealed that knowledge has a significant positive impact on attitude towards halal products. Similarly, Ayyub (2015) also revealed that knowledge was one of the determinants of the non-Muslim's attitude towards halal food in the UK. Hence, adopting the knowledge construct in this study seems justified and the following hypothesis is proposed as follows:

Hypothesis 4: Knowledge influences the customers' attitude towards halal personal care products.

5.3.2.5 Safety and Health Concern

Several studies have suggested the link between safety and health concern and attitude towards halal products (e.g. Ambali and Bakar 2014; Hussain et al. 2016). Explained in more details, Ambali and Bakar's (2014) study on people attitude and awareness on halal products in Malaysia revealed that the attitude towards halal products was positively influenced by their level of safety and health concern. Meanwhile, a survey by Hussain et al. (2016) who were investigating the integrating factors influencing consumers' halal product purchase in Pakistan also found safety and health concern has a significant positive impact on attitude towards halal products. This leads the authors to the fifth hypothesis:

Hypothesis 5: Safety and health concern affects the customers' attitude towards halal personal care products.

5.3.2.6 Media Exposure

The impacts of media exposure on attitude have been supported by numerous studies related to halal products (e.g. Kamarulzaman et al. 2015; Rahim et al. 2013). To elaborate, in a study exploring the effect of electronic media on Muslim minority in Britain, Kamarulzaman et al. (2015) found that electronic media exposure played a significant role in influencing British Muslim's attitude towards halal food products. On the same notes, in a research investigating the awareness and perception of Muslim consumers on halal non-food products in Malaysia, Rahim et al. (2013) also discovered that individuals who were more exposed to media would show a positive attitude towards halal non-food products. Therefore, adopting the media exposure construct in this study seems justified, and the next hypothesis is proposed as follows:

Hypothesis 6: Media exposure influences the customers' attitude towards halal personal care products.

5.3.2.7 Friends', Family Members', and Colleagues' Influences

Several studies related to Islamic financial services and information technology have recognized the significant relationship between interpersonal referents (i.e. friends, family members, and colleagues) and subjective norm (Husin and Rahman 2013; Husin et al. 2016). Explained in more details, in a conceptual paper to investigate the factors influencing the customers' intention to participate in family takaful scheme, Husin and Rahman (2013) postulated that interpersonal referents such as friends, family members, and colleagues were significant antecedents who may exert social pressure on individuals' intention to participate in family takaful scheme. Similarly, applying DTPB in a study to investigate the roles of mass media, word-of-mouth, and subjective norm in family takaful purchase intention, Husin et al. (2016) found that subjective norm was significantly influenced by word-of-mouth referents. Although the influence of interpersonal referents has yet to be empirically tested in the studies related to halal consumer products, the relevancy of these three determinants should not be overlooked. Therefore, the authors strongly believe that these three determinants of subjective norm should be included in the framework, thus, the subsequent hypotheses are proposed as follows:

Hypothesis 7: Friends' influence affects subjective norm
Hypothesis 8: Family members' influence affects subjective norm
Hypothesis 9: Colleagues' influence affects subjective norm

5.3.2.8 Resource-Facilitating Conditions

The effect of self-efficacy and resource-facilitating conditions on perceived behavioural control has been supported by a number of studies related to Islamic financial services and information technology (e.g. Bhattacherjee 2000; Husin and Rahman 2013). For example, in a conceptual paper to investigate the factors influencing the customers' intention to participate in family takaful scheme, Husin and Rahman (2013) postulated that self-efficacy (i.e. self-confidence) and resource-facilitating conditions were significant antecedents of perceived behavioural control. Similarly, Bhattacherjee's (2000) study on individuals' underlying motivation to accept electronic brokerage technology among e-brokerage users showed that perceived behavioural control was significantly affected by one's self-confidence in skills to perform the intended behaviour (i.e. self-efficacy) and beliefs about availability of resources to facilitate the behaviour (i.e. resource-facilitating conditions). Again, even though the effect of self-efficacy (i.e. self-confidence) and resource-facilitating conditions have yet to be empirically tested in the studies related to halal consumer products, the relevancy of these two determinants cannot be ignored. Therefore, the authors are of the opinion that these two determinants of perceived behavioural control should be included in the framework; thus, the subsequent hypotheses are proposed as follows:

Hypothesis 10: Self-efficacy (i.e. self-confidence) influences perceived behavioural control

Hypothesis 11: Resource-facilitating conditions influence perceived behavioural control

5.3.2.9 Religiosity

Religion refers to one's beliefs about the complete authoritativeness and integral truth of a religious teachings and scriptures (Moschis and Ong 2011). It acts as a foundation on which human beings shape their attitudes and behaviour (Essoo and Dibb 2004). Meanwhile, religiosity can be defined as the intensity of being religious and pious (De Run et al. 2010; O'Connell 1978). More specifically, it is the extent to which a person is devoted to his religion which is mirrored through his attitudes and behaviour (Johnson 2001). The strength of consumers' religiosity affects certain aspects of the person's psychological and physical wellbeing (Mukhtar and Butt 2012). In addition, although customers' choices are usually influenced by their religious environments, the strength of influence may vary according to their level of religiosity (Ibrahim and Ismail 2015). Therefore, the authors believe that a more religious Muslim would try to lead their daily life in line with their religious teachings. Furthermore, it seems rationale to assume that those with higher level of religiosity would prefer to sacrifice their worldly pleasures when it clashes with the teachings of their religion. In line with the above justifications, the authors are of the opinion that when compared to Muslims with lower level of religiosity, Muslims with higher level of religiosity are usually having stronger intention to purchase halal personal care products, thus resulting in their positive response to consume them. Therefore, the authors propose that one's level of religiosity strengthens or alters the relationships between the TPB constructs and the dependent variable.

Several halal-related studies have investigated the moderating effect of religiosity on the relationship between the TPB constructs and the dependent variable (e.g. Al-Nahdi 2008; Bonne et al. 2007; Husin and Rahman 2013). Selectively, Al-Nahdi's (2008) study on the customers' intention to patronage halal restaurants in Malaysia revealed that religiosity moderates the relationship between the two main constructs of the framework (i.e. subjective norm and perceived behavioural control) and intention to patronage halal restaurants such that the relationship between subjective norm and perceived behavioural control and patronage intention is stronger for those customers with high levels of religiosity than for those customers with low levels of religiosity. However, religiosity did not seem to moderate the relationships between attitude and intention to patronage halal restaurant. Meanwhile, a survey by Bonne et al. (2007) who were investigating the determinants of halal meat consumption in France found that religiosity moderated the relationship between the TPB constructs (i.e. attitude, subjective norm, and perceived behavioural control) and the dependent variable (i.e. intention to consume halal meat). Following the footsteps of the above studies, examining the moderating effect of religiosity on the relationship between the TPB constructs and the dependent variable seems justified. This leads the authors to the subsequent hypotheses:

Hypothesis 12: Religiosity moderates the relationship between attitude and intention to purchase halal personal care products such that the relationship between attitude and purchase intention is stronger for those customers with high levels of religiosity than for those customers with low levels of religiosity

Hypothesis 13: Religiosity moderates the relationship between subjective norm and intention to purchase halal personal care products such that the relationship between subjective norm and purchase intention is stronger for those customers with high levels of religiosity than for those customers with low levels of religiosity

Hypothesis 14: Religiosity moderates the relationship between perceived behavioural control and intention to purchase halal personal care products such that the relationship between perceived behavioural control and purchase intention is stronger for those customers with high levels of religiosity than for those customers with low levels of religiosity

5.4 Implications of The Study

5.4.1 Theoretical Implications

This study extends the purchase intention research on halal personal care products by applying the Decomposed Theory of Planned Behaviour (DTPB) as the underpinning theory of the study. By decomposing the attitudinal, normative, and perceived control beliefs into relevant multidimensional constructs, the authors expect to have a higher explanatory power and a more precise understanding of the antecedents or determinants of behaviour. Most of the purchase intention studies on halal personal care products emphasize on the main construct of TPB as the main factors that will affect one's purchase intention, and they seemed to ignore the importance of the antecedents or determinants of attitude, subjective norm, and perceived behavioural control in predicting the customers' behavioural intention. Therefore, this study attempts to close this theoretical gap by incorporating the relevant antecedents or determinants of attitude, subjective norm, and perceived behavioural control in DTPB model as a new approach in predicting customers' behavioural intention in the context of halal personal care products. On top of that, this study further extends DTPB by integrating the moderating role of religiosity on the relationship between the TPB constructs (i.e. attitude, subjective norm, and perceived behavioural control) and the dependent variable (i.e. purchase intention). According to Mukhtar and Butt (2012), the strength of consumers' religiosity affects certain aspects of the person's psychological and physical wellbeing. In addition, although customers' behaviour is usually influenced by their religious environments, the strength of influence may vary according to their level of religiosity (Ibrahim and Ismail 2015). Therefore, in line with the findings and arguments of the above studies, the authors expect that one's level of religiosity strengthens or alters the relationships between the TPB constructs and the dependent variable.

5.4.2 Practical Implications

In this study, the authors decomposed the attitudinal, normative, and perceived control beliefs into relevant multidimensional constructs in order to provide a more precise understanding of the antecedent of the customers' purchase intention towards halal personal care products. Better understandings of specific determinants of attitude, subjective norm, and perceived behavioural could help marketers and product managers formulate and pursue relevant marketing strategies that could significantly affect individual's behavioural intention, thus enhancing the organization's competitiveness in the market. In addition, by focusing on specific beliefs, the model will become more relevant to practitioners who are interested in examining a more complete set of antecedents or determinants that could better predict the customers' behavioural intention towards the products.

5.5 Limitations of The Study

Although this research has been able to fill both the conceptual and theoretical gaps, it has a number of limitations. Firstly, this study concentrates mainly on the quantitative methods. However, other methods of data collection such as mail surveys or a combination of qualitative (in-depth interviews, focus groups, etc.) and quantitative methods can be considered in the future. Secondly, this DTPB model is only tested on halal non-food sector (i.e. halal personal care products). Therefore, future studies could extend the model to include other halal products and service sectors such as food, financial, and pharmaceutical segments. It will be interesting to learn whether this model can also be applied into other halal-related studies. Finally, due to limited publication, only a limited number of halal-related studies utilizing DTPB are discussed in this study. Notwithstanding the above limitations, this study contributes towards a better understanding of the factors that may influence customers' intention to purchase halal personal care products.

5.6 Conclusion

In this study, the authors adapted decomposed theory of planned behaviour (DTPB) in predicting the customers' intention to purchase halal personal care products. Based on the extensive literature search, the authors identified relevant determinants and antecedents of attitude, subjective norm, and perceived behavioural control. Although DTPB is specifically tailored to understand the adoption of information technology (IT), antecedents such as interpersonal referents (i.e. friends' influence, family members' influence, and colleagues' influences), self-efficacy (i.e. self-confidence), and resource-facilitating conditions (i.e. time, money, and information) can still be applied in research of other natures (Husin and Rahman 2013; Husin et al. 2016) including halal personal care products. In addition, through this literature review, the authors also discovered the moderating effect of religiosity on the relationship between the TPB constructs (i.e. attitudes, subjective norm, and perceived behavioural control) and the dependent variable (i.e. purchase intention). To the best of the researchers' knowledge, none of the purchase intention studies on halal personal care product has utilized DTPB as the theoretical framework of their research. On top of that, this is the first study utilizing this particular model in examining the moderating effect of religiosity on the relationship between the TPB constructs and the dependent variable.

References

Abdul Aziz, Y., & Chok, N. V. (2013). The role of Halal awareness, Halal certification, and marketing components in determining Halal purchase intention among non-Muslims in Malaysia: A structural equation modeling approach. *Journal of International Food and Agribusiness Marketing, 25*(1), 1–23.

Aboelmaged, M. G. (2009). Predicting e-precurement adoption in a developing country: An empirical integration of technology acceptance model and theory of planned behaviour. *Industrial Management and Data Systems, 110*(3), 392–414.

Ajzen, I. (1991). The theory of planned behaviour. *Organizational Behaviour and Human Decision Processes, 50,* 179–211.

Ajzen, I., & Fishbein, M. (1980). *Understanding Attitudes and Predicting Social Behaviour*. Eaglewood Cliffs, NJ: Prentice-Hall.

Ajzen, I., & Madden, T. J. (1986). Prediction of goal-directed behaviour: attitudes, intentions, and perceived behavioural control. *Journal of Experimental Social Psychology, 22*(5), 453–474.

Alam, S. S., & Sayuti, N. M. (2011). Applying the Theory of Planned Behavior (TPB) in halal food purchasing. *International Journal of Commerce and Management, 21*(1), 8–20.

Al-Nahdi, T. S. (2008). *Intention to patronage Halal restaurants among Malaysian Muslims: An issue of Halal perception. Master of Business Administration (MBA) Thesis.*

Ambali, A. R., & Bakar, A. N. (2014). People's awareness on halal foods and products: Potential issues for policy-makers. *Procedia-Social and Behavioral Sciences, 121,* 3–25.

Ayyub, R. M. (2015). Exploring perceptions of non-Muslims towards Halal foods in UK. *British Food Journal, 117*(9), 2328–2343.

Bailey, A. A. (2006). Retail employee theft: A theory of planned behaviour perspective. *International Journal of Retail and Distribution Management, 34*(11), 802–816.

Bhattacherjee, A. (2000). Acceptance of e-commerce services: The case of electronic brokerages. *IEEE Transactions on Systems, Man, and Cybernetics-Part A: Systems and Humans, 30*(4), 411–420.

Bonne, K., Vermeir, I., Bergeaud-Blackler, F., & Verbeke, W. (2007). Determinants of halal meat consumption in France. *British Food Journal, 109*(5), 367–386.

Chan, K., & Tsang, L. (2011). Promote healthy eating among adolescent: A Hong Kong study. *Journal of Consumer Marketing, 28*(5), 354–362.

De Run, E. C., Jee, T. W., & Lau, W. (2010). *Malaysia*. Wellington: Asia Business Research Corporation Limited.

Engle, R. L., Dimittriadi, N., Gavidia, J. V., Schlaegel, C., Delanoe, S., Alvarado, I., et al. (2010). Entrepreneurial intent: A twelve-country evaluation of Ajzen's model of planned behaviour. *International Journal of Entrepreneurial Behaviour and Research, 16*(1), 35–37.

Essoo, N., & Dibb, S. (2004). Religious influences on shopping behaviour: An exploratory study. *Journal of Marketing Management, 20,* 683–712.

Fishbein, M., & Ajzen, I. (1975). *Belief, attitudes, intention and behaviour: An introduction to theory and research*. Reading, MA: Addison-Wesley.

Gentry, L., & Calantone, R. (2002). A comparison of the three models to explain Shop-bot use on the web. *Psychology and Marketing, 19*(11), 945–956.

George, J. (2002). Influences on the intent to make internet purchases. *Internet Research, 12*(2), 165–180.

GIFR. (2015). *The Global Halal Industry: An overview. Global Institute of Forensic Research*. Retrieved February 6, 2016 from http://www.gifr.net/gifr2013/ch_13.pdf.

Gopi, M., & Ramayah, T. (2007). Applicability of Theory of Planned Behaviour in predicting intention to trade online: Some evidence from a developing country. *International Journal of Emerging Markets, 2*(4), 348–360.

Hajipour, B., Gharache, M., Hamidizadeh, M. R., & Mohammadian, F. (2015). Raising halal cosmetic awareness among the respective consumers. *International Journal of Academic Research in Business and Social Sciences, 5*(7), 338–349.

Haque, A., Sarwar, A., Farzana, Y., Tarofder, A. K., & Hossain, M. A. (2015). Non-Muslim consumers' perception toward purchasing halal food products in Malaysia. *Journal of Islamic Marketing, 6*(1), 133–147.
Hashim, A. J. C. M., & Musa, R. (2014). Factors influencing attitude towards halal cosmetic among young adult urban Muslim women: A focus group analysis. *Procedia-Social and Behavioral Sciences, 130,* 129–134.
HDC. (2014). The Halal Industry: the new source of economic growth. Retrieved from Retrieved January 31, 2016, from http://www.hdcglobal.com.
Hunter, M. (2012). *The emerging Halal cosmetic and personal care market: integrating the organization towards the philosophy of Tawhid. Working Paper, University Malaysia Perlis.*
Husin, M. M., & Rahman, A. A. (2013). What drives consumers to participate into family Takaful schemes? A literature review. *Journal of Islamic Marketing, 4*(3), 264–280.
Husin, M. M., Ismail, N., & Rahman, A. A. (2016). The roles of mass media, word of mouth and subjective norm in family Takaful. *Journal of Islamic Marketing, 7*(1), 59–73.
Hussain, I., Rahman, S. U., Zaheer, A., & Saleem, S. (2016). Integrating factors influencing consumers' halal products purchase: application of theory of reasoned actions. *International Food and Agribusiness Marketing, 28*(1), 35–58.
Iakovleva, T., Kolvereid, L., & Stephan, U. (2011). Entrepreneurial intentions in developing and developed countries. *Education and Training, 53*(5), 353–370.
Ibrahim, H., & Ismail, H. (2015). A generational cohort study of the relationship between religious intensity and religious assurance for the purchase of non-food products. *International Journal of Economics and Financial Issues, 5*(Special Issue), 330–334.
Jas, P. (1988). Aspects of food choice behaviour in adolescents. *Nutrition and Food Science, 98* (3), 163–165.
Johnson, B. (2001). Does adolescent religious commitment matter? A reexamination of the effects of religiosity on delinquency. *Journal of Research in Crime and Delinquency, 38*(1), 22–43.
Kalafatis, S., Pollard, M., East, R., & Tsogas, M. H. (1999). Green marketing and Ajzen theory of planned behaviour: a cross-market examination. *Journal of Consumer Marketing, 16*(5), 441–460.
Kamarulzaman, Y., Veeck, A., Abdul Muhmin, A. G., Luqmani, M., & Qureashi, Z. A. (2015). religious community building through digital media : the search for halal food in muslim minority regions. In *40th Annual Macromarketing Conference.*
KasehDia Consulting. (2012). *The 7th World Halal Forum, 4–5 April 2012, Kuala Lumpur, Malaysia. Post Event Report.*
Khalid, M. N., & John, M. P. (2008). An exploratory study into the adoption of internet banking in a developing country: Malaysia. *Journal of Internet Commerce, 7,* 29–73.
Khalifa, M., & Limayem, M. (2003). Drivers of internet shopping. *Communications of the ACM, 46*(12), 233–239.
Khan, A., & Azam, M. K. (2016). Factors Influencing Halal Products Purchase Intention in India: Preliminary Investigation. *The IUP Journal of Marketing Management, 15*(1), 20–35.
Lada, S., Tanakinjal, G. H., & Amin, H. (2009). Predicting intention to choose halal products using theory of reasoned action. *International Journal of Islamic and Middle Eastern Finance and Management, 2*(1), 66–76.
Limayem, M., Khalifa, M., & Frini, A. (2000). What makes consumers buy from internet? A logitudinal study of online shopping. *IEEE Transactions on Systems, Man, and Cybernatics—Part A: Systems and Humans, 30*(4), 421–432.
MITI. (2015). Exports of Halal Cosmetic and Personal Care Products Hit RM1.7 Billion, Emerging as the Fastest Growing Consumer Segment. Retrieved May 5, 2016, from http://www.miti.gov.my/index.php/pages/view/3114.
Mohd Hashim, A. J. C., & Musa, R. (2013). Modelling the effects of the attitude of young adult urban Muslim women towards halal cosmetic products: New insights for championing the halal economy. *International Journal of Education and Research, 1*(7), 1–8.

Mokhtar, A., Nooreha, H., & Nik Mustapha, N. H. (2012). *Guidelines for implementing value-based total performance excellence model in business organizations*. Manila, Philippines: Presentations at the Islamic Perspective Forum.

Morris, M. G., & Dillon, A. (1997). How user perceptions influence software use. *IEEE Software, 14*(4), 58–65.

Moschis, G. P., & Ong, F. (2011). Religiosity and consumer behavior of older adults: A study of subcultural influences in Malaysia. *Journal of Consumer Behaviour, 10*(1), 8–17.

Mukhtar, A., & Butt, M. M. (2012). Intention to choose Halal products: The role of religiosity. *Journal of Islamic Marketing, 3*(2), 108–120.

O'Connell, B. (1978). Dimensions of religiosity among Catholics. *Review of Religious Research, 16*(3), 198–207.

Parthasarathy, M., & Bhattacherjee, A. (1998). Understanding post-adoption behaviour in the context of online services. *Information Systems Research, 9*(4), 362–379.

Rahim, N. F., Shafii, Z., & Shahwan, S. (2013). Awareness and perception of muslim consumers on non-food halal product. *Journal of Social and Development Sciences, 4*(10), 478–487.

Rahim, N. F., Shafii, Z., & Shahwan, S. (2015). Awareness and perception of muslim consumers on halal cosmetics and personal care products. *International Journal of Business, Economics and Management, 2*(1), 1–14.

Rahman, A. A., Asrarhaghighi, E., & Rahman, S. A. (2015). Consumers and Halal cosmetic products: knowledge, religiosity, attitude and intention. *Journal of Islamic Marketing, 6*(1), 148–163.

Ramlee, J. (2013). *Safi rebrands products to reach younger men* (pp. 9–10). New Straits Times: Business Times.

Shih, Y.-Y., & Fang, K. (2004). The use of a decomposed theory of planned behavior to study Internet banking in Taiwan. *Internet Research, 14*(3), 213–223.

Sparks, P., & Shepherd, R. (1992). Self-identity and the theory of planned behavior: assessing the role of identification with "green consumerism". *Social Psychology Quarterly, 55*(4), 388–399.

State of Global Islamic Economy Report. (2014). Retrieved January 25, 2016, from http://www.dinarstandard.com/state-of-the-global-Islamic-economy-report-2014.

Taylor, S., & Todd, P. (1995a). Understanding information technology usage, a test of competing models. *Information Systems Research, 6*(2), 144–176.

Taylor, S., & Todd, P. (1995b). Decomposing and crossover effects in the theory of planned behaviour: A study of consumer adoption intention. *International Journal of Research in Marketing, 12,* 137–155.

Teng, P. K., & Wan Jamaliah, W. J. (2013). Investigating students awareness and usage intention towards halal-labelled cosmetics and personal care products in Malaysia. *In Proceeding of the 4th International Conference on Business and Economic Research (4th ICBER 2013),4–5th March 2013, Bandung, Indonesia*, 367–376.

WHF. (2011). *The 6th World Halal Forum, 4-5 April 2011*. Malaysia, Post Event Report: Kuala Lumpur.

Zolait, A. H. S., & Sulaiman, A. (2009). The influence of communication channels on internet banking adoption. *Asian Journal of Business and Accounting, 2*(1/2), 115–134.

Chapter 6
Factors that Contributes Towards Opportunity Creation and Identification

Abg Zainoren Abg Abdurahman, Ramraini Ali Hassan, Nazura Mohamed Sayuti and Johari Bin Abdullah

Abstract Organizational sustainability has been a major theme in shaping global business arena in which entrepreneurship as the cornerstone. This also has forced entrepreneurship to become an important driver to the government initiative to implant entrepreneurial competencies as its organizational culture. In relation to the development, public universities are urged to diversify their income generation from various sources as to promote financial sustainability through entrepreneurship. Therefore, the readiness of the members of the organization for such environment is crucial. It is important for the university to engage with opportunity identification or creation as it can lead to income generation and profitability. This paper examined the relationship between entrepreneurial competency, social capital, experience and knowledge with opportunity identification and creation. Both academic and non-academic staffs were involved in the study. Findings show that entrepreneurial competency, social capital, experience and knowledge found to be positively significant towards opportunity identification and creation.

Keywords Entrepreneurship · Opportunity creation · Identification orientation

A.Z.A. Abdurahman (✉)
Faculty of Business Management, Universiti Teknologi MARA, Sarawak, Jalan Meranek, Kota Samarahan Sarawak 94300, Sarawak, Malaysia
e-mail: zainoren@sarawak.uitm.edu.my

R.A. Hassan
Faculty of Business, Economic and Accountancy, Universiti Malaysia Sabah, Jalan UMS, Kota Kinabalu 88400, Sabah, Malaysia
e-mail: ramraini@ums.edu.my

N.M. Sayuti
Faculty of Business and Management, Puncak Alam Campus, Universiti Teknologi MARA, 42300 Bandar Puncak Alam, Selangor, Malaysia
e-mail: nazura139@salam.uitm.edu.my

J.B. Abdullah
Faculty of Business Management, Universiti Teknologi MARA, Sarawak Mukah Branch, Jalan Mukah-Oya, Mukah 96400, Sarawak, Malaysia
e-mail: johariabdullah@sarawak.uitm.edu.my

F. Noordin et al. (eds.), *Proceedings of the 2nd Advances in Business Research International Conference*, https://doi.org/10.1007/978-981-10-6053-3_6

6.1 Introduction

Malaysian government since 2015 had been cutting off budget allocations for public universities besides encourages public universities boost up their income generation (Sharma 2015). In relation to the current development, this paper aims to explore the perceptions of the university staffs in identifying and creating business opportunity in Universiti Teknologi MARA (UiTM). There have been limited studies on perception towards factors that contribute to entrepreneurial opportunities particularly among public universities in Malaysia. The importance of the contributing factors is very significant to device capacity building strategies among members of organization orientation towards opportunity. Ability to create and identify opportunity can lead to entrepreneurial success (Ardichvili et al. 2003). Entrepreneurial success can be reflected as ability to earn profit from the opportunity. Thus, this paper attempts to determine the relationship entrepreneurial competency, social capital, experience and knowledge towards the opportunity creation and identification.

6.2 Literature Review

Extensive literature review had been conducted to determine the items for instruments from previous studies of the independent and dependent variable. The review findings encompassed the entrepreneurial competencies, social capital, experience, knowledge, opportunity identification and creation.

6.2.1 Entrepreneurial Competency

Ability to solve problem is one of the entrepreneurial competencies that can lead to success. New value proposition can be developed when it solve customers' problem. However, venturing into new start up requires proper study to minimize unforeseen risks that might affect the entrepreneur's newly start-ups. Hence, ability to mitigate risks is also the entrepreneurial competencies (Naldi et al. 2007). In addition, facing the unknown circulated with uncertainty need self-confidence by imposing strong self-belief to enable the entrepreneur to make the first few strategic moves by risking the resources (Wilson et al. 2007). Besides, willingness to learn new things helps the entrepreneur to indulge themselves with new idea and approach (Shane 2000) in executing their strategies for sustainable survival and competitive advantage (Alvarez and Barney 2007). However, entrepreneur at the same time needs to understand their customers and also respect them at the same time in order to create trust and matured relationship (Davidsson and Honig 2003).

6.2.2 Social Capital

Networking is important in entrepreneurship as it can lead to sustainable opportunities that sustain the survival of the venture (Abdullah et al. 2009). Relationship can be with the external general public and also the internal public of the organization. Social capital also refers to the ability of actors to extract benefits from their networks, memberships and social structure (Myint et al. 2005). In addition, Nahapiet and Ghosal (1998) indicated that social capital is multidimensional and occurs at both the individual and the organizational levels. Meanwhile, the important role for an entrepreneur might be a personal relationship. A strong relationship has been argued to bond actors via mechanisms such as reciprocity, trust and the threat of future censure from exchange (Davidsson and Honig 2003). On the other hand, according to Ardichvili et al. (2003), the nature of social networks which include action set, partnerships, weak ties, and inner circle also determines the level of entrepreneurial alertness.

6.2.3 Experience

Baron (2006) suggested that entrepreneurs tend to associate their past experience to interpret and identify new business opportunity. In other words, they use cognitive frameworks they possess to "connect the dots" between changes in the external environment which are the markets, technology, politics, and other factors. The patterns they then perceive in these events or trends eventually suggest ideas for new products or services for the new ventures. Earlier, (Gaglio and Katz 2001) highlighted that individual histories and life experiences eventually turn into individual meanings and interpretations that shape their stock of knowledge and make it idiosyncratic. The idiosyncratic knowledge and information creates an individual knowledge corridor which enables people to recognize opportunities (Kuivaniemi 2010). Hence, experience entrepreneur can identify opportunity better than novice entrepreneurs (Leonie 2013).

6.2.4 Knowledge

Knowledge is not easily transferable to others. It enables one to see certain patterns in market behaviour, subtle differences in quality of goods, or ways to identify whether resources are being used efficiently (Holcombe 2003). Conversely, Ardichvili et al. (2003) indicated prior knowledge as one of the antecedents of the entrepreneurial opportunity identification and development. According to Von Hippel (1994), mostly people will tend to notice information that is related to information that they already know. In addition, Shane 2000 assumed that entrepreneurs will discover opportunities because prior knowledge triggers recognition of the value of the new information. Besides, Shane (2000) people who learn new knowledge will most likely to use it for new opportunity discovery. Meanwhile, Li et al. (2015) concurred that prior knowledge significantly and indirectly affected opportunity recognition through its impact on entrepreneurial alertness. The entrepreneurial alertness of non-entrepreneurial university students significantly influenced their opportunity recognition. On the other hand, the prior knowledge of entrepreneurial university students greatly influenced their opportunity recognition. On the other hand, leveraging external actors by exploiting their knowledge can help to create opportunity (Berglund 2007). It is important to note that knowledge acquisition and sharing can lead to opportunity creation such as research and development done by the universities researchers (Dang and McKelvey 2016).

6.2.5 Entrepreneurial Opportunity

An opportunity is an image in the person's mind, particularly an entrepreneur (Penrose 1959, p. 42). In relation to that, entrepreneurs take advantage on opportunity to generate profit (Kirzner 1999). Entrepreneurial opportunity can be defined "*…as situations in which new goods, services, raw materials, markets and organizing method can be introduced through the formation of new means, ends, or means-ends relationships…*" (Eckhardt and Shane 2003, p. 336). Opportunity can be categorized into two types of formation which are (1) opportunity creation or Schumpeterian and (2) opportunity identification or Kirznerian (Jong and Marsili 2010).

6.2.5.1 Opportunity Creation

In principle, opportunity creation emphasizes on the newness that had never been seen before which are derived due to invention and innovation. The newness in its value proposition will destruct the current equilibrium the present market where it will take over (Jong and Marsili 2010). However, Berglund (2007) indicated opportunity creation may require expert entrepreneurs engage with external actors to adjust and translate existing solutions but require strategically leveraging relationships. On the other hand, opportunity creation is based on entrepreneurs' subjective perceptions and created through social interactions and learning processes. All these trigger entrepreneurs' subjective notions of opportunity and environment (Sarasvathy 2001; Alvarez and Barney 2007).

6.2.5.2 Opportunity Identification

In discovery theory, competitive imperfections are assumed to arise exogenously, from changes in technology, consumer preferences, or some other attributes of the context within which an industry or market exists (Krizner 1973). In addition, Shane (2003) were cited that technological changes, political and regulatory changes, and social and demographic changes as examples of the kinds of events that can disrupt the competitive equilibrium that exists in a market or industry, thereby forming opportunities. Besides, opportunity identification is all about searching systematically by scanning the environment to identify opportunities that enable the production of new products or services. However, it is also important to note the duration and direction of the process in order to avoid confusion in searching the opportunity that might involve global search (Levinthal 1997).

6.3 Methodology

Extensive literature review had been conducted to enable the development of questionnaire as an instrument to generate data for analysis from the selected respondents. The instrument consists of three sections where Section A captures the demographic profile of respondent, whereas Section B captures respondent's feedback on statements on both dependent variables which are opportunities identification and creation. Lastly Section C captures the items under personal competencies, social capital, knowledge and experience. Section C and D respondent's feedback are based on the 5-Likert scale of 1 = strongly disagree to 5 = strongly agree. Prior to the field study, pilot test had been conducted involving 10 respondents. Cronbach's alpha reliability test had shown all the dimensions which are entrepreneurial competencies, social capital, past experience, and knowledge are reliable ranging from 0.784 to 0.954. The reliability refers to the extent to which scale produces consistent result if repeated measurements are taken on the characteristic. According to (Nunnally 1978), all the reliabilities exceeded the 0.70 were considered acceptable. Meanwhile, based on Hair et al. (2006) suggested that Cronbach alpha greater than 0.50 is within acceptable value in assessing reliability for basic research. A total of 254 questionnaires were distributed among the academic and non-academic staff of Universiti Teknologi MARA Sarawak in accordance with the rule of thumb (Krejcie and Morgan 1970) with the population of 750 total staff at the university.

6.4 Findings

From the distribution of 254 questionnaires, a total of 239 completed questionnaires return with the yield of 94.1%. Cronbach's alpha reliability test had been conducted on all dimensions which are entrepreneurial competency, social capital, past experience, knowledge, opportunity identification, and opportunity creation. Results had indicated that all dimensions are within the acceptable range of 0.67 and above. The descriptive statistical analysis had shown that among all the factors identified, entrepreneurial competency had the highest mean value of 4.15. Hence this indicates that respondents had agreed with entrepreneurial competency. The lowest mean is shown by past experience with 3.40, but overall respondent had agreed on identified factors (Table 6.1).

In accordance with Table 6.2, the descriptive statistics showed that continuous learning as the highest mean value of 4.34 for the entrepreneurial competency factor with the lowest standard deviation 0.653. In addition, other items such as self-confidence, risk taking, problem solving also have high mean value ranging from 4.04 to 4.15.

On the other hand, Table 6.3 has shown that the item communicate with other people had the highest mean score of 4.10 for the factor of social capital. In addition, the standard deviation for the item is 0.885. Likewise, mean value for other items is also above neutral which are near to agree ranging from 3.44 to 3.94. The items are relationship with family, relationship with friends, social media engagement, and relationship with organization.

In Table 6.4, the descriptive statistics on past experience factor indicated that previous working tasks item had the highest mean value of 4.08 with the lowest

Table 6.1 Descriptive statistic analysis

Descriptive statistics		
Factors	N	Mean
Entrepreneurial competency	239	4.15
Social capital	239	3.80
Past experience	239	3.40
Knowledge	239	3.80
Total	239	3.78

Table 6.2 Entrepreneurial competency factor

Descriptive statistics			
Items	N	Mean	Std. Deviation
1. Understanding others	239	4.11	0.750
2. Self-confidence	239	4.15	0.700
3. Continuous learning	**239**	**4.34**	**0.653**
4. Risk taker	239	4.04	0.824
5. Solve problem	239	4.10	0.849
Total	239		

Table 6.3 Social capital factor

Descriptive statistics			
Items	N	Mean	Std. Deviation
6. Relationship with family	239	3.44	0.976
7. Relationship with friends	239	3.79	0.878
8. **Communicate with people**	239	**4.10**	0.885
9. Social media engagement	239	3.94	0.939
10. Relationship with organization	239	3.74	0.975
Total	239		

Table 6.4 Past experience factor

Descriptive statistics			
Items	N	Mean	Std. Deviation
11. **Previous working tasks**	239	**4.08**	0.827
12. Specific product and service	239	3.72	0.864
13. Part-time business	239	3.29	1.173
14. Previous business problem	239	2.77	1.263
15. Business skills	239	3.34	1.159
Total	239		

Table 6.5 Knowledge factor

Descriptive statistics			
Items	N	Mean	Std. Deviation
16. Learning by interacting with others	239	3.99	0.775
17. **Formal learning**	239	**4.06**	0.742
18. Learning from my family	239	3.50	1.037
19. Learning from my friends	239	3.78	0.887
20. Learning from my mentor	239	3.64	1.154
Total	239		

standard deviation of 0.827 compared to other items. The other items which are specific product and service, part-time business, and business skills accorded the mean value of above 3.00 ranging 3.34 to 3.72. In contrast, previous business problems mean value is below 3.00 at 2.77 and standard deviation of 1.263.

With reference to Table 6.5, descriptive statistics for the item formal learning in the knowledge factor indicated that the item formal learning had the highest mean

Table 6.6 Pearson's correlation between opportunity identification and identified factors

Factors	Correlation	Opportunity identification
Entrepreneurial competency	Pearson's correlation	**0.375**[a]
	Sig. (two-tailed)	0.000
	N	239
Social capital	Pearson's correlation	**0.461**[a]
	Sig. (two-tailed)	0.000
	N	239
Past experience	Pearson's correlation	**0.616**[a]
	Sig. (two-tailed)	0.000
	N	239
Knowledge	Pearson's correlation	**0.494**[a]
	Sig. (two-tailed)	0.000
	N	239

[a]Correlation is significant at the 0.01 level (two-tailed)

value of 4.06 and the lowest standard deviation of 0.742. Nevertheless, the other items which are learning by interacting with others, learning from friends, learning from my mentor and learning from my family are above 3.00 ranging from 3.50 to 3.99 mean value.

Based on Table 6.6, all correlation between the opportunity identification and the identified factors which are entrepreneurial competency, social capital, past experience and knowledge is positively significant. According to Guttmann rules of thumb, the correlation is positively significant, but the relationship is weak at $p = 0.375$ for entrepreneurial competency. However, for social capital and knowledge, relationship is moderately strong which are $p = 0.461$ and $p = 0.494$, respectively. On the other hand, the result shows the respondent experience has a strong and positive correlation relationship at $p = 0.616$ with opportunity identification. Hence, the result shows that there are strong tendency for the respondent to capitalize past experience to identify entrepreneurial opportunity. Baron (2006) indicated that individuals gain experience in a particular domain, their prototypes and other cognitive frameworks do indeed become more clearly defined, richer in content, and more focused on key attributes of that content domain (Fig. 6.1).

Based on Table 6.7, all correlation values between the opportunity creation and the identified factors which are entrepreneurial competency, social capital, past experience and knowledge are positively significant. According to Guttmann rules of thumb, the correlation for entrepreneurial competency is positively significance, but the relationship is weak at $p = 0.313$. In addition, the result also shows the respondent knowledge, social capital, and past experience have a moderate positive

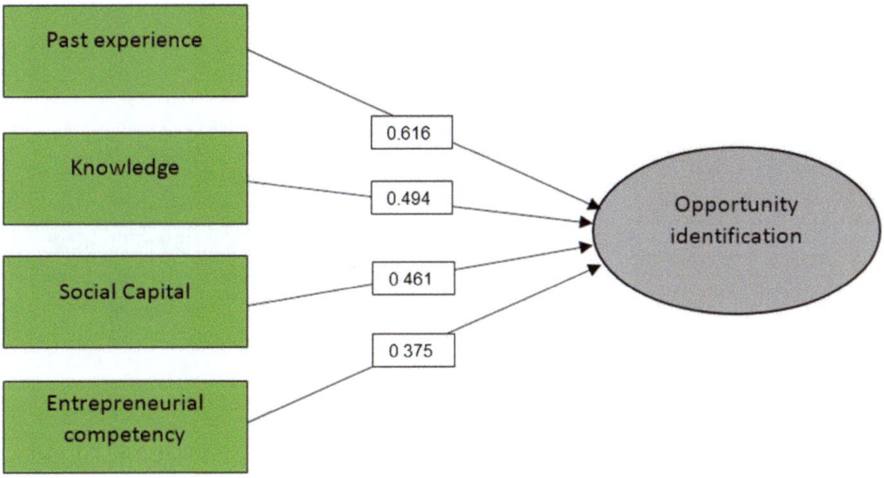

Fig. 6.1 Framework of factors that contribute to opportunity identification

Table 6.7 Pearson's correlation between opportunity creation and identified factors

Factors	Correlation	Opportunity creation
Entrepreneurial competency	Pearson's correlation	**0.313**[a]
	Sig. (two-tailed)	0.000
	N	239
Social capital	Pearson's correlation	**0.473**[a]
	Sig. (two-tailed)	0.000
	N	239
Past experience	Pearson's correlation	**0.460**[a]
	Sig. (two-tailed)	0.000
	N	239
Knowledge	Pearson's correlation	**0.506**[a]
	Sig. (two-tailed)	0.000
	N	239

[a]Correlation is significant at the 0.01 level (two-tailed)

relationship ranging from $p = 0.506$, $p = 0.473$ and $p = 0.460$ accordingly. Kuivaniemi (2010) has mentioned that the idiosyncratic knowledge and information creates an individual knowledge corridor which it enables people to recognize and create opportunity (Fig. 6.2).

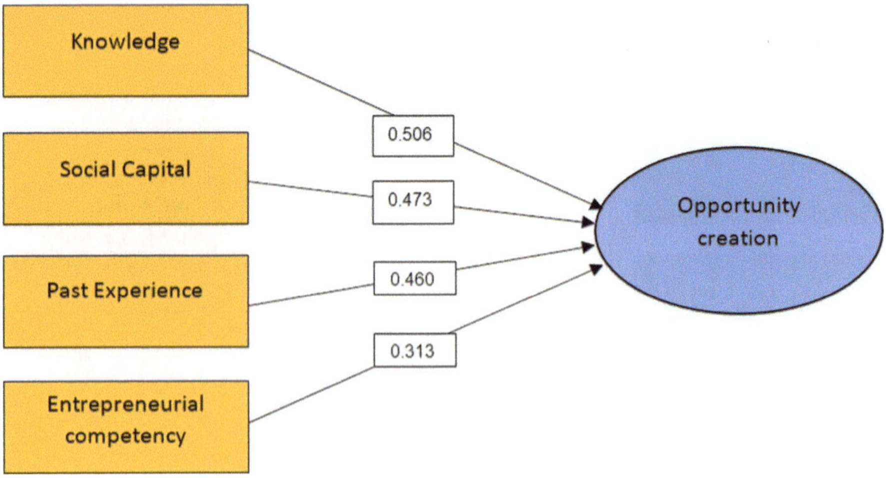

Fig. 6.2 Framework of factors that contribute to opportunity creation

6.5 Conclusion

This paper highlights the factors that contribute to opportunity identification and opportunity creation. The factors identified are entrepreneurial competency, social capital, past experience and knowledge in accordance with mean value indicated by the respondent of the study. However, based on Pearson's correlation, it is found that all factors are significantly and positively correlated with opportunity identification. Nevertheless in terms of the order of importance, past experience has the strongest correlation with opportunity identification. Likewise, Pearson's correlation between the identified factors and opportunity creation had indicated that knowledge factor is the most important factor, but it is at the moderate strength. On the other hand, other identified factors are also significantly and positively correlated with opportunity creation. The findings of the study really make sense as opportunity identification need past experience to enable the entrepreneur to discover or spot opportunity. The findings concurred to (Corbett 2005; Baron 2006) who indicated experience as the mechanism to opportunity identification. On the other hand, it is found that knowledge factor is the important factor for opportunity creation which is in line with Dang and McKelvey 2016. Earlier, Berglund 2007 indicated that knowledge needs to be exploited by leveraging the external actors in order to create opportunity.

References

Abdullah, F., Hj Hamali, J., Deen, A., Saban, G., & Abdurahman, A. A. (2009). Developing a framework of success of Bumiputera entrepreneurs. *Journal of Enterprising Communities: People and Places in the Global Economy, 3*(1), 8–24.

Alvarez, S. A., & Barney, J. B. (2007). Discovery and creation: Alternative theories of entrepreneurial action. *Organizações em contexto, 3*(6).

Ardichvili, A., Cardozo, R., & Ray, S. (2003). A theory of entrepreneurial opportunity identification and development. *Journal of Business Venturing, 18,* 105–123.

Baron, R. A. (2006). Opportunity recognition as pattern recognition. *Academy of Management Perspectives*, 104–118.

Berglund, H. (2007). Opportunities as existing and created: A study of entrepreneurs in the Swedish mobile internet industry. *Journal of Enterprising Culture, 15*(3), 243–273.

Corbett, A. C. (2005). Experiential learning within the process of opportunity identification and exploitation. *Entrepreneurship Theory and Practice, 29,* 473–491.

Dang, R. J., & McKelvey, M. (2016). Knowledge management processes and the formation of entrepreneurial opportunities. *Journal of Innovation Economics & Management*, 31–59. doi:10.3917/jie.019.0031.

Davidsson, P., & Honig, B. (2003). The role of social and human capital among nascent entrepreneurs. *Journal of Business Venturing, 18,*(3) 301–331.

De Jong, J. P., & Marsili, O. (2010). Schumpeter versus Kirzner: An empirical investigation of opportunity types. *EIM Research Reports*.

Gaglio, C. M., & Katz, J. A. (2001). The psychological basis of opportunity identification: entrepreneurial alertness. *Small Business Economics, 16*(2), 95–111.

Hair, J. F., Black, W. C., Babin, B. J., Anderson, R. E., & Tatham, R. L. (2006). SEM: confirmatory factor analysis. *Multivariate data analysis. Pearson Prentice Hall, Upper Saddle River*, 770–842.

Holcombe, R. G. (2003). The origins of entrepreneurial opportunities. *The Review of Austrian Economics, 16*(1), 25–43.

Kirzner, M. I. (1999). Creativity and/or alertness: A reconsideration. *Review of Austrian Economics*, 5–17.

Krejcie, R. V., & Morgan, D. W. (1970). Determining sample size for research. *Educational and Psychological Measurement, 30,* 607–610.

Krizner, I. (1973). *Competition and Entrepreneurship*. Chicago and London: University of Chicago Press.

Kuivaniemi, L. (2010). Evaluation and reasoning in the entrepreneurial opportunity process: Narratives from sex industry entrepreneurs. *Studies in Business and Economics*, 18–52.

Leonie, B. (2013). *Entrepreneurial experience and opportunity identification: the role of intuition and cognitive versatility.* Retrieved from http://wrap.warwick.ac.uk/58187/.

Levinthal, D. A. (1997). Adaptation on rugged landscapes. *Management Science, 43*(7), 934–950.

Li, Y., Wang, P., & Liang, Y. J. (2015). Influence of entrepreneurial experience, alertness, and prior knowledge on opportunity recognition. *Social behavior and personality an International Journal, 43*(9), 1575–1584.

Myint, Y. M., Vyakarnam, S., & New, M. J. (2005). The effect of social capital in new. *Strategic Change*, 165–177.

Nahapiet, J., & Ghosal, S. (1998). Social capital, intellectual capital and the organizational advantage. *Academy of Management Review, 23*(2), 242–266.

Naldi, L., Nordqvist, M., Sjöberg, K., & Wiklund, J. (2007). Entrepreneurial orientation, risk taking, and performance in family firms. *Family business review, 20*(1), 33–47.

Nunnally, C. (1978). *Psychometric theory, 2nd Edition* New York: McGraw-Hill.

Penrose, E. T. (1959). *The theory of the growth of the firm.* Oxford: Oxford University Press.

Sarasvathy, D. S. (2001). Causation and effectuation: Toward a Theoretical Shift from Economic Inevitability to Entrepreneurial Contingency. *Academy of Management Review*, 243–263.

Shane, S. (2000). Prior Knowledge and the discovery of entrepreneurial opportunities. *Organization Science, 11*(4), 448–469.

Shane, S. A. (2003). *A General Theory of Entrepreneurship: The Individual-opportunity Nexus. New horizons in entrepreneurship*. Northampton, MA: Edward Elgar.

Sharma, Y. (2015). Universities bear the brunt of cuts as economy slows. *University World News, 388*(00424). Retrieved August 23, 2016, from http://www.universityworldnews.com/article.php?story=20151029210957170.

Von Hippel, E. (1994). "Sticky information" and the locus of problem solving: implications for innovation. *Management science, 40*(4), 429–439.

Wilson, F., Kickul, J., & Marlino, D. (2007). Gender, entrepreneurial self-efficacy, and entrepreneurial career intentions: implications for entrepreneurship education. *Entrepreneurship theory and practice, 31*(3), 387–406.

Chapter 7
The Influence of Intellectual Capital and Corporate Entrepreneurship Towards Small and Medium Enterprises' (SMEs) Sustainable Competitive Advantage: Building a Conceptual Framework

Ahmad Rusydan Ab. Kadir, Azira Aminallah, Azman Ibrahim, Joehary Sulaiman, Mohd Fadzli Mohd Yusoff, Mohd Mahfudz Idris, Mohd Roslee Bahar, Rahayu Hasanordin, Siti Sakinah Ab. Rahim and Zaitun Abd Malek

Abstract In order to compete and staying alive in current dynamic global competitive environment, SMEs in Malaysia must have not only competitive advantage, but sustainable competitive advantage. Sustainability will ensure SMEs to withstand market onslaught and adaptable to volatile market changes. Even though Malaysian SME performance is improving, it is still way below the target of 41% SME-GDP contribution and lowers than other neighbouring ASEAN countries like Singapore, Thailand and Indonesia. As a result, Malaysian SMEs can capitalize their valuable internal resources like intellectual capital to gain sustainable competitive advantage. In addition, intellectual capital can be used to pervade corporate entrepreneurship into usable concept in SMEs that can eventually promote sustainable competitive advantage. This paper presents the current research on intellectual capital and corporate entrepreneurship in achieving sustainable competitive advantage at SMEs in Malaysia. It focuses on two main questions: How intellectual capitals boost sustainable competitive advantage in SMEs? How Corporate Entrepreneurship enhance sustainable competitive advantage in SME?

Keywords Sustainable competitive advantage · Intellectual capital · Corporate entrepreneurship

A.R.Ab. Kadir (✉) · A. Aminallah · A. Ibrahim · J. Sulaiman · M.F.M. Yusoff · M.M. Idris · M.R. Bahar · R. Hasanordin · S.S.Ab.Rahim · Z.A. Malek
Faculty of Business and Management, Arshad Ayub Graduate Business School, Universiti Teknologi MARA, Shah Alam, Malaysia
e-mail: ahmad.rusydan@gmail.com

F. Noordin et al. (eds.), *Proceedings of the 2nd Advances in Business Research International Conference*, https://doi.org/10.1007/978-981-10-6053-3_7

7.1 Introduction

SMEs have a major significant role in ASEAN economy. SMEs represent more than 96% of all enterprises that generate 50–95% employment. In addition, SMEs to GDP contribution are from 30 to 59% and it represents around 19–31% of export to the economies of all ASEAN state members. SME is vital to Malaysian economy since 1970s, and they are now considered as the new engine as well as the driver for nation economic growth and development (Hasan et al. 2016). Under the proposed SME Master Plan 2012–2020, Malaysian SMEs envision to become globally competitive all across sectors that enhance the nation's wealth and contribute to the social wellbeing. This is in line with the government aspiration to achieve high income nation by 2020. Four goals have been set up under the SME Development Framework. They are to increase business formation, increase the number of high growth and innovative firms, increase productivity and intensifying formalization of SMEs. These goals can be achieved by focusing on strategic areas such as innovation and technology adaptation, market access, human capital development, legal and regulatory environment, access to financing and infrastructure (SME Corp 2016). In term of achievement, Malaysian SMEs are still lagging in term of GDP contribution as compared to its neighbouring ASEAN countries (APEC.org 2014). Even though the figure has increased from 32.3 in 2010–36.3% in 2015, it is still below the 41% target for year 2020.

There are many contributing factors that help SMEs to perform better. In knowledge-based economy, knowledge is a powerful resource. The capitalization of intellectual capital can help to fully utilize internal resources. According to the Research-based Theory of Competitive Advantage, internal resources are more important than the market environment in strategic formulation in order to achieve sustainable competitive advantage (Grant 1991). Intellectual capital is an "intellectual material—knowledge, information, intellectual property, experience—that can be put use to create wealth" as well as "the sum of everything everybody in the company knows that gives it a competitive edge" (Stewart and Ruckdeschel 1998). There are three dimensions of intellectual capital, namely human capital, structural capital and relational capital (Martín-de-Castro et al. 2011). SMEs should capitalize on intellectual capital by devoting appropriate resources to its development at the human, organizational and relational levels to respond rapidly to change, allowing them to sense opportunities and threats and subsequently benefiting from competitive advantages (Daou et al. 2013).

Corporate entrepreneurship is a source for promoting and sustaining corporate competitiveness (Covin and Miles 1999). Corporate entrepreneurship is an entrepreneurship within an organization that includes formal and informal activities at the firm level that concentrate on discovering and seeking new business opportunities via corporate venturing, innovation and strategic renewal (Guth and Ginsberg 1990; Sharma and Chrisman 2007). Recent studies suggest that corporate entrepreneurship has positive influence on the overall performance of SMEs (Bierwerth et al. 2015; Kaya 2015). In addition, corporate entrepreneurship can assist SMEs in achieving sustainable competitive advantage (Corbett et al. 2013; Koentjoro and Eliyana 2015; Teng 2007), especially in this current highly competitive global economy to adapt and renew themselves. However, in order to harvest its intangible resources for competitive advantage, firms need a capability to convert corporate entrepreneurship into usable concepts (Zahra 2015).

Michael Porter defined the two types of competitive advantage an organization can achieve relative to its rivals: lower cost or differentiation. This advantage derives from attributes that allow an organization to outperform its competition, such as superior market position, skills or resources. In Porter's view, strategic management should be concerned with building and sustaining competitive advantage. The term competitive advantage refers to the ability gained through attributes and resources to perform at a higher level than others in the same industry or market. Sustainable competitive advantages refer to resources that have value, rare, inimitable and irreplaceable (Barney 1991). Managers and management scholars have traditionally embraced the premise that sustainable competitive advantage is vital in an organization and it can be achieved with innovation (Corbett et al. 2013). However, companies need a capability to convert the knowledge that permeates their corporate entrepreneurship activities into usable concepts (Zahra 2015). In addition, corporate entrepreneurship has shown that it can mediate in improving firm performance (Bakar and Mahmood 2014; García-Morales et al. 2014; Kearney et al. 2013) as well as innovation (Chen et al. 2015).

Previous researches in SMEs showed that intellectual capital has strong significant relationship to sustainable competitive advantage (Kamukama 2013; Todericiu and Stăniţ 2015; Yaseen et al. 2016), improve SMEs' performance and profitability (Alipour 2012; Khalique et al. 2015; Lu et al. 2014). In addition, innovation fully mediates intellectual capital and competitive advantage's relationship, while organizational learning moderates the same relationship (Chahal and Bakshi 2014). However, to our knowledge, there is a paucity in research that uses corporate entrepreneurship as the mediator in intellectual capital and sustainable competitive advantage's relationship. In line with Malaysia's inspiration to become a high income nation with SMEs as one of the main engine for growth, this research could be able to contribute for the improvement of our SMEs.

Therefore, this paper will focus on two main questions:

1. How intellectual capitals boost sustainable competitive advantage in SMEs?
2. How Corporate Entrepreneurship enhance sustainable competitive advantage in SME?

7.2 Literature Review

7.2.1 The Impact of Sustainable Competitive Advantage on SME

Sustainable competitive advantage refers to the ability to maintain and improve the competitive market position by a company, in our case SMEs to survive against competitors for certain long period of time (Todericiu and Stăniţ 2015). To remain competitive advantage in business, Nada and Ali (2015) have suggested that SMEs strongly need to innovate in their services. Innovation is one of the key elements which could differentiate SMEs from their competitors hence attracts customers. In details, the study by Marques and Ferreira (2009) has explained that the process innovation and R&D investment are the most important variables which leads to higher competitive advantage. Furthermore, many previous studies have linked innovation (technical and non-technical) of the company including SMEs to the competitive advantage (as cited in Weerawardena and Mavondo 2011).

In the other view, Van Gils and Zwart (2004) believed that small- and medium-sized firms should improve their knowledge management process and as well as assign strategic alliance partner for their growth development to achieve sustainable competitive advantage. The implementation of knowledge management on SMEs could also be a part of innovation effort to improve the firms position in the competitive market. The above finding on the importance of knowledge management was also observed in other study by Egbu et al. (2005), who emphasized that the implementation of correct strategies, tools and technologies of knowledge management could definitively help SMEs to sustain in competitive advantage, with embracing a knowledge culture which is vital in the current knowledge economy. Jardon and Susana Martos (2012) have further elaborated that the use of knowledge management based on intellectual capital is essential in enhancing strategic factors trough organizational capabilities of SMEs to remain competitive in their business.

Addition to that, the knowledge management on SMEs based on information technology in the term of resources integration, information usage and the facilities availability was also proven to have significance effect towards competitive advantage of the firm (Ong and Ismail 2008). This is parallel to the study by Pavic et al. (2007), who emphasized the needs of internet technology integration, with right attitude, knowledge and management skills on overall SMEs strategy to gain competitive advantage. These studies are the proofs that SMEs have to strategize their firm in adapting knowledge management through the latest technology in order to innovate and hence to sustain in competitive advantage against other competitors.

7.2.2 Intellectual Capital and Sustainable Competitive Advantage

Intellectual capital can be seen as collective knowledge which can be exploited to produce an output for useful purposes. In the context of business, intellectual capital is considered as an asset for an organization to use in gaining their competitive advantage as well as driving its revenue and profits that, in turn, will also promoting to the nation's economic development. This was supported by Yaseen et al. (2016) which had stated that intellectual capital is considered as a determining factors that drive organization's innovation and as well as economic growth. Intellectual capital can be seen as collective knowledge which can be exploited to produce an output for useful purposes. In the context of business, intellectual capital is considered as an asset for an organization to use in gaining their competitive advantage (Chahal and Bakshi 2014; Kamukama 2013; Todericiu and Stăniţ 2015; Yaseen et al. 2016) as well as driving its performance, revenue and profits (Alipour 2012; Gogan et al. 2016; Lu et al. 2014) that, in turn, will also promoting to the nation's economic performance (Seleim and Bontis 2013).

Past studies largely investigated on intellectual capital discovered that the concept of intellectual capital is varied. As for an example Gogan et al. (2016) and Todericiu and Stăniţ (2015) justified that intellectual capital is an intangible asset which an organization owned such as human capital, structural capital and relational capital that can be determined by the failure or success of the organization. This was agreed by Bontis (1998) and Tovstiga and Tulugurova (2009) in their paper which also stated that intellectual capital including the combination of human capital, relational capital and structural capital which derived an organization to succeed in the future.

However, recent study also suggests that intellectual capital has insignificant relationship with financial performance (Bontis et al. 2015). Moreover, some of the components in IC like human capital (Khalique et al. 2015b; Yaseen et al. 2016) as well as customer and social capital (Khalique et al. 2015a) have negative relationship with firm's performance.

In order for an organization to stay survive and sustained in competitive markets, it is necessarily for them to continuously enhance its competitive advantage which cannot be replicated by its competitors. In particular, sustainable competitive advantages refer to an extra value that an organization creates from matching up its core competencies to the opportunities which providing greater value of strategies through differentiation from their competitors. Furthermore, an organization may use and combine their resources more effectively than others so that they could leverage the resources to create greater value (Evans 2016).

7.2.3 Intellectual Capital and Corporate Entrepreneurship

To recapitulate, this paper defined intellectual capital as an intangible capital which consists of three (3) constructs, namely human capital, structural capital and relationship capital. Human capital relates to expertise, skills, competency, creativity and innovative of the employees for the organization, while structural capital refers to overall processes and procedures of the organization for value creation. Meanwhile, the third construct, relationship capital, refers to engagement of the team with external stakeholders inclusive of customers, suppliers and vendors.

There is a growing recognition on the significant of intellectual capital towards organization as a tool to compete. In today's era of globalized economy, organizations need to undertake entrepreneurial activities to achieve competitive success (Bloodgood et al. 2013). In addition, organizations need to become more entrepreneurial in order to survive and prosper following the global intense competition (Dess et al. 1999). Entrepreneurial activities in established mid-sized and large organizations are known as Corporate Entrepreneurship (Morris et al. 2008).

Intellectual capital has positive influence on corporate entrepreneurship (Hayton 2005), and it mediates the relationship between corporate entrepreneurship and firm's performance (Simsek and Heavey 2011). In addition, intellectual capital is a value-creating factor in what concerns product innovation at innovative SMEs where human, relational and structural capital effectively reveal a significant impact on product innovation performance (Costa et al. 2014). As a result, SMEs should capitalize on intellectual capital by devoting appropriate resources to its development at the human, organizational and relational levels to respond rapidly to change, allowing them to sense opportunities and threats and subsequently benefiting from competitive advantages (Daou et al. 2013). Moreover, resource-based SMEs should use intellectual capital along with other resources to build organizational capabilities that, joint with the territory, affect strategic factors, allowing them to achieve better results (Jardon and Catalina 2015). This model characterizes elements of the human capital (attitude, training and staff skills), the structural capital (culture, technology and internal organization of the company) and the relational capital (customer and supplier relationships, cooperation and image of the company). Therefore, SMEs can use corporate entrepreneurship to turn intellectual capital into valuable internal resources to boost performance, increase profitability, enhance innovation thus creating sustainable competitive advantage.

7.2.4 Corporate Entrepreneurship and Sustainable Competitive Advantage

Corporate entrepreneurship has long been recognized as a potentially viable means for promoting and sustaining corporate competitiveness (Covin and Miles 1999). Corporate entrepreneurship includes formal and informal activities at the firm level that concentrate on discovering and seeking new business opportunities via corporate venturing, innovation and strategic renewal (Guth and Ginsberg 1990; Sharma and Chrisman 2007). Recent studies suggest that CE have positive influence on the overall performance of SMEs (Bierwerth et al. 2015; Kaya 2015). In addition, CE can assist SMEs in achieving sustainable competitive advantage (Corbett et al. 2013; Koentjoro and Eliyana 2015; Teng 2007), especially in this current highly competitive global economy to adapt and renew themselves. However, in order to harvest its intangible resources for competitive advantage, firms need a capability to convert CE into usable concepts (Zahra 2015).

Previous studies show that corporate entrepreneurship mediates the performance of SMEs with external environment (Kearney et al. 2013), transformational leadership (Bakar and Mahmood 2014), technological skills and absorptive capacity (García-Morales et al. 2014) as well as IT capabilities (Chen et al. 2015). Therefore, authors believe that sustainable competitive advantage can be achieved through intellectual capital and corporate entrepreneurship in SMEs. Hayton (2005) examined the relationship between intellectual capital and business in terms of heterogeneity and aggregation of intellectual capital. By differentiation, it includes interest in human capital, innovative work, corporate society, data frameworks and creation forms. Intellectual capital is connected with information, innovation and the capacity of representatives. Intellectual capital can be defined as a knowledge that can be converted into value. (Edvinsson and Sullivan 1996).

Based on the literature review, there is a paucity in research that shows clear relationship between corporate entrepreneurship and intellectual capital that resulting sustainable competitive advantage among SMEs in Malaysia. Indeed, intellectual capital is always associated with sustainable competitive advantage, especially in this current knowledge-based economy. Therefore, SMEs that are able to capitalize and exploit intellectual capital by turning their human capital, structural capital and relational capital into sources of sustainable competitive advantage through corporate entrepreneurship are expected to survive the current dynamic and highly competitive market.

7.3 Conceptual Framework

Based on the literature review, a conceptual framework has been developed. Intellectual capital is the independent variable, corporate entrepreneurship is the mediating variable and sustainable competitive advantage is the dependent variable. Based on the input-process-output structural framework (Fig. 7.1) which imply on how different input, intermediate and output variables form causal relationship in a system. In this study, it is proposed that intellectual capital is static resources that need to go through processes of corporate entrepreneurship to achieve sustainable competitive advantage of SMEs.

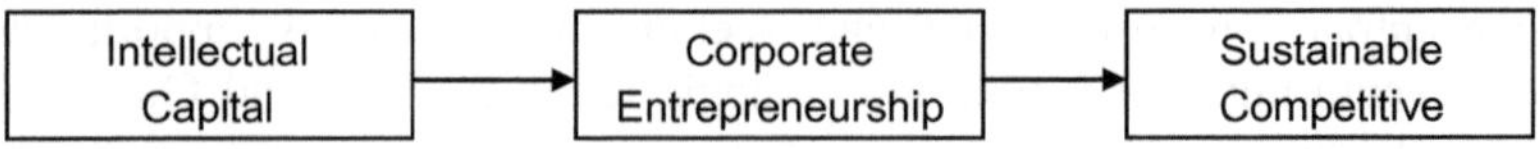

Fig. 7.1 Conceptual framework

7.4 Conclusion

This paper has successfully developed a conceptual framework that is helpful for future research in this area. Besides, this study has provided new insight view on SME studies and shift the development of business research from looking at the performance and success factors to different angle which is identifying factors to improve the SME survival. The understanding of SME survival significance may lead to the effort in promoting intellectual capital and corporate entrepreneurship that leads to sustainable competitive advantage in business. Theoretically, the main variables found to be significant to SME survival but empirical data are required to prove these connections. Nevertheless, as this is a conceptual paper with reference to the previous studies. There are no data collected to enable generalization to other countries. Further study is encouraged to assess the developed conceptual framework with the aim to guide SME to stay competitive and can be expanded for the business to grow and flourish.

References

Alipour, M. (2012). The effect of intellectual capital on firm performance: an investigation of Iran insurance companies. *Measuring Business Excellence, 16*(1), 53–66. doi:10.1108/13683041211204671.

Bakar, M. S., & Mahmood, R. (2014). Linking transformational leadership and corporate entrepreneurship to performance in the public higher education institutions in malaysia, *4*(3), 109–122.

Barney, J. (1991). Firm Resources and sustained competitive advantage. *Journal of Composite Materials, 17*(1), 99–120. http://doi.org/0803973233.

Bierwerth, M., Schwens, C., & Ru, R. I. (2015). Corporate entrepreneurship and performance : A meta-analysis, 255–278. http://doi.org/10.1007/s11187-015-9629-1.

Bloodgood, J. M., Hornsby, J. S., & Hayton, J. C. (2013). Organizational resourcefulness: The role of purposeful resource focus vacillation in implementing corporate entrepreneurship. *Advances in Entrepreneurship, Firm Emergence and Growth, 15*(2013), 95–124. http://doi.org/10.1108/S1074-7540(2013)15.

Bontis, N. (1998). Intellectual capital: An exploratory study that develops measures and models. *Management Decision, 36*(2), 63–76.

Bontis, N., Janosevic, S., & Dzenopoljac, V. (2015). Intellectual capital in Serbia's hotel industry. *International Journal of Contemporary Hospitality Management, 27*(6), 1365–1384. http://doi.org/http://dx.doi.org/10.1108/IJCHM-12-2013-0541.

Chahal, H., & Bakshi, P. (2014). Effect of intellectual capital on competitive advantage and business performance: Role of innovation and learning culture. *International Journal of Learning and Intellectual Capital, 11*(1), 52–70. http://doi.org/10.1504/IJLIC.2014.059227.

Chen, Y., Wang, Y., Nevo, S., Benitez-Amado, J., & Kou, G. (2015). IT capabilities and product innovation performance: The roles of corporate entrepreneurship and competitive intensity. *Information & Management, 52*(6), 643–657. doi:10.1016/j.im.2015.05.003.

Corbett, A., Covin, J. G., O'Connor, G. C., & Tucci, C. L. (2013). Corporate entrepreneurship: State-of-the-Art research and a future research agenda. *Journal of Product Innovation Management, 30*(5), 812–820. doi:10.1111/jpim.12031.

Costa, R. V., Fernández, C. F. J., & Dorrego, P. F. (2014). Critical elements for product innovation at Portuguese innovative SMEs: An intellectual capital perspective. *Knowledge Management Research and Practice, 12*(3), 322–338. doi:10.1057/kmrp.2014.15.

Covin, J. O., & Miles, M. P. (1999). Corporate entrepreneurship and the pursuit of competitive advantage. *Entrepreneurship: Theory & Practice*, *23*(3), 47–63. http://doi.org/Article.

Daou, A., Karuranga, E., & Su, Z. (2013). Intellectual capital in mexican SMEs from the perspective of the resource-based and dynamic capabilities views, *29*(6), 1673–1689.

Dess, G. G., Lumpkin, G. T., & McKee, J. E. (1999). Linking corporate entrepreneurship to strategy, structure, and process: Suggested research directions. *Entrepreneurship: Theory and Practice*, *23*(3), 85–85.

Edvinsson, L., & Sullivan, P. (1996). Developing a model for managing intellectual capital. *European Management Journal, 14*(4), 356–364.

Egbu, C. O., Hari, S., & Renukappa, S. H. (2005). Knowledge management for sustainable competitiveness in small and medium surveying practices. *Structural Survey*, *23*(1), 7–21.

Evans, N. G. (2016). Sustainable competitive advantage in tourism organizations: A strategic model applying service dominant logic and tourism's defining characteristics. *Tourism Management Perspectives, 18,* 14–25. doi:10.1016/j.tmp.2015.12.015.

García-Morales, V. J., Bolívar-Ramos, M. T., & Martín-Rojas, R. (2014). Technological variables and absorptive capacity's influence on performance through corporate entrepreneurship. *Journal of Business Research, 67*(7), 1468–1477. doi:10.1016/j.jbusres.2013.07.019.

Van Gils, A., & Zwart, P. (2004). Knowledge acquisition and learning in Dutch and Belgian SMEs: The role of strategic alliances. *European Management Journal*, *22*(6), 685–692.

Gogan, L. M., Artene, A., Sarca, I., & Draghici, A. (2016). The impact of intellectual capital on organizational performance. *Procedia—Social and Behavioral Sciences, 211*(September), 194–202. doi:10.1016/j.sbspro.2015.11.085.

Grant, R. M. (1991). The resource-based theory of competitive advantage: Implications for strategy formulation. *California Management Review*, *33*(3), 114–135.

Guth, W. D., & Ginsberg, A. R. I. (1990). *Guest Editors' Introduction: Corporate Entrepreneurship, 11,* 5–15.

Hasan, H., Jais, M., Razak, M. R. A., Wahid, S. N. S., Ab Halim, R., & Riduan, A. (2016). Perceived service quality of small and medium enterprises (SMEs) on banks' lending and loan service quality in Malacca. In *Regional conference on science, technology and social sciences (RCSTSS 2014)* (pp. 127–135). Singapore: Springer. About SME Masterplan (2012–2020). (n. d). Retrieve from http://www.smecorp.gov.my/index.php/en/policies/2015-12-21-09-16-12/about-sme-masterplan.

Hayton, J. C. (2005). The effect of intellectual capital on entrepreneurial orientation in high-technology new ventures. *R&D Management*, *35*(2), 137–155. http://doi.org/papers://BA75DBD3-74D3-4A2D-AAAC-910414082C6C/Paper/p12396.

Jardon, C. M., & Catalina, N. (2015). Intellectual capital as a source of growth in subsistence small businesses in Latin America. *International Journal of Entrepreneurship and Small Business, 26*(1), 96. doi:10.1504/IJESB.2015.071322.

Jardon, C. M., & Susana Martos, M. (2012). Intellectual capital as competitive advantage in emerging clusters in Latin America. *Journal of Intellectual Capital*, *13*(4), 462–481.

Kamukama, N. (2013). Intellectual capital: Company's invisible source of competitive advantage. *Competitiveness Review: An International Business Journal, 23*(3), 260–283. doi:10.1108/10595421311319834.

Kaya, N. (2015). Corporate entrepreneurship, generic competitive strategies, and firm performance in small and medium-sized enterprises. *Procedia—Social and Behavioral Sciences, 207*, 662–668. doi:10.1016/j.sbspro.2015.10.136.

Kearney, C., Hisrich, R. D., & Antoncic, B. (2013). The mediating role of corporate entrepreneurship for external environment effects on performance. *Journal of Business Economics and Management, 14*(supl), S328–S357. doi:10.3846/16111699.2012.720592.

Khalique, M., Azad Jammu, M., & Ordóñez de Pablos, P. (2015a). Intellectual capital and performance of electrical and electronics SMEs in Malaysia. *International Journal Learning and Intellectual Capital, 12*(3), 251–269. doi:10.1504/IJLIC.2015.070166.

Khalique, M., Bontis, N., Shaari, J. A. N. Bin, & Isa, A. H. M. (2015b). Intellectual capital in small and medium enterprises in Pakistan. *Journal of Intellectual Capital, 16*(1), 224–238.

Koentjoro, S., & Eliyana, A. (2015). Resource orchestration: consolidation, integration, entrepreneurial and affective commitment in creating sustainable competitive advantage in the family firm Sugiarto Koentjoro anis Eliyana faculty of economics & business management Airlangga universit. *International of Business and Social Science, 6*(3), 128–136.

Lu, W. M., Wang, W. K., & Kweh, Q. L. (2014). Intellectual capital and performance in the Chinese life insurance industry. *Omega (United Kingdom), 42*(1), 65–74. doi:10.1016/j.omega.2013.03.002.

Marques, C. S., & Ferreira, J. (2009). SME innovative capacity, competitive advantage and performance in a 'Traditional' industrial region of Portugal. *Journal of Technology Management & Innovation, 4*(4), 53–68.

Martín-de-Castro, G., Delgado-Verde, M., López-Sáez, P., & Navas-López, J. E. (2011). Towards "an intellectual capital-based view of the firm": origins and nature. *Journal of Business Ethics, 98*(4), 649–662. doi:10.1007/s10551-010-0644-5.

Morris, M. H., Kuratko, D. F., & Covin, J. G. (2008). *Corporate entrepreneurship & innovation*. SouthWestern: Thomson Publishers.

Nada, N., & Ali, Z. (2015). Service value creation capability model to assess the service innovation capability in SMEs. *Procedia CIRP, 30*, 390–395.

Ong, J. W., & Ismail, H. B. (2008). Sustainable competitive advantage through information technology competence: Resource-based view on small and medium enterprises. *Communications of the IBIMA, 1*(7), 62–70.

Pavic, S. C. L. K., Koh, S. C. L., Simpson, M., & Padmore, J. (2007). Could e-business create a competitive advantage in UK SMEs?. *Benchmarking: An International Journal, 14*(3), 320–351.

Seleim, A., & Bontis, N. (2013). National intellectual capital and economic performance: Empirical evidence from developing countries. *Knowledge and Process Management, 20*(3), 131–140. doi:10.1002/kpm.

Sharma, P., & Chrisman, S. J. J. (2007). Toward a reconciliation of the definitional issues in the field of corporate entrepreneurship. *Entrepreneurship: Concepts, Theory and Perspective*, 83–103. http://doi.org/10.1007/978-3-540-48543-8_4.

Simsek, Z., & Heavey, C. (2011). The mediating role of knowledge-based capital for corporate entrepreneurship effects on performance: A study of small- to medium-sized firms. *Strategic Entrepreneurship Journal, 5*(1), 81–100. doi:10.1002/sej.108.

SMEs in the APEC Region. (2014, May 19). Retrieve from https://www.apec.org/media/Files/AboutUs/Infographics/20140519_infograph_sme_hires.jpg.

SME Masterplan (2012–2020). (n.d). Retrieve from http://www.smecorp.gov.my/index.php/en/policies/2015-12-21-09-16-12/about-sme-masterplan.

Stewart, T., & Ruckdeschel, C. (1998). *Intellectual capital: The new wealth of organizations*.

Teng, B. S. (2007). Corporate entrepreneurship activities through strategic alliances: A resource-based approach toward competitive advantage. *Journal of Management Studies, 44*(1), 119–142. doi:10.1111/j.1467-6486.2006.00645.x.

Todericiu, R., & Stăniţ, A. (2015). Intellectual capital—The key for sustainable competitive advantage for the SME's sector. *Procedia Economics and Finance, 27*(15), 676–681. doi:10.1016/S2212-5671(15)01048-5.

Tovstiga, G., & Tulugurova, E. (2009). Intellectual capital practices: A four-region comparative study. *Journal of Intellectual Capital, 10*(1), 70–80.

Weerawardena, J., & Mavondo, F. T. (2011). Capabilities, innovation and competitive advantage. *Industrial Marketing Management, 40*(8), 1220–1223.

Yaseen, S. G., Dajani, D., & Hasan, Y. (2016). The impact of intellectual capital on the competitive advantage: Applied study in Jordanian telecommunication companies. *Computers in Human Behavior, 62,* 168–175. doi:10.1016/j.chb.2016.03.075.

Zahra, S. A. (2015). Corporate entrepreneurship as knowledge creation and conversion: the role of entrepreneurial hubs. *Small Business Economics, 44*(4), 727–735. doi:10.1007/s11187-015-9650-4.

Chapter 8
The 11th Malaysia Health Plan: Demand for Investigation on Health Consumers' Intention Toward National Web-Based Health Information Service

Siti Noraini Mohd Tobi, Maslin Masrom and Azman Mohammed

Abstract It is found that the effective way to promote health education to the mass is with the support of technology and such in the case is by using online health information service which is similarly to the Web-based health information service. The main highlight of the article is regarding the Web-based health information service that has been created particularly to educate the health consumers regarding health issues. Meanwhile, the ultimate objective of this paper is to address the demand for a national study on health consumers' intention to use a Web-based health information service. The paper also offered some views on the statement of problems regarding the intended topic and provided further justification on why the study should be conducted. Some pertinent recommendations with regard to the issue are also discussed.

Keywords Web-based health information service · Health consumer intention Health education · National study

S.N. Mohd Tobi (✉)
Center for Management and Administrative Studies, Faculty of Business and Management, Universiti Teknologi MARA, 42300 Bandar Puncak Alam, Selangor, Malaysia
e-mail: snoraini7601@puncakalam.uitm.edu.my

M. Masrom
Razak School of Engineering and Advanced Technology, Universiti Teknologi Malaysia, Jalan Sultan Yahya Petra, 54100, Kuala Lumpur Johor, Malaysia
e-mail: maslin.kl@utm.my

A. Mohammed
Health Education Division, Ministry of Health Malaysia,
Federal Government Administrative Centre, 62590 Putrajaya, Malaysia
e-mail: azmanmohd@moh.gov.my

F. Noordin et al. (eds.), *Proceedings of the 2nd Advances in Business Research International Conference*, https://doi.org/10.1007/978-981-10-6053-3_8

8.1 Introduction

Many of today's and tomorrow's leading causes of death, disease and disability are caused by unhealthy lifestyles and environments, e.g., cardiovascular disease, cancer, chronic lung diseases, depression, violence, substance abuse, injuries, nutritional deficiencies, HIV/AIDS/STI and health infections (WHO 2015). In some developing countries, up to 60% of all new HIV infections occur among 15- to 24-year-olds (WHO 2015). In year 2014, World Health Statistic revealed that the three highest causes of years of life lost due to premature death are coronary heart disease, lower respiratory infections (such as pneumonia) and stroke (WHO Department of Communications 2014). In 47 countries (mostly high-income), the non-communicable diseases and injuries (e.g., cardiovascular disease, diabetes and cancer) have caused more than 90% of years of life lost (WHO Department of Communications 2014), while more than 100 countries are transitioning rapidly toward a greater proportion of deaths from non-communicable diseases and injuries (WHO Department of Communications 2014).

In Malaysia, the non-communicable diseases have surpassed the communicable diseases in terms of morbidity and mortality (Health Informatics Center Planning and Development Division 2012). The non-communicable disease such as cardiovascular disease, diabetes and cancer are the major causes of admissions and deaths in government hospitals (Health Informatics Center Planning and Development Division 2012). The National Health Morbidity Surveys (NHMS) conducted in 1996 (NHMS II) and 2006 (NHMS III) showed that the prevalence of diabetes and hypertension is increasing in trend. The prevalence of diabetes mellitus has increased twofold in NHMS III (14.6%) as compared to NHMS II (8.3%), and higher prevalence of hypertension and cardiovascular disease has also been observed in NHMS III (Ministry of Health Malaysia 1996, 2006).

Furthermore, by the year 2020, it is estimated that people of 60 years of age will contribute to 11.2% of the total population, with a consequent increase in morbidity (Ministry of Health Malaysia 2006). The expected increase in the number of elderly will result in a consequent increase in morbidity conditions, which may consume a large portion of funds for health.

8.2 Need for Online Health Empowerment

WHO has long argued that the adoption of healthy lifestyles and environments is a key element of such preventive actions (WHO 2015). In fact, in today modern living society the prevention of chronic diseases has emerged as a major focus of public health interest. However, it has been made aware that it is difficult to change and modify behaviors of individuals and communities since there is a wide gap between community's knowledge and their behavior in which the community still does not take ownership of their health issues. Lots of health messages and information have been disseminated to the public, but these have yet to be translated into actions and behavioral changes. Thus, the community empowerment becomes instrumental where ultimately it is communities, families and individuals who must change their behavior in order to be healthier.

For this reason, there is an urgent need to orient health systems more toward health promotion and to build their capacity to promote health, and one of its ways is by developing an innovative and updated health promotion means, which are the Web-based health information service (WBHIS). WBHIS is an example of online health education under the pillars of ehealth, and it is considered as an effective way to promote health education to the mass with the support of technology using online health information services. It was also highlighted as, when diseases caused by lifestyles start to threaten the whole society, health information service is considered as a preventive measure to alleviate this threat (Romanow et al. 2012). Having access to any of the ehealth applications such as online health education services, similarly the WBHIS could enhance the preventative measurement. The community also needs to participate in ehealth for their own health benefits. Their participation can be improved through developing their skills and abilities to build capacity. Furthermore, it is also highlighted that the telemedicine service acceptance has been slow in actual healthcare settings despite the proliferation of telemedicine technology (Rho and Choil 2014). This is what perhaps the public healthcare providers believe that health consumers lack interest in using ehealth (Löfstedt 2007). Others suggest that the problem is that it is unclear what kind of services healthcare consumers want and uncertain how best to provide this services (Howitt et al. 2002; Ross et al. 2000). Now, what is clear is that the future of ehealth is critically dependent on developing a clear understanding of consumers' attitudes toward and perceptions of the service. Only then can ehealth offerings be developed that match consumers' needs and wants, a prerequisite for successful service delivery (Lanseng and Andreassen 2007).

8.3 Malaysia National WBHIS

MyHEALTH Portal (MHP) is a national WBHIS setup by the Ministry of Health Malaysia in 2005. It is one of the national initiatives by Malaysia Government to bring great advances to the country through the innovative use of information and communication technology (ICT) to enable accurate, appropriate and up-to-date information about the health information to be disseminated in a timely, equitable and interactive manner. The main functions of MHP are to provide online health information for Malaysians and become a source of comprehensive, credible, accurate and latest information on health covering prevention, treatment, and rehabilitation developed by local health and medical experts. There are four main objectives of this portal: to empower Malaysians to take responsibility for their health; to equip Malaysians with knowledge, understanding and skills in order to enable them to make informed health decision; to encourage participation and involvement of Malaysians in managing their health and to encourage Malaysians to undertake health risk assessment (Malaysia Health Education Division 2014). This portal carries certain health-related topics such as Health for Kids; Teenagers; Prime Years; Golden Years; Nutrition; Medication and You; Oral Health Alert; Frequently Asked Questions (FAQ) and also maintains a Health Forum. The portal can be accessed at URL http://www.myhealth.gov.my.

8.4 Problem Statements

It was found that health consumers' intention to use would be an important element that contributes to a successful implementation of a new IT introduction (Jian et al. 2012). Relatively, MHP has been introduced in Malaysia since 2005, but the outcome is known to be limited within the health consumers and within the Ministry as well. As of today, it was found that there is only one elementary study conducted on MHP, and it is limited only to the health consumers' awareness concerning the existence of MHP (Malaysia Institute for Health Behavioral Research 2014). Furthermore, it is of importance to investigate the actual health consumer's intention to use of MHP as the government had spent a large amount of money, and there is no point in spending time and money on health education if it does not work. This statement is further supported by few statistics such as in the elementary study of MHP which revealed only 24% of respondents know about MHP, but only 9% had used it (Malaysia Institute for Health Behavioral Research 2014). Besides that, evidence also revealed that the portal usage is still far from the target number as expected by Malaysia Health Education Division (which is the operating division) that is 3 million hits in 2014. A statement also made by Malaysia National Audit Department which highlighted that Ministry of Health had spent the unnecessarily immense amount of money through its miscellaneous health campaigns, yet the outcome is unachievable and unclear (National Audit Department 2012). Due to above circumstances, a further study is fundamental to investigate MHP behavioral intention among Malaysian health consumers to examine the actual MHP further usage while answering the alarming issues highlighted above. Furthermore, there is a need for behavioral intention study as an intention to use has been established as a good predictor for technology use (Venkatesh et al. 2003, 2007).

It is also crucial to determine the successful implementation of WBHIS-MHP with regard to an understanding of what influences users to use WBHIS-MHP. It is found that health consumers' intention to use WBHIS-MHP among Malaysian population is not well understood with regard to the factors that influence its usage and the relationship among predictors of WBHIS-MHP usage. A further study is mutually acknowledged as essential to help solve the puzzle in understanding the factors that influence users' intention to use MHP. Due to the fact that Ministry of Health has spent a large amount of budget for MHP, it is important to depict and explore the causal circumstances for further corrective actions. The above statement is further supported with a preliminary interview with the senior principal assistant director of Health Education Division, Ministry of Health, which revealed that further investigations into factors that contribute toward the public usage of this portal are necessary as this would help them to act accordingly based on the findings, thus maximizing the portal usage while reducing the healthcare cost. Furthermore, it is important to understand the process of technology diffusion's factor among end users for effectively implementing adoption and coping with frequent changes in the environment (Lee 2003). To consider other possible factors, it had been firmly stressed that WBHIS presents other challenges to the user beyond just the general technology adoption (Torres 2011; Limayem et al. 2003). Also, the future of ehealth is critically dependent on developing a clear understanding of consumers' attitudes toward and perceptions of the service which is a prerequisite for successful service delivery (Lanseng and Andreassen 2007).

In addition, evidence has shown that there will be an expected increase in a number of elderly in 2020 that is 11.2% from the total number of population and Malaysia soon will achieve the status of as an aging population country in the year 2030 with 15% number of elderly (WHO 2014). This will result in a consequent increase in morbidity conditions consuming a large portion of funds for health (Ministry of Health Malaysia 2006). Apart of that, evidence also revealed that lifestyle-related diseases tend to occur more frequently among young generation than among elder adults (WHO 2015). The above situations demand a need for academic attention to investigate healthcare service issues covering multi-ages of health users including young and elder adults. Therefore, it is imperative to undertake WBHIS-intention study that will be covering wider ages of respondents with regard to the significant factors that influence health consumers' intention to use MHP.

8.5 Recommendation

All of above have established a justification that there is a crucial need to conduct further study to investigate deeper on health consumers' intent to utilize national WBHIS-MHP. As highlighted, measuring user acceptance of government's health information portal using one framework alone is not sufficient where there are other factors that potentially influenced the usage (Wilson and Lankton 2004). These potential factors could have a direct influence toward the utilization of national WBHIS-MHP. Likewise, it is also crucial to study individual's attitude and behavioral intention toward health promotion and education as person's behavior is predicted by their attitude toward the particular behavior and how they think other people would view them if they did the actual behavior (Ajzen 1991). Both of these factors determine a person's behavior intention, which leads to whether the actual behavior will be carried or not. The above-mentioned factors would be imperative to be investigated in answering the gaps highlighted above while at the same time contributes to the knowledge by anticipating various factors that will significantly influence citizens' intentional use of WBHIS-MHP.

8.6 Conclusion

The adoption of healthy lifestyles and environments is the key element of preventive actions toward healthy living and to uphold the health promotion through ehealth applications such as the Web-based health information service is one of the keys. This paper has offered some views on the statement of the problem regarding the intended topic and justified why it should be done. At the end, it is summed up by few recommendations on potential factors influencing the use of MyHEALTH Portal among Malaysian health consumers.

Acknowledgements Authors would like to acknowledge Universiti Teknologi MARA, Universiti Teknologi Malaysia and the Health Education Division, Ministry of Health Malaysia for supporting the research.

References

Ajzen, I. (1991). The theory of planned behavior. *Organizational Behavior and Human Decision Process, 50,* 179–211. doi:10.1016/0749-5978(91)90020-T.

Health Informatics Center Planning and Development Division Ministry of Health Malaysia. (2012). Health Facts 2012. http://www.moh.gov.my/images/gallery/stats/heal_fact/health_fact_2012_page_by_page.pdf.

Howitt, A., Clement, S., De Lusignan, S., Thiru, K., Goodwin, D., & Wells, S. (2002). An evaluation of general practice websites in the UK. *Family Practice, 19*(5), 547–556.

IHBR. (2014). *MyHEALTH Portal Research Survey*. Ministry of Health Malaysia: Unpublished Study.

Jian, W. S., Abdul, S. S., Sood, S. P., Lee, P., Hsu, M. H., Ho, C. H., et al. (2012). Factors influencing consumer adoption of USB-based personal health records in Taiwan. *BMC Health Services Research, 12,* 277. doi:10.1186/1472-6963-12-277.

Lanseng, E. J., & Andreassen, T. W. (2007). Electronic healthcare: a study of people's readiness and attitude toward performing self-diagnosis. *International Journal of Service Industry Management, 18*(4), 394–417.

Lee, S. G. (2003). An integrative study of mobile technology adoption based on the technology acceptance model, theory of planned behaviour and diffusion of innovation theory. ETD collection for University of Nebraska-Lincoln. Paper AAI3104619. http://digitalcommons.unl.edu/dissertations/AAI3104619.

Limayem, M., Hirt, S. G., & Cheung, M. K. (2003). How Habit Limits the Predictive Power of intention: The case of information systems continuance.

Löfstedt, U. (2007). Public E-services research – A critical analysis of current research in Sweden. *International Journal of Public Information Systems, 2,* 101–112.

MHED. (2014). *Klik Portal MyHEALTH [Brochure]*. Putrajaya: Ministry of Health Malaysia.

Ministry of Health Malaysia. National Health and Morbidity Survey II (1996). http://www.moh.gov.my/index.php/file_manager/dl_item/624746305a584e305833426b5a69394f51305176546b684e553138794d44457858305a4251315266553068465256517563475247d.

Ministry of Health Malaysia. National Health and Morbidity Survey III (2006). http://NHMS_2006_FACT_SHEET.pdf.

National Audit Department (2012). National Audit Report 2012. https://www.audit.gov.my/docs/BI/LKAN2011/FSB/AUDITOR%20GENERAL'S%20REPORT%202011%20%20ON%20AUDIT%20OF%20FINANCIAL%20MANAGE.pdf.

Rho, M. J., & Choil, I. Y. (2014). Predictive factors of telemedicine service acceptance and behavioral intention of physicians. *International Journal of Medical Informatics, 83,* 559–571.

Romanow, D., Cho, S. Y. & Straub, D. (2012). Riding the Wave: Past Trends and Future Directions for Health IT Research. MIS Quarterly. *36*(3): iii-A18.

Ross, J., Chapman, C., Murray, C., Stevenson, M., Natin, D., & Rogstad, K. (2000). How much interest is the internet to patients? *Sexually Transmitted Infections., 76,* 393–394.

Torres, C. A. (2011). *Examining the Role of Anxiety and Apathy in Health Consumers' Intentions to Use Patient Health Portals for Personal Health Information Management.* Doctor Philosophy: The Florida State University, Ann Arbor.

Venkatesh, V., Morris, M. G., Davis, F. D., & Davis, G. B. (2003). User acceptance of information technology: toward a unified view. *MIS Quarterly 27*(3), 425–478.

Venkatesh, V., Davis, F. D., & Morris, M. G. (2007). Dead or alive? the development, trajectory, and future of technology adoption research. *Journal of the Association for Information Systems., 8*(4), 267–286.

WHO (2014). Health and Ageing Country Factsheet. http://www.wpro.who.int/topics/ageing/ageing_fs_malaysia.pdf.

WHO (2015). School and Youth Health. http://www.who.int/school_youth_health/en/.

WHO Department of Communications (2014). World Health Statistics 2014. http://www.who.int/mediacentre/news/releases/2014/world-health-statistics-2014/en/.

Wilson, E. V., & Lankton, N. K. (2004). Modeling patient's acceptance of provider-delivered ehealth. *Journal of the American Medical Informatics Association, 11*(4), 241–248.

Chapter 9
The Effects of e-Service Quality on Users' Satisfaction: A Case of e-Filing at LHDN

Mohd. Khirzan Badzli A Rahman, Abdul Kadir Othman and Nurulhuda Amrin

Abstract Lembaga Hasil Dalam Negeri (LHDN) had introduced e-Filing services, which allow taxpayers to submit their tax return forms electronically via the Internet, which is an alternative means to the traditional form submission. The success of e-Filing depends on the delivery of e-service quality and satisfaction to its users. This paper aims to investigate the effects of e-service quality on user satisfaction with regard to the users of e-Filing in Klang Valley, Malaysia. A total of 377 respondents were involved in the study, and by using SPSS version 22 the results of regression analysis revealed that all e-service quality dimensions except reliability have significant influence on user satisfaction of using e-Filing of LHDN. The results indicate that responsiveness, ease of use, security/privacy and website design are the factors of e-service quality that must accompany with e-Filing service so that users' satisfaction can be assured.

Keywords e-Service quality · e-Filing · User satisfaction

9.1 Introduction

The *Lembaga Hasil Dalam Negeri Malaysia (LHDN)* or Inland Revenue Board of Malaysia has introduced a new system called e-Filing to individual taxpayers in 2004 to allow the taxpayers to enjoy the services at their own convenience. Since its

Mohd.K.B.A. Rahman (✉)
Institute of Business Excellence, Universiti Teknologi MARA, Shah Alam, Malaysia
e-mail: khirzan@puncakalam.uitm.edu.my

A.K. Othman
Faculty of Business and Management, Universiti Teknologi MARA, Puncak Alam, Malaysia
e-mail: abdulkadir@salam.uitm.edu.my

N. Amrin
Centre for Post Graduate and Professional Study, Faculty of Business and Management, Universiti Teknologi MARA, Shah Alam, Malaysia
e-mail: nurulhuda.amrin@gmail.com

F. Noordin et al. (eds.), *Proceedings of the 2nd Advances in Business Research International Conference*, https://doi.org/10.1007/978-981-10-6053-3_9

introduction, the number of e-Filing submission has increased significantly. The increment has benefited not only the taxpayers but also the government where it enables LHDN to reduce its cost since the introduction of e-Filing system. The LHDN annual report stated that the agency saved around RM8.17 million in 2008 due to the increasing usage rate of e-Filing system by the citizens (LHDN 2014).

Most of the previous studies were basically focused on finding the best determinant to attract the taxpayers to adopt the new approach of submission from manual to electronic (Ramayah et al. 2008; Lai and Choong 2009; Azmi and Bee 2010). However, Sheng and Liu (2010) suggested that e-service quality has a positive effect on customers' satisfaction. Thus, to enrich the literature, this study examined the relationship between e-service quality and user satisfaction in using LHDN e-Filing.

9.2 Literature Review

9.2.1 LHDN e-Filing Service

Beginning in 2004, the taxpayers in Malaysia have been given an option to choose the manual or Internet-based tax filing method. Manual filing is cumbersome, time-consuming and paper-intensive for both parties. Error checking on paper is fault-intensive and was traditionally done by the tax agency staff. The Internet-based method allows the tax payer to return their income tax forms via e-Filing application. This application is protected by Public Key Infrastructure technology which has a pair of secret keys that are harder to be hacked or cracked. E-Filing users can log-in and use this application at their convenience. This facility helps taxpayers to fill out, calculate and send forms with ease, accurate and secure, and refund processing is faster (LHDN 2014). Thus, this offers superior quality and tailored services which are key contributors to user satisfaction (Wisniewski 2001).

9.2.2 User Satisfaction

Studies show that user satisfaction is vital in today's business world (Hanif et al. 2010) and researchers believed that service quality is the key to measure user satisfaction (Pitt et al. 1995). Users will reach their level of satisfaction after the organization provided them with quality services (Zeithaml et al. 2006). Therefore, to retain online customers and acquire user satisfaction, a high priority should be given to e-service quality. E-service quality is meant to satisfy customers by meeting their expectations.

9.2.3 e-Service Quality Model

Parasuraman et al. (1988) have first introduced a model to measure service quality. Later, Zeithaml et al. (2002) developed an E-S-QUAL scale based on seven dimensions. Zeithaml (2002) further said that e-service quality (e-SQ) is comprehensive and it includes both pre- and post-Web site service aspects. This denotes that e-service quality is one of the key determinants of success and failure of an organization because e-service quality is the overall customer assessment and judgment of e-service delivery in the virtual marketplace (Santos 2003). Al-Tarawneh (2012) posited that e-service quality dimensions comprising reliability, Website design, responsiveness, security, personalization and ease of use are directly related to customer's perception of e-service quality.

Reliability is associated with the technical functioning of the site, particularly the extent to which it is available and functioning properly (Zeithaml 2002). According to Santos (2003), promises made by service providers are one of the important elements to maintain e-service quality to users. Consistently, Parasuraman et al. (2005) indicated that reliability is the extent to which the site's promises about order delivery and item availability is fulfilled. Al-Tarawneh (2012) found that reliability refers to the ability to perform the promised service accurately and consistently, including frequency of updating the Web site, prompt reply to customer enquiries and accuracy of online transaction. Therefore, the following hypothesis is developed:

H_1 There is a relationship between reliability and user satisfaction on LHDN e-Filing service.

Responsiveness provides effective handling of problems and returns through the site (Parasuraman et al. 2005). Evidently, the responsiveness of Web-based services has highlighted the relationship between e-service quality and customer satisfaction (Yang and Jun 2002), able to measure the ability of a company to provide appropriate information to customers when a problem occurs (Zeithaml 2002), leads to the quick response and the ability to get help if there is a problem or question (Han and Baek 2004), and relates to flexibility, prompt delivery, consistency and accuracy of service delivered (Al-Tarawneh 2012). Thus, the hypothesis below is highlighted:

H_2 There is a relationship between responsiveness and user satisfaction on LHDN e-Filing service.

Ease of use refers to the functions of a device that help customers find what they need without difficulty, have good search functionality and allow the customer to maneuver easily and quickly back and forth through the pages (Al-Tarawneh 2012). It was also defined as how easy the Website is for citizens to interact with. The great importance of this dimension has also been noted by other researchers (Santos 2003). Hence, the following hypothesis is suggested:

H_3 There is a relationship between ease of use and user satisfaction on LHDN e-Filing service.

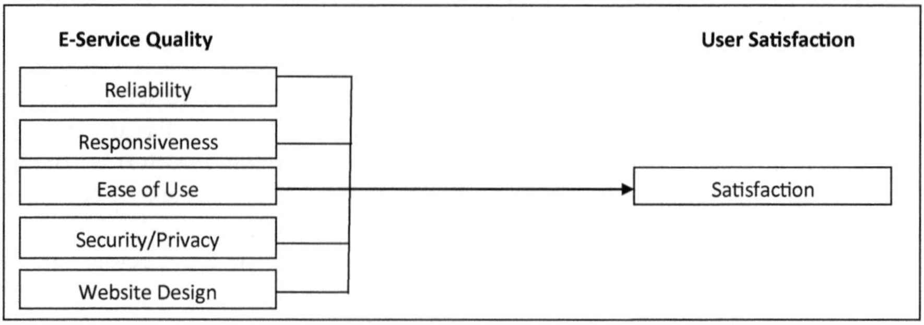

Fig. 9.1 Conceptual framework of the study

Security is considered to be one of the most important drivers of e-service satisfaction (Wingfield and Rose 2001). Security is described as the degree to which the site is safe and protects the customers' information and the users feel confidence from risk of danger while using it (Parasuraman et al. 2005). Evidently, security is important as a critical aspect of e-service (Zhao et al. 2010) and addresses the technical specifications of a Website (Al-Tarawneh (2012), protecting users from the risk of fraud and ensuring that the whole transaction is carried out accordingly (Yomnak 2007). Consequently, the hypothesis below is highlighted:

H_4 There is a relationship between security/privacy and user satisfaction on LHDN e-Filing service.

Website Design refers to the quality of the information presented and layout of the Website, like the proper use of color, graphics and size (Papadomichelaki et al. 2012). Consistently, Hoffman and Krauss (2004) said that the visual impact of a Web page can have a significant influence on user experience and has important implications for effective communication. Al-Tarawneh (2012) argued that design is a part of a multidisciplinary pursuit pertaining to the planning and production of Web sites, including, but not limited to, technical development, information structure, visual design and networked delivery As a result, the following hypothesis is developed:

H_5 There is a relationship between Website design and user satisfaction on LHDN e-Filing service.

As this study intends to investigate the effects of e-service quality on user satisfaction, the proposed conceptual framework is as follows (Fig. 9.1)

9.3 Methodology

This study employed a quantitative research design with the objective of investigating the relationship between e-service quality and user satisfaction on e-Filing system of LHDN. The populations were 1,070,939 taxpayers in the Klang Valley who used e-Filing (LHDN 2014). Klang Valley was chosen due to the characteristics of respondents who are IT savvy as compared to other parts of the country. Since the members of the population are difficult to locate, the snowball sampling method was chosen for this study. Following Krejcie and Morgan (1970), the required sample size is 384 and the unit of analysis is the individual e-Filing user. Adopted questionnaire from previous studies was used as an instrument to collect the data. The questionnaire was verified by professionals for its content and face validity. Reliability test was conducted by examining the Cronbach's alpha values, and a variable is said to be reliable when the Cronbach's alpha value is more than 0.70 (George and Mallery 2003). Data were analyzed using the Statistical Package Social Science (SPSS) version 22. Descriptive statistic, Pearson correlation and a multiple regression analysis were employed to test the hypotheses.

9.4 Findings and Discussions

A total of 384 questionnaires were distributed to users of LHDN e-Filing in the area of Klang Valley and were collected to be analyzed recording in the response rate of 100%. From 384 questionnaires that have been collected, 377 questionnaires were regarded as valid for analysis.

9.4.1 Profile of Respondents

In terms of gender, the number of male respondents is slightly higher with 52.8% than that of female respondents (47.2%). Most respondents are in the group age of 31–35 years old (27.3%), and Malays (64.7%) were the highest number of respondents followed by Chinese (24.4%) and Indian (10.9%). 57.3% of the respondents possessed a bachelor degree, and 75.6% were working in the private sector. On monthly income, 37.7% of the respondents were in the income range of RM5001–RM7500, followed by 36.1% respondents who earned between RM2501 and RM5000.

9.4.2 Results of Factor Analyses

Following Hair et al. (2010), factor analysis was used to examine the underlying structure in the data matrix in order to identify parsimonious sets of variables. Table 9.1 shows the results of factor analysis for the independent variables.

Principal component's factor analysis with varimax rotation was used to determine factor's dimensionality. As shown in Table 9.1, the KMO value of 0.896 indicates that the data were sufficient to proceed with factor analysis. Meanwhile, the Bartlett's test of sphericity shows a significant value with approx. Chi-square is

Table 9.1 Factor analysis for independent variable: e-service quality

	Component				
	1	2	3	4	5
The menu items on the LHDN e-Filing site are easy to understand	0.853				
The texts on the LHDN e-Filing site are easy to understand	0.817				
It would be easy for me to become skillful at using the site	0.803				
The texts on the LHDN e-Filing site are easy to read	0.789				
The label items on the LHDN e-Filing site are easy to understand	0.789				
Learning to operate the LHDN e-Filing site is easy for me	0.775				
I find the LHDN e-Filing site is easy to use and navigate	0.726				
The LHDN e-Filing site protects my personal records		0.885			
I am confident of the security of LHDN e-Filing site		0.823			
The LHDN e-Filing site does not share my personal information with other sites		0.778			
LHDN e-Filing site assures me of the security it provides		0.728			
The security mechanisms at LHDN e-Filing site are adequate		0.713			
The LHDN e-Filing Website is visually appealing			0.794		
Pages at LHDN e-Filing site do not hang after entering details/information			0.742		
The user interface of the LHDN e-Filing Web site has a well-organized appearance.			0.741		
The LHDN e-Filing site is always accessible for users			0.682		
It is quick to complete a transaction at the LHDN e-Filing site			0.583		
Administrators of LHDN e-Filing tell you exactly when the service will be performed				0.795	
Administrators of LHDN e-Filing are always willing to help you				0.786	
Administrators of LHDN e-Filing give you prompt service				0.712	
Administrators of LHDN e-Filing are never too busy to respond to your questions				0.668	

(continued)

Table 9.1 (continued)

		Component				
		1	2	3	4	5
LHDN e-Filing provides its services at the time it promises to do so						0.811
LHDN e-Filing site doesn't always live up to its promise						0.799
LHDN e-Filing site insists on error-free records						0.771
% of variance explained (after rotation)		20.9	15.8	13.6	12.6	12.4
Total variance explained		75.248				
Kaiser–Meyer–Olkin measure of sampling adequacy		0.896				
MSA		0.836–0.944				
Bartlett's test of sphericity	Approx. Chi-square	8746.529				
	Df	300				
	Sig.	0.000				

8746.529 ($p < 0.001$), indicating the significant of correlation matrix and appropriateness of factor analysis. Moreover, the MSA values are in the range between 0.836 and 0.944, indicating sufficient data for each variable.

The results of factor analysis show the existence of five factors explaining 75.25% of the variance. The first factor consists of seven items with loadings ranged from 0.726 to 0.853. Since the items measure ease of use construct, the initial name was retained. The second factor contains five items measuring security/privacy. Thus, the original name was used. These items had loadings in the range of 0.713 and 0.885. The third factor reflects Website design; thus, the name was maintained. The five items loaded with values ranged from 0.583 to 0.794. The fourth factor represents items that measure responsiveness; therefore, its original name was used. The fifth factor contains three items that measure reliability construct. The factor has loadings ranged from 0.771 to 0.811. The name reliability was retained.

Principal component's factor analysis with varimax rotation was also used to determine factor's dimensionality of the dependent variable. As shown in Table 9.2, the KMO value of 0.874 indicates that the data were sufficient to proceed with factor analysis. Meanwhile, the Bartlett's test of sphericity shows a significant value with approx. Chi-square is 2055.859 ($p < 0.001$), indicating the significant of correlation matrix and appropriateness of factor analysis. Moreover, the MSA values are in the range between 0.801 and 0.935, indicating sufficient data for each variable. The result of factor analysis shows the existence of unidimensional nature of user satisfaction construct with loadings in the range of 0.735 and 0.842. Therefore, the name is retained.

Table 9.2 Factor analysis for dependent variable: user satisfaction

		Component
		1
Overall, I am satisfied in using the LHDN e-Filing site		0.842
I am satisfied with the LHDN e-Filing Website characteristics related to design		0.835
I am satisfied with the LHDN e-Filing service related to reliability		0.818
It is very pleasant experience to use the LHDN e-Filing site		0.8
I find the LHDN e-Filing site never disappoint me at some point		0.787
I am satisfied with the LHDN e-Filing service related to speed and responsiveness		0.774
I am satisfied with the Website characteristics related to ease of use		0.767
I am satisfied with the LHDN e-Filing service related to security and privacy provided		0.735
% of variance explained (after rotation)		63.273
Total variance explained		63.273
Kaiser–Meyer–Olkin measure of sampling adequacy		0.874
MSA		0.801–0.935
Bartlett's test of sphericity	Approx. Chi-square	2055.859
	df	28
	Sig.	0.000

9.4.3 Results of Descriptive, Reliability and Correlation Analyses

Referring to Table 9.3, the mean scores for all variables are all above 3.5 with the values of standard deviation range from 0.49 to 0.63. The reliability test was conducted on each variable by examining the Cronbach's alpha values. Table 4.10 shows the values for independent variables are in the range of 0.875–0.940. And, the Cronbach's alpha value for the dependent variable is 0.911. These values show that all items measuring the intended variables are highly reliable. Based on the results of correlation analysis, all independent variables are moderately to highly correlated with each other with the highest correlation between reliability and responsiveness ($r = 0.636$) and the lowest correlation between reliability and ease of use ($r = 0.479$), indicating the convergent validity. Looking at the correlation between the e-service quality dimensions and user satisfaction, the variables are moderately to highly correlated with the highest correlation between Website design and user satisfaction ($r = 0.785$) and the lowest correlation between ease of

Table 9.3 Results of descriptive, reliability and correlation analyses

No		Mean	SD	1	2	3	4	5	6
1	Reliability	3.78	0.49	(0.875)					
2	Responsiveness	3.56	0.63	0.636**	(0.881)				
3	Ease of use	3.80	0.56	0.479**	0.498**	(0.940)			
4	Security privacy	3.62	0.53	0.499**	0.512**	0.538**	(0.914)		
5	Website design	3.50	0.57	0.526**	0.582**	0.547**	0.563**	(0.871)	
6	User satisfaction	3.67	0.49	0.569**	0.674**	0.628**	0.761**	0.758**	(0.911)

Notes ** Correlation is significant at the 0.01 level (one-tailed); N = 377; Cronbach's alphas are along the diagonal in the parentheses

use and user satisfaction ($r = 0.674$), indicating concurrent validity. The results indicate that the e-service quality dimensions have potential influence of user satisfaction.

9.4.4 Results of Regression Analysis

The regression analysis was performed to determine the dimensions of e-service quality that have significant influence on users' satisfaction. Table 9.4 shows that the R^2 value of 0.883 indicates that 88.3% of the variance in the regression model was explained by the five independent variables. The regression model is significant (F (5, 372) = 264.211, $p < 0.01$). The Durbin Watson value of 1.779 denotes the absence of autocorrelation problem in the model.

Based on the regression coefficients, four out of five independent variables are significant to influence user satisfaction. They are responsiveness ($\beta = 0.211$, $p < 0.01$), ease of use ($\beta = 0.122$, $p < 0.01$), security/privacy ($\beta = 0.392$, $p < 0.01$) and Website design ($\beta = 0.349$, $p < 0.01$). Reliability did not significantly influence user satisfaction ($\beta = -0.003$, $p > 0.05$).

Table 9.4 Results of a multiple regression analysis

Independent variables	Standardized beta (β)
Reliability	−0.003
Responsiveness	0.211**
Ease of use	0.122**
Security/privacy	0.392**
Website design	0.349**
R	0.883
R^2	0.780
F change	264.211
Sig. F value	0.000
Durbin Watson	1.779

The results of regression analysis show that reliability did not significantly influence users' satisfaction in using LHDN e-Filing service. This finding also contradicts with the one found by Nupur (2010), in his study that shows that there is positive relationship between reliability and user satisfaction. The probable reason for the finding is that the online version of the tax return form reliably provides all the information required by the users. This form is similar to the traditional one and the only different lies in its online version. Because of its similar function, users found that there is nothing much different is using online or traditional tax return service. Therefore, the H_1 that says that there is a relationship between reliability and user satisfaction on LHDN e-Filing service is not supported.

The result of regression analysis also shows significant relationship between responsiveness and user satisfaction on LHDN e-Filing service. The outcome is consistent with the research findings discovered by Lee and Lin (2005), which stated that responsiveness is strongly correlated with user satisfaction. Users highly value responsiveness of the service provider regardless whether the service is offered via online or conventional method. Therefore, the hypothesis H_2 that says there is a relationship between responsiveness and user satisfaction on LHDN e-Filing service is supported.

The result shows that there is a strong relationship between ease of use and user satisfaction on LHDN e-Filing service. As cited by Abels et al. (1999) and Yang (2001), as far as the individual independent variable is concerned, ease of use significantly impacts the dependent variable user satisfaction as users highly appreciate the difference in performing the task using online and conventional methods. This attribute is found to be a significant determinant of the e-service quality. Therefore, the hypothesis that highlights there is a relationship between ease of use and user satisfaction on LHDN e-Filing service is supported.

The result shows that there is a strong relationship between security/privacy and user satisfaction on LHDN e-Filing service. This finding is supported by previous research efforts undertaken by Al-Tarawneh (2012) in which security is confirmed as the strongest variable as it matters the most. Users prefer security/privacy of the service over other attributes. The importance of this attribute for e-Filing users was also previously noted by Zafar (2011) where user satisfaction can be measured through quality aspects such security/privacy. Therefore, the hypothesis that says there is a relationship between security/privacy and user satisfaction on LHDN e-Filing service is supported.

The result shows that there is a strong relationship between Website design and user satisfaction on LHDN e-Filing service. The result of this research is in line with Ahmed (2011), where the researcher found that Website design variable has strong influence on users' satisfaction because of its appealing appearance, accessible and quick to perform the required task. Furthermore, this research is also directly in line with Al-Tarawneh (2012) in which Website design is confirmed as one of the strongest variables in e-service quality. Therefore, the hypothesis that mentions there is a relationship between Website design and user satisfaction on LHDN e-Filing service is supported.

9.5 Conclusions and Recommendations

Based on the findings, it can be concluded that for gender, the number of male respondents is slightly exceeded the number of female respondents. Majority of the respondents are in the group age of 31–35 years old. Moreover, majority of the respondents are Malays. Majority of the respondents possessed a bachelor's degree, working in private sectors and earn RM5001–RM7500 as their monthly income. The results also proved that there are significant relationship between reliability, responsiveness, ease of use, security/privacy and Website design, and user satisfaction on LHDN e-Filing service.

As Internet technologies become increasingly sophisticated, a high-quality e-service is the important factor toward the success of government organizations. By understanding the characteristics of e-service quality that enhance users' satisfactions, this study allows LHDN to understand which area in e-services that should be emphasized that will contribute toward increasing users' satisfaction. This study is also significant to further increase the levels of e-service quality in LHDN. Based on the results, LHDN as the government organization can also avoid investing costly resources in offering e-service quality features that may not work effectively. The organization will be able to find out the right strategies in retaining also expanding the size of its users in future besides making the existing users influence other taxpayers to opt to e-Filing service once they feel satisfied with the service performance. The future studies could also consider analyzing the continuance intention toward e-filing system. The outcome of the study could enable the LHDN to design better strategies to satisfy the possible different needs and wants of the different segments of users in order to ensure that the great number of e-Filing users will be using e-Filing system continuously.

References

Abels, E. G., White, M. D., & Hahn, K. (1999). A user-based design process for Web sites. *OCLC Systems & Services: International Digital Library Perspectives, 15*(1), 35–44.

Ahmed, K. (2011). *Online Service Quality and Customer Satisfaction: A Case Study of Bank Islam Malaysia Berhad*. Online at http://mpra.ub.unimuenchen.de/30782/MPRA. Paper No. 30782.

Al-Tarawneh, K. A. (2012). Measuring e-service quality from the customers' perspective: An empirical study on banking services. *International Research Journal of Finance and Economics, 91*(1), 123–137.

Azmi, A. C., & Bee, N. L. (2010). The acceptance of the e-filing system by Malaysian taxpayers: A simplified model. *Electronic Journal of e-Government, 8*(1), 13–22.

George, D., & Mallery, M. (2003). *Using SPSS for Windows step by step: A simple guide and reference*. Boston, MA: Allyn Y Bacon. [Links].

Hair, J. F., Black, W. C., Babin, B. J., & Anderson, R. E. (2010). *Multivariate data analysis* (7th ed.). Upper Saddle River, NJ: Pearson Prentice Hall.

Han, S., & Baek, S. (2004). Antecedents and consequences of service quality in online banking: An application of the SERVQUAL instrument. *Advances in Consumer Research, 31*(2), 208–214.

Hanif, M., Hafeez, S., & Riaz, A. (2010). Factors affecting customer satisfaction. *International Research Journal of Finance and Economics, 60,* 44–52.

Hoffmann, R., & Krauss, K. (2004, October). A critical evaluation of literature on visual aesthetics for the web. In *Proceedings of the 2004 Annual Research Conference of The South African Institute of Computer Scientists and Information Technologists on IT Research in Developing Countries* (pp. 205–209). South African Institute for Computer Scientists and Information Technologists.

Krejcie, R. V., & Morgan, D. W. (1970). Determining sample size for research activities. *Educational and Psychological Measurement.*

Lai, M. L., & Choong, K. F. (2009). Self-Assessment tax system and compliance complexities: Tax practitioners' perspectives. In *2009 Oxford Business & Economics Conference.*

Lee, G. G., & Lin, H. F. (2005). Customer perceptions of e-service quality in online shopping. *International Journal of Retail & Distribution Management, 33*(2), 161–176.

LHDN. (2014). Laporan tahunan 2014. Retrived from http://www.hasil.gov.my/pdf/pdfam/Laporan_Tahunan_2014_BM.pdf.

Nupur, J. M. (2010). E-banking and customers' satisfaction in Bangladesh: An analysis. *International Review of Business Research Papers, 6*(4), 145–156.

Papadomichelaki, X., & Mentzas, G. (2012). E-govqual: A multiple-item scale for assessing e-government service quality. *Government Information Quarterly, 29*(1), 98–109.

Parasuraman, A., Zeithaml, V. A., & Berry, L. L. (1988). Servqual. *Journal of Retailing, 64*(1), 12–37.

Parasuraman, A., Zeithaml, V. A., & Malhotra, A. (2005). ES-QUAL: A multiple-item scale for assessing electronic service quality. *Journal of Service Research, 7*(3), 213–233.

Pitt, L. F., Watson, R. T., & Kavan, C. B. (1995). Service quality: A measure of information systems effectiveness. *MIS Quarterly, 19*(2).

Ramayah, T., Ramoo, V., & Ibrahim, A. (2008). Profiling online and manual tax filers: Results from an exploratory study in Penang, Malaysia. *Labuan e-Journal of Muamalat and Society, 2,* 1–8.

Santos, J. (2003). E-service quality: A model of virtual service quality dimensions. *Managing Service Quality, 13*(3), 233–246.

Sheng, T., & Liu, C. (2010). An empirical study on the effect of e-service quality on online customer satisfaction and loyalty. *Nankai Business Review International, 1*(3), 273–283.

Wingfield, N., & Rose, M. (2001, February). Amazon is split on fees to plug books. *The Wall Street Journal Europe, 8.*

Wisniewski, M. (2001). Using SERVQUAL to assess customer satisfaction with public sector services. *Managing Service Quality: An International Journal, 11*(6), 380–388.

Yang, Z. (2001, May). Consumer perceptions of service quality in internet-based electronic commerce. In *Proceedings of the EMAC Conference* (Vol. 811).

Yang, Z., & Jun, M. (2002). Consumer perception of e-service quality: From internet purchaser and non-purchaser perspectives.

Yomnak, T. (2007). *Perceptions of service quality and customer satisfaction of Thai online shopping services.* Dissertation Abstracts International, *68*(03).

Zafar, H. (2011). Security Risk Management at a Fortune 500 Firm: A Case Study. *Journal of Information Privacy and Security, 7*(4), 23–53.

Zeithaml, V. A. (2002). Service excellence in electronic channels. *Managing Service Quality, 12*(3), 135–139.

Zeithaml, V. A., Bitner, M. J., & Gremler, D. D. (2006). *Services marketing: Integrating customer focus across the firm.*

Zeithaml, V. A., Parasuraman, A., & Malhotra, A. (2002). Service quality delivery through web sites: A critical review of extant knowledge. *Journal of the Academy of Marketing Science, 30*(4), 362–375.

Zhao, J. J., Zhao, S. Y., & Zhao, S. Y. (2010). Opportunities and threats: A security assessment of state e-government websites. *Government Information Quarterly, 27*(1), 49–56.

Chapter 10
Exchange Rate Exposure: Does International Involvement Matter?

Jaratin Lily, Imbarine Bujang and Abdul Aziz Karia

Abstract This paper investigates the effect of exchange rate movements on large non-financial firms' share returns in Malaysia and Singapore using multi-bilateral exchange rates namely the Euro (EUR), US Dollar (USD) and Chinese Renminbi (CNY). Our empirical results show that only a few firms in both Malaysia and Singapore are exposed to exchange rate movements. More firms in Singapore are exposed to exchange rate movements than Malaysia, especially to EUR and CNY. Surprisingly, only three of the large non-financial firms in Singapore are exposed to USD and none in Malaysia. In both Malaysia and Singapore, the majority of the exposed firms have a high level of foreign sales ratio (more than 25%), but in the case of Singapore, it seems that a firm with a low level of foreign involvement (<5%) is also exposed to the studied currencies. The results disclosed that the majority of exposed Singapore firms would mainly benefit from CNY appreciation and USD depreciation, meanwhile Malaysian firms benefited from CNY appreciation and EUR depreciation. The insignificant exchange rate movements in most firms imply that these large firms mitigate the effect of the exchange rate movements through hedging programmes. Future research should include more firms and countries with different levels of market capitalisation to better understand the stylised effect of exchange rate exposure in firm-level analysis.

Keywords Exchange rate exposure · Firm level · Malaysia · Singapore

J. Lily (✉) · I. Bujang · A.A. Karia
Faculty of Business Management, Universiti Teknologi MARA Sabah, Kota Kinabalu, Sabah, Malaysia
e-mail: jaratin@ums.edu.my

J. Lily
Faculty of Business, Economics and Accountancy, Universiti Malaysia Sabah, Jalan UMS, 88400 Kota Kinabalu, Sabah, Malaysia

F. Noordin et al. (eds.), *Proceedings of the 2nd Advances in Business Research International Conference*, https://doi.org/10.1007/978-981-10-6053-3_10

10.1 Introduction

The general concept of economic exchange rate exposure is the level of impact (sensitivity) on the net worth of a firm due to the exchange rate movements (Adler and Dumas 1983, 1984; Bartram and Bodnar 2007; Fama and French 1993; Jorion 1990). The exchange rate exposure may affect cash flows from contracts denominated in foreign currencies (e.g., sales) and the value of its foreign assets and liabilities which also affect its competitive position (Alssayah and Krishnamurti 2013; Entorf et al. 2011; Jorion 1990).

Most previous empirical studies use a trade-weighted exchange rate index as a proxy for firm-specific exchange rate movements (De Jong et al. 2006). Although a trade-weighted index can capture the home currency's value in aggregate and help investors to understand its portfolio share return sensitivity towards the currency environment that a country would encounter in average (Agyei-Ampomah et al. 2012), this trade-weighted exchange rate index does not inform investors of which particular individual currency affects their particular share returns (Bartram and Bodnar 2007; Lin 2011; Parsley and Popper 2006).

In addition, there are extensive studies on the factors influencing exchange rate exposure such as firm size, market capitalisation, foreign sales and growth opportunities (e.g., Chue and Cook 2008; De Jong et al. 2006; Ye, Hutson and Muckley 2014). However, these studies only indicated the factors important to explain the level of exchange rate exposure as an aggregate and did not indicate individual firms' share return reaction towards the factors (El-Masry et al. 2007).

Therefore, the aim of this study is to analyse the effect of exchange rate movements on large non-financial firm's share returns in Malaysia and Singapore. Malaysia and Singapore are among the most dynamic countries in the ASEAN region. The study intends to answer the following research questions: (1) How exposed are these large firms to the exchange rate movements? (2) To what extent can a firm's foreign involvement explain the magnitude of firm-level foreign exchange exposure?

10.2 Literature Review

Since Aggarwal's (1981) study, there have been various theoretical models and empirical studies on the exchange rate exposure at country, market or firm levels in developed and emerging markets. Empirical studies in developing or developed markets offer little support for the theoretical predictions where the proportion of exposed firms tends to be lower than expected (Bacha et al. 2013; El-Masry et al. 2007; Lin 2011; Parsley and Popper 2006). For instance, in Parsley and Popper's (2006) study during non-pegged regimes, the percentage of firms that are significantly exposed to the USD in selected Asian countries is 0% in Philippines, 2% in Indonesia, 3% in Taiwan, 4% in Korea, 10% in Thailand, and 27% in Malaysia, respectively. Furthermore, a study by El-Masry et al. (2007) on the UK non-financial firms indicated only 23% and 26% of the firms have significant exposure to USD and Japanese Yen, respectively. Meanwhile, Malaysian listed firms' exposure to Japanese Yen and Pound Sterling is 12.5% and 29%, respectively (Bacha et al. 2013). This phenomenon is called the exchange rate exposure puzzle (Bartram and Bodnar 2007; Kang et al. 2016).

With the main objective of the firm to maximise the shareholders'market value (Copeland and Copeland 1999), the determination of the foreign exchange rate fluctuations on firms' market values has attracted considerable attention (Agyei-Ampomah et al. 2012). The main factors tested in the developed market are foreign sales, foreign assets, profit margin, firm size, market to book value, usage of financial derivative and debt ratio (Agyei-Ampomah et al. 2012; Makar and Huffman 2013). Foreign sales are usually used as a proxy for international involvement. In theory, a large firm is expected to have a higher level of exposure because of its high level of foreign involvement. Nevertheless, the contrary can be hypothesised because such firms have the tendency to hedge the exchange rate risks (Aggarwal and Harper 2010; El-Masry et al. 2007). A larger firm should have necessary personnel and knowledge resources to mitigate the negative effect of the exchange rate movements to its value or cash flows. Thus, this study will segregate the sample firms based on their foreign involvement (proxy by foreign sales ratio) to examine the effect of the exchange rate movements on returns.

In summary, despite intensive tests on exchange rate exposure since the 1970s, the exchange rate exposure theory continues to stand upon mixed evidence. This scenario has motivated this research on the existence of exchange rate exposure in Malaysia and Singapore where both are considered small open economies with significant international trade.

10.3 Data and Methodology

10.3.1 Data

The empirical analysis in this study uses monthly data from June 2005 to March 2016. The data start from June 2005 due to the pegged value of CNY and Malaysian ringgit towards USD until June 2005. The foreign exchange rate consists of Chinese Yuan (CNY), European Dollar (EUR) and US Dollar (USD). China and Eurozone are among the main trading partners for most ASEAN countries including Malaysia and Singapore. Except for the CNY exchange rate for Malaysia, which was obtained from the database of Malaysia's Central Bank, bilateral foreign exchange rates (domestic currency units per foreign currency units) for Malaysia and Singapore, Consumer Price Index (CPI) for USA, China (excluding Macau and Hong Kong) and the Eurozone, and firms' foreign sales ratios were obtained from Datastream International. In this study, the monthly Morgan Stanley Capital

International (MSCI) Investable Market Index (IMI) country index (local currency) was applied as a proxy for country market indexes. The MSCI IMI country index captures large, mid and small capital representation for each country.

Our sample comprises the constituent firms of each country's top 30 equity market index by market capitalisation index as at the end of 2015. However, for the purpose of this study, only non-financial firms were selected for further analysis. Financial firms were excluded due to being highly regulated (Aggarwal and Harper 2010; Alssayah and Krishnamurti 2013; El-Masry 2006). The firms must also have historical data for share return observations for the sample period. Thus, the final number of firms for both Malaysia and Singapore is 15 firms, respectively. The sample was also divided into four groups according to their average 5-year foreign sales ratio (<5%, 5 to <25%, 25 to <50%, and >50%) to study the effect of foreign involvement on the sensitivity of firm's share returns towards exchange rate movements (Aggarwal and Harper 2010; El-Masry et al. 2007). Aggarwal and Harper (2010) indicated that firms with less 5% foreign sales ratio as those with little foreign involvement.

10.3.2 Empirical Model

10.3.2.1 Exchange Rate Exposure Model

This research adopts the estimated two-factor exchange rate exposure model by Jorion (1990) as followed:

$$R_{i,t} = \alpha + \beta_1 RM_t + \beta_2 USD_t + \beta_3 EUR_t + \beta_4 CNY_t + \varepsilon_t \tag{10.1}$$

where α is constant, $R_{i,t}$ is share return of firm i, over time period t, RM_t is market portfolio return, ε_t is error term which is independently and identically distributed (i.i.d), and $\beta_1 - \beta_4$ are the exposure to the real exchange rate movements for respective currency. By adjusting real exchange rates for inflation, a more accurate effect of exchange rate on share return can be obtained because most ASEAN countries including Malaysia and Singapore apply managed floating exchange rate regimes (Bacha et al. 2013). The study follows Lin's (2011) calculation of the real exchange rate as follows:

$$E^R_{j,t} = E^N_{j,t} \times \frac{P_F}{P_H} \tag{10.2}$$

where $E^N_{j,t}$ is the nominal exchange rate (Home/Foreign) of currency j, P_F is the price level in the foreign country, P_H is the price level in the home country.

With all the studied variables integrated at $I(0)$, the firm's coefficients are estimated using ordinary least squares (Muller and Verschoor 2007) with dynamic dependent and control variables. This study also applied GARCH (1,1) specification if there is evidence of conditional heteroscedasticity in the error terms (e.g., Bacha et al. 2013; Ye et al. 2014) with the robust standard error (Bollerslev and Wooldridge 1992) or Student's t-distribution (Bollerslev 1987) to overcome the non-normal distribution (Alberg et al. 2008).

10.3.2.2 Unit Root Analysis

The study applied the Dickey-Fuller (DF), or Augmented Dickey-Fuller (ADF) (Dickey and Fuller 1979) and the Phillips-Perron (PP) (Phillips and Perron 1988) to test the hypothesis of a unit root to check if the variables under consideration were integrated over $I(0)$, $I(1)$ or if they were mutually integrated. The optimal lag length was chosen based on the lowest Schwarz Information Criterion (SIC) value.

10.4 Results

10.4.1 Descriptive Analysis

Most of the studied variables demonstrated skewness and high kurtosis (more than 3) that had shown non-normal distribution. Furthermore, both the ADF and PP unit root tests indicated all variable series were found to be stationary regardless of the constant and the trend included in the test equations at 5% significance level. The results of these statistical summaries are available upon request.

10.4.2 Firm-specific Exposure

Table 10.1 indicates the firm-specific exposure by the number of currencies in Malaysia and Singapore. Our results showed that only a few firms in both Malaysia (3 firms) and Singapore (6 firms) are exposed to exchange rate movements. All the

Table 10.1 Firm-specific exposure by number of currencies

	Malaysia		Singapore	
No. of currencies exposed	No. of firms	Percentage	No. of firms	Percentage
Zero	12	80	9	60
One	0	0	3	20
Two	3	20	2	13.3
Three	0	0	1	6.7
Total	15	100	15	100

Table 10.2 Firm-specific exposure by foreign sales ratio and coefficient sign in Malaysia

Particular	CNY (Coeff.)	EUR (Coeff.)	USD (Coeff.)
Foreign sales ratio: >50%			
Kuala Lumpur Kepong	1.2361**	−1.1217**	−0.0011
IOI	1.1452**	−0.7848*	0.1622
YTL	−0.0655	0.04591	0.0223
Sime Darby	0.3169	−0.5893	−0.0003
Genting Group	−0.3530	0.2390	−0.0654
Foreign sales ratio: 25 to 50%			
MISC Berhad	−1.1798*	1.0540*	0.1962
Genting Malaysia	0.6069	−0.7999	0.2547
Foreign sales ratio: 5 to <25%			
PPB Group	0.3521	−0.1587	0.1147
Hap Seng	−0.5559	1.0301	0.1391
British American Tobacco (Malaysia)	−0.4537	0.1646	−0.1371
Telekom Malaysia	−0.4058	0.2290	−0.0828
Foreign sales ratio: <5%			
Tenaga Nasional	−0.3606	−0.0295	0.3116
Digi	−0.5952	0.5484	−0.0216
Foreign sales ratio: NA			
Petronas Gas	−0.1481	0.0726	−0.0330
Petronas Dagangan	−0.0878	0.2245	0.0458

Notes ***, **, * denote significant at the 1%, 5% and 10% levels, respectively, NA: Non-available

exposed firms in Malaysia are exposed to two currencies (20%), while the majority of the exposed firms in Singapore are exposed to one currency (20%).

Tables 10.2 and 10.3 show the results of the firm-specific exposure by foreign sales ratio and coefficient sign in Malaysia and Singapore, respectively. The exposed firms in Malaysia are mostly exposed to EUR and CNY. In Singapore, firms are exposed mostly to the CNY, and equally exposed to EUR and USD, though most of the exposure is weak. Surprisingly, only three sampled firms in Singapore are exposed to the USD and none in Malaysia. In addition, the majority of the exposed Malaysian and Singapore firms have a high level of foreign sales ratio (more than 5%). However, in the case of Singapore, it seems that a firm with a low level of foreign involvement (<5%) is also exposed to all studied currencies.

Moreover, the study showed that those Malaysian firms exposed to CNY (positive coefficient) and EUR (negative coefficient) would mainly benefit from the appreciation of CNY and depreciation of EUR although one sampled firm has the reverse effect. In other words, the positive (negative) exchange rate movement

Table 10.3 Firm-specific exposure by foreign sales ratio and coefficient sign in Singapore

Particular	CNY (Coeff.)	EUR (Coeff.)	USD (Coeff.)
Foreign sales ratio: > 50%			
Sembcorp Marine	0.3398	0.7397**	−0.7701
Golden Agri-resources	0.8531	0.6398	−0.4820
Sembcorp Industries	0.3983	0.0199	−0.3672
Wilmar International	1.8378*	0.3218	−2.0625**
Foreign sales ratio: 25 to 50%			
Comfort Delgro	0.4944	0.1299	−0.2211
Keppel	−0.1048	0.2011	−0.2297
Singapore Technologies Engineering	0.5911*	−0.0810	−0.5618*
Foreign sales ratio: 5 to <25%			
Singapore Airlines	0.1433	−0.2922*	0.0625
SIA Engineering	−0.0717	−0.0079	0.1303
SATS	−0.4128	0.3438	0.3469
Foreign sales ratio: <5%			
Singapore Press Holding	0.0068	−0.0313	0.1655
Genting Singapore	1.0910*	0.4831**	−1.2690**
Starhub	0.7264	−0.0140	−0.3613
Foreign sales ratio: NA			
Singapore Telecom	0.9820**	0.1193	−0.6391
Jardine Cycle and Carriage	−0.3476	0.2949	−0.2080

Notes ***, **, * denote significant at the 1%, 5% and 10% levels, respectively, NA: Non-available

coefficients of the sampled firms in Malaysia indicated that the exposed firms are net importers from Europe but net exporters to China. In Singapore, the majority of the exposed sampled firms benefit from the depreciation of USD (net importers) but an appreciation of CNY and EUR (net exporters).

10.4.3 Diagnostic Tests

A series of diagnostic tests were performed to evaluate the model adequacy employed in this study to make sure the data fits the model. Most of the test results confirm the model adequacy for autocorrelation and heteroscedasticity issues. The results of these diagnostic tests are available upon request.

10.5 Discussion and Recommendation

10.5.1 Discussion

In this study, we investigated the foreign exchange rate exposure on the large non-financial firms' share returns in Malaysia and Singapore. This paper extends the previous literature by introducing multi-bilateral exchange rates rather than using a trade-weighted currency index (Parsley and Popper 2006), as well as identifying how the firms are exposed due to foreign involvement (El-Masry et al. 2007).

First, we queried as to how exposed are these large firms to the exchange rate movements? Our study results showed that few sampled firms in both Malaysia (3 firms) and Singapore (6 firms) are exposed to exchange rate movements though most of the exposure is weak. The exposed firms in Malaysia have a significant exposure to the EUR and CNY, while Singaporean firms are exposed more to CNY, and equally exposed to EUR and USD. More specifically, most of the exposed Singapore firms will mainly benefit from the appreciation of CNY and EUR (net exporters) but depreciation of USD (net importers). In Malaysia, the exposed non-financial firms benefit from the CNY appreciation (net exporters) and EUR depreciation (net importers). Surprisingly, none of these sampled firms was exposed to USD in Malaysia, and only three firms in Singapore, which is inconsistent with some previous studies (e.g., Bacha et al. 2013; Kang et al. 2016). These results support the argument of multiple exchange rate movement exposures to share returns in the previous studies (e.g., Bacha et al. 2013; Bartram 2004; Bartram and Bodnar 2007; Parsley and Popper 2006). As most of the exposed firms are exposed to the EUR and CNY, there is a possibility that these large firms are actively hedging the USD to mitigate the negative impact from this currency's movements.

Second, we examined the extent to which a firm's foreign involvement can explain the magnitude of firm-level foreign exchange exposure. The majority of the exposed sampled firms in Malaysia and Singapore have significant foreign involvement (foreign sales ratio more than 5%), but in the case of Singapore, a firm with a low level of foreign involvement (<5%) is also exposed to all studied currencies. Consistent with common expectations that a firm with a higher foreign involvement is more exposed to exchange rate movements (El-Masry et al. 2007), our results provide evidence that the proportion of significant foreign exchange rate exposure is higher for firms with higher foreign sales revenue in Malaysia and Singapore.

However, our results indicate that the expectation that large firms are highly involved in international operations is not always true because some of the sampled firms have little foreign involvement (less than 5% foreign sales ratio). One explanation for the low level of foreign sales is the business nature of these firms which focuses on local markets. In addition, a hedging strategy might explain why the majority of sampled firms are not exposed to any of the studied currencies, especially USD, which is one of the most important currencies in international business. These large firms may structure their financial and operational hedging strategies to reduce the aggregate foreign exchange rate exposure (Koutmos and Martin 2003; Lin 2011).

Our findings on the contemporaneous impact of studied exchange rate movements to the share returns of the sampled firms imply some degree of market efficiency in both Malaysian and Singaporean markets. Our results have shown that large firms are also exposed to other currencies instead of USD. Thus, the firm's understanding of the effect of other currencies to their share returns is also important to fully manage their exchange rate exposure through hedging strategies.

10.5.2 Recommendation

This study investigated exchange rate exposure of large firms in Malaysia and Singapore only. Future research should include more firms and countries with different levels of market capitalisation to better understand the stylised effect of exchange rate exposure in the firm-level analysis. Future research should also look into the possibility that the relationship between exchange rate movements and share returns is asymmetric and has a lagged effect due to the possibility of the firms to adopt hedging strategies to mitigate the aggregate effect of exchange rate exposure. In practical implications, the significant effect of different bilateral exchange rates implies the importance of introducing multiple exchange rate rates in the exposure model (e.g., Bacha et al. 2013; Bartram 2004; Bartram and Bodnar 2007; Parsley and Popper 2006). Hence, the firm's financial manager should constantly monitor the effect of multiple currencies on their share returns to mitigate their exchange rate exposure through the hedging strategies.

References

Adler, M., & Dumas, B. (1983). International portfolio choice and corporation finance: a synthesis. *Journal of Finance, 38*(3), 925–984.

Adler, M., & Dumas, B. (1984). Exposure to currency risk: definition and measurement. *Financial Management, 13*(2), 41–50. http://www.jstor.org/stable/3665446.

Aggarwal, R. (1981). Exchange rates and stock prices: a study of U.S. capital markets under floating exchange rates. *Akron Business and Economic Review, 12*(3), 7–12.

Aggarwal, R., & Harper, J. T. (2010). Foreign exchange exposure of "domestic" corporations. *Journal of International Money and Finance, 29*(8), 1619–1636. doi:10.1016/j.jimonfin.2010.05.003.

Agyei-Ampomah, S., Mazouz, K., & Yin, S. (2012). The foreign exchange exposure of UK non-financial firms: A comparison of market-based methodologies. *International Review of Financial Analysis, 29*, 251–260. doi:10.1016/j.irfa.2012.05.006.

Alberg, D., Shalit, H., & Yosef, R. (2008). Estimating stock market volatility using asymmetric GARCH models. *Applied Financial Economics, 18*(15), 1201–1208. doi:10.1080/09603100701604225.

Alssayah, A., & Krishnamurti, C. (2013). Theoretical framework of foreign exchange exposure, competition and the market value of domestic corporations. *International Journal of Economics and Finance, 5*(2), 1–14. doi:10.5539/ijef.v5n2p1.

Bacha, O. I., Mohamad, A., Zain, S. R. S. M., & Rasid, M. E. S. M. (2013). Foreign exchange exposure and impact of policy switch—the case of Malaysian listed firms. *Applied Economics, 45*(20), 2974–2984. doi:10.1080/00036846.2012.684790.

Bartram, S. M. (2004). Linear and nonlinear foreign exchange rate exposures of German nonfinancial corporations. *Journal of International Money and Finance, 23*(4), 673–699. doi:10.1016/j.jimonfin.2004.03.002.

Bartram, S. M., & Bodnar, G. M. (2007). The exchange rate exposure puzzle. *Managerial Finance, 33*(9), 642–666. doi:10.1108/03074350710776226.

Bollerslev, T. (1987). A conditionally heteroskedastic time series model for speculative prices and rates of return. *The Review of Economics and Statistics, 69*(3), 542–547. doi:10.2307/1925546.

Bollerslev, T., & Wooldridge, J. M. (1992). Quasi-maximum likelihood estimation and inference in dynamic models with time-varying covariances. *Econometric Reviews, 11*(2), 143–172. doi:10.1080/07474939208800229.

Chue, T. K., & Cook, D. (2008). Emerging market exchange rate exposure. *Journal of Banking and Finance, 32*(7), 1349–1362. doi:10.1016/j.jbankfin.2007.11.005.

Copeland, T., & Copeland, M. (1999). Managing corporate FX approach maximizing. *Financial Management, 28*(3), 68–75.

De Jong, A., Ligterink, J., & Macrae, V. (2006). A firm-specific analysis of the exchange-rate exposure of Dutch firms. *Journal of International Financial Management and Accounting, 17* (1), 1–28.

Dickey, D. A., & Fuller, W. A. (1979). Distribution of the estimators for autoregressive time series with a unit root. *Journal of the American Statistical Association, 74,* 427–431. doi:10.2307/2286348.

El-Masry, A. (2006). The exchange rate exposure of UK non-financial companies: Industry level analysis. *Managerial Finance, 32*(2), 115–136. doi:10.1108/03074350710776217.

El-Masry, A., Abd-Elsalam, O. H., & Abdel-Salam, O. (2007a). Exchange rate exposure: Do size and foreign operations matter? *Managerial Finance, 33*(9), 741–765. doi:10.1108/03074350710776262.

El-Masry, A., Abdel-Salam, O., & Alatraby, A. (2007b). The exchange rate exposure of UK non-financial companies. *Managerial Finance, 33*(9), 620–641. doi:10.1108/03074350710776217.

Entorf, H., Moebert, J., & Sonderhof, K. (2011). The foreign exchange rate exposure of nations. *Open Economies Review, 22*(2), 339–353. doi:10.1007/s11079-009-9128-6.

Fama, E. F., & French, K. R. (1993). Common risk factors in the returns on stocks and bonds. *Journal of Financial Economics, 33,* 3–56.

Jorion, P. (1990). The exchange-rate exposure of U.S. multinationals. *The Journal of Business, 63* (3), 331–345.

Kang, S., Kim, S., & Lee, J. W. (2016). Reexamining the exchange rate exposure puzzle by classifying exchange rate risks into two types. *Global Economic Review, 45*(2), 116–133. doi:10.1080/1226508X.2015.1072730.

Koutmos, G., & Martin, A. D. (2003). Asymmetric exchange rate exposure: Theory and evidence. *Journal of International Money and Finance, 22*(3), 365–383. doi:10.1016/S0261-5606(03)00012-3.

Lin, C.-H. (2011). Exchange rate exposure in the Asian emerging markets. *Journal of Multinational Financial Management, 21*(4), 224–238. doi:10.1016/j.mulfin.2011.04.002.

Makar, S., & Huffman, S. (2013). The FX exposure puzzle: Insights from SEC disclosures. *Managerial Finance, 39*(4), 342–361. doi:10.1108/03074351311306175.

Muller, A., & Verschoor, W. F. C. (2007). Asian foreign exchange risk exposure. *Journal of the Japanese and International Economies, 21*(1), 16–37. doi:10.1016/j.jjie.2006.06.001.

Parsley, D. C., & Popper, H. A. (2006). Exchange rate pegs and foreign exchange exposure in east and south east Asia. *Journal of International Money and Finance, 25*(6), 992–1009. doi:10.1016/j.jimonfin.2006.07.009.

Phillips, P., & Perron, P. (1988). Testing for a unit root in time series regression. *Biometrika, 75,* 335–346. doi:10.1093/biomet/75.2.335.

Ye, M., Hutson, E., & Muckley, C. (2014). Exchange rate regimes and foreign exchange exposure: The case of emerging market firms. *Emerging Markets Review, 21,* 156–182. doi:10.1016/j.ememar.2014.09.001.

Chapter 11
Shock and Volatility Transmission Between Oil Prices and Stock Returns: Case of Oil-Importing and Oil-Exporting Countries

Nurul Nazurah Atu, Imbarine Bujang and Norlida Jaafar

Abstract This study examines shock and volatility transmission between oil prices and stock returns in oil-importing and oil-exporting countries, including the USA, China, Saudi Arabia, Malaysia and a Brent oil market. We used daily data starting from January 1, 2004, until December 31, 2014. By using a bivariate vector autoregressive–generalised autoregressive conditional heteroscedasticity (VAR-GARCH) model, the empirical results suggest that there is a unidirectional shock transmission from oil to stock and bidirectional volatility transmission between oil prices and stock returns in the Standard and Poor 500 (S&P 500). Additionally, bidirectional shock and volatility transmission was discovered between oil prices and stock returns in the Tadawul All Share Index (TASI) and FTSE Bursa Malaysia KLCI (FBMKLCI). Nevertheless, there is no evidence found in the Shanghai Stock Exchange (SSE) Composite. The empirical results also suggest that the transmissions appear more often from oil to stock markets.

Keywords Oil prices · Stock returns · VAR-GARCH model

N.N. Atu (✉) · I. Bujang
Faculty of Business Management, Universiti Teknologi MARA,
Kota Kinabalu, Sabah, Malaysia
e-mail: nurulnazurah90@gmail.com

I. Bujang
e-mail: imbar074@sabah.uitm.edu.my

N. Jaafar
Faculty of Business Management, Universiti Teknologi MARA,
Shah Alam, Selangor, Malaysia
e-mail: norlidaj@salam.uitm.edu.my

F. Noordin et al. (eds.), *Proceedings of the 2nd Advances in Business Research International Conference*, https://doi.org/10.1007/978-981-10-6053-3_11

11.1 Introduction

Tremendous economic growth has made crude oil the most crucial source of energy in the business production purposes. Crude oil is among the physical commodities with the greatest influence on economic growth. Oil prices fell drastically between June and December 2014 marking an end to a four-year period of relative price stability around $105 per barrel as claimed by the World Bank Group (2015). Moreover, World Bank Group (2015) indicated that the reasons for the sharp drop in oil prices are due to trends in supply and demand, changes in the Organisation of Petroleum Exporting Countries (OPEC) objectives, receding geopolitical concerns about supply disruptions and appreciation of the US dollar. This has had implications for the macroeconomy and finance sector.

Also, efficient market hypothesis (EMH) theory developed by Fama (1970) stated that a market is called efficient when the prices fully reflect all the available data. Numerous researchers used this theory associated with the stock market and viewed it as information collection and processing since the asset price will react according to the arrival of new information. Therefore, it is reasonable to anticipate that the stock market would take in the data regarding the impact of oil price shocks and assimilate quickly into stock prices.

The findings of previous research regarding the influence of oil price shocks on stock returns have been both consistent and contradictory. Some found that the influence of oil price shocks on stock returns exists (Jones and Kaul 1996; Sadorsky 1999; Papapetrou 2001; Zarour 2006; Park and Ratti 2008), while others concluded that it does not exist (Huang et al. 1996; Maghyereh 2004). Additionally, the influences of oil price shocks on stock returns differ between nations. The empirical results exhibit that oil price shocks had adverse impacts on stock returns (Sadorsky 1999; Papapetrou 2001; Cunado and Perez de Gracia, 2014), while other studies found it had a positive impact (Park and Ratti, 2008; Zarour 2006; Narayan and Narayan 2010). The effects of oil price shocks on stock returns differ depending on whether the country is an oil importer or oil exporter (Park and Ratti 2008). When the oil prices increase, it will raise wealth and income for the oil-exporting or oil-producing countries and affect stocks positively. Thus, it is a positive relationship between oil prices and stock returns (Awartani and Maghyereh 2013). Previous studies focused on the impact of oil price shocks on stock returns and disregarded the shock and volatility transmission between oil price and stock returns. Respectively, several studies discovered that shock and volatility transmission between oil prices and stock returns is unidirectional and bidirectional (Arouri et al. 2011, 2012; Chaibi and Gomes 2013; Gencer and Demiralay 2014). Nonetheless, the mixed results from previous studies are due to the data collection used and selection of either the industry- or market-level data, which affect the result of the study. The time duration of the data also affects the results as suggested by Gencer and Demiralay (2014).

Therefore, the main objective of this paper is to examine shock and volatility transmission between oil prices and stock returns in oil-importing and oil-exporting countries. The remaining sections of this paper are organised as follows: Sect. 11.2 discusses the literature review from the previous studies. Section 11.3 introduces the methodology used in this paper, and Sect. 11.4 presents the data and preliminary analysis. Section 11.5 discusses the empirical results, and the last section concludes the paper.

11.2 Literature Review

A preliminary work examining the impact of oil price shocks on stock markets was done by Jones and Kaul (1996). They discovered that the impact of oil price shocks on the US and Canada stock markets is influenced by current and future real cash flow, but not in the UK and Japan. A number of previous studies have attempted to examine the impact of oil price shocks on stock returns by using VAR models (Huang et al. 1996; Sadorsky 1999; Papapetrou 2001; Maghyereh 2004; Park and Ratti 2008). Huang et al. (1996) discovered that oil future returns do not have a great influence on the S&P 500 index, but have a significant influence on individual corporation stock returns. Similarly, Maghyereh (2004) found very weak evidence on the relationship between oil price shocks and stock market returns in 22 emerging countries. He stated that the shocks in the oil market are slowly transmitted in the emerging stock markets. By using monthly data, Sadorsky's (1999) findings are consistent with Papapetrou (2001) whereby oil price shock has a negative influence on stock return. Even so, through Park and Ratti's (2008) findings, the influences of oil price shocks on oil-exporting countries are positive, while the oil-importing countries are negative. Another study conducted by Zarour (2006) found that the oil price shock gives greater impact on the Oman market than the Gulf Cooperation Council (GCC) market. Bahrain, Saudi Arabia and Abu Dhabi reacted negatively, while other GCC markets reacted positively to oil return shock.

The recent volatility of oil prices has had a negative impact on stock market returns in most countries as claimed by Cunado and Perez de Gracia (2014). Their results are coherent with previous studies (Sadorsky 1999; Papapetrou 2001; Park and Ratti 2008). Agren (2006) suggested that strong evidence of volatility spillover is found in Japan, Norway, the UK and the USA, yet there is weak evidence found in Sweden. Meanwhile, Malik and Hammoudeh (2007) found that only Saudi Arabia had significant volatility transmission from the Saudi Arabia market to the oil market, but the GCC stock markets received volatility from the oil market. There is a significant transmission of shocks and volatility discovered by Malik and Ewing (2009) between oil prices and only some sector returns in the USA. Moreover, Chaibi and Gomes (2013) revealed that shock and volatility transmission between oil and some frontier stock markets is unidirectional, yet bidirectional is found in many markets. They also stated that the spillover runs more often from oil to stock markets. Also, Gencer and Demiralay (2014) claimed that unidirectional volatility transmission exists from the oil market to five sectors (Banking, Chemicals–Petroleum–Plastics (C-P-P), Industrials, Services and BIST 100). They also reported that oil-dependent sectors had been more affected by oil return volatility than non-oil-dependent sectors. Most of the relationships are unidirectional from the oil market to the Tunisian stock market as signified by Hamma et al. (2014). Several recent studies employed VAR-GARCH to examine volatility spillover between oil price and stock sector return (Hammoudeh et al. 2009; Arouri et al. 2011, 2012; Jouini 2013). Hammoudeh et al. (2009) included service, banking and industrial sectors for Kuwait, Qatar and Saudi Arabia, while financial, insurance and service sectors were included for the UAE. They suggest that previous conditional volatility is stronger than past shocks in anticipating future volatility.

The existence of significant spillover effect is unidirectional from oil to some sectors for return (Telecommunications and Information Technology (IT), Industrial Investment, Insurance, Energy and Utilities and Banks and Financial Services). Nevertheless, bidirectional shock transmission between oil and market index and Telecommunications and IT was suggested by Jouini (2013). Abdalla (2013) revealed that shock and past volatility from oil market had a significant influence on the stock market in Saudi Arabia. Furthermore, Arouri et al. (2011) discovered unidirectional transmission from oil markets to the stock market in Europe, while spillover in the USA was bidirectional. This study is equivalent to their study in the following year, wherein they investigated the impact of oil volatility on European equity market (Arouri et al. 2012). Subsequently, Lin and Appiah (2014) found significant results of spillover effects what was stronger in Nigeria than Ghana.

Moreover, Narayan and Narayan (2010) found that oil prices, stock prices and nominal exchange rates are cointegrated and share a long-run correlation. Meanwhile, oil price shocks have a positive impact on stock prices, and they argued that it is inconsistent with the theoretical expectations. This finding supports Ravinchandran and Alkhathlan's (2010) study of GCC countries. They confirmed that in the long period the consequences of oil price volatility on GCC stock returns exist as these nations are major suppliers of crude oil that expected to react when the oil price fluctuates. In contrast to Ravinchandran and Alkhathlan (2010), Arouri et al. (2010) employed weekly data and linear and nonlinear models to find that stock markets in Qatar, Oman, Saudi Arabia and the UAE responded to the volatility of oil prices but not in Bahrain and Kuwait. This result is consistent with Azar and Basmajian (2013) who suggested that oil price has nonlinear effects on the Saudi Arabia stock market, while oil price shocks insignificantly impacted on the Kuwait stock market. Consequently, we employed the VAR-GARCH model proposed by Ling and McAleer (2003) to extend a better understanding of shock and volatility transmission between oil prices and stock returns. This bivariate GARCH model provides meaningful estimates of the model's parameters with fewer computational complications.

11.3 Methodology

11.3.1 VAR-GARCH Model

The bivariate GARCH model used in this study to examine shock and volatility transmission between oil prices and stock returns is the VAR-GARCH model proposed by Ling and McAleer (2003). The conditional mean and variance of VAR-GARCH are as follows:

$$R_t = \mu + \phi R_{t-1} + \varepsilon_t,\ \varepsilon_t = D_t \eta_t \tag{11.1}$$

where $R_t = (r_t^S, r_t^O)', r_t^S \text{ and } r_t^O$ are the stock and oil returns, respectively, $\mu = (\mu^S, \mu^O)'$ is a 2-vector of the constant term, ϕ is a square matrix of order 2 of coefficients allowing for cross-sectional dependency of conditional mean between oil price and stock markets, $\varepsilon_t = (\varepsilon_t^S, \varepsilon_t^O)', \varepsilon_t^S \text{ and } \varepsilon_t^O$ being the error terms of the conditional mean equations for stock and oil returns, respectively, $\eta_t = (\eta_t^S, \eta_t^O)'$ refers to a sequence of independently and identically distributed random errors, and $D_t = diag\left(\sqrt{h_t^S}, \sqrt{h_t^O}\right)'$ with $h_t^S \text{ and } h_t^O$ is the conditional variances of $r_t^S \text{ and } r_t^O$, respectively, and given by:

$$h_t^S = C_S^2 + \beta_{S1}^2 h_{t-1}^S + \alpha_{S1}^2 (\varepsilon_{t-1}^S)^2 + \beta_{S2}^2 h_{t-1}^O + \alpha_{S2}^2 (\varepsilon_{t-1}^O)^2 \tag{11.2}$$

$$h_t^O = C_O^2 + \beta_{O1}^2 h_{t-1}^O + \alpha_{O1}^2 (\varepsilon_{t-1}^O)^2 + \beta_{O2}^2 h_{t-1}^S + \alpha_{O2}^2 (\varepsilon_{t-1}^S)^2 \tag{11.3}$$

Both Eqs. (11.2) and (11.3) show how volatility is transmitted over time and across the oil and stock markets. The cross-values of error terms, $(\varepsilon_{t-1}^O)^2$ and $(\varepsilon_{t-1}^S)^2$, which capture the impact, direct effects of shock transmission, and also those of lagged conditional volatilities, which it indicates the return shocks in the oil market and to the corresponding stock sector at time (t−1). Additionally, h_{t-1}^O and h_{t-1}^S explain for the volatility transmission between markets. The null hypothesis is that the alpha 2 and beta 2 coefficients are equal to zero and there is no spillover of volatility from either direction, oil to stock or stock to oil. The roots of the question $|I_2 - AL - BL = 0|$ must be outside the unit circle, and the expressions $(I_2 - AL)$ and BL are left coprime and satisfy some other identifiability conditions to guarantee stationarity as developed by Jeantheau (1998), where L is a lag polynomial, I_2 is a (2 × 2) identity matrix, and A and B are defined as:

$$A = \begin{pmatrix} \alpha_{S1}^2 & \alpha_{S2}^2 \\ \alpha_{O2}^2 & \alpha_{O1}^2 \end{pmatrix} and\, B = \begin{pmatrix} \beta_{S1}^2 & \beta_{S2}^2 \\ \beta_{O2}^2 & \beta_{O1}^2 \end{pmatrix} \tag{11.4}$$

The conditional covariance between stock and oil returns can be described as $h_t^{SO} = p\sqrt{h_t^S h_t^O}$, given that p is the constant conditional correlation (CCC).

The empirical model simultaneously allows long-run volatility persistence as well as shock and volatility transmissions between the oil and stock markets under consideration. Note that the CCC assumption can be viewed as restrictive given that the correlation coefficient is likely to vary over time according to changes in economic and market conditions. By following Ling and McAleer (2003), the quasi-maximum likelihood estimation (QMLE) method is employed to estimate the empirical model in order to take into consideration the fact that the normality condition is frequently rejected for the majority of the macroeconomic and financial series.

11.4 Data and Preliminary Analysis

This paper used daily data which for crude oil and stock market indices. The time span of the study is starting from January 1, 2004, until December 31, 2014. For the crude oil market, the study employed the Brent crude oil price and four countries' stock market index, which included the USA and China representing as oil-importing countries, while Saudi Arabia and Malaysia represented oil-exporting countries. Many researchers from previous studies used the Brent oil price instead of West Texas Intermediate (WTI) because the price reflects about two-thirds of the traded crude oil and serves as an indicator of oil prices for valuing crude oil (Abdalla 2013; Gencer and Demiralay 2014; Jouini 2013; Arouri et al. 2011, 2012). In addition, the study selects the USA and China to represent oil-importing countries as to the Energy Information Administration (EIA) (2015) stated that China had become the biggest global net importer of oil in the first quarter of 2014 followed by the USA. Meanwhile, Saudi Arabia was chosen to represent oil-exporting country since it is the biggest holder of crude oil and the leading exporter of total petroleum liquids in 2013 claimed EIA (2014a, b). It has the largest crude oil production capacity in the world by having 16% of the world's proved oil reserves. Malaysia was included in this study because the EIA (2014a, b) indicated that it is the second largest oil and natural gas producer in Southeast Asia and continued as a net oil exporter of crude oil and products of petroleum in 2013, even though there is a narrowing gap between consumption and production in the previous few years. Moreover, only a few previous studies have chosen Malaysia to examine shock and volatility transmission between oil prices and stock returns. Through the descriptive statistics are for four stock market indices and Brent oil returns, all the return series are in a non-normal distribution as signified by the skewness, kurtosis and Jarque–Bera test. Consequently, all return series have to convert the data into natural logarithm transformation equation as follows, $r_t = \log\left(\frac{P_t}{P_{t-1}}\right)$, where r_t refers to the return of the index at time t, while P_t denotes the current index closing price and P_{t-1} is the previous day index of closing price.

Table 11.1 Results of unit root tests

Stock indices/data	Level		
	ADF	PP	KPSS
S&P 500 index	−42.21616***	−60.45392***	0.085048
SSE Composite index	−53.75273***	−53.81655***	0.160975
Tadawul All Share Index	−49.81958***	−49.79203***	0.203804
FTSE Bursa Malaysia KLCI	−47.50668***	−47.49172***	0.064683
Brent oil market	−45.74356***	−45.72899***	0.08879

Note The Mackinnon's 1% critical value is −3.961241 for ADF and PP tests. The critical value for the KPSS test is 0.216000 at a 1% significance level. *, ** and *** indicate statistical significance at the 10%, 5% and 1% levels, respectively

Table 11.2 Results of regression of stock and oil price returns

Stock Indices	S&P 500	SSE Composite	TASI	FBMKLCI
α	0.000220	0.000261	0.000195	0.000265
t statistic	0.963946	0.880257	0.630017	1.937619
p value	(0.3352)	(0.3788)	(0.5287)	(0.0528)*
β	−0.024404	0.034232	0.106183	0.055331
t statistic	−1.751227	1.895548	5.615007	6.633059
p value	(0.0800)*	(0.0581)*	(0.0001)***	(0.0001)***
R-squared	0.001068	0.001251	0.010874	0.015109

Note *, ** and *** indicate statistical significance at the 10%, 5% and 1% levels, respectively

Three unit root tests are employed in this study, viz. augmented Dickey–Fuller (ADF), Phillips–Perron (PP) and Kwiatkowski–Phillips–Schmidt–Shin (KPSS) tests. Based on Table 11.1, both ADF and PP tests suggest it is significant at the 1% level for all return series by rejecting the null hypothesis. Meanwhile, the results of the KPSS test show it failed to reject the null hypothesis, indicating the return series is stationary. Therefore, all return series are stationary at the level of data.

The result of linear regression in Table 11.2 reports that only oil price returns have a negative impact on stock returns in the S&P 500 and positive impact on stock returns in SSE Composite, TASI and FBMKLCI. Both S&P 500 and SSE Composite probability values of the t statistic show significance at the 10% level, while both TASI and FBMKLCI were significant at the 1% level. Subsequently, the R^2 coefficient of determination reported a very weak model to fit the data as it is not close to 100%, with only 0.1068, 0.1251, 1.0874 and 1.5109%.

Table 11.3 demonstrates that the results of the ARCH-LM test provide strong evidence for rejecting the null hypothesis, which is significant at the 1% level for all return series. This finding suggests the presence of ARCH effect in the residual series and supports the decisions to use a GARCH methodology to examine the shock and volatility transmission between oil prices and stock returns.

Table 11.3 Result of ARCH-LM test for returns series

Stock indices	ARCH-LM test statistic	Probability Chi-square (1)
S&P 500	131.8099***	0.0000
SSE Composite	66.58044***	0.0000
TASI	62.89641***	0.0000
FBMKLCI	31.17644***	0.0000
Brent oil	152.8155***	0.0000

Note *, ** and *** indicate statistical significance at the 10%, 5% and 1% levels, respectively

11.5 Empirical Results

As shown in Table 11.4, the estimated ARCH and GARCH coefficients of oil and all stock market returns are statistically significant at the 1% level. This signifies the presence of strong ARCH and GARCH effects. For the oil-S&P 500, there is a unidirectional shock transmission from oil to stock which is significant at the 1% level. The past of oil shocks positively impacted on the current volatility of the stock returns. Nonetheless, bidirectional volatility transmission was discovered between oil prices and stock returns. Both current volatility of stock and oil are negatively affected by past oil and stock volatility. Subsequently, there is no evidence in the oil-SSE Composite. As for the oil-TASI, the past oil and stock shocks and volatility positively and negatively impacted the current volatility of stock and oil in both directions. This finding is consistent with Abdalla (2013) who found a bidirectional shock and volatility transmission between oil prices and stock returns in TASI. Furthermore, the reaction of oil price to the Saudi Arabia stock market shock would be explained by the fact that Saudi Arabia is a strong oil exporter as suggested by Jouini (2013). The world oil market stability may be associated with the major oil-exporting countries. We also found a bidirectional shock and volatility transmission between oil prices and stock returns in oil-FBMKLCI. Both current volatility of stock and oil are positively affected by past of oil and stock shocks. Meanwhile, past volatility of the oil market positively impacted on the current volatility of the stock market and negatively impacted from the stock to the oil market.

Additionally, the estimates of CCC discovered that all stock markets are significantly positively correlated with oil returns. This result is in favour of potential earnings from investing in all these markets. To make important investment decisions in those stock markets, investors should be conscious of everything that happens in the oil market. As for the results of diagnostic tests of ARCH (10), it exhibits that only the S&P 500 and FBMKLCI show significant result which implies there is an ARCH effect in the standardised residuals. Therefore, the bivariate VAR-GARCH model that we used is only sufficient to capture the shock and volatility transmission between oil and stock returns in the SSE Composite and TASI. Meanwhile, for the result of LB (10), the existence of serial correlation in the standardised residuals is only found in the SSE Composite.

Table 11.4 Result of VAR-GARCH model

Market/data	S&P 500	SSE Composite	TASI	FBMKLCI
Mean				
C_{OO}	0.015133	0.024681	0.040070	0.018439
σ_{OO}	0.1744434***	0.168386***	0.168087***	0.158370***
σ_{OS}	0.258587***	0.103446***	0.119129***	0.343129***
C_{SS}	0.059444***	0.030932	0.108197***	0.036642***
σ_{SO}	−0.013094	−0.008142	0.045823***	0.003177
σ_{SS}	−0.057523**	0.000677	0.087178***	0.140401***
Variance				
C_{OO}	0.015008***	0.005736	0.010849***	0.458325***
C_{SS}	0.018949***	0.014099**	0.023544**	0.092405***
A_{OO}	0.039408***	0.047001***	0.043292***	0.048260***
A_{SS}	0.097289***	0.047424***	0.137980***	0.093534***
A_{OS}	0.040625***	−0.000324	0.014267**	0.451396***
A_{SO}	0.000795	−0.000672	0.039454**	0.010107***
B_{OO}	0.955230***	0.947262***	0.951760***	−0.724968***
B_{SS}	0.848465***	0.943153***	0.8484646***	2.452617***
B_{OS}	−0.043353***	0.004138	−0.012945**	7.151460***
B_{SO}	−0.023506**	0.004825	−0.023506**	−0.351168***
CCC	0.064655***	0.041843**	0.064655***	0.080856***
Log-L	−8802.1180	−10112.1158	−9590.7863	−7851.6846
ARCH (10)	110.69*	85.32	79.46	170.76***
LB (10)	90.64	61.16**	49.90	25.54

Note CCC is the constant conditional correlation between stock and oil. Log-L denotes the log-likelihood. ARCH (10) and LB (10) refer to the empirical statistics of statistical test for conditional heteroscedasticity and Ljung–Box tests for autocorrelations on return of order 10 applied to standardised residuals. N/A signifies not available. *, ** and *** indicate statistical significance at the 10%, 5% and 1% levels, respectively

This study also supports Park and Ratti's (2008) findings in terms of oil prices shock but not in the volatility, whereby the influence of oil price shocks on oil-exporting countries is positive as can be seen in TASI and FBMKLCI. However, the oil price volatility has a negative impact on the S&P 500 as oil-importing countries. An increase in the oil prices consequently leads to higher industry cost, which will negatively affect the stock market. The empirical results also show that the transmissions appear more often from oil to stock markets, which is consistent with Chaibi and Gomes (2013).

11.6 Conclusion

This study examined shock and volatility transmission between oil prices and stock returns in oil-importing and oil-exporting countries using the VAR-GARCH model. Empirical results suggest that in the oil-S&P 500, there is a unidirectional shock transmission from oil to stock and bidirectional volatility transmission between oil and stock returns. Yet, there is insignificant result in the SSE Composite. Meanwhile, bidirectional shock and volatility transmission was found between oil prices and stock returns in TASI and FBMKLCI. The empirical results also show that the transmissions appear more regularly from oil to stock markets. Moreover, the S&P 500, TASI and FBMKLCI are efficient because they react to the arrival of new information in the oil market, which is supported by Fama's (1970) EMH theory. However, this study suggested that the SSE Composite is inefficient and does not reasonably react with the fluctuation of oil prices. Therefore, this study assists the investors to make crucial investment decisions. Since the SSE Composite is not affected by the oil price shock and volatility, it is a good indication to the investors as well as for international portfolio managers.

References

Abdalla, S. Z. S. (2013). Modelling the impact of oil price fluctuations on the stock returns in an emerging market: The case of Saudi Arabia. *Interdisciplinary Journal of Research in Business, 2*(10), 10–20.

Agren, M. (2006). Does oil price uncertainty transmit to stock market? (No. 2006: 23). Working Paper, Department of Economics, Uppsala University.

Arouri, M. E. H., Lahiani, A., & Bellalah, M. (2010). Oil price shocks and stock market returns in oil-exporting countries: The case of GCC Countries. *International of Economics and Finance, 2*(5), 132–139.

Arouri, M. E. H., Jouini, J., & Nguyen, D. K. (2011). Volatility spillovers between oil prices and stock sector returns: Implications for portfolio management. *Journal of International Money and Finance, 30*(7), 1387–1405.

Arouri, M. E. H., Jouini, J., & Nguyen, D. K. (2012). On the impacts of oil price fluctuations on European equity markets: Volatility spillovers and hedging effectiveness. *Energy Economics, 34*(2), 611–617.

Awartani, B., & Maghyereh, A. I. (2013). Dynamic spillovers between oil and stock markets in the gulf cooperation council countries. *Energy Economics, 36*(1), 28–42.

Azar, S. A., & Basmajian, L. (2013). Oil prices and the Kuwaiti and the Saudi stock markets: The contrast. *International Journal of Economics and Financial Issues, 3*(2), 294–304.

Chaibi, A. & Gomes, M. (2013). Volatility spillovers between oil prices and stock returns: A focus on Frontier Markets. Working Paper, IPAG Business School.

Cunado, J., & Perez de Gracia, F. (2014). Oil price shocks and stock market returns: Evidence for some European countries. *Energy Economics, 42,* 365–377.

Energy Information Administration. (2014, September 10). Saudi Arabia overview. Retrieved from http://www.eia.gov/beta/international/analysis.cfm?iso=SAU.

Energy Information Administration. (2014, September 29). Saudi Arabia overview. Retrieved from http://www.eia.gov/beta/international/analysis.cfm?iso=MYS.

Energy Information Administration. (2015, May 14). China overview. Retrieved from http://www.eia.gov/beta/international/analysis.cfm?iso=CHN.

Fama, E. F. (1970). Efficient capital markets: A review of theory and empirical work. *The Journal of Finance, 25*(2), 383–417.

Gencer, H. G., & Demiralay, S. (2014). Shock and volatility spillovers between oil prices and Turkish sector returns. *International Journal of Economics and Finance, 6*(2), 174–180.

Hamma, W., Jarboui, A., & Ghorbel, A. (2014). Effect of oil price volatility on Tunisian stock market at sector level and effectiveness of hedging strategy. *Procedia Economics and Finance, 13,* 109–127.

Hammoudeh, S. M., Yuan, Y., & McAleer, M. (2009). Shock and volatility spillovers among equity sectors of the Gulf Arab stock markets. *The Quarterly Review of Economics and Finance, 49*(3), 829–842.

Huang, R. D., Masulis, R. W., & Stoll, H. R. (1996). Energy shocks and financial markets. *Journal of Futures Markets, 16*(1), 1–27.

Jones, C. M., & Kaul, G. (1996). Oil and the stock markets. *The Journal of Finances, 51*(2), 463–491.

Jouini, J. (2013). Return and volatility interaction between oil prices and stock markets in Saudi Arabia. *Journal of Policy Modeling, 35*(6), 1124–1144.

Lin, B., Jr, P. K. W., & Appiah, M. O. (2014). Oil price fluctuation, volatility spillover and the Ghanaian equity market: Implication for portfolio management and hedging effectiveness. *Energy Economics, 42*, 172–182.

Ling, S., & McAleer, M. (2003). Asymptotic theory for a vector ARMA-GARCH model. *Econometric Theory, 19*(02), 280–310.

Malik, F., & Hammoudeh, S. (2007). Shock and volatility transmission in the oil, US and Gulf equity markets. *International Review of Economics and Finance, 16*(3), 357–368.

Malik, F., & Ewing, B. T. (2009). Volatility transmission between oil prices and equity sector returns. *International Review of Financial Analysis, 18*(3), 95–100.

Maghyereh, A. (2004). Oil price shocks and emerging stock markets: A generalized VAR approach. *International Journal of Applied Econometrics and Quantitative Studies, 1*(2), 27–40.

Narayan, P. K., & Narayan, S. (2010). Modelling the impact of oil prices on Vietnam's stock prices. *Applied Energy, 87*(1), 356–361.

Park, J., & Ratti, R. A. (2008). Oil price shocks and stock markets in the US and 13 European countries. *Energy Economics, 30*(5), 2587–2608.

Papapetrou, E. (2001). Oil price shocks, stock market, economic activity and employment in Greece. *Energy Economics*, *23*(5), 511–532.

Ravichandran, K., & Alkhathlan, K. A. (2010). Impact of oil prices on GCC stock market. *Research Applied Economics, 2*(1), 1–12.
Sadorsky, P. (1999). Oil price shocks and stock market activity. *Energy Economics, 21*(5), 449–469.
Zarour, B. A. (2006). Wild oil prices, but brave stock markets! The case of Gulf Cooperation Council (GCC) stock markets. *Operational Research, 6*(2), 145–162.
World Bank Group. (2015). *Global economic prospects, January 2015: Having fiscal space and using it*. Washington, DC: World Bank. doi:10.1596/978-1-4648-04444-1.

Chapter 12
Effect of Cash Holding Towards Firm's Efficiency: Moderating Effect of Earning Quality

Siti Julea Binti Supar, Imbarine Bujang and Taufik Abdul Hakim

Abstract This conceptual paper attempts to assess the moderating effect of earning quality on the relation of cash holding towards the firm's efficiency by sector in Malaysia. Failure in utilizing the cash within the firms may lead to the existence of agency conflict which later will cause the firm value to drop. This situation later will cause the manager to change the figures of earning in the financial report throughout the reporting period that will lead to poor earning quality. The earning quality will influence the efficiency of the firms as the financial report will reflect the actual economic activity. Changes in financial report may lead to the misallocation of resources and directly affect the efficiency of the firms. Generally, the findings have the important information that can be used in proposing the new policy in managing the cash for each sector in Malaysia.

Keywords Cash holdings · Earning quality · Firm efficiency · Agency conflict

12.1 Introduction

In a perfect capital market, firms will have an easy access to finance a project with the external financing. Modigliani and Miller (1958) also believe that firms will easily have the access to enter into the capital market and prefer to hold less cash as if they are in a perfect capital market since it is easy to obtain the external financing in order to finance their project. In addition, firms are believed to give the remaining cash to their shareholders in the form of dividend after they have invested all the

S.J.B. Supar (✉) · I. Bujang · T.A. Hakim
Faculty of Business Management, Universiti Teknologi MARA (UiTM), Shah Alam, Sabah, Malaysia
e-mail: aellea_julea99@yahoo.com

I. Bujang
e-mail: imbar074@sabah.uitm.edu.my

T.A. Hakim
e-mail: taufikabdhakim@yahoo.com

F. Noordin et al. (eds.), *Proceedings of the 2nd Advances in Business Research International Conference*, https://doi.org/10.1007/978-981-10-6053-3_12

available funds in a positive return investment in a perfect market condition (Pinkowitz et al., 2006). This situation makes cash seem to be unimportant to be held within a firm. However, this is not always the case.

The perfect capital market does not exist due to several identified reasons. It is believed that the inexistence of perfect capital market is due to the restriction in finance and the higher cost of the external financing (Jensen & Meckling, 1976; Myers & Majluf, 1984). Majority firms hold sufficient amount of cash within the company in order to prevent from using the expensive external financing. There are several reasons that caused the external financing become expensive in which it includes the agency cost, cost of transaction, information asymmetric and many more (Jensen & Meckling, 1976; Myres & Majluf, 1984).

A study by Campello et al. (2010) indicates that firms will not carry out any plan for investment if the condition of capital market is not good due to the imperfect market condition. This may help the company to avoid the costly external financing by not doing any project or investment in such situation. Despite the situation, a company still needs to earn profit and maintain its sustainability even in imperfect capital market. An et al. (2012) suggests that a company should manage well the liquidity position for its daily operational expenses and investment opportunities in order to fully utilize the internal financing as well as to avoid the expensive external sources of finance. In addition, Tahir and Alifiah (2015) have stated that the imperfect condition of capital market does become the main reason for firms to hold more cash within the company. Therefore, the condition of imperfection in capital market highlights the importance of holding cash within the firms.

However, majority of research efforts conducted previously only focused on the (i) relationship between cash holdings and the efficiency and (ii) relationship between cash holdings and earning quality of the firms. In contrast, Mahmud et al. (2009) have conducted a study on the relationship between the earning quality and efficiency of the firms without considering the level of cash holding of the firms as cash plays an important role in a company. The researchers later found an inconsistency in finding the significance of relationship between the two variables as the researchers assessed the performance of the firms using the return on assets (ROA) and Tobin's Q methods. However, these two methods used to capture the efficiency of the firms are not able to generate a comparative result that can be used to make a comparison between firms in the same industry (Soh, 2015).

Furthermore, most of the studies related to cash holding only focused on the developed countries. The result derived from other countries cannot be implemented in another country. Therefore, this study will be focusing on the developing country that is Malaysia. Sarif (2011) pointed out that Malaysia has been recognized as the advanced emerging market by British stock market (FTSE) in June 2011 because of the active development in economy. In addition, a study by Wasiuzzaman (2014) claimed that Malaysia is different as it has different structures of firm compared to other countries. The difference in the structure of firms in Malaysia caused the manager of the company to invest in low quality of investment that gives low returns for the company (Claessens et al., 1998). The reason why Malaysia is different from other countries is most firms in Malaysia are family firms. Claessens et al. (2000) found that ten largest families are conquering almost one forth industry in Malaysia. This is why the structure of firms in Malaysia is different. Kuan et al. (2011) have also pointed out that decision making involving the cash holdings for family firms is not the same as for non-family firms.

Apart from that, Tahir and Alifiah (2015) have also highlighted that most of the previous researchers did not classify the firms according to its industry as it is important to study the background of business separately according to its sector. The classification of firms according to its industry will provide a better understanding on the business environment as well as give the researcher more reliable results for the research efforts. This has been supported by Kayo and Kimura (2011) in which they have also pointed out that every sector or industry has its own different background of structure in financial that will influence the final results of a study.

Moreover, in the forms of macroeconomic levels, Wasiuzzaman (2014) has found that the economic condition of a country has a positive relationship with the cash holdings of firms. Soh (2015) has pointed out that the macroeconomic variables, such as gross domestic product (GDP), inflation and interest rates have the biggest impact on the efficiency of the firms. It can be assumed that the level of cash holding will be less during the economic downturn because of the poor condition that forced the company to take any available chances to enhance the performance of the firm so that the company can still be able to survive in the market. This has also been supported by a study by Pan (2006), where the researcher has found that the economic condition of a country will also have influenced towards the final findings on assessing the efficiency of firms where the economy itself will affect the performance of the firms. Thus, this study attempts to examine the moderating effect of earning quality on the relation of cash holding towards the firm's efficiency by sector in Malaysia. The remainder of this paper will be organized as follows: Sect. 12.2 will discuss the literature review for this study, while the data and the method used will be discussed in the next section.

12.2 Literature Review

There is no existence of perfect capital market in the world because the restriction in financial as well as the higher cost involves in external financing (Jensen & Meckling, 1976; Myers & Majluf, 1984). As if there is an existence of perfect capital market, Pinkowitz et al. (2006) pointed out that the manager of a company will tend to make an investment in all projects that offer a positive net present value (NPV) by using the entire cash that is being held by the firm. Not only that, the manager will also give back the extra cash to their shareholders in dividend form. This is because it is easy for firms to have access to external funding in perfect capital market. But no such perfect capital market exists in the world. Thus, this makes cash as one of the important assets in a company.

Despite the importance of cash for firms, the amount of cash for each firm is different from one another. It is believed that the amount of cash that is being held by a firm can be influenced by the purposes or motives for keeping cash within the company itself. The three main motives for holding cash within the firms according to Keynes (1936) are the transaction motives, precautionary motives and speculative motives. However, a study by Wasiuzzaman (2014) found that there are no exact motives for holding cash due to some of significant variables like growth opportunity, cash flow, liquid substitute, capital and more. Prior studies, moreover, have found that the decision on cash holding for a firm is affected by two main factors that are the opportunities in investment and the facilities in accessing the external financing. The other factors that also have influenced towards the decision on cash holdings are the firm characteristics and also the board characteristics.

However, the imperfect conditions of capital market do force the firms to hold more cash due to the expensive cost of external financing. Therefore, this makes the imperfect market condition as the main reason for a company to keep more cash within them (Tahir & Alifiah, 2015). Moreover, firms that hold high level of cash are able to survive and perform well so as to attract many investors to invest and become the stakeholder of the firms. A company with a good performance will be able to generate more profit in the future. This situation may create the investor's interest to invest with the company since the investors will try to avoid a company that has a higher chance of risk in default payment (Tahir & Alifiah, 2015).

In addition, it has been found by many researchers that the contribution of cash holding will determine the efficiency of the firms due to the existence of significant relationship. However, there are various results on this matter as some researcher found that there is a positive relationship, while the others have found that the cash holdings and firm's efficiency are negatively correlated. Some studies found that there will be an improvement in firm's efficiency if the firms having a high level of cash holding show the positive relationship (for example, Abushammala & Sulaiman, 2014; Mikkelson & Partch, 2003; Das, 2015; Fresard, 2010). Meanwhile, not all of the findings are similar as some researchers have argued and found that a higher level of cash holding will hinder the efficiency of the company (for example, Raheman & Nasr, 2007; Couderc, 2005; Pan, 2006).

It is found that having hoard of cash obviously can bring a positive effect as well as negative effect towards a firm. The high level of cash may complement some firms in terms of the performance, while some may create the agency conflict problem to occur within the company itself (Ferreira & Vilela, 2004). The existence of agency conflict occurs when the manager does not take the shareholder's interest into consideration in decision making for an investment. This agency conflict will cause the firm value to drop as the manager tends to invest in a low-quality project so as to maintain and accumulate more cash under the manager controls (Al-Dhamari & Ku Ismail, 2015) instead of investing in a project that could maximize the shareholders wealth (Gill & Shah, 2012).

This situation later will attract lots of investor from either inside or outside the country that may have the potential to threaten the position of the manager. Al-Dhamari and Ku Ismail (2015) have also claimed that many investors including foreign investors will be attracted towards firm faced with a decreasing in firm value in which later will caused the manager to feel insecure with their position in that particular company. Thus, the manager tends to make some changes towards the figure of earning in the financial report or statement throughout the reporting period in order to secure their position in the firm.

The impact of changes in figures of earnings will affect the reliability of the financial statement issued by the company. The reason for this implication is the earning quality can be defined as the extent of the financial statement to reflect the actual economic activity of firms (Mahmud et al., 2009). Furthermore, Healy and Wahlen (1999) believed that the financial report will become less reliable if it does not accurately reflect the actual economic activity of the firms and lead to the misallocation of resources. The firms later will resulted in poor earning quality as the report issued by the company is opposite from the actual economic activity of the firms.

It is found that the poor earning quality that resulted from the existence of agency conflict will lead to uncertainty or risk that will eventually give an impact towards the performance of the firms (Maham & Shabanha, 2015). The performance of the firms is affected because of the inability to predict the future operating performance in which this will prevent them from allocating the resources efficiently due to the poor earning quality. Furthermore, a study by Dechow and Schrand (2004) has found that a good earning quality will become a great tool to forecast the future company's operating performance as it shows that the financial statement issued reflects the current performance of the company. Therefore, firms are able to improve their performance as the firms have issued a more useful and reliable financial statement.

12.3 Data and Methodology

Six different industries in Malaysia are chosen to be the sample for this study where the other regulated sectors such as financial and utilities sectors are excluded from this study due to its difference and unique financial structure compared to the other industries. The six selected industries are the consumer products, industrial products, construction, trading or services, properties and plantation. Later, the firms from each sector will be classified according to its level of cash holdings whether the firm has high-level or low-level of cash holdings. According to a study made by Mikkelson and Partch (2003), a firm is classified as high level of cash holding if the firm holds more than 25% of cash and cash equivalent for at least 5 years and above. The data collected are mainly from secondary data, Datasream software. Two-stage of regression is being applied in this study. Various forms of test are conducted later by using the STATA software in order to compute the data and to solve the problem that arises in this research.

12.3.1 Dependent Variable

In order to compute the efficiency of firms for this study according to sector, the researcher has decided to use the data envelopment analysis (DEA) approach. As this model is nonparametric approach, there is no assumption being made regarding its form of production technology (Soh 2015). Thus, the technical efficiency (TE) is more suitable to be adopted as a measure as it can capture the efficiency of firm at its firm level rather than the total factor productivity (TFP).

Following Soh (2015), this study also attempts to estimate the efficiency by using the output orientation where the net sales represent the output variable and the input variables are the total debt, total shareholders' equity and the expenses on salaries or wages. The output orientation is more suitable for this study instead of the input orientation due to the agency conflict that arises within the company.

$$x_{gj} = \text{input } g(g = 1,\ldots,m), \text{DMU } j(j = 1,\ldots,n)$$
$$y_{hj} = \text{output } h(h = 1,\ldots,s)$$
$$a_j = \text{non-negative weights attached to DMU } j\text{'s input and output}$$

The above series show that by using some of m inputs to generate s output, there will be n DMUs. Thus, below is the equation for DEA models by implying the $F_o(x_j, y_j) = \text{maximum } \emptyset$ to represent the output-orientation Farrell efficiency:

$$\sum_j^n =_1 a_j y_{gj} \geq \emptyset y_{gj}, g = 1,\ldots,s$$
$$\sum_j^n =_1 a_j x_{hj} \leq \emptyset x_{hj}, h = 1,\ldots,m$$
$$a_j \geq 0, j = 1,\ldots,n$$

The result for this approach is in interval range, 0–1, where the closer the result towards 1, the more efficient the firm is.

12.3.2 Independent Variable

The researcher decides to use cash ratio (CR) or also known as cash-to-net assets instead of using cash and cash equivalents to represent cash holdings. This is because the cash ratio is commonly used in computing the liquidity assets and much more suitable in computing the efficiency of the firms (Soh, 2015; Chen & Mahajan, 2010; Opler et al., 1999). Therefore, below is the cash ratio or also known as the cash-to-net asset equation applied in this study:

$$CR = \frac{\text{Cash}}{\text{Net Asset}}$$

where,

CR	= cash ratio
Cash	= sum of cash and cash equivalents and marketable securities
Net asset	= subtraction of total asset and the cash and cash equivalents and marketable securities.

According to Opler et al. (1999), this cash ratio or also known as cash-to-net asset is formulated to capture the amount of cash available from the total asset of the firm as they believed that the main function of all kind of asset is to generate return for the company. The natural logarithm will take place after the cash ratio is calculated. The lagged cash ratio will also be included in the regression model later as it is believed that the value for today is influenced by the previous period.

12.3.3 Moderating Variable

This study will implement the accrual quality (AQ) method introduced by Dechow and Dichev (2002) in order to estimate the earning qualities for each firm according to its industry. The approach introduced by the researchers is capturing the accrual quality for three different periods that includes last period, present period and next period.

This approach also required a firm to have at least 8-year data compatible with this study since the time period for this study is 14 years that is from year 2001 to 2014. This model also needs to use the logarithm of total accrual quality as the result of highly skewed (Al-Dhamari & Ku Ismail, 2015). Therefore, below is the accrual quality equation applied in this study:

$$TCA_{it} = \alpha + \beta_i CFO_{t-1} + \beta_i CFO_{it} + \beta_i CFO_{i+t} + \varepsilon_{it}$$

where TCA_{it} is the total current accrual of the firm i in year t, scaled or deflated by average net asset; CFO_{t-1} is the operation cash flow in year $t - 1$, scale or deflated by average net asset; CFO_{it} is the operation cash flow in year t, scale or deflated by average net asset; CFO_{t+1} is the operation cash flow in year $t + 1$, scale or deflated by average net asset. The equation to find total current accrual (TCA_{it}) is as follows:

$$TCA_{it} = \Delta CA_{it} - \Delta CL_{it} - \Delta CASH_{it} + \Delta STDEBT_{it} - DEPN_{it}$$

where ΔCA_{it} is the changes in current asset; ΔCL_{it} is the changes in current liabilities; $\Delta CASH_{it}$ is the changes in cash; $\Delta STDEBT_{it}$ is the changes in debt in current liabilities; $DEPN_{it}$ is the depreciation and amortization.

Therefore, the earning qualities of a firm can be captured using this method by looking at the accrual quality (AQ). Accrual quality (AQ) for this study is the standard deviation of the industry-specific yearly residual. A firm is indicated to have higher quality if the accrual quality is also higher but shows a small value of standard deviation residuals. However, if the result shows a large value of standard deviation residual with lower accrual quality, it means that the firm is having a lower earning quality.

12.3.4 Controlling Variables

Several variables that are believed to have correlation with the efficiency of firms will also be included in this study to generate a strong result. The variables are assumed as the control variables in this study, which include the firm size, firm growth, capital expenditure, leverage, inflation, gross domestic product (GDP) and also the interest rate. The measurement method of the control variables is shown in Table 12.1.

12.3.5 Model Formulation

Each model will be tested in the second stage of regression where each of the selected sectors in Malaysia according to the level of cash holdings. The sectors included in this study are the consumer products, industrial products, construction, trading or services, properties and plantation. Model I is to estimate the relationship between the contribution levels of cash holding towards the performance of the firm by looking at the firm's efficiency. Meanwhile, the earning qualities will be added in Model II to estimate whether it has an influence over the relationship in Model I.

Table 12.1 Summary measurement and expected sign of control variables

Variable	Measurement
Firm size (FS)	Natural logarithm (Ln) of total asset
Firm growth (FG)	Sales for the current year minus the sales for the previous year over the previous year sales
Capital expenditure (CE)	Total fixed asset acquired plus capital expenses over the net sales
Leverage (LEV)	Long-term debt over total value of long-term debt plus market capitalization
Inflation (INF)	Annual inflation rate
Gross domestic product (GDP)	Annual gross domestic product
Interest rates (INT)	Annual base lending rate

In Model III, some control variables that are believed to have some correlation with the efficiency of the firms are added in the equation in order to produce a wise estimation. The equation for each model that is going to be tested for both high and low levels of cash holding is shown below:

Model I

$$FE_{it} = \alpha_i + \beta_{i1} CR_{it} + \beta_{i2} CR_{t-1} + \varepsilon_{it}$$

Model II

$$FE_{it} = \alpha_i + \beta_{i1} CR_{it} + \beta_{i2} CR_{t-1} + \beta_{i3} AQ_{it} + \varepsilon_{it}$$

Model III

$$\begin{aligned} FE_{it} = {} & \alpha_i + \beta_{i1} CR_{it} + \beta_{i2} CR_{t-1} + \beta_{i3} AQ_{it} + \beta_{i4} FG_{it} + \beta_{i5} FS_{it} + \beta_{i6} CE_{it} \\ & + \beta_{i7} CE_{t-1} + \beta_{i8} LEV_{it} + \beta_{i9} INF_{it} + \beta_{i10} GDP_{it} + \beta_{i11} INT_{it} + \varepsilon_{it} \end{aligned}$$

where FE_{it} is the efficiency of the firm in year t derived from the DEA model; CR_{it} is cash ratio in year t; CR_{t-1} is the cash ratio in year $t - 1$; AQ_{it} is the standard deviation of the industry-specific yearly residual; *FG* is the firm growth in year t; *FS* is the firm size in year t; *CE* is the capital expenditure in year t; CE_{t-1} is the capital expenditure in year $t - 1$; *LEV* is the leverage in year t; *INF* is the inflation in year t; *GDP* is the gross domestic product in year t; *INT* is the interest rates in year t.

12.4 Conclusion

Therefore, this study will contribute to the body of knowledge in efficiency of firms by assessing the contribution of cash holdings and earning quality. A new strategy or policy direction for cash management can be implemented later so as to assist firms in each sector in managing their cash. If the firms apply the appropriate strategy or policy of cash management according to their sector, the performance of the firm itself will improve. This situation will offer benefits not only to the firms but also to the shareholder and the investor as they will be able to gather more information before deciding which firm or sector that they should be involved with.

References

Abushammala, S. N. M., & Sulaiman, J. (2014). Cash holdings and corporate profitability: Some evidence from Jordan. *International Journal of Innovation and Applied Studies, 8*(3), 898–907.

Al-Dhamari, R. A., & Ku Ismail, K. N. I. (2015). Cash holding, political connections, and earning quality. *International Journal of Managerial Finance, 11*(2), 215–231.

An, H., Hardin, W., & Wu, Z. (2012). Information asymmetry and corporate liquidity management: Evidence from real estate investment trusts. *Journal of Real Estate Finance and Economics, 45*(3), 678–704.

Campello, M., Graham, J. R., & Harvey, C. R. (2010). The real effects of financial constraints: Evidence from a financial crisis. *Journal of Financial Economics, 97,* 470–487.

Chen, N., & Mahajan, A. (2010). Effects of macroeconomic condition on corporate liquidity: International evidence. *International Research Journal of Finance and Economics, 35,* 112–129.

Claessens, S., Djankov, S., & Lang, L. (2000). Separation of ownership and control in East Asian corporations. *Journal of Financial Economics, 58*(1/2), 81–112.

Claessens, S., Fan, J. P. H., Djankov, S., & Lang, H. H. P. (1998). *Diversification and efficiency of investment of East Asian corporations.* Working Paper No. 2033, Policy Research Dissemination Centerm, The World Bank, Washington, DC, 25 April.

Couderc, N. (2005). Corporate cash holdings: Financial determinant and consequences. In *2005 EFMA Corporate Governance Symposium*, Working Paper.

Das, S. (2015). Analysis of cash holding for measuring the efficiency of cash management: A study on IT sector. *Management Science Letters, 5,* 51–58.

Dechow, P. M., & Dichev, I. D. (2002). The quality of accruals and earnings: The role of accrual estimation errors. *The Accounting Review, 77*(S1), 35–59.

Dechow, P. M., & Schrand, C. (2004). Earning quality. *The Research Foundation of CFA Institute.*

Ferreira, M. A., & Vilela, A. (2004). Why do firms hold cash? Evidence from EMU countries, European governance. *Financial Management, 10*(2), 295–319.

Fresard, L. (2010). Financial strength and product market behavior: The real effects of corporate cash holdings. *The Journal of Finance, 65*(3), 1097–1122.

Gill, A., & Shah, C. (2012). Determinants of corporate cash holdings: Evidence from Canada. *Journal of Economics and Finance, 4*(1), 70–79.

Healy, P., & Wahlen, J. (1999). A review of the earning management literature and its implications for standard setting. *Accounting Horizons, 13,* 365–383.

Jensen, M. C., & Meckling, W. H. (1976). Theory of the firm: Managerial behavior, agency costs and ownership structure. *Journal of Financial Economics, 3,* 305–360.

Kayo, E. K., & Kimura, H. (2011). Hierarchical determinants of capital structure. *Journal of Banking & Finance, 35*(2), 358–371.

Keynes, J. M. (1936). *The general theory of employment, interest and money.* London: Harcourt Brace.

Kuan, T. H., Li, C. S., & Chu, S. H. (2011). Cash holdings and corporate governance in family controlled firms. *Journal of Business Research, 64*(7), 757–764.

Maham, K., & Shabanha, Z. H. (2015). The relationship between earning quality and cash holding by companies. *International Journal of Review in Life Sciences, 5*(5), 673–677.

Mahmud, R., Ibrahim, M. K., & Pok, W. C. (2009). Earning quality attributes and performance of Malaysian public listed firms. Retrieved from http://papers.ssrn.com/sol3/papers.cfm?abstract_id=1460309.

Mikkelson, W. H., & Partch, M. M. (2003). Does persistent large cash reserve hinder performance? *Journal of Financial and Quantitative Analysis, 38,* 275–294.

Modigliani, F., & Miller, M. H. (1958). The cost of capital, corporation finance and the theory of investment. *The American Economic Review, 48*(3), 261–297.

Myers, S. C., & Majluf, N. S. (1984). Corporate financing and investment decisions when firms have information that investors do not have. *Journal of Financial Economics, 13,* 187–221.

Opler, T., Pinkowitz, L., Stulz, R., & Williamson, R. (1999). The determinants and implications of corporate cash holdings. *Journal of Financial Economics, 52,* 3–46.

Pan, C. H. (2006). *Why are firms with entranced manager more likely to pay dividends?* Working Paper, Ohio State University.

Pinkowitz, L., Stulz, R., & Williamson, R. (2006). Does the contribution of corporate cash holdings and dividends to firm value depend on governance? A cross-country analysis. *The Journal of Finance, 61*(6), 2725–2751.

Raheman, A., & Nasr, M. (2007). Working capital management and profitability—Case of Pakistani firms. *International Review of Business Research Papers, 3*(1), 279–300.

Sarif, E. (2011, June 22). Malaysia promoted to advanced emerging market. *The Star Online*. Retrieved from http://www.thestar.com.my/business/business-news/2011/06/22/malaysia-promoted-to-advanced-emerging-market/.

Soh, W. N. (2015). *High and low cash holdings by corporations in Malaysia and Korea: Relevance to efficiency, valuation and risks.* Doctoral thesis, University Putra Malaysia.

Tahir, S., & Alifiah, M. N. (2015). Corporate cash holdings behavior and financial environment: A critical review. *International Journal of Economics and Financial Issues, 5,* 277–280.

Wasiuzzaman, S. (2014). Analysis of corporate cash holdings of firms in Malaysia. *Journal of Asia Business Studies, 8*(2), 118–135.

[illegible]

Chapter 13
Revisiting Exchange Rate Exposure: A Case Study of Malaysia and Singapore

Jaratin Lily, Imbarine Bujang, Abdul Aziz Karia and Mori Kogid

Abstract This paper investigates the relationship of foreign exchange rate movements on national market returns in Malaysia and Singapore using multi-bilateral exchange rates Euro (EUR), Japanese Yen (JPY) and Chinese Renminbi (CNY). The contemporaneous, asymmetric and lagged exchange exposure framework is used to investigate the nature of these exchange rate movements towards national market returns. Our study results show that both Malaysia and Singapore market returns are exposed to those currencies. The relationship of JPY and CNY exchange rate movements towards national market returns is contemporaneous in both countries. Meanwhile, EUR has a contemporaneous effect on national market returns in Malaysia but a lagged 1-month relationship in Singapore. Only JPY exchange rate returns have significant asymmetric effects on national market returns in Singapore. Future research should be conducted at industry and firm levels for more countries to better understand the stylised exchange rate exposure for mitigation purposes. Choice of the market index should also be taken into consideration when investigating the exchange rate exposure at the country level.

Keywords Exchange rate exposure · Country level · Malaysia · Singapore

13.1 Introduction

While there has been extensive research on exchange rate exposure at country level in emerging countries, including in ASEAN involving Malaysia and Singapore (e.g. Chue and Cook 2008; Du et al. 2014), few studies have examined the

J. Lily (✉) · I. Bujang · A.A. Karia
Faculty of Business Management, Universiti Teknologi MARA,
Kota Kinabalu, Sabah, Malaysia
e-mail: jaratin@ums.edu.my

J. Lily · M. Kogid
Faculty of Business, Economics and Accountancy, Universiti Malaysia,
Jalan UMS, 88400 Kota Kinabalu, Sabah, Malaysia

F. Noordin et al. (eds.), *Proceedings of the 2nd Advances in Business Research International Conference*, https://doi.org/10.1007/978-981-10-6053-3_13

exchange rate exposure at the national level using multi-bilateral currencies (De Jong et al. 2006). Furthermore, a study by Bacha et al. (2013) focused on Malaysia and did not consider the asymmetric and lagged effect in the relationship between the share returns and exchange rate movements. The recent study by Ye et al. (2014) also did not include asymmetric and lagged term in their firm's exchange rate exposure model. Lin (2011) investigated exchange rate exposure at the country level in Asian countries using the asymmetric framework but did not include Malaysia and Singapore in the sample study.

Hence, the issue of how the national market returns react to the exchange rate movements is important to both government and investors for long-term decision-making. This study seeks to determine whether the relationship between exchange rate returns and country market returns is contemporaneous, lagged or asymmetric. Therefore, this study extends the knowledge of exchange rate exposure in Malaysia and Singapore by investigating the exchange rate exposure at the market level by applying a lagged and asymmetric framework and introducing multiple bilateral exchange rate movements in the model.

13.2 Literature Review

With the evolvement of the financial market and accessibility of financial data, there is a possibility to engage in market level analysis, especially in emerging countries. Market level studies (Entorf et al. 2011; Koutmos and Martin 2003; Lin 2011) showed that the exchange rate movement affected the national share market. Empirically, exchange rate exposure can be measured by looking at the significance of the exchange rate movement coefficient on the regressions with a firm's share returns or market index returns (e.g. Adler and Dumas 1983, 1984; Aggarwal and Harper 2010; Hutson and Laing 2014; Jorion 1990). Although estimating exchange exposure is important to both the industry and firm levels, investors and mutual fund managers would probably be more concerned about the existence and nature of exchange rate exposure at the market level (Entorf et al. 2011; Lin 2011). Lin (2011) argued that if the investors realise that their market portfolio is exposed to exchange rate risk, they may be willing to pay a premium to avoid it.

Some of the arguments behind the lack of support for the contemporaneous exchange rate exposure are due to the possibility of having lagged effect (Aggarwal and Harper 2010; Al-shboul and Anwar 2014; Bartram and Bodnar 2012; Chue and Cook 2008; Muller and Verschoor 2006b) and asymmetric effect (Koutmos and Martin 2003) on the relationship. According to lagged effect argument, the exchange rate movements take time to have an impact on the share return, because the investors need to gather more information before making a decision on their investment (Inci and Lee 2014). Meanwhile, the asymmetric exchange rate exposure is mainly due to asymmetric pricing-to-market (PTM) behaviour and resulting pass-through effects (Flodén et al. 2008), asymmetric hedging and hysteretic behaviour (Koutmos and Martin 2003; Miller and Reuer 1998; Muller and

Verschoor 2006a), investors' mispricing errors (Koutmos and Martin 2003), government intervention (Lin 2011; McKenzie 2002). For instance, in Koutmos and Martin's (Koutmos and Martin 2003) country-sector model study, more than 40% of the significant exposures turn out to be asymmetric.

In summary, despite intensive tests on exchange rate exposure since the 1970s, the exchange rate exposure theory continues to stand upon mixed evidence, especially in the case of methodology and empirical evidence.

13.3 Data and Methodology

13.3.1 Data

The empirical analysis in this study used monthly data on the exchange rates (domestic currency units per foreign currency units), market index (country and world) and Consumer Price Index (CPI) from January 2000 to March 2016. The foreign exchange rate consisted of Chinese Yuan (CNY), European dollar (EUR) and Japanese Yen (JPY). China, Japan and Eurozone are among the main trading partners for most ASEAN countries including Malaysia and Singapore. In this study, we employed monthly Morgan Stanley Capital International (MSCI)[1] ACWI Investable Market Index (IMI) and MSCI IMI country index as a proxy for world and country market indexes, respectively. Both indexes were in USD value. The MSCI ACWI IMI captures large, mid and small capital representation across developed markets and emerging markets. According to MSCI, Malaysia is categorised as an emerging market, while Singapore is a developed market. Thus, this world market index is appropriate to absorb all macroeconomic effects in those markets. With the exception of the CNY exchange rate for Malaysia, which was obtained from the Central Bank of Malaysia, the other variables were obtained from the Datastream International.

13.3.2 Empirical Model

13.3.2.1 Exchange Rate Exposure Model

The study estimates the contemporaneous and lagged exchange rate exposure for each country using the two-factor asset pricing country model (Entorf et al. 2011) as in the following equations;

$$R_{m,t} = \alpha_i + \beta_i R_{wt} + \chi_i R_{cny,t} + \delta_i R_{eur,t} + \phi_i R_{jpy,t} + \varepsilon_{it} \tag{13.1}$$

[1]MSCI website, http://www.msci.com, provides access to their database.

$$R_{m,t} = \alpha_i + \beta_i R_{w,t} + \sum_{i=o}^{p} \chi_i R_{cny,t-i} + \sum_{i=o}^{q} \delta_i R_{eur,t-i} + \sum_{i=o}^{r} \phi_i R_{jpy,t-i} + \varepsilon_t \quad (13.2)$$

where $R_{m,t}$ is the country's market portfolio return, over the time period t; $R_{w,t}$ is the world market portfolio return, over time period t; χ_i, δ_i and ϕ_i are the real exchange rate exposure parameters for CNY, EUR and JPY, respectively. Following De Jong's (2006) study, we tested for two lagged effects in Eq. (13.2). Meanwhile, the asymmetric exchange rate exposure model (Koutmos and Martin 2003; Lin 2011) is as follows:

$$R_{m,t} = \alpha_i + \beta_i R_{wt} + \gamma_i R_{xt} + \gamma_i^D D_x R_{xt} + \varepsilon_{it} \quad (13.3)$$

where R_x is exchange rate return for currency x at time t; D_x is a dummy variable that takes the value of unity when the exchange rate return of currency x is negative or appreciation in local currency ($D_x = 1$ if $R_x < 0$), zero otherwise. The unknown parameter γ_i^D measures the asymmetry in exchange rate exposure irrespective of the sign of the coefficient. With the inclusion of market returns, the response of R_{xt} will be equal to γ_i when $R_{xt} > 0$ and $\gamma_i + \gamma_i^D D_x$ for $R_{xt} < 0$ (Brooks et al. 2010; Lin 2011). Incorporating bilateral exchange rate of CNY, EUR and JPY in model (13.3), the exchange rate exposure with asymmetric behaviour is as follows:

$$R_{m,t} = \alpha_i + \beta_i R_{wt} + \left(\chi_i + \chi_i^D D_{cny,t}\right) R_{cyn,t} + \left(\delta_i + \delta_i^D D_{eur,t}\right) R_{eur,t} + \left(\phi_i + \phi_i^D D_{jpy,t}\right) R_{jpy,t} + \varepsilon_{it} \quad (13.4)$$

The study follows Lin's (2011) study in calculating the real exchange rate in a simple form as follows:

$$E_{j,t}^R = E_{j,t}^N \times \frac{P_F}{P_H} \quad (13.5)$$

where $E_{j,t}^N$ is the nominal exchange rate (Home/Foreign) of currency j, P_F is the price level in the foreign country, P_H is the price level in the home country. In this study, Malaysia and Singapore were referred to as the home country. After taking log and difference in Eq. (13.2), it will be:

$$\Delta \ln\left(E_{j,t}^R\right) = \Delta \ln\left(E_{j,t}^N\right) - \Delta \ln(P_H) + \Delta \ln(P_F) \quad (13.6)$$

If inflation in the foreign country is stable and non-stochastic,[2] the inflation rate of a foreign country will be zero $(\Delta \ln(P_F) = 0)$.

[2]One of convergence criteria to join the Euro is price stability or inflation controlled. Available at http://ec.europa.eu/economy_finance/euro/adoption/who_can_join/index_en.htm. Access 02 April 2016.

This also study applied GARCH (1,1) specification if there is evidence of the conditional heteroscedasticity in the error terms which have been applied by previous exchange rate exposure studies (e.g. Bacha et al. 2013; Ye et al. 2014). To address the fat-tailed distribution property that exhibits significant kurtosis and skewness (Alberg et al. 2008), this study applied the robust standard error (e.g. Bollerslev and Wooldridge 1992) or the Student's t distribution (e.g. Bollerslev 1987) in the GARCH specification model.

13.3.2.2 Unit Root Analysis

The study tested the hypothesis of a unit root using several unit roots tests through Dickey–Fuller (DF), or Augmented Dickey–Fuller (ADF) (Dickey and Fuller 1979), and the Phillips–Perron (PP) (Phillips and Perron 1988) to check if the variables were integrated over $I(0)$, $I(1)$ or if they were mutually integrated. The optimal lag length was chosen based on the lowest Schwarz Information Criterion (SIC) value.

13.4 Results

13.4.1 Descriptive Analysis

As expected in financial data, most of the studied variables demonstrated skewness and high kurtosis (more than 3) that displayed non-normal distribution. Furthermore, both the ADF and PP unit root tests produced similar results, indicating that all variable series were found to be stationary regardless of the constant and the trend included in the test equations at the 5% significance level. The results of these statistical summaries are available upon request.

13.4.2 Exchange Rate Exposure

Tables 13.1, 13.2 and 13.3 illustrate the results of the relationship between exchange rate returns and country market returns in Malaysia and Singapore. In the case of Malaysia, all the bilateral exchange rate returns (CNY, EUR and JPY), although the effect of EUR is weak, were significant with negative coefficients and contemporaneous relationship (see Table 13.1). None of the bilateral exchange rate movements affected Malaysia market return asymmetrically (see Table 13.2), but CNY and JPY lagged 1-month returns had a significant relationship with Malaysia market returns (see Table 13.3).

Table 13.1 Contemporaneous exchange rate exposure model

	Malaysia		Singapore	
Variables	Coefficient	z-statistics	Coefficient	z-statistics
Constant	0.1239	0.4534	−0.0129	−0.0389
ACWI	0.3662***	5.0182	0.7241***	7.1184
CNY	−0.5691**	−2.9981	−1.3197***	−6.4842
EUR	−0.2542*	−1.8616	−0.1911	−1.5404
JPY	−0.2245**	−2.1196	−0.5079***	−4.8011
Diagnostic tests	Q (4) = 0.5023 Q^2 (4) = 1.7456 JB = 0.7911 Log likelihood = −556.8952		Q (4) = 7.9317* Q^2 (4) = 0.7773 JB = 2.1661 Log likelihood = −552.5085	

Notes Figures in ( ) indicate the number of lag. ***, **, * denote significant at the 1%, 5% and 10% levels, respectively. JB = Jarque–Bera statistic, Q = Q-statistic

Table 13.2 Asymmetric exchange rate exposure model

	Malaysia		Singapore	
Variables	Coefficient	z-statistics	Coefficient	z-statistics
Constant	0.1735	0.2543	0.4405	0.7380
ACWI	0.3631***	−4.9015	0.6864***	7.4521
CNY	−0.6360*	−1.7200	−0.6508*	−1.7246
DCNY	0.1848	0.3538	−1.3312	−1.9847
EUR	−0.1651	−0.6400	−0.3009	−1.1758
DEUR	−0.1910	−0.4775	0.3076	0.6908
JPY	−0.2800	−1.2386	−0.9534***	−4.8193
DJPY	1.1095	0.3524	0.8489**	3.0198
Diagnostic tests	Q(4) = 1.7427 Q^2 (4) = 3.4668 JB = 0.9053 Log likelihood = −556.6226		Q(4) = 6.3764 Q^2 (4) = 1.6267 JB = 2.2001 Log likelihood = −547.5471	

Notes Figures in ( ) indicate the number of lag. ***, **, * denote significant at the 1%, 5% and 10% levels, respectively. JB = Jarque–Bera statistic, Q = Q-statistic. Exposure parameters are based on Eq. (13.4). 'D' indicates Dummy variable (e.g. DCNY indicates dummy variable for CNY)

For contemporaneous exchange rate exposure in Singapore, all bilateral exchange rate movements had negative coefficients, but only CNY and JPY currencies were significant. The insignificance of EUR exposure in Singapore was puzzling because the Euro market is an important international market for Singapore since the currency introduction (Bartram and Karolyi 2006). However, it appeared that there was evidence of lagged effect relationship between EUR exchange rate movements and country market returns (see Table 13.3). Lagged 1-month EUR exchange rate returns had a negative coefficient indicating appreciation in Singapore (negative exchange rate returns) and will benefit the local share returns. Interestingly, only JPY had an asymmetric effect on the Singapore market

Table 13.3 Lagged exchange rate exposure model

	Malaysia		Singapore	
Variables	Coefficient	z-statistics	Coefficient	z-statistics
Constant	0.3754	1.2623	0.1289	0.3613
ACWI	0.4152***	5.9101	0.7208***	8.0274
CNY	−0.6117**	−3.5635	−1.3956***	−6.9149
CNY(−1)	−0.4276**	−2.7390	0.2071	1.0348
CNY(−2)	−0.1646	−0.9946	−0.4854**	−2.4816
EUR	−0.2317*	−1.8233	−0.2162*	−1.7706
EUR (−1)	0.1539	1.3629	0.3641**	2.5846
EUR(−2)	0.0685	0.6502	−0.0881	−0.6366
JPY	−0.1403	−1.4240	−0.4479**	−3.9054
JPY(−1)	0.2594**	2.4115	0.0114	0.0901
JPY(−2)	−0.0185	−0.2316	−0.0179	−0.1718
Diagnostic tests	Q(4) = 0.6954 Q^2 (4) = 1.6098 JB = 4.4748 Log likelihood = −539.7027		Q(4) = 7.1774 Q^2 (4) = 1.4873 JB = 1.2924 Log likelihood = −538.1184	

Notes Figures in ( ) indicate the number of lag. ***, **, * denote significant at the 1%, 5% and 10% levels, respectively. JB = Jarque–Bera statistic, Q = Q-statistic

returns, indicating that JPY exchange rate movement affected the country market returns differently during the currency's appreciation and depreciation (see Table 13.2).

13.4.3 Diagnostic Tests

A series of diagnostic tests were performed to evaluate the model adequacy employed in this study to make sure the data fit the model. Most of the test results confirmed the model adequacy.

13.5 Discussion and Recommendation

13.5.1 Discussion

In this study, we investigated whether the relationship between exchange rate returns and country market returns (Malaysia and Singapore) is contemporaneous, lagged or asymmetric by introducing multi-bilateral exchange rates to investigate the impact of a particular currency on the country market index (Parsley and Popper 2006). Our results have shown evidence of contemporaneous exchange rate exposure in both Malaysia and Singapore's national returns towards all studied currencies except EUR in Singapore. More specifically, Malaysia and Singapore experience negative impact of domestic currency depreciation towards the exposed currencies (net importer).

In a lagged effect relationship, Malaysia experienced a lagged effect of both CNY (1-month) and JPY (1-month), while such was the case for Singapore for CNY (2-month) and EUR (1-month). The lagged effects indicate that exchange rate movements in Malaysia (CNY and JPY) and Singapore (EUR and CNY) will take time to affect the market movements in both markets, respectively. This implies that investors or interested parties need to gather more information before making any decision in financial markets (Inci and Lee 2014). Meanwhile, only JPY has an asymmetric effect on the Singapore market returns (none of them in Malaysia), indicating that JPY exchange rate movement affects the country market returns differently during the currency's appreciation and depreciation. This may be due to the aggregated effect issue, where the market index consists of both exporters and importers, indicating that the asymmetric relationship effect is more appropriate in a firm level analysis (Varga 2013).

The results have shown that the contemporaneous impact of these exchange rate movements implies some degree of market efficiency in both markets. Moreover, regardless of the coefficient sign of exchange rate exposure in the results, there is evidence that country market index is exposed to multiple exchange rate movements (e.g. Bacha et al. 2013; Parsley and Popper 2006). Thus, investors and mutual fund managers should be more concerned about the effect of exchange rate movements towards their portfolio for long-term decision-making (Entorf et al. 2011; Lin 2011). Furthermore, the study results also imply that managing only one currency, such as the US dollar, does not fully protect a country from other currency exposure. Knowing that country market returns are exposed to exchange rate movements without understanding which particular currency may affect the market returns will make decisions on hedging strategy more difficult.

However, caution should be made when interpreting the coefficient sign of exchange rate movements at the country level, because the effect could be depending on the choice of country market index employed in the exchange rate exposure model. As the market index prices are the aggregate selected firms' share prices, the exchange rate movement relationship with the country market index may vary depending on the firm's types and international involvements within the market index, thus sometimes may be biased to certain industries only.

13.5.2 Recommendation

This study investigates exchange rate exposure at a country level for Malaysia and Singapore. Future research should be done on the industry and firm level with more countries to better understand the nature of this exposure, such as which firms from which industry are more exposed to the exchange rate movements (CNY, EUR and

JPY). Including more countries across different markets in the sample would help researchers identify the exchange rate exposure stylised effect and pattern in finding the suitable methodology framework to capture the effect of exchange rate movements towards share returns, especially in emerging markets. In addition, choice of market index returns should be taken into consideration when evaluating the exchange rate exposure, especially in emerging and frontier markets to investigate the effect of using different types of country market indexes. For practical implication especially for the policymakers, it is important to align various policy variables to stabilise the economy including foreign exchange rates to avoid fluctuations in the overall economy. Ignoring the direct and indirect effect of the exchange rate exposure may cause the government to face economic instability in the long run, due to increasing bankruptcy among local firms. Policymakers may intervene in foreign exchange markets to advance a variety of economic objectives: controlling inflation, maintaining competitiveness or maintaining financial stability.

References

Adler, M., & Dumas, B. (1983). International portfolio choice and corporation finance: A synthesis. *The Journal of Finance, 38*(3), 925–984.

Adler, M., & Dumas, B. (1984). Exposure to currency risk: Definition and measurement. *Financial Management, 13*(2), 41–50. https://www.jstor.org/stable/3665446.

Aggarwal, R., & Harper, J. T. (2010). Foreign exchange exposure of "domestic" corporations. *Journal of International Money and Finance, 29*(8), 1619–1636. doi:10.1016/j.jimonfin.2010.05.003.

Al-shboul, M., & Anwar, S. (2014). Foreign exchange rate exposure: Evidence from Canada. *Review of Financial Economics, 23*(1), 18–29. doi:10.1016/j.rfe.2013.12.001.

Alberg, D., Shalit, H., & Yosef, R. (2008). Estimating stock market volatility using asymmetric GARCH models. *Applied Financial Economics, 18*(15), 1201–1208. doi:10.1080/09603100701604225.

Bacha, O. I., Mohamad, A., Zain, S. R. S. M., & Rasid, M. E. S. M. (2013). Foreign exchange exposure and impact of policy switch—The case of Malaysian listed firms. *Applied Economics, 45*(20), 2974–2984. doi:10.1080/00036846.2012.684790.

Bartram, S. M., & Bodnar, G. M. (2012). Crossing the lines: The conditional relation between exchange rate exposure and stock returns in emerging and developed markets. *Journal of International Money and Finance, 31*(4), 766–792. doi:10.1016/j.jimonfin.2012.01.011.

Bartram, S. M., & Karolyi, G. A. (2006). The impact of the introduction of the Euro on foreign exchange rate risk exposures. *Journal of Empirical Finance, 13*(4–5), 519–549. doi:10.1016/j.jempfin.2006.01.002.

Bollerslev, T. (1987). A Conditionally heteroskedastic time series model for speculative prices and rates of return. *The Review of Economics and Statistics, 69*(3), 542–547. doi:10.2307/1925546.

Bollerslev, T., & Wooldridge, J. M. (1992). Quasi-maximum likelihood estimation and inference in dynamic models with time-varying covariances. *Econometric Reviews, 11*(2), 143–172. doi:10.1080/07474939208800229.

Brooks, R. D., Iorio, A. Di, Faff, R. W., Fry, T., & Joymungul, Y. (2010). Asymmetry and time variation in exchange rate exposure: An investigation of Australian stocks returns. *International Journal of Commerce and Management, 20*(4), 276–295. doi:10.1108/10569211011094613.

Chue, T. K., & Cook, D. (2008). Emerging market exchange rate exposure. *Journal of Banking & Finance, 32*(7), 1349–1362. doi:10.1016/j.jbankfin.2007.11.005.

De Jong, A., Ligterink, J., & Macrae, V. (2006). A firm-specific analysis of the exchange-rate exposure of Dutch firms. *Journal of International Financial Management & Accounting, 17* (1), 1–28.

Dickey, D. A., & Fuller, W. A. (1979). Distribution of the estimators for autoregressive time series with a unit root. *Journal of the American Statistical Association, 74,* 427–431. doi:10.2307/2286348.

Du, D., Hu, O., & Wu, H. (2014). Emerging market currency exposure: Taiwan. *Journal of Multinational Financial Management, 28,* 47–61. doi:10.1016/j.mulfin.2014.10.001.

Entorf, H., Moebert, J., & Sonderhof, K. (2011). The foreign exchange rate exposure of nations. *Open Economies Review, 22*(2), 339–353. doi:10.1007/s11079-009-9128-6.

Flodén, M., Simbanegavi, W., & Wilander, F. (2008). When is a lower exchange rate pass-through associated with greater exchange rate exposure? *Journal of International Money and Finance, 27*(1), 124–139. doi:10.1016/j.jimonfin.2007.04.013.

Hutson, E., & Laing, E. (2014). Foreign exchange exposure and multinationality. *Journal of Banking & Finance, 43,* 97–113. doi:10.1016/j.jbankfin.2014.03.002.

Inci, A. C., & Lee, B.-S. (2014). Dynamic relations between stock returns and exchange rate changes. *European Financial Management, 20*(1), 71–106. doi:10.1111/j.1468-036X.2011.00621.x.

Jorion, P. (1990). The exchange-rate exposure of U.S. multinationals. *The Journal of Business, 63* (3), 331–345.

Koutmos, G., & Martin, A. D. (2003). Asymmetric exchange rate exposure: theory and evidence. *Journal of International Money and Finance, 22*(3), 365–383. doi:10.1016/S0261-5606(03)00012-3.

Lin, C.-H. (2011). Exchange rate exposure in the Asian emerging markets. *Journal of Multinational Financial Management, 21*(4), 224–238. doi:10.1016/j.mulfin.2011.04.002.

McKenzie, M. (2002). The economics of exchange rate volatility asymmetry. *International Journal of Finance and Economics, 7*(3), 247–260.

Miller, K. D., & Reuer, J. J. (1998). Asymmetric corporate exposures to foreign exchange rate changes. *Strategic Management Journal, 19*(12), 1183–1191. doi:10.1002/(SICI)1097-0266(1998120)19:12<1183:AID-SMJ1>3.0.CO;2-S.

Muller, A., & Verschoor, W. F. C. (2006a). Asymmetric foreign exchange risk exposure: Evidence from U.S. multinational firms. *Journal of Empirical Finance, 13*(4–5), 495–518. doi:10.1016/j.jempfin.2006.01.003.

Muller, A., & Verschoor, W. F. C. C. (2006b). Foreign exchange risk exposure: Survey and suggestions. *Journal of Multinational Financial Management, 16*(4), 385–410. doi:10.1016/j.mulfin.2005.09.001.

Parsley, D. C., & Popper, H. A. (2006). Exchange rate pegs and foreign exchange exposure in East and South East Asia. *Journal of International Money and Finance, 25*(6), 992–1009. doi:10.1016/j.jimonfin.2006.07.009.

Phillips, P., & Perron, P. (1988). Testing for a unit root in time series regression. *Biometrika, 75,* 335–346. doi:10.1093/biomet/75.2.335.

Varga, R. F. F. (2013). Currency exposure, second-moment exchange rate exposure and asymmetric volatility of stock returns: The effects of financial crises on Taiwanese firms. *Journal of Applied Finance and Banking, 3*(2), 15–37.

Ye, M., Hutson, E., & Muckley, C. (2014). Exchange rate regimes and foreign exchange exposure: The case of emerging market firms. *Emerging Markets Review, 21,* 156–182. doi:10.1016/j.ememar.2014.09.001.

Chapter 14
The Impact of Reducing Tick Size on Malaysian's Stock Market Liquidity

Diana Baharuddin, Imbarine Bujang and Hamizah Hassan

Abstract This paper provides a unique opportunity to investigate the impact reduction in tick size towards Malaysian's stock market liquidity by utilising spread and trading volume as proxies to market liquidity. The main function of tick size it is a tool to improvise the market liquidity, it is a tool to beautify the market liquidity. Using the components of FTSE-BMKLCI and closing daily data compiled starting from the implementation new tick size regime, from 3 August 2009 until the end of trading day 31 December 2014, this study found that, with the reduction in tick size, it reduces the spread significantly and there is a significant impact on trading volume.

Keywords Liquidity · Tick size · Spread · Trading volume

14.1 Introduction

On 3 August 2009, the Kuala Lumpur Stock Exchange (KLSE) known as Bursa Malaysia broke new ground by introducing changes to the tick size structure. In February 2001, the Securities Commission (SC) of Malaysia released the capital market plan (CMP) consisting of six main objectives that outline the framework that needs to be achieved in conjunction with 152 recommendations (SC 2001). Among the recommendations, there is a policy set to reduce tick sizes for stock

D. Baharuddin (✉) · I. Bujang
Faculty of Business Management, Universiti Teknologi MARA, Kota Kinabalu
Sabah, Malaysia
e-mail: dianabaharuddin89@gmail.com

I. Bujang
e-mail: imbar047@sabah.uitm.edu.my

H. Hassan
Faculty of Business and Management, Universiti Teknologi MARA,
ShahAlam, Selangor Darul Ehsan 40450, Malaysia
e-mail: hamiza013@salam.uitm.edu.my

F. Noordin et al. (eds.), *Proceedings of the 2nd Advances in Business Research International Conference*, https://doi.org/10.1007/978-981-10-6053-3_14

Table 14.1 Structure of pre- and post-changes in tick size

Stock price range	Tick size (Cent)	
	Pre	Post
Below RM1.00	0.50	0.50
RM1.00–RM2.99	1	1
RM3.00–RM4.99	2	1
RM5.00–RM9.99	5	1
RM10–RM24.99	10	2
RM25.00–RM99.98	25	2
RM100.00 and above	50	10

Note For bonds, debentures, warrants and call warrants, the minimum bid structure will have the same minimum trading spreads as for shares. Tick size for different price ranges are shown before (pre) and after (post) 3 August 2009, which became the new rule of minimum price range and effectively on Bursa Malaysia

trading in Bursa Malaysia to improve the market liquidity (Taunson and Poshakwale 2014). By using smaller tick size, Bursa Malaysia (2009) believes that it could strengthen the market complexity and improve the liquidity among traders.

A question that arises is how to beautify the market liquidity. Kadan (2006) mentioned that one of the policy tools that can be used by the financial market to enhance market liquidity is by using tick size. He further argued that reducing the tick size could enhance the market liquidity and increase the gains traded in the market,[1] particularly for stock exchanges. Bursa Malaysia (2009) defines tick size or minimum bid as the minimum price variation between the buying and selling price for a stock.[2] Table 14.1 summarises tick size differentiations pre- and post-implementation of the new tick size structure from different price ranges.

This topic has drawn significant interest to the market exchangers and academicians from all over the world in investigating the consequences of using smaller tick size on market liquidity. Evidence can be found from Australia (Aitken and Forde 2005), the USA (Ahn et al. 1996; and Goldstein and Kavajecz 2000), Japan (Ahn et al. 2007), Singapore (Lau and Mclnish 1995), Thailand (Pavabutr and Prangwattananon 2009), Indonesia (Allen and Sudiman 2009) and Hong Kong (Gerace and Smark 2012). One motivation to conduct this research is the paucity of research investigating the impact of a reduction in tick size on market liquidity in the Malaysian stock market.

[1]Harris (2002) found that liquidity derives from different perspectives such as traders need liquidity to encourage them implement inexpensive trading strategies, exchanges need liquidity to fascinate traders to commerce with them and regulators fancy liquidity as the liquid market will produce less volatility.

[2]Harris (1997) delineates tick size as minimum price increment at what prices traders use. Meanwhile, Pavabutr and Prangwattananon (2009) define tick size as minimum price changes allowed for stock quotations.

The trend to use smaller tick size in trading mechanisms has created dozens of "natural experiment" that attempt to reduce transactions cost (spread) and promote trading activities. Harris (1994) mentioned that a larger tick size increases the execution cost (bid–ask spread) because tick size and bid–ask spread are binding constraints and impose unnecessarily large execution cost. In simple terms, using large tick size could increase the cost, whereas using smaller tick size might reduce the incentive for traders. Harris (1994) also concludes that smaller tick size would significantly reduce the spread. This means that implementing the use of smaller tick size is expected to reduce the cost to attract more traders to provide liquidity. Krishnan and Mishra (2013) found that trading volume could become an indicator of liquidity, as a higher volume of trade is a sign of high liquidity. However, according to Pavabutr and Prangwattananon (2009), a well-known result when investigating the impact of using smaller tick size is lower spreads and the impact on trading volume to increase trading activities remains uncertain. Nevertheless, most researchers documented that reductions in tick size does not increase volume to a statistically significant extent (Ahn et al. 2007; Aitken and Forde 2005; Bacidore 1997; Huson et al. 1997). However, a recent paper by Gerace and Smark (2012) provides evidence of an increase in trading volume when the Hong Kong Stock Exchange (HKEx) reduced the minimum tick size.

Taunson and Poshakwale (2014) examined the post-changes or the reduction in tick size using data from Malaysia. Their analysis used trading volume as an indicator to measure the market liquidity. Their findings revealed that as tick size decreases, it has a positive impact on pricing efficiency by using future index data and hence improves the effectiveness of index futures. However, as they use trading volume as a proxy to liquidity, they found that the coefficient of tick size and trading volume is negative, and increases the volume traded, yet the regression coefficient is not statistically significant. This result reveals that the reduction in tick size and whether it enhances the market liquidity or vice versa in the context of the Malaysian stock market are still ambiguous.

Prior to the reduction in tick size in Malaysia, Chung et al. (2005) examined the structure of tick size using data from Bursa Malaysia. They investigated the ability of using seven different tick sizes from Bursa Malaysia and utilised spread and depth as proxies of liquidity. From their empirical findings, they suggested that KLSE's stepwise tick system unnecessarily executes large execution cost to higher priced stocks and stocks that have larger tick size binding constraints to a larger spread. In short, their results suggest that larger tick size for higher stock prices are damaging to market liquidity. Considering the conclusions of Taunson and Poshakwale (2014) and Chung et al. (2005), the question could arise as to what happens to the market liquidity after the market exchanger implements the new tick size regime by taking into consideration the spread and trading volume as indicators for market liquidity. Does the market liquidity become liquid? Are the spread and tick size binding constraints even using daily data? Is the trading volume statistically significant when tick size is smaller? To provide an answer to these questions, this study investigates the impact of a reduction in tick size towards market liquidity in the Malaysian stock market by employing trading volume and spreads as proxies to market liquidity as well as using components of the FTSE Bursa Malaysia Composite Index (FTSE-BMKLCI) as the sample of study.

This paper divides into five sections. The next section explains the impact reduction in tick towards market liquidity by using spread and trading volume as their proxies to liquidity. Section three explains the description of dataset and measurement of the dataset used in this study. Section four presents the results, and the final section provides concluding remarks.

14.2 Tick Size Reduction and Market Liquidity

Numerous researchers have empirically investigated the consequences of a reduction in tick size along with the foremost objective to enhance the market liquidity (Ahn et al. 2007; Aitken and Forde 2005; Bacidore 1997; Goldstein and Kavajecz 2000). Harris (1991) was the first to research the minimum price variation or tick size using US exchange-listed stock. The US equity market uses decimal fraction whereby the upshot of decimalisation would be in a smaller price increment (Harris 1997). The advocators under Harris (1997) remark that decimals are easier than using fractional prices and that decimalisation is necessary to modernise the US market. Likewise, Harris (1997) pointed out that small tick would have narrow spread, thus leading the traders to post smaller orders. It gives advantages to the small market traders and professional traders. However, it harms large traders and all public traders that use limited orders to compete with dealers.

Harris (1994) raises several important issues whereby (i) the effect of a reduction in tick size may lead to reducing the quote depth, and with it, the liquidity premium lowers for liquidity providers, (ii) reduction in minimum price increment leads to greater risk in liquidity provision and smaller minimum price variation leads to a shift in power from public traders to dealers and slower traders to faster traders and (iii) the strategies used by large public limit order traders to defend themselves against front runners involve higher transaction costs, lower displayed sizes and lower market transparency. Harris (1994) thus proposed that decreases in the bid–ask spread may be obtained if traders could use smaller minimum price variation and offers significant cost saving to small investors. Additionally, Harris (1994) suggested that decreasing the minimum price variation would reduce displayed quotation sizes and does not necessarily indicate a decrease in market depth.

Easley and O'Hara (1992) highlighted that tick size and spreads are correlated. This means that any changes in tick size can cause a change in transaction cost (bid–ask spreads), thereby making the market more liquid. Chordia, Roll and Subrahmanyam (2000) revealed that spread and depth recorded a decline in June 1997, due to corresponding with a reduction in tick size from 1/8 to 1/16 on the NYSE. It shows that, as tick size reduces, bid–ask spread declines. Their study included six explanatory variables that consist of short- and long-term interest rate, default spreads, market volatility, recent market movements and indicator variables for the day of the week, for holiday effect and major economic announcements. It shows that trading activity and market depth increased prior to macroeconomic announcements of GDP and the unemployment rate reduced.

Ahn et al. (1996) examined the impact of tick size reduction on bid–ask spread, market depth and trading volume for AMEX, pointing out that for stocks traded at prices between US$1 and US$5, the minimum price variations significantly reduced the quoted price and affected the spreads. However, as tick size reduces, they did not show any trading volume increases. Ahn et al. (2007) then examined the changes in minimum tick size in the Tokyo Stock Exchange (TSE). Their study postulated that (i) the TSE uses a minimum price range that uses different price range pre- and post-changes and (ii) TSE is mainly order driven whereby there are no market maker on TSE and liquidity is provided by limited orders submitted electronically by the public investor with the intention to see whether the smaller tick size will enhance market liquidity under the order driven market. Ahn et al. (2007) found that the quoted spread declined significantly by 20–50% (by 24–60). Reduction in the spread is greater for firms with greater tick size reduction, better trading activities and high transitory components in their bid–ask spread. Although investors are more aggressive in posting quotes, there is no definite evidence of increases in trading volume, which was concluded by other researchers such as Huson et al. (1997), Bacidore et al. (2001), and Aitken and Forde (2005).

On the other hand, Gerace and Smark (2014) examined the impact of reducing tick sizes on the HKSE. They used 40 ordinary shares as a sample and used cross-sectional analysis. They found that, as tick size decreases, bid–ask spread decreases, quoted depth decreases and they show an increase in trading volume. Pruit et al. (2000) also showed an increase in trading volume from a reduction in tick size.

To summarise, the aforementioned researchers rarely used trading volume as proxies to market liquidity. They included trading volume into spread and depth regression to examine the relationship. It proves that the conflicting reduction in tick size remains vague as to whether trading volume will increase following the reduction in tick size. According to Krishnan and Mishra (2013), trading volume can serve as an indicator of market liquidity, as it adds to high trade volume and there is a sign of high liquidity. This suggests that instead of determining the relationship between spread and trading volume, trading volume can be mutually used as a proxy of market liquidity. Hence, this study uses spread and trading volume as proxies to market liquidity to examine the impact of a reduction in tick size on Malaysian stock market liquidity.

14.3 Data and Methodology

Due to limitations of the intraday database, this study uses daily data for all datasets. This is supported by Chung et al. (2005) who used daily closing data to calculate the spread.[3] As this paper focuses on the impact of the implementation of new tick size structure on market liquidity in the Malaysian stock market, the data can be collected and accessed through BMKC (Bursa Malaysia Knowledge Centre) database from 3 August 2009 until 31 December 2014. The compilation dataset contains stock prices such as closing price, bid and ask price, number of shares traded, value of shares traded and market capital for each of the 25 components of the FTSE-BMKLCI based on closing daily data. As a time series analysis, the component needs to be average for all the companies based on the variables that encompass this research.

A useful starting point to study the effect of tick size towards spreads and trading volume as proxies to market liquidity is to identify the variables used in this study. To measure spread, the researcher computed the relative spread from Chung et al. (2005) where they used closing daily ask price and bid price at time t. RLS_t is the relative spread at time t, P_t^A is ask price at time t and P_t^B is bid price at time t. Another variable used in this study as proxy to market liquidity is trading volume. Trading volume is still a popular proxy to measure liquidity (Chordia et al. 2001). According to Fleming (2003), market liquidity is considered close to trading frequency, which means trading frequency equals the number of trades executed within specified time. Thus, this study uses trading volume (TV) or number of shares traded during time t. Moreover, control variables are included in this study as it can enhance the regression and are believed to have an effect on spreads (Harris 1994) and trading volume. The control variables included in this study are inverse price, firm size and turnover, whereby each of these data traded during time t.

$$RLS_t = \frac{2^*\left(P_t^A - P_t^B\right)}{P_t^A + P_t^B} \tag{1}$$

$$TV_t = Number\ of\ Shares\ traded_t \tag{2}$$

$$Inverse\ Price = \frac{1}{Price_t} \tag{3}$$

$$Firm\ Size = Market\ Capitalization_t \tag{4}$$

[3]Chung et al. (2005) used data compilation from KLSE (Bursa Malaysia) during the years 1996–2001. Facing a data limitation of spreads and depth, they used daily closing bid–ask spread throughout the study. They remarked that this approach will not introduce any biasness in their results as long as the variation in spreads and depth is consistent across the period.

$$Turnover = \frac{Total\,Value\,of\,Shares\,Traded_t}{Market\,Capitalization_t} \tag{5}$$

$$LNRLS_t = \beta_0 + \beta_1 Dummy\,Tick_t + \beta_2 DLNFS_t + \beta_3 DLNIP_t + \beta_4 LNTR_t + \varepsilon_t \tag{6}$$

$$LNTV_t = \beta_0 + \beta_1 Dummy\,Tick_t + \beta_2 DLNFS_t + \beta_3 DLNIP_t + \beta_4 LNTR_t + \varepsilon_t \tag{7}$$

As depicted in Eqs. 6 and 7, the variables of LNRLS, LNTV and LNTR have transformed into natural logarithms and data at 1% level rejecting the null hypothesis (data are stationary at level) using the augmented Dickey–Fuller (ADF) test and Philip–Perron (PP) test. However, LNFS and LNIP require transformation into first difference to ensure it has no unit root. Thus, DLNFS and DLNIP achievable at first difference of data are stationary using the same unit root tests.where $LNTV_t$, $LNRLS_t$ and $LNTR_t$ are natural logarithms on trading volume, natural logarithm relative spread and natural logarithm turnover at time t correspondingly. $DLNFS_t$ and $DLNIP_t$ indicate first difference natural logarithm firm size and first difference natural logarithm inverse price at time t, respectively. To determine the impact of tick size towards market liquidity, the creation of dummy tick is applied. To date, the measurement for tick size is still unknown. According to Ascioglu et al. (2010), no possible model can be used to measure tick size. Thus, most researchers create tick size as a dummy variable. Gerace and Smark (2012) and Taunson and Poshakwale (2014) created tick size as a dummy variable to examine pre- and post-changes in tick size. Given the fact that this study is confronted with limited data (limited number of access to the components of FTSE-BMKLCI), thus this study examine the post-changes in tick size. Since this study fully makes use of data after the reduction in tick size (started from 3 August 2009 until 31 December 2014), it is presumed that all the data are fully absorbed with the new rules. This creation of dummy tick is expected to see the binding constraint result between tick size and spread (positive relationship), whereas for trading volume the expected result is a negative relationship between tick size and trading volume.

14.4 Result

Before regressing the dataset using ordinary least square (OLS) method, the dataset needs to be tested for stationarity to avoid any spurious regression. Some of the datasets were found to be stationary at level such as natural logarithm relative spread (LNRLS), natural logarithm trading volume (LNTV) and natural logarithm turnover (LNTR), whereas inverse price and firms size need to be transformed into first difference to deal with the stationarity of the data. Thus, first difference natural logarithm of firm size (DLNFS) and first difference natural logarithm of inverse price (DLNIP) are transformed to make it stationary. Thus, the final time series regression can be undertaken.

The results of regression analysis on LNRLS and LNTV as dependent variables with dummy tick as independent variable and DLNFS, DLNIP and LNTV as

Table 14.2 Summary results of variable analysis

Particular/independent variable	Dependent variables	
	LNRLS (Eq. 6)	LNTV (Eq. 7)
Dummy tick		
β	0.1180	−0.0169
t-statistic	4.4584	−1.6646
p-value	(0.0001)***	(0.0962)*
DLNFS		
β	−0.1671	0.9137
t-statistic	−0.0748	1.0255
p-value	(0.9404)	(0.3053)
DLNIP		
β	−2.7364	0.4427
t-statistic	−1.8970	0.7078
p-value	(0.0580)*	(0.4792)
LNTR		
β	0.0478	0.9735
t-statistic	1.4514	81.1473
p-value	(0.1469)	(0.0001)***
Constant		
β	−5.8703	8.6333
t-statistic	−25.6911	106.0460
p-value	(0.0001)***	(0.0001)***
R-Squared	0.0453	0.9085
F-statistic	15.7517	3294.570
Prob(F-statistic)	0.0000	0.0000
Included Obs.	1332	1333

Note Regression ordinary least square (OLS) suffers heteroskedasticity and serial correlation; therefore, the problems can be treated by using Newey–West test to treat the standard errors and covariance. Above result shows the analysis of OLS with adjustment of Newey–West. The superscripts *, ** and *** denote significance level at 10%, 5% and 1%

control variables are depicted in Table 14.2. This regression was conducted for the period of 3 August 2009 (implementation date for new tick size rule) until the end of the trading day 31 December 2014 using Newey–West test after the adjustment of standard error and variance. The first set analysis to be explained is LNRLS regression analysis. The results reveal that the coefficient between of dummy tick and LNRLS is 0.1180 or 0.12%. This finding suggests that after the reduction in tick size, on average for relative spreads, stock prices below RM10 mostly traded by 0.12% compared to the price above RM10. The coefficient between dummy tick and LNRLS shows a strong positive relationship with a p-value of 0.0001. This means that the dummy tick variable and LNRLS are significant at the 1% level, denoting the rejection of null hypothesis at the 99% confidence level. This suggests that the implementation of using smaller tick size in the Malaysian stock market could reduce the usage of spread. It indicates as tick size decreases, spreads will also decrease. This finding is consistent with past studies such as Harris (1994) and

Gerace and Smark (2012) who found spreads and tick size are a binding constraint or positive relationship, as a decrease in tick size will lead to the reduction in relative spreads.

In support of the control variable to enhance the regression analysis, inverse price or DLNIP plays a vital role, especially when dealing with the spread. This study found a negative relationship between DLNIP and LNRLS. This contrasts with Harris (1994) and Chung et al. (2005) who found a positive relationship between the spread and inverse price. This indicates that, on average, with an increase of 1% in price, the relative spread will decrease by 2.74%, whereas for DLNFS against LNRLS, it shows a negative relationship, as an increase of 1% in DLNFS, will decrease LNRLS by 0.17%. In contrast, LNTR shows a positive relationship between LNTR and LNRLS as an increase of 1% in LNTR will increase LNRLS by 0.05%. These results are consistent with Harris (1994) and Chung et al. (2005). For the control variable, the inverse price seems to affect the LNRLS variable although the finding shows a negative relationship between DLNIP and LNRLS.

As for trading volume as a proxy for liquidity or LNTV regression (Table 14.2), column two shows the relationship between dummy tick and trading volume is negative or has an inverse relationship with coefficient −0.0169 or −0.02%. As tick size decreases, the stock price below RM10 shows lesser traded volume compared to stock price above RM10 by 0.02%. More importantly, by looking at the coefficient of dummy tick and LNTV, the result shows a negative coefficient and slightly fails to reject at 5% but still under consideration of 10% significance level. This finding leads the researcher to reject the null hypothesis at 90% confidence level, which indicates as tick size decreases, the volume traded in the market increases. This finding is consistent with Taunson and Poshakwale (2014) who concluded a negative relationship between tick size and trading volume. Although it is not statistically significant, interestingly, this study was able to provide statistical significance at the 10% level.

The control variable included in LNTV regression found that all were positively correlated with dependent variable. The coefficient between DLNFS and DLNIP is positive, and both are not statistically significant to the trading volume with 0.91% and 0.44%, respectively. Similarly, the LNTR coefficient is positive and shows statistical significance with LNTV. The result shows that an increase of 1% in LNTR will increase LNTV by 0.97%. This result denotes that turnover appears to be an important control variable for trading volume.

In summary, these findings provide evidence from the regression of ordinary least square (OLS) adjusted with Newey–West test and confirm that tick size reduction has a significant effect on relative spread (Harris 1994; Pavabutr and Prangwattananon 2009; Gerace and Smark 2012). It concludes with a clear positive relationship and strongly rejects the null hypothesis at 99% confidence level. Meanwhile, the regression of tick size and trading volume shows an inverse relationship. This finding is supported by Harris (1994) who suggested that as tick size decreases, trading volume will increase due to expectations of transaction cost or relative spread decrease (Harris 1994). Even though trading volume slightly rejects the null hypothesis at 10% significance level, it still provides evidence of a statistically significant inverse relationship between tick size and trading volume.

14.5 Conclusion

Effective on 3 August 2009, the new rule of minimum price variation or tick size was revamped by Bursa Malaysia with the aim of enhancing the market liquidity. Following the new application, this paper examined the impact reduction in tick size towards Malaysian stock market liquidity by utilising spread and trading volume as measurements for market liquidity. Fleming (2003) mentioned that market with low transaction cost (spread) is characterised as a liquid market, whereas trading volume is considered liquid when the volume of shares is highly traded in the market (Krishnan and Mishra 2013). This study proves a positive relationship between tick size and spread. As modelled by Harris (1994), using a cross-sectional regression model, the sign coefficient is positive and statistically significant. Their findings highlight that the spread decreases following the reduction in tick size. This analytical result is consistent with Harris (1994) that following the reduction in tick size, the spread becomes smaller to provide liquidity in the market.

For trading volume, the result of this paper provides a negative relationship between tick size and trading volume. Again, Harris (1994) suggested that if the spread is lower, the volume traded should increase. However, a number of empirical papers documented that as tick size is smaller, the volume did not increase (Ahn et al. 1996, 2001; Aitken and Forde 2005). Another study conducted by Taunson and Poshakwale (2014) used data from Bursa Malaysia and documented a negative relationship that is not statistically significant. Interestingly, this paper provides a negative and statistically significant result. This signifies that, following the reduction in tick size, the volume traded is high as supported by Gerace and Smark (2012) and Krishnan and Mishra (2013) who documented that high volume trade is an indication of the market becoming more liquid. We believe with the implantation of smaller tick size in Malaysia, itleads the spread to become smaller and there is significant impact on trading volume toenhance the market liquidity.

References

Ahn, H. J., Cai J., Chan, K., & Hamao, Y. (2007). Tick size change and liquidity provision on the Tokyo Stock Exchange. *Journal of the Japanese and International Economies, 21*(2), 173–194.

Ahn, H., Cao, C. Q., & Choe, H. (1996). Tick size, spread, and volume. *Journal of Financial Intermediation, 5*(1), 2–22.

Aitken, M., & Forde, C. C. (2005). Do reductions in tick sizes influence liquidity? *Accounting and Finance Published by Blackwell Publishing 45*(2), 171–184.

Allen, D. E., & Sudiman, J. (Eds.). (2009). *Does tick size change improve liquidity provision?: Evidence from the Indonesia stock exchange*. Churchlands: School of Acc., Finance and Economics [u.a].

Angel, J. J. (1997). Tick size, share prices, and stock splits. *The Journal of Finance, 52*(2), 655–681.

Ascioglu, A., Comerton-Forde, C., & McInish, T. H. (2010). An examination of minimum tick sizes on the Tokyo Stock Exchange. *Japan and the World Economy, 22*(1), 40–48.

Bacidore, J. (1997). The impact of decimalization on market quality: An empirical investigation of the Toronto Stock Exchange. *Journal of Financial Intermediation, 6*(2), 171–184.

Bacidore, J. M. (2001). Decimalization, adverse selection, and market maker rents.*Journal of banking & finance, 25*(5), 829–855.

Bessembinder, H. (2000). Tick Size, Spreads, and Liquidity: An Analysis of Nasdaq Securities Trading near Ten Dollars. *Journal of Financial Intermediation, 9*(3), 213–239.

Bursa Malaysia's (2009). Reduction of tick size poised to boost liquidity in equitiesmarket. Retrieved February 27, 2015, fromhttp://www.bursamalaysia.com/corporate/media-centre/media-releases/956

Capital Market Masterplan. (2001). Kuala Lumpur, Malaysia: Securities Commission. https://www.sc.com.my/wp-content/uploads/eng/html/cmp/EXECUTIV.PDF..

Chordia, T., Roll, R., & Subrahmanyam, A. (2000). Commonality in liquidity. *Journal of Financial Economics, 56*(1), 3–28.

Chordia, T., Subrahmanyam A., & Ashuman V. R. (2001). Trading activity andexpected stock returns. *Journal of Financial Economics, 59*, 3–25.

Chung, K. H., Kim, K. A., & Kitsabunnarat, P. (2005). Liquidity and quote clustering in a market with multiple tick sizes. *Journal of Financial Research, 28*(8), 177–195.

Easley, D., & O'Hara, M. (1992). Time and the process of security price adjustment. *The Journal of Finance, 47*(2), 577–605.

Fleming, M. J. (2003). Measuring treasury market liquidity. *Federal Reserve Bank ofNew York (FRBNY) Economic Policy Review*, 83–108.

Gerace, D., Smark, C., & Freestone, T. (2012). Impact of reduced tick sizes on the Hong Kong Stock Exchange. *Journal of New Business Ideas and Trends, 10*(2), 54–71.

Goldstein, M. A., & Kavajecz, K. A. (2000). Eighths, sixteenths, and market depth: Changes in tick size and liquidity provision on the NYSE. *Journal of Financial Economics, 56*(1), 125–149.

Harris, L. (1991). Stock price clustering and discreteness. *The Review of Financial Studies 1991, 4* (3), 389–415.

Harris, L. (1994). Minimum price variations, discrete bid-ask spread and quotation sizes. *The Review of Financial Studies (1986–1998); Spring 1994, 7*(1), 149.

Harris, L. (1997). *Decimalization: A review of arguments and evidence*. Working Paper, University of Southern California.

Harris, L. (2002). *Trading and exchanges—Draft copy*. New York: Oxford University Press Fall 2002.

Huson, M., Kim, Y., & Mehrotra, V. C. (Eds.). (1997). *Decimal quotes, market quality, and competition for order flow: Evidence from the Toronto Stock Exchange*. Edmonton: Institute for Financial Research, University of Alberta. Kadan, O. (2006). So who gains from a small tick size? *Journal of Financial Intermediation, 15*(1), 32–66.

Kadan, O. (2006). So, who gains from a small tick size. *Journal of FinancialIntermediation, 15*, 32–66.

Krishnan, R., & Mishra, V. (2013). Intraday liquidity pattern in Indian stock market. *Journal of Asian Economics, 28*, 99–114.

Kuo, S. W., Huang, C. S., & Chen, C. C. (2010). Impact of the change in tick size on transaction costs and liquidity: An empirical investigation of the Taiwan Stock Exchange. *Asia-Pacific Journal of Financial Studies, 39*(4), 524–551.

Lau, S. T., & Mclnish, T. H. (1995). Reducing tick size on the Stock Exchange of Singapore. *Pacific-Basin Finance Journal, 3*(4), 485–496.

Pavabutr, P., & Prangwattananon, S. (2009). Tick size change on the Stock Exchange of Thailand. *Review of Quantitative Finance and Accounting, 32*(4), 351–371.

Pruit, S. W., Van Ness, B. F., & Van Ness, R. A. (2000). The impact reduction in tick increments in Major US market on spreads, depth and volatility. *Review of Quantitative Finance and Accounting, 15*(2), 153–167.

Taunson, J., & Poshakwale, S. (2014, March). *Tick size reduction, liquidity, and stock index futures pricing efficiency: Evidence from emerging Malaysian market*. Paper presented at Global Finance Conference, Dubai, UAE.

Chapter 15
Predicting the Financial Fragility in Malaysia

Nurziya Muzzawer, Imbarine Bujang and Balkis Haris

Abstract Financial fragility is a priority topic for many policymakers, practitioners, and researchers due to its impact on the economy. Financial fragility is also termed financial instability leading to financial crisis. This paper attempts to predict the existence of financial fragility by examining its impact through the proxy of corporate and government-linked companies and their role in Malaysia's macroeconomics. The data set was taken from years 2005 to 2015 on a quarterly basis. By employing ordinary least square (OLS) time series analysis, our result found that government bond spreads can better explain the macroeconomic variables than corporate bond spreads. Corporate bond spreads only have a relationship with the inflation rate. As another indicator for financial fragility, KLCI stock returns are found to have a significant relationship with all macroeconomic variables.

Keywords Financial fragility · Bond spreads · Stock returns · Macroeconomics performance

15.1 Introduction

In the history of development economics, financial fragility has been considered the root of financial crises in both the banking and corporate sectors (Penas and Tümer-Alkan 2010). Bernake and Gertler (1990) characterised financial fragility as

N. Muzzawer (✉) · B. Haris
Faculty of Business Management, Universiti Teknologi MARA (UiTM), Shah Alam, Malaysia
e-mail: nurziyamuzzawer@gmail.com

B. Haris
e-mail: balkish@salam.uitm.edu.my

I. Bujang
Faculty of Business Management, Universiti Teknologi MARA (UiTM), Shah Alam, Sabah, Malaysia
e-mail: imbar074@sabah.uitm.edu.my

F. Noordin et al. (eds.), *Proceedings of the 2nd Advances in Business Research International Conference*, https://doi.org/10.1007/978-981-10-6053-3_15

a situation where there is weak balance sheets performance (higher liabilities than its net worth). Driscoll (1991) defined financial fragility as a situation where the non-financial sector has difficulty meeting their debt repayment commitment leading to increased defaults among lending institutions. This is consistent with the definition by Davis (1992) that financial fragility is a vulnerability to default in the non-financial sector. Driscoll (1991) also mentioned that financial fragility could increase the likelihood of financial shocks leading to financial instability and crisis. This is supported by Radelet and Sachs (1998), Kaminsky and Reinhart (1999) who emphasised that financial fragility is an important factor leading to financial crisis.

There has been an increased interest in investigating the existence of financial fragility due to financial crises recurring since 1929 when the US stock market collapsed known as the Great Depression. Asia experienced a similar situation during the Asian Financial Crisis in 1997–1998. A few years later, the world took another hit plummeting the world economy as a result of the 2008 Global Financial Crisis. This crisis led to the collapse of a number of large institutions in the USA (Dick et al. 2008), and the interconnectivity of global economies means that the entire world fell into a recession. To prevent such crises from recurring, there is renewed interest in reducing the existence of financial fragility.

This study adopts the definition of financial fragility by Tsomocos (2003), Aspachs et al. (2007), and Lee et al. (2013) who defined financial fragility as a combination of high probability of default and low profitability. In other words, the higher default is a sign of financial fragility. For example, if everyone paid their debts in full and on the due date, there would be no default. However, if everyone was unable to pay their debts and everyone is in default, this will have a grievous impact on the economy and lead to financial crisis. As mentioned by Minsky (1977), economic vulnerability occurs when the expectation of possible default reduces; creditors will offer lower borrowing rates to debtors even though they know that the debtors will invest in risky projects which then allows the financial institution to increase their leverage and invest more in riskier projects leading to higher defaults.

This study examines financial fragility by using the probability of default for risk measurement and equity index returns as a measurement for profitability in Malaysia. Default probability has been found to be an empirically useful measure (Bernoth and Pick 2011). Cihak (2006) showed that distance to default is one of the most frequently used market-based risk indicators. Also, Hillegeist et al. (2004) and Demirovic and Thomas (2007) found that market-based risk measures are more reliable than other measures relying on financial statements. The probability of default in this study is measured by government bond spread and corporate bond spread. Bond spreads have been widely used by other researchers as a measurement of credit risk and have been found to have a predictive power in economic activity (Bernake 1983; Friedman and Kuttner 1989; Bonser-Neal and Morley 1997; Saito and Takeda 2000; Gertler and Lown 2000; Bleaney et al. 2012; Mohapi and Botha 2013; Simon et al. 2012; Guender and Tolan 2015; Schock 2015).

15.2 Literature Review

15.2.1 *Issues on Measurement of Financial Fragility in the Banking and Corporate Sectors*

In this contemporary era, many researchers have investigated the early signals of financial crisis by measuring financial fragility in the banking sector. Most of the researchers believed that vulnerability in banking sector performance leads to increase in financial fragility. For example, Demirguc-Kunt and Detragiache (1998) found that banking crisis tends to appear when the macroeconomic environment is weak, typically when GDP is low, inflation rate is high, and the interest rate is high. Zwet and Swank (2000) found that the financial sector of the emerging countries is more fragile than highly developed countries. Antonio and Carlos (2001) found that low bank capital tends to increase banking fragility in the form of credit risk. Loayza and Ranciere (2006) found that an increase in private domestic credit to GDP ratio as a measurement of financial fragility of banks leads to a low rate of GDP per capita. This is consistent with the findings of Demirgue-Kunt and Detragiache (1997) who found that increases in the credit risk, which is the probability of default on loans, can lead to low GDP growth. Ghosh (2010) found that increased bank soundness leads to increases in loan supply, while increases in credit growth lead to the fragility in Indian banking sector. Bruno et al. (2013) found that increases in asset prices and optimum bank behaviour lead to an increase in leverage that enhances financial fragility.

Even though these previous studies used different indicators for financial fragility, indicators from banking sector performance can be used to predict the existence of financial fragility. However, one question that needs to be asked is can the indicators from corporate and government-linked companies also be used to predict the existence of financial fragility? A few studies have explored financial fragility in the corporate sector, but they only focus based on their respective countries (Vlieghe 2001; Bruneau et al. 2012; Lemus et al. 2012). Vlieghe (2001) found that the high rate of corporate failures is a sign of financial fragility in the corporate sectors in the UK, whereas Bruneau et al. (2011) found that macroeconomic variables have an effect on the bankruptcy rate of the firms and the business cycle in France. Lemus et al. (2012) involved investigated the indicators that differentiate between firms that are more likely to default and those less likely to default in the private corporate sector in Colombia. The findings show that firms default when it is heavily connected with the financial intermediaries and do not have strict policies in extending credit to customers.

Meanwhile, in Malaysia, little attention has been paid to explain whether the performance of the corporate and government sector can be used as a predictor of financial fragility. For example, Beh et al. (2014) investigated the determinants of bank fragility in Malaysia. The result revealed that all factors like reserve, exchange rate, and financial crisis have a significant and positive relationship with bank liquidity except for interest rate which has a negative and insignificant relationship. Ahmad and Mazlan (2015) explained the trend of bank fragility for both local- and foreign-based commercial banks in Malaysia by developing the Bank Sector Fragility Index proposed by Kibritçioglu (2003). The findings revealed that the likelihood of Malaysian commercial banks to be fragile is significantly determined by total loans to total assets and interbank rate. These recent studies in Malaysia mostly predict the financial fragility in banking sector performance and pay little attention to the performance of the corporate sector and government-linked companies in Malaysia. This paper seeks to fill this lacuna in the literature. This study attempts to predict the existence of financial fragility in Malaysia using the corporate sector and government-linked companies rather than using the banking sector.

15.2.2 Indicators to Measure Financial Fragility

In this study, the indicators used to measure financial fragility are based on definitions given for financial fragility by Tsomocos (2003), Aspachs et al. (2007), and Lee et al. (2013) who defined financial fragility as a combination of the high probability of default and low profitability. The measurements used for probability of default are government bond spreads and corporate bond spreads, while profitability is measured by stock returns.

Bond spreads have been widely used by other researchers as a measurement of credit risk. Bond spreads are differences between yields of different types of bonds but have the same maturity period (Gilchrist et al. 2009). For example, we have yields of corporate bonds and treasury bonds which mature in 10 years. The different yields between 10-year corporate bonds and 10-year treasury bonds are called bond spreads. Sometimes bond spreads are the differences between long-term bond and short-term bond as argued by Bonser-Neal and Morley (1997) who evaluated the ability of the yield spread to forecast real economic activity. The result was that the relationship between bond spreads and real GDP growth rate is significantly positive. They used bond spread between long-term and short-term government bonds for 10-year and 3-month bonds. The expectation theory explained the relationship between the short-term and long-term rates of interest which suggested that the long-term interest rate is equal to the all expected short-term rates. The spread between long- and short-term yields reflects the market forecast of changes in short-term rates (Heng et al. 2005). Saito and Takeda (2000) found that both corporate and government bond spreads have a positive relationship with real GDP growth; however, the corporate bond spread has higher r-squared than government bond spread, indicating relatively higher predictive power which is supported by Gertler and Lown (2000).

Bleaney et al. (2012) showed that there is a negative relationship between corporate bond spreads and economic variables, namely real gross domestic product, industrial production index, and employment growth, while there is a positive relationship with the unemployment rate. In addition, Guender and Tolan (2015) found that corporate bond spreads have predictive power for real GDP, industrial production index, and unemployment rate before and during the establishment of the Economic and Monetary Union of Europe. They also found a positive relationship between government bond spread and industrial production rate in Spain and Germany while showing a negative relationship with the unemployment rate in Spain. The overall findings from the past studies conclude that the relationship between a government bond and corporate bond spread has a positive and negative relationship, respectively. Other countries recorded an insignificant relationship.

15.3 Data and Methodology

15.3.1 Data

All the data information is based on Malaysian data and collected from DataStream, Department of Statistics Malaysia, Bank Negara Malaysia (BNM), and Bond Pricing Agency Malaysia (BPAM) Sdn Bhd. The data were gathered from third quarter of year 2005 till second quarter of year 2015 (10-year period). The empirical analysis is based on quarterly data basis, and all data are transformed to natural logarithm form.

Independent variables consist of financial fragility indicators such as government bond spreads (GOBS), corporate bond spreads (COBS), and Kuala Lumpur Composite Index stock return (SR). GOBS and COBS measured by the difference of yields between 10-year and 3-month bonds, while KLCI stock return calculated from current price divided previous price. The dependent variables consist of macroeconomic variables such as gross domestic product growth rate (GDP), gross domestic product per capita (GDPPC), consumer price index rate (CPI), and treasury bills 3 months (TBILLS). Export (EXP) and private consumption (PVC) are used as control variables in this study.

15.3.2 Empirical Model

The empirical models used in the analysis of time series data technique before testing unit root were as follows:

$$\begin{aligned}
&\textbf{Model1}: && \textbf{lnGDP}_\textbf{t} && = \beta_0 + \beta_1 lnGOBS_t + \beta_2 lnCOBS_t + \beta_3 lnSR_t + \beta_4 lnEXP_t + \beta_5 lnPVC_t + e_t \\
&\textbf{Model2}: && \textbf{lnGDPPC}_\textbf{t} && = \beta_0 + \beta_1 lnGOBS_t + \beta_2 lnCOBS_t + \beta_3 lnSR_t + \beta_4 + lnEXP_t + e_t \\
&\textbf{Model3}: && \textbf{lnCPI}_\textbf{t} && = \beta_0 + \beta_1 lnGOBS_t + \beta_2 lnCOBS_t + \beta_3 lnSR_t + e_t \\
&\textbf{Model4}: && \textbf{lnTBILLS}_\textbf{t} && = \beta_0 + \beta_1 lnGOBS_t + \beta_2 lnCOBS_t + \beta_3 lnSR_t + e_t
\end{aligned}$$

From the above model by using time series data technique, $lnGDP_t, lnGDPPC, lnCPI_t$, and $ln\ TBILLS_t$ were represented as dependent variables that the researcher attempts to investigate whether these variables will influence by $lnGOBS_t, lnCOBS_t, lnSR_t$, which is represented as independent variables and used as financial fragility indicators. *EXP* (export) and *PVC* (private consumption) are used as control variables. β_1 and β_2 were the coefficients that explained the size effect of the dependent variables and independent variables. When all the independent variables were equal to zero, a becomes the predicted value for dependent variables.

15.3.3 Unit Root Test

For the purpose of this study, this study employs the most popular approaches such as augmented Dickey–Fuller (ADF), Phillips–Perron, and Kwiatkowski–Phillips–Schmidt–Shin (KPSS) tests to test the unit root and stationary of the data.

15.3.4 Diagnostic Testing

In this study, the diagnostic testing such as multicollinearity, autocorrelation, and heteroscedasticity test will be adopted. The variance inflation factor (VIF) will be used to check the multicollinearity problem. For detection of autocorrelation problem, this study has decided to use Breusch–Godfrey serial correlation LM test, while White test will be used to detect the heteroscedasticity problem.

15.3.5 Ordinary Least Square (OLS) Regression

Ordinary least squares (OLS) regression is a generalised linear modelling technique that may be used to model a single response variable which has been recorded on at least an interval scale. This test will show the result on the relationship between the variables in this study and to analyse whether there is a significant relationship between the variables. The OLS regression is analysed with Newey–West adjustment in order to solve the autocorrelation and heteroscedasticity problem (Newey and West 1987).

15.4 Hypothesis

Hypotheses are developed based on the objectives stated in this study. This study included four hypotheses which can be proven based on findings and results of this study.

Hypothesis One

H_1: There is a relationship between financial fragility indicators and gross domestic product

Hypothesis Two
H_1: There is a relationship between financial fragility indicators and gross domestic product per capita

Hypothesis Three
H_1: There is a relationship between financial fragility indicators and inflation rate

Hypothesis Four
H_1: There is a relationship between financial fragility indicators and interest rate

The null hypothesis will be rejected if there is an evidence of a significant relationship either positive or negative on parameter of coefficient which proves that financial fragility indicators actually will influence the macroeconomics in a country.

15.5 Findings

15.5.1 Result of Unit Root Test

The results from unit root tests revealed that all variables are stationary at levels based on the KPSS test. Meanwhile, ADF and PP tests were not stationary at level data. Thus, this study decides to use the KPSS test as the overall decision criterion for the stationarity test. Table 15.1 gives the result from KPSS test statistic.

Table 15.1 Result of stationarity tests based on Kwiatkowski–Phillips–Schmidt–Shin (KPSS) intercept and linear trends

Variables	At level
lnGDP	0.086243
lnGDPPC	0.059000
lnCPI	0.076925
lnTBILLS	0.101754
lnGOBS	0.089371
lnCOBS	0.118976
lnSR	0.048994
lnEXP	0.084258
lnPVC	0.098436

Notes The asymptotic critical value is 0.146000 based on 5% level

15.5.2 Result Based on Multiple Regressions

Results from the diagnostic testing revealed that there is no serious multicollinearity problem. However, some of the model regressions suffered from autocorrelation and heteroscedasticity. Therefore, based on Table 15.2, the result of OLS regression is analysed with Newey–West adjustment to solve the autocorrelation and heteroscedasticity problem.

Table 15.2 shows the relationship between financial fragility indicators and macroeconomic variables used in this study. The result revealed that only corporate bond spreads (COBS) as an indicator of financial fragility do not have a relationship with lnGDP, lnGDPPC, and lnTBILLS except for lnCPI which has a significant positive relationship. Government bond spreads (GOBS) and stock returns (SR) had a significant relationship with all the macroeconomic variables. The lnGOBS and lnSR showed a positive relationship with lnGDP indicating that for every unit increase in lnGOBS and lnSR change, there is a 12.19% and 114.5% increase in the lnGDP, respectively. For lnGDPPC model, lnGOBS and lnSR showed a negative and positive relationship with lnGDPPC at 1% and 5% levels, respectively. Furthermore, both lnGOBS and lnSR showed a significant negative relationship with lnCPI and lnTBILLS indicating that for every unit increase in lnGOBS and

Table 15.2 Result based on ordinary least square (OLS) for log gross domestic product, log gross domestic product per capita, log consumer price index and log treasury bills

Dependent variables	lnGDP	lnGDPPC	lnCPI	lnTBILLS
lnGOBS	**0.121877 (1.718294)***	**−0.131672 (−2.535680)*****	**−0.134894 (−1.778205)***	**−0.205422 (−4.806158)*****
lnCOBS	−0.077661 (−1.060679)	0.014505 (0.129476)	**0.209110 (3.359757)*****	−0.012290 (−0.206766)
lnSR	**1.144826 (2.553890)*****	**1.196031 (2.296713)****	**−2.396191 (−3.103601)*****	**−0.661233 (−2.554634)*****
lnEXP	**0.268330 (2.908040)*****	**0.984162 (14.34923)*****	N/A	N/A
lnPVC	**0.605240 (2.517527)*****	N/A	N/A	N/A
R-squared	0.871045	0.887473	0.485246	0.654670
F-statistic	(45.93142)***	(69.00880)***	(11.31212)***	(22.74939)***
No. of observations	40	40	40	40

Notes The Newey-West adjusted t-statistics are given in the parentheses below the coefficient figures. P-values denotes as *, **, and ***. Where * denotes significant at the 10% level, ** denotes significant at the 5% level, and *** denotes significant at the 1% level. N/A: Not applicable

lnSR, there is a decrease in lnCPI and TBILLS. Among the four models, lnGDPPC is found to have a high r-squared at 88.74% which can be explained by independent variables, followed by lnGDP and lnTBILLS at 87.10 and 65.47%, respectively, while lnCPI showed the lowest r-squared at 48.52% can be explained by financial fragility indicators used in this study.

15.6 Conclusions

The findings showed that the relationship between financial fragility indicators and macroeconomics in Malaysia has a significant and insignificant relationship. The result from all hypotheses testing revealed that government bond spreads and stock returns as financial fragility indicators rejected the null hypothesis which indicates that there is a relationship between government bond spreads and stock returns with all macroeconomic variables. Meanwhile, corporate bond spreads failed to reject the null hypothesis for hypotheses one, two, and four which indicates that there is no relationship between corporate bond spreads and macroeconomic variables except for inflation rate.

As can be concluded in this study, the performance of government bond spreads as a measurement of the probability of default and stock returns as a measurement of profitability in financial fragility indicators have a better predictor power for financial fragility than the performance of corporate bond spreads in Malaysia. Interestingly, these results are in line with the definition given in this study where the probability of default increases and profitability decreases, and it indicates that the economy is more financially fragile, and GDP as a proxy of the economic condition will fall. Our findings support Minsky's financial instability hypothesis. When the expectation of the possibility of default decreases and creditors are willing to offer lower borrowing rates even though debtors invest in riskier projects, it allows financial institutions to increase leverage and invest in riskier assets leading to higher default and making the economic system more vulnerable.

This paper suggests that more studies be conducted in the future on predicting the financial fragility in Malaysia. Few studies have investigated financial fragility in Malaysia. Hence, this paper recommends that future researchers investigate financial fragility to help the policymakers as well as the practitioners in Malaysia to be well prepared for any consequences of vulnerability in the economy.

References

Ahmad, N., & Mazlan, N. F. (2015). Banking fragility sector index and determinants: a comparison between local-based and foreign-based commercial banks in Malaysia. *International Journal of Business and Administrative Studies, 1*(1), 5–17.

Antonio Ahumada C. & Carlos Budnevich L. (2001). *Some measures of financial fragility in the chilean banking system: An early warning indicators application*. Central Bank of Chile, 117.
Aspachs, O., Goodhart, C. A., Tsomocos, D. P., & Zicchino, L. (2007). Towards a measure of financial fragility. *Annals of Finance, 3*(1), 37–74.
Beh, L. S., Chew, P. H., Leow, Y. V., Lim, L. S., & Ling, W. X. (2014). *Determinants of banking fragility in Malaysia* (Doctoral dissertation, UTAR).
Bernake, B. S. (1983). Non-monetary effects of the financial crisis in the propagation of the great depression. *American Economic Review, 73*, 488–500.
Bernanke, B., & Gertler, M. (1990). Financial fragility and economic performance. *The Quarterly Journal of Economics, 105*(1), 87–114.
Bernoth, K., & Pick, A. (2011). Forecasting the fragility of the banking and insurance sectors. *Journal of Banking & Finance, 35*(4), 807–818.
Bleaney, M., Mizen, P., & Veleanu, V. (2012). *Bond spreads as predictors of economic activity in eight European economies*. Centre for Finance and Credit Markets, 12/11.
Bonser-Neal, C., & Morley, T. R. (1997). Does the yield spread predict real economic activity? A multicountry analysis. *Economic Review-Federal Reserve Bank of Kansas City, 82*(3), 37.
Bruneau, C., De Bandt, O., & El Amri, W. (2011). *Macroeconomic fluctuations and corporate financial fragility*. Banque de France, Working Paper No. NER-R 226.
Bruneau, C., De Bandt, O., & El Amri, W. (2012). Macroeconomic fluctuations and corporate financial fragility. *Journal of Financial Stability, 8*(4), 219–235.
Bruno, O., Cartapanis, A., & Nasica, E. (2013). *Bank leverage, financial fragility, and prudential regulation. University of Nice Sophia-Antipolis.*
Cihak, M. (2006). *How do central banks write on financial stability*?. International Monetary Fund, 06/163.
Davis, E. P. (1992). *Debt, financial fragility, and systematic risk* (pp. vii). Oxford: *Clarendon Press*.
Demirguc-Kunt, A., & Detragiache, E. (1997). *The determinants of banking crises: evidence from industrial and developing countries*. World Bank Policy Research Working Paper, (1828).
Demirguc-Kunt, A., & Detragiache, E. (1998). *The determinants of banking crises in developing and developed countries*. International Monetary Fund Staff Papers (Vol. 15(1), March 1998).
Demirovic, A., & Thomas, D. C. (2007). The relevance of accounting data in the measurement of credit risk. *European Journal of Finance, 13*(3), 253–268.
Dick, K., Martin, A. W., James, K. J., Ben, D., Wayne, M. M., William, H. C., et al. (2008). *The U.S. financial crisis: the global dimension with implications for U.S. policy*. CRS Report for Congress, November 2008.
Driscoll, M. (1991). *Deregulation, credit rationing, financial fragility and economic performance*. OECD Department of economics and statistics, 98.
Friedman, B. M. & Kuttner, K. (1989). Why does the paper-bill spread predict real economic activity?. In *National bureau of economic research* (pp. 213–254).
Gertler, M., Lown, & C. S. (2000). The Information in the high yield bond spread for the business cycle: Evidence and some implications. In *National bureau of economic research working paper*, (7549).
Ghosh, S. (2010). Credit growth, bank soundness and financial fragility evidence from indian banking sector. *South Asia Economic Journal, 11*(1), 69–98.
Gilchrist, S., Yankov, V., & Zakrajsek, E. (2009). Credit market shocks and economic fluctuations: evidence from corporate bond and stock markets. *Journal of Monetary Economics, Elsevier, 56*(4), 471–493.
Guender, A., & Tolan, B. (2015). The predictive ability of a risk-adjusted yield spread for economic activity in Europe. *Empirica*, 1–27.
Heng, N. V., Nassir, A. M., Ariff, M., & Mohamad, S. (2005). Predictive power of forward rates: Evidence from Malaysian government securities (MGS) market. *Investment Management and Financial Innovations, 2,* 61–71.
Hillegeist, S. A., Keating, E. K., Cram, D. P., & Lundstedt, K. G. (2004). Assessing the probability of bankruptcy. *Review of Accounting Studies, 9*(1), 5–34.

Kaminsky, G. L., & Reinhart, C. M. (1999). The twin crises: The causes of banking and balance-of-payments problems. *American economic review*, 473–500.
Kibritçioglu, A. (2003). Monitoring banking sector fragility. *The Arab Bank Review, 5*(2), 51–66.
Lee, J. H., Ryu, J., & Tsomocos, D. P. (2013). Measures of systemic risk and financial fragility in Korea. *Annals of Finance, 9*(4), 757–786.
Lemus, J. S., Corredor-Waldron, A., & Rueda, J. G. (2012). Fragility determinants of the private corporate sector in Colombia. *Temas*, (66).
Loayza, N. V., & Ranciere, R. (2006). Financial development, financial fragility, and growth. *Journal of Money, Credit and Banking*, 1051–1076.
Minsky, H. (1977). *A theory of systemic fragility* (pp. 138–152). Financial crises: Institutions and markets in a fragile environment.
Mohapi, T. A., & Botha, I. (2013). The explanatory power of the yield curve in predicting recessions in South Africa. *International Business & Economics Research Journal, 12*(6), June 2013.
Newey, W. K., & West, K. D. (1987). A simple positive Semi –definite heteroskedasticity and autocorrelation consistent covariance matrix. *Econometrika, 55*(3), 703–708.
Penas, M. F., & Tümer-Alkan, G. (2010). Bank disclosure and market assessment of financial fragility: evidence from Turkish banks' equity prices. *Journal offinancial services research, 37* (2–3), 159–178.
Radelet, S., & Sachs, J. (1998). The east Asian financial crisis: diagnosis, remedies, prospects. *Brookings Papers on Economic Activity, 1,* 1–78.
Saito, Y., Takeda, Y. (2000). *Predicting the US real GDP growth using yield spread of corporate bonds*. International Department Bank of Japan, Working Paper Series 00-E-3.
Simon, G., Vladimir, Y., & Egon, Z. (2012). Credit spreads and business cycle fluctuations. *American Economic Reviews, 102*(4), 1692–1720.
Schock, M. (2015). *Predicting economic activity via eurozone yield spreads: impact of credit risk.* Institute of Public Economics, Leibniz University of Hannover, Germany, 542.
Tsomocos, D. P. (2003). *Equilibrium analysis, banking, contagion, and financial fragility*. Bank of England, 175.
Vlieghe G. W. (2001). *Indicators of fragility in the UK corporate sector*. Monetary Assessment and Strategy Division, Bank of England.
Zwet, A. V. D., & Swank, J. (2000). Financial fragility and macroeconomic performance: A comparison between the emerging countries and highly developed countries. *De Nederlandsche Bank*, 52.

Chapter 16
Measuring Bank Stability: A Comparative Analysis Between Islamic and Conventional Banks in Malaysia

Norzitah Abdul Karim, Syed Musa Syed Jaafar Alhabshi, Salina Kassim and Razali Haron

ABSTRACT The present study provides new empirical evidence of bank stability measures for 50 banks in Malaysia, for a period from 1999 to 2015. There are two methods of measuring bank stability that is using Z-score and CAMELS variables. After calculating, these variables are ranked, with the highest average is ranked as one, and the lowest average is ranked last, or fifty. This is following the method by (Roman and Procedia Economics and Finance, *6*(13), 703–712 Roman and Şargu 2013) and (Procedia—Social and Behavioral Sciences, *24*, 1530–1545 Dincer et al. 2011) and extending it by introducing the average of total ranking for all variables. The empirical findings suggest that both local Islamic and conventional banks are ranked favourable in overall average bank stability score, sensitivity to market risk, asset quality, earning and profitability, but local conventional banks are recorded favourable ranking in liquidity. Comparing the two types of local banks, conventional banks are ranked better in liquidity, sensitivity to market risk and earning and profitability.

Keywords Bank stability · Z-score · CAMELS · Ranking

N.A. Karim (✉)
Universiti Teknologi MARA, IIUM Institute of Islamic Banking and Finance (IIiBF), International Islamic University, Kuala Lumpur, Malaysia
e-mail: norzitah@salam.uitm.edu.my

S.M.S.J. Alhabshi · S. Kassim · R. Haron
IIUM Institute of Islamic Banking and Finance (IIiBF), International Islamic University, Kuala Lumpur, Malaysia
e-mail: syedmusa@iium.edu.my

S. Kassim
e-mail: ksalina@iium.edu.my

R. Haron
e-mail: hrazali@iium.edu.my

F. Noordin et al. (eds.), *Proceedings of the 2nd Advances in Business Research International Conference*, https://doi.org/10.1007/978-981-10-6053-3_16

16.1 Introduction

The recent global financial crisis has induced a series of failure of many conventional banks and led to an increased interest in the Islamic banking. The financial crisis also highlighted the importance of a stable financial system that can weather financial and economic shocks. The issue of financial and bank stability has always been the interest of all central banks since it has direct implications on the sustainability of the banking industry itself.

Despite its critical importance, the concept of bank stability has still not been properly defined or agreed (Segoviano and Goodhart 2009; Gersl and Hermanek 2010; Schinasi 2004; Creel et al. 2014; Swamy 2014). There is a lack of consensus on the measure, indicators and quantification of banking or financial stability or instability (Segoviano and Goodhart 2009; Gersl and Hermanek 2010). A review of literature reveals that commonly used bank stability measures are Z-score and CAMELS. Thus, there is an urgent need to discuss both measures and compare the measures for both Islamic and conventional banks. The remaining of this paper is structured as follows. Section 16.2 discusses the empirical finding of Z-score and CAMELS as the measures of bank stability. Section 16.3 looks at the data and methodology. Section 16.4 presents the findings, and the last section provides a conclusion of the study with some recommendations for future research.

16.2 Literature Review

Empirical Evidence of Z-score as A Measure of Bank Stability

The principle of "Safety First" was developed based on Roy (1952)s dissatisfaction over the simple rule of maximising return and also his traumatic wartime experience (Sullivan 2011). The application of the principle of Safety First means that when having wide range of possibilities including disasters, the gross return should not be less than some quantity, that is the disaster level (Roy 1952). The development of this principle leads to the Z-score measure which indicates the distance from insolvency combining accounting measures of profitability, leverage and volatility (Rajhi and Hassairi 2013). The Z-score is inversely related to the probability of a bank's insolvency, i.e. the probability that the value of its assets will become lower than the value of the debt which means that higher Z-score corresponds to a lower risk of insolvency (Rajhi and Hassairi 2013). Due to the recent global financial crisis, it has become a great interest and draws enormous attention to the bank insolvency risk (Rahman 2010); thus, the Z-score has become important than ever (Strobel 2011). Rahman (2010) in her research noted that financing structures of the banks affect the risk exposure, bank's profitability, capital structure decisions, degree of risk tolerance and economic performance. According to Rahman (2010), there are three methods of measuring risks namely Z-score, CAPM risk measures and Zrisk index. Rahman (2010) in her research used Zrisk index with the rationale

Table 16.1 Definition of principle of safety first's Z-score

Principle of safety first	Definition
Minimising risk (Z-score)	The Z-score is a measure of the distance-to-default, which measures the market value of a bank's assets in relation to the book value of its liabilities. Thus, the higher is Z-score, the less likely of probability of insolvent and hence, the stable is the bank

Source Adapted from Rajhi and Hassairi (2013)

that it is the most appropriate because Malaysian Islamic banks are relatively small and not publicly traded on the stock exchange. Rahman (2010) extended the work by Hannan and Hanweck (1988) where Zrisk is calculated as E(ROA) + CAP/σROA, where E(ROA) is the expected return on assets, CAP is the ratio of equity capital to total assets, and σROA is the standard deviation of ROA. The usage of Zrisk as a measure of risk is also noted in the research by Ahmad et al. (2008). This usage of Zrisk is similar in term of formula to Z-score.

Bourkhis and Nabi (2013) and Beck et al. (2013) used Z-score ratio as the indicator for bank's soundness. According to Bourkhis and Nabi (2013), Z-score ratio is an important measure for bank soundness because it is inversely related to the probability of bank's insolvency. Z-score is denoted as follows: $Z = (\mu + K)/\sigma$ where μ denotes the bank's average return on assets (ROA), K is the equity capital in percentage of total assets, and σ is the standard deviation of the ROA as a proxy for return volatility. The probability of insolvency is defined as the probability that losses exceed equity, i.e. therefore, an increase in the Z-score is equivalent to a decrease in the upper bound of the insolvency risk. Under the assumption of bank's return normality, the Z-score can be interpreted as the number of standard deviations below the mean by which profits would have to fall in order to deplete equity. The bank's soundness is measured by Z-score that is the average return on asset plus equity divided assets divided by standard deviation of return on assets (Beck et al. 2013). Thus, the definition of Z-score is summarised in Table 16.1.

16.3 Empirical Evidence of CAMELS as a Measure of Bank Stability

According to Roman and Şargu (2013) and Christopoulos et al. (2011), financial ratios based on CAMEL have been used to assess the soundness of banks in the USA since 1979. Later, these ratios have been extended and used as a tool to assess the soundness of banks for the supervisory authorities in different countries (Roman and Şargu 2013). The International Monetary Fund (IMF) measures financial vulnerability and soundness using handful dimensions of Financial System Soundness with acronym CAMEL, which signifies five major dimensions of a bank namely Capital adequacy, Asset quality, Management quality, Earnings ability and Liquidity

(Roman and Şargu 2013). Nevertheless, it has been extended to include the sixth dimension "S", so that the CAMEL approach became the CAMELS approach, which includes the sensitivity of the bank to the changes in the market (Roman and Şargu 2013). This "S" captures the sensitivity of market to include indicators like interest rate, foreign exchange and inflation risk which in overall capture the system risk (Gasbarro et al. 2002). Currently, CAMELS becomes the regulatory bodies monitoring instruments and also bank's evaluation of its performance (Roman and Şargu 2013). The IMF and the World Bank recommend the usage of CAMELS as the measures for financial soundness of the banking sector (Roman and Şargu 2013) and current health of financial institution (IMF 2000). It should be noted that although these indicators are measures of the past problems, or backward looking, IMF (2000) acknowledged that these indicators have some impact on the current situations and thus are useful indicators of the current health of the financial system.

Klomp and Haan (2013) in their studies of risk includes the IMF's core set of "Financial Soundness Indicators" or CAMEL dimensions—i.e. capital adequacy, asset quality, management, earnings and profitability, and liquidity (IMF 2000). Regulatory bodies used CAMEL in assessing the financial soundness and vulnerability of the banks (Klomp and Haan 2013). Nevertheless, there is no specified combination of indicators used for CAMEL dimension, but Klomp and Haan (2013) used 14 indicators for CAMEL dimension in their studies. It is noted that most of the research using CAMELS tend to rank the banks (see, for example Joshi et al. 2014; Roman and Şargu 2013; Kumar et al. 2012; Christopoulos et al. 2011; Gasbarro et al. 2002). The components of CAMELS are summarised in Table 16.2.

Table 16.2 Components of CAMELS

Component	Definition
Capital adequacy	Capital adequacy is evaluated on the basis of both the bank's sizes as well as the composition of its assets and liabilities and used as a measure of its financial strength and stability
Asset quality	Examiners assess the credit risks in the various loans in the bank's portfolio and classify these loans as: good, substandard, doubtful, or loss
Management efficiency	Examiners attempt to gauge not only the bank's management but also its board of directors. Competence, management acumen, integrity, and willingness to comply with banking regulations are some of the factors assessed
Earning and profitability	There is an evaluation of the earnings as well as their level relative to peers. One objective is to assess the impact on the bank's capital of internally generated funds
Liquidity	Regulators assess liquidity by examining credit conditions, deposit volatility, loan commitments, and other contingent claims against the bank, capital, current stock of liquid assets, and the bank's perceived ability to raise funds on short notice
Sensitivity to market risks	Regulators assess how sensitive the bank's asset, liability and net worth values are to changes in market condition like interest

Sources Adapted from Greenbaum and Thakor (2007), Olalekan and Adeyinka (2013)

16.4 Data and Methodology

The main data source for this study comes from BankScope database produced by the Bureau Van Dijk. The sample consists of 33 commercial banks and 17 Islamic banks operating in Malaysia. However, only 10 local Islamic banks and 8 local commercial banks are discussed here. The last discussion is on the remaining banks' categories by BankScope as commercial or Islamic banks. Covering the sample period from 1999 to 2015, the Z-score and CAMELS measures are chosen as the method of analysis. Table 16.3 summarises the variables used and ways of measuring or calculating these variables. Subsequent to calculation of these variables, the average from year 1999 to 2015 is calculated for each of the bank. The best highest average is allocated as rank one, next accordingly and the lowest average is ranked last, or rank fifty. This is following the method by Roman and Şargu (2013) and Dincer et al. (2011). It has later been extended by introducing the average of total ranking for all variables. Next, the rank numbers from each variables are added together to form a total rank for each bank. The lowest sum of ranking denotes the most stable bank because the bank obtains top ranking for each variables. The total rank takes a score from 7, being the most stable, to score of 350, being the least stable. Finally, the average on the total average of rank is calculated, which takes a score between 7, being the most stable, and 50, being the least stable. The limitation of this study is that the stability of a particular bank is discussed with respect to the stability of a group of 50 banks, hence not the individual bank's absolute stability.

Table 16.3 Variables and measurements of bank stability

Variable	Measurement
Z-score	ROA plus earning to total asset/standard deviation ROA
Capital adequacy	Capital adequacy, equity to total asset, Tier I, Tier 2/Risk Weighted asset, Total capital, debt to equity
Asset quality	Change in NPA, connected lending, coverage of NPL, impaired loan, leverage ratio, Net NPA to total asset, Net NPA to net advances, NPL to total asset, total liabilities to total asset, total NPL to total liabilities
Management efficiency	Business per employee, deposit interest as % total deposit, growth in number of banks, interest expense to deposits
Earning and profitability	Dividend payout, cost to income, interest income to total income, net profit to average asset, non-interest income to total income, ROA, ROE
Liquidity	Central bank credit to FI, circulating asset to total asset, deposit to monetary aggregate, liquid asset to total asset, liquid asset to total deposit, total loan to total deposit, net loan to s/term deposit, liquid asset to s/term deposit
Sensitivity to market risk	Total asset to total sector asset

Sources Roy (1952), IMF (2000), Gasbarro et al. (2002), Christopoulos et al. (2011), Kumar et al. (2012), Roman and Şargu (2013), Joshi et al. (2014)

16.5 Analysis and Discussions

Even though 50 banks are analysed, only the result of 18 banks is discussed and presented here. These banks include important banks as highlighted by Central Bank of Malaysia as being the local Islamic and local conventional banks. The Islamic banks include Affin Islamic Bank Berhad, Alliance Islamic Bank Berhad, Bank Islam Malaysia Berhad, Bank Muamalat Malaysia Berhad, CIMB Islamic Bank Berhad, Hong Leong Islamic Bank Berhad, Maybank Islamic Berhad, Public Islamic Bank Berhad and RHB Islamic Bank Berhad, while the conventional banks are Affin Bank, Alliance Bank Berhad, CIMB Bank Berhad, Hong Leong Bank Berhad, Maybank, Public Bank Berhad and RHB Bank Berhad. In addition, only the final result of average total ranking for each variable is discussed, leaving out the details discussion on the ranking of the measurements. However, the last discussion will include all 50 banks but looking at the extreme case of highest and lowest in terms of the average of total ranking of all variables of bank stability.

In Fig. 16.1, in the period of 1999 to 2015, the result is favourable for overall average bank stability score, sensitivity to market risk, asset quality, earning and profitability for Islamic banks as compared to other 50 banks, as noted with ranking of below 40 (rank 1 is the most favourable, and 50 is the least favourable). Capital adequacy, management efficiency and liquidity reported mixed trends for local Islamic banks. However, two local Islamic banks are ranked unfavourable in z-score. This may signal the likelihood of being the least stable as compared to the other 50 banks.

In Fig. 16.2, in the period of 1999 to 2015, there is favourable overall average bank stability score, sensitivity to market risk, asset quality, earning and profitability and liquidity for local conventional banks as compared to other 50 banks, as noted with ranking of below 30 (rank 1 is the most favourable, and 50 is the least favourable). Capital adequacy, management efficiency and Z-score reported mixed trends. However, two local conventional banks are ranked unfavourable in Z-score,

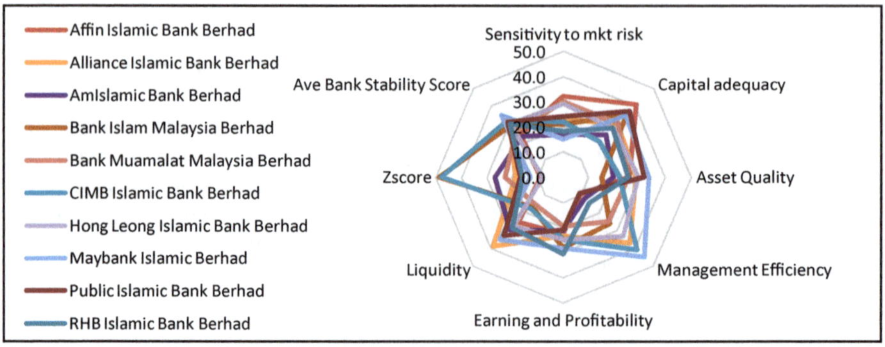

Fig. 16.1 Stability of local Islamic banks (based on average total ranking)

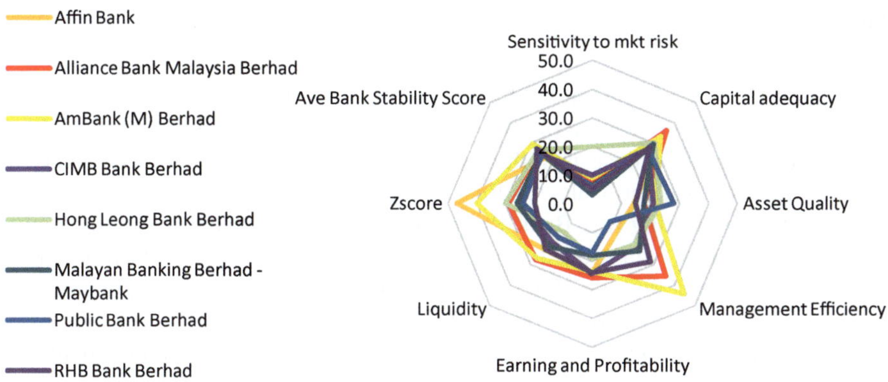

Fig. 16.2 Stability of conventional commercial banks (based on average total ranking)

may signal they are more likely of probability of insolvent and hence, the least stable as compared to the other 50 banks.

Comparing Figs. 16.1 and 16.2, it is noted that conventional bank recorded more favourable rank as compared to the Islamic banks counterparts, in most of the variables of bank stability. In addition, conventional banks are ranked better in liquidity, sensitivity to market risk and earning and profitability.

Figure 16.3 shows the average of total ranking of all variables of bank stability, which includes Z-score and CAMELS in the period of 1999 to 2015. The figure implies the stability of the bank in comparison with the other 50 banks in Malaysia. From the figure below, it is noted that Bank Kerjasama Rakyat Malaysia Berhad (Bank Rakyat) recorded the lowest average total ranking of Z-score and CAMELS variables. This indicates that Bank Rakyat is the most stable bank as compared to the other 50 banks. On the other hand, Public Bank (L) Ltd recorded the highest average total ranking of Z-score and CAMELS variables, indicating that Public Bank (L) Ltd is the least stable bank as compared to the other 50 banks in Malaysia.

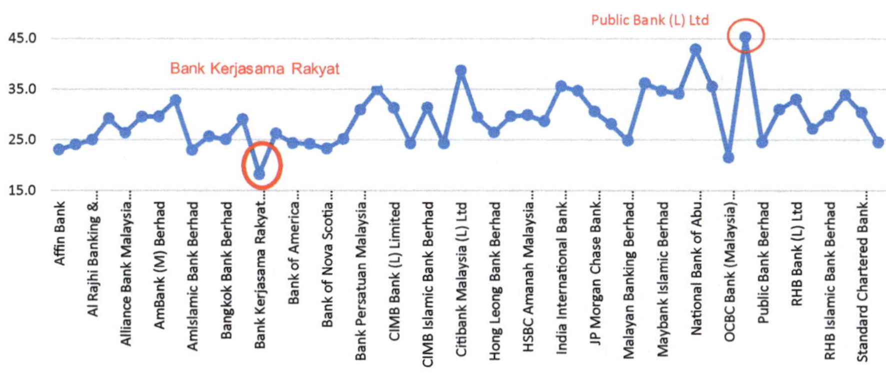

Fig. 16.3 Bank stability (based on average total ranking of Z-score and CAMELS)

16.6 Conclusions

The ranking of the commercial banks in Malaysia based on the Z-score and CAMELS could be indicative of their stability with reference to the other banks in group. Based on these measures, this study finds that of the 50 banks in Malaysia, Bank Kerjasama Rakyat Malaysia Berhad (Bank Rakyat) has the lowest average total ranking, indicating that Bank Rakyat is the most stable bank as compared to the other 50 banks, while on the other hand, Public Bank (L) Ltd recorded the highest average total ranking of Z-score and CAMELS variables indicating the least stable bank as compared to the other 50 banks in Malaysia.

The empirical findings also suggest that local Islamic and conventional banks are ranked favourable in overall average bank stability score, sensitivity to market risk, asset quality, earning and profitability, but local conventional banks also recorded favourable ranking in liquidity. Comparing the two types of local banks, conventional banks are ranked better in liquidity, sensitivity to market risk and earning and profitability. These results could have important implications for better policy strategy to increase the stability of the banking sector in Malaysia. The bank stability can be achieved through effective macro- and micro-prudential policies, for example, with the focus on effective capital and liquidity regulatory framework. This leads to a recommendation for future areas of research in the area of effective capital and liquidity framework in achieving the bank stability.

References

Ahmad, R., Ariff, M., & Skully, M. J. (2008). The determinants of bank capital ratios in a developing economy. *Asia-Pacific Financial Markets, 15*(3–4), 255–272. doi:10.1007/s10690-009-9081-9.

Beck, T., Demirgüç-Kunt, A., & Merrouche, O. (2013). Islamic vs. conventional banking: Business model, efficiency and stability. *Journal of Banking & Finance, 37*(2), 433–447. doi:10.1016/j.jbankfin.2012.09.016.

Bourkhis, K., & Nabi, M. S. (2013). Islamic and conventional banks' soundness during the 2007–2008 financial crisis. *Review of Financial Economics, 22*(2), 68–77. doi:10.1016/j.rfe.2013.01.001.

Christopoulos, A. G., Mylonakis, J., & Diktapanidis, P. (2011). Could Lehman brothers' collapse be anticipated? An examination using CAMELS rating system. *International Business Research, 4*(2), 11–20. doi:10.5539/ibr.v4n2p11.

Creel, J., Hubert, P., & Labondance, F. (2014). Financial stability and economic performance *. *Economic Modelling, 266800*, 1–26. doi:10.1016/j.econmod.2014.10.025.

Dincer, H., Gencer, G., Orhan, N., & Sahinbas, K. (2011). A performance evaluation of the Turkish banking sector after the global crisis via CAMELS ratios. *Procedia—Social and Behavioral Sciences, 24*, 1530–1545. doi:10.1016/j.sbspro.2011.09.051.

Gasbarro, D., Sadguna, I. G. M., & Zumwalt, J. K. (2002). The changing relationship between CAMEL ratings and bank soundness during the Indonesian banking crisis. *Review of Quantitative Finance and Accounting, 19*(3), 247–260. doi:10.1023/a:1020724907031.

Gersl, A, & Hermanek, J. (2010). Financial Stability Indicators: Advantages and Disadvantages of their Use in the Assessment of Financial System Stability. *Occasional Publications-Chapters in Edited*, (2005), 69–79. Retrieved from http://ideas.repec.org/h/cnb/ocpubc/fsr06-2.html.

Greenbaum, S. I., & Thakor, A. V. (2007). *Contemporary Financial Intermediation.*

Hannan, T. H., & Hanweck, G. A. (1988). Bank insolvency risk and the market for large certificates of deposit. *Journal of Money, Credit and Banking*, *20*(2), 203. doi:10.2307/1992111.

IMF. (2000). Macroprudential indicators of financial system soundness. *IMF Occasional Papers, 192,* 45–47.

Joshi, A., Sharma, L. D., & Indira. (2014). Seeking the best Indian bank : An implementation to CAMEL Bank. *Pezzottaite Journals*, *3*(4), 1349–1359.

Klomp, J., & Haan De, J. (2013). Bank regulation, the quality of institutions and banking risk in emerging and developing countries : An empirical analysis. *Mimeo*, 1–57.

Kumar, M. A., Harsha, G. S., Anand, S., & Dhruva, N. R. (2012). analyzing soundness in Indian banking : A CAMEL approach. *Research Journal of Management Sciences*, *1*(3), 9–14. Retrieved from www.isca.in.

Olalekan, A., & Adeyinka, S. (2013). Capital adequacy and banks' profitability: an empirical evidence from Nigeria. *American International Journal of Contemporary Research, 3*(10), 87–93.

Rahman, A. A. (2010). Financing structure and insolvency risk exposure of Islamic banks. *Financial Markets and Portfolio Management, 24*(4), 419–440. doi:10.1007/s11408-010-0142-x.

Rajhi, W., & Hassairi, S. A. (2013). Islamic banks and financial stability: a comparative empirical analysis between MENA and southeast Asian countries. *Région et Développement, 37*(1), 1–31.

Roman, A., & Şargu, A. C. (2013). Analysing the financial soundness of the commercial banks in Romania: An approach based on the camels framework. *Procedia Economics and Finance, 6*(13), 703–712. doi:10.1016/S2212-5671(13)00192-5.

Roy, A. (1952). Safety first and the holding of assets. *Econometrica: Journal of the Econometric Society*, *20*(3), 431–450. Retrieved from http://www.jstor.org/stable/1907413.

Schinasi, G. J. (2004). Defining Financial Stability. *IMF Working Papers*, *4*(187), 1. doi:10.5089/9781451859546.001.

Segoviano, M. A., & Goodhart, C. (2009). Banking stability measures. *IMF Working Paper, WP/09/4*, 1–56. doi:10.5089/9781451871517.001.

Strobel, F. (2011). Bank insolvency risk and different approaches to aggregate Z -score measures: A note. *Applied Economics Letters, 18*(16), 1541–1543. doi:10.1080/13504851.2010.548775.

Sullivan, E. J. (2011). *Research in the history of economic thought and methodology* (Vol. 29). Bingley: Emerald Group Publishing.

Swamy, V. (2014). Testing the interrelatedness of banking stability measures. *Journal of Financial Economic Policy, 6*(1), 25–45. doi:10.1108/JFEP-01-2013-0002.

Chapter 17
The Effect of Religiosity, Financial Knowledge, and Financial Behaviour on Financial Distress Among Undergraduate Students

Nelson Lajuni, Imbarine Bujang and Abdul Aziz Karia

Abstract This paper aims to make a specific contribution relating to the determinants of financial distress among undergraduate students in Malaysia. Therefore, this paper tends to assess the relationship between religiosity, financial knowledge, and financial behaviour on financial distress to examine whether public universities' students are equipped with sufficient financial knowledge, depth of religiosity, and right financial behaviour to face this issue. First, the literature on personal financial distress is reviewed with a view to the identification of useful models and concepts. The small number of reference especially on personal financial distress in that literature is noted, especially here in Malaysia. The debate will focus issues on the influence of religiosity, financial knowledge & financial behaviour towards financial distress among undergrad students. Finally, a proposed theoretical framework is recommended to examine on how religiosity, financial knowledge, and financial behaviour influence personal financial distress. We anticipate that behavioural traits will emerge as having a stronger impact on the incidence of financial distress than religiosity or financial knowledge. We expect the results will raise questions about whether policy can be oriented towards improving financial habits and mitigating the impact of behavioural characteristics on personal finances. It presents an ideal approach whereby policymakers are confronted with the latest research findings

N. Lajuni (✉)
Faculty of Business, Economics and Accountancy, Universiti Malaysia Sabah,
Jalan UMS, 88400 Kota Kinabalu, Sabah, Malaysia
e-mail: nelson@ums.edu.my; nlajuni@gmail.com

I. Bujang · A. Aziz Karia
Faculty of Business Management, Kota Kinabalu Campus, Universiti Teknologi MARA,
88997 Kota Kinabalu, Sabah, Malaysia
e-mail: imbar074@sabah.uitm.edu.my

A. Aziz Karia
e-mail: abdulaziz@sabah.uitm.edu.my

F. Noordin et al. (eds.), *Proceedings of the 2nd Advances in Business Research International Conference*, https://doi.org/10.1007/978-981-10-6053-3_17

concerning the determinants of financial distress, how they can be applied, how the policymakers can attempt to increase and improve the financial knowledge and inculcate positive financial behaviour in Malaysia through education. In return, it will permit researchers to study "cases" over time and to gain greater depth of knowledge concerning not only the presence of behavioural success-related traits, but also an understanding of how policymakers navigate the public universities' students towards financial knowledge and eventually reduce financial distress by fine-tuning their levels of readiness.

Keywords Financial distress · Financial knowledge · Financial behaviour PLS-SEM

17.1 Introduction

Entering university may open up students' mind that they are now facing a challenging time in their lives when they are constantly required to make an important financial decision daily without the presence of their parents. For many undergraduate students, the first year in university can be considered as a major transitional phase where parental supervision and control are reduced and the students begin to achieve some degree of financial independence where they need to make decision regularly in the absence of their parents. Living independently in the university means that students are now facing with financial responsibilities, such as paying bills, doing budgeting, and managing the credits for the first time in their lives. However, studies by Lyons et al. (2006) revealed that how well the students deal with these challenges depends on their financial knowledge and behaviours they acquired before entering university. Other studies by Markovich and DeVaney (1997), Chen and Volpe (1998), Beal and Delpachitra (2003), and Murphy (2005) revealed that college students were incapably prepared for these burdens and they often poorly manage their finances based on several studies conducted in the USA and other countries. In fact, Xiao, Shim, Barber, and Lyons found that the coursework, workshops, and other educational experiences are considered the best ways for colleges and universities to inspire the advancement of sound financial practices among students. With the goal of assisting university students to reduce financial distress, researchers are beginning to scrutinize students' knowledge about finances to determine how they acquire financial management skills and to ascertain the best approaches for teaching these skills (Shim et al. 2009). This study suggests that financial distress among undergraduate students can be best handled through exogenous variables such as religiosity, financial knowledge, and financial behaviour to take care of financial distress.

17.2 Literature Review

17.2.1 Financial Distress

Financial distress is a subjective phenomenon. Two individuals in the same financial situation may have different levels of perceived financial distress. Distress about financial matters is increasingly prevalent in society, with half or more adults reporting moderate to high levels of stress and worry about money matters in survey after survey (2nd American Express 2004; The MetLife Study of Employee Benefit Trends 2003). Previous studies on financial stress concern about personal finances linked to health (Bagwell and Kim 2003; Drentea 2000; Drentea and Lavrakas 2000; Jacobson, et al. 1996; O'Neill 2004; O'Neill, Xiao, Sorhaindo, and Garman, 2005a, 2005b, 2005c) as has debt burden and credit card debt (Drentea and Lavrakas 2000). It has been known for decades that financial stressors contribute to marital stress and discord (Freeman et al. 1993; Olson et al. 1983). Financial distress also has been associated with lower self-esteem (Kernis et al. 1991) and dissatisfaction with one's financial situation (Garman and Sorhaindo 2005).

17.2.2 Religiosity

One of the most universal and influential social institutions is religion. In fact, according to Shweder (1991), religion has a substantial influence on people's attitudes, values, and behaviours at both the individual level and societal level. For example, Sabri and Falahati (2014) found that there were dissimilarities between Muslim and Non-Muslim students. The results reveal higher effect of secondary socialization or influence agents on Non-Muslim students, while for Muslim students, the effect of their financial knowledge and primary socialization agents, including parents and religion, is greater. John (1999) and Hira (1997) defined secondary socialization agents comprised agents such as magazines, mass media, advertisements, peer group, mobile phones, and the Internet, while primary socialization agents comprised mother, father, siblings, school, and religion. Even though there is considerable literature focused on culture and its influence on various aspects of consumer behaviour (Mokhlis 2009), little research has examined the effect of religion specifically on financial behaviour, financial knowledge, or especially on financial distress.

17.2.3 Financial Knowledge

However, some studies normally operationalize financial knowledge using measures either related to general financial knowledge or specific areas of financial knowledge, e.g. credit card annual percentage rate. In some cases, financial knowledge is also commonly associated with a selection of financial behaviours such as cash flow management, credit management, saving, and investing (Hilger et al. 2003; Perry and Morris 2005). Financial knowledge according to Norvilitis and MacLean (2010) was found to be a predictor of debt and overall financial well-being for college students. Lower financial knowledge was found to be significantly related to increased debt levels in another related study by Norvilitis et al. (2006). Contrary to previous research, Robb and Sharpe (2009) discovered college students have relatively low levels of financial knowledge. Their study found that higher financial knowledge was significantly associated with higher levels of credit card debt.

17.2.4 Financial Behaviour

Financial knowledge measurement should mirror individual conditions and agreed that financial knowledge concerned about people being informed and confident in making decision in all aspects including spending behaviours (Roy 2003). Irresponsible overspending on consumption is part of several symptoms of insufficient personal financial knowledge according to Beal and Delpachitra (2003). Ibrahim et al. (2009) discovered that many students are unable to manage their income in a proper manner because they simply spend it out and treated as necessary expense once they hold abundant of money. For educated students, more expenses will be spent on housing, reading, and education rather than on food, clothing, cyber cafe, etc. In fact, financial prudence could enlighten the future among the youth and generate wealth to circumvent any debt and wasteful spending which lead to financial soundness. Many students were not having adequate basic consumer financial principles of earning, saving, spending, and investing. Ultimately, it raises concerns about their financial futures and their ability to be effective consumer (Pillai et al. 2010). Training related to financial knowledge is thus highly recommended, and it should be conducted starting from high schools, colleges, and universities as there is a need to improve the financial knowledge among the students who have a mass spending pattern (Davidson 2006).

17.2.5 Framework and Hypothesis Development

The above-mentioned literature hypothesized that religiosity, financial knowledge, and financial behaviour have direct effect on the financial distress among undergraduate students. The research framework of the study is depicted in Fig. 17.1.

Therefore, three hypotheses are formulated to address the research problems and objectives of the study.

Fig. 17.1 Research framework

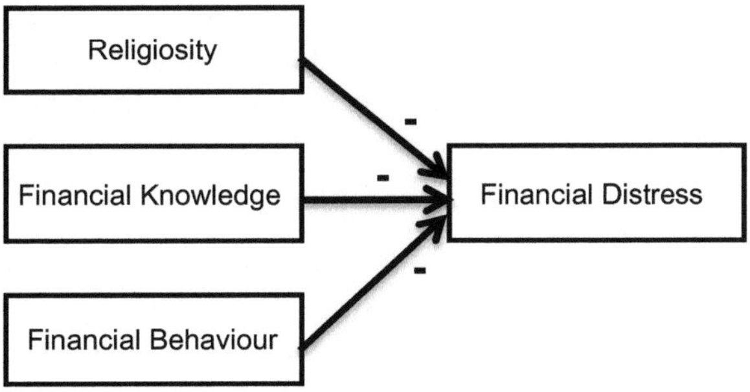

H$_1$: Religious student is associated with having lower financial distress.
H$_2$: Financial knowledgeable student has lower financial distress.
H$_3$: Student with positive financial behaviour has lower financial distress.

17.3 Research Methodology

We will use quantitative approach and adopted positivist paradigm in this study. The samples for this study are undergraduate students currently studying at public universities here in Malaysia. To make sure the sample characteristics corresponded to the ideas of the study, a non-probability quota sampling technique will be employed to guarantee the collected data are indeed from valid sources. Sample size estimation is determined using G-power analysis and the complexity of the study, e.g. the number of constructs and items (Onwuegbuzie and Collins 2007). Figure 17.1 depicts the questionnaire that contained statements of three variables investigated. The variables are measured using multiple items (Hayduk and Littvay 2012). Partial least squares structural equation modelling (PLS-SEM) will then be employed to examine the data and test the hypotheses.

17.4 Expected Results

By integrating evidence on behavioural physiognomies apart from financial knowledge, socio-economic, and demographic factors, this study is expected to extend the results previously existing in the current literature in scrutinizing the topic of what are the key drivers of financial distress. Specifically, a key area of this study focuses on whether undergraduate students are equipped with sufficient financial knowledge, depth of religiosity, and right financial behaviour will affect their ability to manage their finances and stay out of financial trouble or financial distress. We anticipated that the behavioural factors may turn out to be an important determinant of financial difficulties, where people who are imprudent are more likely to get into financial distress than people who are prudent, and this result applies even if a person is well educated and financially knowledgeable. Similarly, impatient or disorganized people are also more likely to experience financial distress. The results may suggest that policy efforts to prevent financial distress must go beyond exclusively trying to improve financial knowledge and education levels (McCarthy 2011).

We expect behavioural traits will emerge as having a stronger impact on the incidence of financial distress than religiosity or financial knowledge. We are expecting the results raise questions about whether policy can be oriented towards improving financial habits and mitigating the impact of behavioural characteristics on personal finances. It presents an ideal approach whereby policymakers are confronted with the latest research findings concerning the determinants of financial distress, how they can applied, how the policymakers can attempt to increase its chances of improving the financial knowledge and inculcate positive financial behaviour in Malaysia through education.

17.5 Discussions and Conclusion

We are expecting in future that the number of people facing financial difficulties will increase. This situation is disturbing, as the implications will not only affect individuals, but also will cause in enormous costs for the entire financial system. Therefore, it is crucial for the policymakers to understand precisely why people get involved into financial trouble, so that appropriate action or policy could be devised to prevent people from getting into difficulties in the future (McCarthy 2011). Using representative data from the undergraduate students of public universities in Malaysia, we expect to validate on how exogenous variables such as religiosity, financial knowledge, and financial behavioural factors such as an individual's capacity for self-control, planning, and patience are important determinants of who gets into financial distress.

Thus, understanding financial distress among young people is thus of critical importance for policymakers in several areas; investigating the reasons why policies on financial education introduced by government through Bank Negara are currently less effective thus could suggest which policies are significant and relevant to be implemented. It can aid those who wish to devise effective financial education programmes targeted to protect younger consumers so that bankruptcy cases could be reduced through improving financial education. Therefore, financial knowledge among public university students cannot be taken for granted. These students need help to make sound financial decisions in future, and at the same time, the authority needs to realize that a "one-time or one-size-fits-all" financial education programme is likely to be ineffective in stimulating financial distress for future financial security for Malaysian context.

References

2nd American Express national survey finds worker financial stress lingering into 2004: (2004, April 1). Press release, American Express Financial Services.

Bagwell, D. C., & Kim, J. (2003). Financial stress, health status, and absenteeism in credit counseling clients. *Journal of Consumer Education, 21,* 50–58.

Beal, D. J., & Delpachitra, S. B. (2003). Financial literacy among Australian university students. *Economic Papers, 22*(1), 65–78.

Chen, H., & Volpe, R. P. (1998). An analysis of personal financial literacy among college students. *Financial Services Review, 7* (2), 22 107–128.

Davidson, I. B. (2006). Financial literacy important for future. *Montana Business Quarterly, 44* (3). Retrieved from http://www.accessmylibrary.com/coms2/summary_0286-33521732_ITM.

Drentea, P. (2000). Age, debt and anxiety. *Journal of Health and Social Behavior, 41*(4), 437–450.

Drentea, P., & Lavrakas, P. J. (2000). Over the limit: The association among health status, race and debt. *Social Science and Medicine, 50,* 517–529.

Freeman, C., Carlson, J., & Sperry, L. (1993). Alderian marital therapy strategies with middle income couples facing financial stress. *American Journal of Family Therapy, 21*(4), 324–332.

Garman, E. T., & Sorhaindo, B. (2005). Delphi study of experts' rankings of personal finance concepts important in the development of the In charge financial distress/financial wellbeing scale. *Consumer Interests Annual, 51,* 184–194.

Hayduk, L. A., & Littvay, L. (2012). Should researchers use single indicators, best indicators, or multiple indicators in structural equation models? *BMC Medical Research Methodology, 12*(1), 12–159.

Hilgert, M., Hogarth, J., & Beverly, S. (2003). Household financial management: The connection between knowledge and behavior. *Federal Reserve Bulletin*, 309–322.

Hira, T. K. (1997). Financial attitudes, beliefs and behaviors: Differences by age. *Journal of Consumer Studies and Home Economics, 21,* 271–290.

Ibrahim, D., Harun, R., & Mohamed Isa, Z. (2009). A study on financial literacy of Malaysian degree students. *Cross-Cultural Communication, 5*(4), 51–59.

Jacobson, B. H., Aldana, S. G., Goetzel, R. Z., Vardell, K. D., Adams, T. B, & Pietras, R. J. (1996). The relationship between perceived stress and self-reported illness-related absenteeism. *American Journal of Health Promotion,* 54–61.

John, D. R. (1999). Consumer socialization of children: A retrospective look at twenty-five years of research. *Journal of Consumer Research, 26,* 183–213.

Kernis, M. H., Grannemann, B. D., & Mathis, L. C. (1991). Stability of self-esteem as a moderator of the relation between level of self-esteem and depression. *Journal of Personality and Social Psychology, 61,* 80–84.

Lyons, A. C., Scherpf, E., & Roberts, H. (2006). Financial education and communication between parents and children. *The Journal of Consumer Education, 23,* 64–76.

Mokhlis, S. (2009). Relevancy and measurement of religiosity in consumer behavior research. *International Business Research, 2*(3), 75–84.

Markovich, C. A., & DeVaney, S. A. (1997). College seniors' personal finance knowledge and practices. *Journal of Family and Consumer Sciences, Fall*, 61–65.

Murphy, A. J. (2005). Money, money, money: An exploratory study on the financial literacy of Black college students. *College Student Journal, 39*(3), 478–488.

McCarthy, Y. (2011, February). *Behavioural characteristics and financial distress.* Paper presented at the Conference on Household Finance and Consumption (Luxembourg).

Norvilitis, J., & MacLean, M. (2010). The role of parents in college students' financial behaviors and attitudes. *Journal of Economic Psychology, 31*(1), 55–63.

Norvilitis, J. M., Merwin, M. M., Osberg, T. M., Roehling, P. V., Young, P., & Kamas, M. M. (2006). Personality factors, money attitudes, financial literacy, and credit card debt in college students. *Journal of Applied Social Psychology, 36*(6), 1395–1413.

Olson, D. H., McCubbin, H. I., Barnes, H., Larsen, A., Muxen M., & Wilson, M. (1983). *Families: what makes them work?* Beverly Hills: Sage Publications.

O'Neill, B. (2004, December). Small steps to health and wealth. *The Forum For Family & Consumer Issues.* Retrieved December 29, 2004, from www.ces.ncsu.edu/depts/fcs/pub/9_3/smallsteps.html.

O'Neill, B., Sorhaindo, B., Xiao, J. J., & Garman, E. T. (2005a). Financially distressed consumers: Their financial practices, financial well-being, and health. *Financial Counseling and Planning, 16*(1), 73–87.

O'Neill, B., Sorhaindo, B., Xiao, J. J., & Garman, E. T. (2005b). Health, financial well-being, and financial practices of financially distressed consumers. *Consumer Interests Annual, 51,* 80–82.

O'Neill, B., Sorhaindo, B., Xiao, J. J., & Garman, E. T. (2005c). Negative health effects of financial stress. *Consumer Interests Annual, 51,* 260–262.

Onwuegbuzie, A. J., & Collins, K. M. T. (2007). A typology of mixed methods sampling designs in social science research. *The Qualitative Report, 12*(2), 281–316.

Perry, V. G., & Morris, M. D. (2005). Who is in control? The role of self-perception, knowledge, and income in explaining consumer financial behavior. *Journal of Consumer Affairs, 39*(2), 299–313.

Pillai, R., Carlo, R., & D'souza, R. (2010). Financial prudence among youth. *Munich Personal RePEc Archive,* 22. Retrieved from http://mpra.ub.uni-muenchen.de/22450/1/MPRA_paper_22450.pdf.

Robb, C. A., & Sharpe, D. L. (2009). Effect of personal financial literacy on college student's credit card behaviour. *Journal of Financial Counseling and Planning, 20*(1), 25–43.

Roy. M. (2003). ANZ survey of adult financial literacy in Australia—telephone survey report (pp. 428). Melbourne: ANZ Banking Group. Retrieved from http://www.anz.com.au/.

Sabri, M. F., & Falahati, L. (2014). Toward a framework of financial wellness determinants: investigating the moderating effect of religion. *Australian Journal of Basic and Applied Sciences, 8*(9), 275–281.

Shim, S., Xiao, J. J., Barber, B. L., & Lyons, A. C. (2009). Pathways to life success: a conceptual model of financial distress for young adults. *Journal of Applied Developmental Psychology, 30* (6), 708–723.

Shweder, R. A. (1991). *Thinking through cultures: expeditions in cultural psychology.* Cambridge, MA: Harvard University Press.

The MetLife study of employee benefits trends: (2003, November). *Findings from the 2003 national survey of employers and employees.* New York: MetLife Insurance Company.

Chapter 18
Effects of Intellectual Capital on Microfinance Institutions' Performance

Maryam Jameelah Hashim, Adewale Abideen Adeyemi and Syed Musa Alhabshi

Abstract The survival and competitive success of microfinance institutions (MFIs) depends on their intellectual capital. The strategic management of intellectual capital provides greater contribution to the company success as compared to the strategic allocation of physical and financial resources. Ultimately, the top management is uncertain on the valuable resources processed by the firm that will cause the success of new strategies. This is due to the fact that they do not understand the nature and value of intellectual capital, how to create, extract and optimize value and wealth through intellectual capital. Therefore, the purpose of this study is to investigate the effect of intellectual capital on the performance of MFIs. This study was conducted in the form of a survey and the respondents comprised MFIs managers who were considered to have knowledge on the internal management and involved in the development of the institutions. Data collected were tested using multiple regression analysis. The results revealed that intellectual capital as a whole has a significant effect on the performance of MFIs. However, the relationship between human capital (knowledge) and structural capital on MFIs performance is insignificant.

Keywords Intellectual capital · Microfinance institutions (MFIs) and performance

---

M.J. Hashim (✉) · A.A. Adeyemi · S.M. Alhabshi
IIBF, International Islamic University, Kuala Lumpur, Malaysia
e-mail: jamieniz@yahoo.com; jamieniz@salam.uitm.edu.my

A.A. Adeyemi
e-mail: adewale@iium.edu.my

S.M. Alhabshi
e-mail: syedmusa@iium.edu.my

M.J. Hashim
Universiti Teknologi MARA, Puncak Alam, Malaysia

F. Noordin et al. (eds.), *Proceedings of the 2nd Advances in Business Research International Conference*, https://doi.org/10.1007/978-981-10-6053-3_18

18.1 Introduction

It is extremely important for microfinance institutions (MFIs) to determine the key challenges in maintaining their operations and remaining sustainable (Kahaso 2012). There is a complete transformation in the current business due to knowledge-based economy. Intellectual capital (IC) is one of the determinants that leads to the growth of knowledge-based economy and improvement of the competitiveness of organization despite being either profit or non-profit oriented (Adnan et al. 2014). Furthermore, IC comprises models, strategies, unique approaches and mental methodologies organizations apply in order to produce, appreciate, compete, solve problems and imitate resources (Akpinar and Akdemir 1999). Therefore, ignoring IC will lead to a dilemma to the organization such as employee's ineffectiveness, low quality of service, lack of knowledge and poor relationship with customers. Employees have pervasive knowledge about their job and what works best for the company. However, this knowledge has never been shared or passed on to other employees. Nevertheless, whenever they leave the company, they will take along their knowledge with them (Akpinar and Akdemir 1999). In this case, it is advisable for MFIs to focus and put high priority on the intellectual capital in order to perform and remain sustainable in the long run. In addition, Tuyon et al. (2011) state that failures of some MFIs are due to institutional problems and financial constraints. An equally important challenge faced by MFIs is managing its intellectual capital. It was further distinguished that the top management is uncertain on the valuable resources possessed by the firm will cause the success of new strategies. This is due to the fact that they do not understand the nature and value of intellectual capital, how to create, extract and optimize value and wealth through intellectual capital (Amrizah and Rashidah 2013). In addition, Adejoke (2010) argued that one of the challenges faced by MFIs is the decreasing numbers of human capital in assisting the clerical work. Besides, he also noted that the main challenge faced is financial sustainability. Furthermore, lack of training opportunities and poor conditions of service also encountered as an issue faced by MFIs. Consequently, those circumstances will lead to inefficiency and a high level of frauds thus reducing the quality of manpower. In the long run, IMFS may experience a high labour turnover whenever there are signs of demotivated staff and poor personnel practices (Acha Ikechukwu 2012). The purpose of this research is to determine the relationship between intellectual capital (IC) comprising human capital, customer capital and structural capital on the performance of MFIs.

18.2 Literature Review

18.2.1 Microfinance Institutions Performance

Two major criteria outreach and sustainability have been used in evaluating the performance of microfinance institutions. Financial sustainability is defined as the development of products and delivery systems that meet the client's needs, at prices that cover all costs of providing these financial services (Adongo and Stork 2005), whereas outreach is defined as the ability of an MFI to provide high-quality financial services to a large number of clients. The indicators of outreach performance include changes in the number of clients, the percentage of female clients, total value of assets, amount of savings on deposits, value of outstanding loan portfolio, average savings deposits size, average credit size and number of branches (Babandi 2011).

18.2.2 Intellectual Capital

Intellectual capital (IC) is reflected as the heart of a knowledge-based economy (Khalique et al. 2013). Although intellectual comes from the word intellect (which means pure intellect), the founder of IC, John Kenneth Galbraith in 1969 presumed it as a degree of intellectual action. The most widely used definition of IC is "knowledge that is of value to an organization". The definition suggests that the management of knowledge (the sum of what is known) creates IC. The main elements of IC are human capital, structural capital, and customer capital (Bontis et al. 2000). It was found that firms with high intellectual capital inherently have strong resources, which are the sources of sustained competitive advantage, as compared to firms with low intellectual capital, or firms, which possess high intellectual capital in only human, structural, and customer capital. This is due to the fact that firms which possess all the intellectual capital components are endowed with more strength to compete in the business as compared to those which possess only a single intellectual capital resource (Amrizah and Rashidah 2013).

18.2.3 Human Capital

The most valuable asset in any business is human resources as compared to other capitals or equipment. However, it was also believed to be the most ignored asset by the firms. Human can be considered valuable asset or liability to an organization (Khan et al. 2010). Human capital refers to experts or employees' skills, knowledge and experience shared with their organization in order to add value (Baron 2011). Therefore, MFIs are required to retain their experts and appreciate their work. This will cause employees to feel more comfortable and loyal to the company. For them to remain loyal to the institution, MFIs should identify their level of satisfaction. It is agreed that human capital is the main source of MFIs and the way they behave towards the institution will lead to greater outreach performance and financial sustainability (Tofael Hossain 2012). In MFIs, human capital consists of higher-level management (including CEOs and managers), executives and other employees.

18.2.4 Structural Capital

Structural capital consists of concepts, models, patents, computers and systems created by employees, yet owned by the organization (Akpinar and Akdemir 1999). Alternatively, it may also acquire elsewhere. In other words, an organization existed from the combination of internal structure and people. Once the organization enhances its technology, develops process and establishes other internal initiatives, structural capital will improve. Therefore, structural capital means the ability of the organization to accommodate its customers' demand. Recent evidence suggests that a good organization structure together with skilled employees providing efficient and quality service will cause greater performance of a microfinance institution (Amrizah and Rashidah 2013). Although organization possesses knowledgeable and skilled employees, it provides less effective structural capital; it is believed that the whole intellectual capital is not stretched to its maximum capacity.

18.2.5 Customer Capital

Customer capital or external capital consists of relationships with customers and suppliers, the government or related industry associations, brand names, trademarks and reputation. According to Akpinar and Akdemir (1999), it refers to the "organization's relationships or network of associates and their satisfaction with and loyalty to the company". Recent evidence confirms that there is a significant positive relationship between Malaysian MFIs and the clients' wellbeing, which leads to higher performance of their micro- and small enterprises (Al-Shami et al. 2013). In order for MFIs to remain sustainable in the long run, supports from local community, customers and suppliers are very important. Besides having a strong financial foundation, MFIs should have a substantial banker–customer relationship (Prawiranata 2013).

18.3 Methodology

As this study attempts to examine the internal factors influencing MFIs, where the information retrieved and shared is from people, therefore, the study opted to use a positivist approach. Positivism is an epistemological perspective and philosophy of science, which holds that the only authentic knowledge is the one based on actual sense experience (Bryman 1989). Positivism is based on the epistemology that objective reality exists versus interpretivism, which is based on the subjective lens of the researcher's perspective and experience.

One of the methods used to confirm the subject matter of this study is through examining the use of intellectual capital by microfinance institutions to achieve better performance. Due to the exploratory nature of this study, a cross-sectional approach was undertaken to measure firms' responses regarding this study, whereby a personally administrated survey was employed in this study using a convenience sampling method. Data were collected from 153 managers of microfinance institutions throughout 22 countries worldwide. Data collected were tested using the SPSS focusing on the correlation among intellectual capital components and their relationship with MFIs performance. This present study is regarded as a causality study, since the purpose is to examine the relationship between intellectual capital components and MFIs performance.

The framework for this study is the outcome of the relationship deduced from the review of the literature. The literature review of intellectual capital based on the works of Bontis et al. (2000); Chen et al. (2005); Khalique et al. (2011) as well as Amrizah and Rashidah (2013) contributed to this theoretical framework. Previously, the intellectual capital framework would have the intellectual capital as an independent variable and organization performance as its dependent variable. Intellectual capital consists of human capital, structural capital and customer capital. It was developed by integrating several direct relationships among study variables to come up with the deduced framework. Figure 18.1 illustrates the theoretical framework.

The framework presented above shows how the links for variables are hypothesized. It is noted that each variable, human capital, customer capital and structural capital, has hypothesized effects on MFIs performance. The proposed hypotheses are:

H1: Human capital has a positive effect on MFIs performance.
H2: Customer capital has a positive effect on MFIs performance.
H3: Structural capital has a positive effect on MFIs performance.

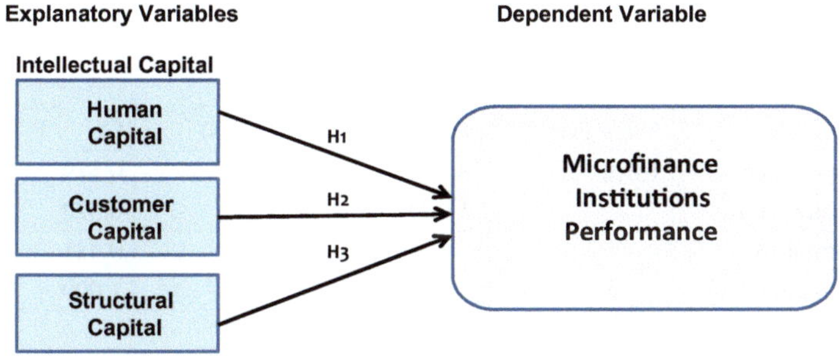

Fig. 18.1 Theoretical framework

18.4 Findings

18.4.1 *Reliability Test*

The most common reliability coefficient is the Cronbach's alpha, which estimates internal consistency by determining the reliability and consistency level of scales used in questionnaires (Pallant 2011). The reliability is expressed as a coefficient between 0 and 1.00. The greater the coefficient is, the more reliable the test will be. The result of the study showed that the Cronbach alphas reliability coefficient for the components of intellectual capital are in the range of 0.789–0.929 and the Cronbach's alpha for the dependent variable, MFIs performance is 0.882, indicating that these scales have a very good internal consistency reliability test. Therefore, based on the results below, no item was removed (Table 18.1).

18.4.2 *Correlation*

In addition to meeting assumptions before the factorization of a set of variables, the strength of the relationships and linear relationships was evaluated by reviewing the correlation matrix produced from the data. Generally, correlations exceeding 0.30 provide enough evidence to indicate that there is enough commonality to justify comprising factors (Tabachnik and Fidell 1996). The output in Table 18.2 indicates that the variables are moderate and positively related.

Table 18.1 Cronbach's Alpha result

Variables		Dimensions	Cronbach's Alpha
Intellectual capital	Human capital	Knowledge	0.789
		Skills	0.854
	Customer capital		0.850
	Structural capital		0.929
MFIs performance			0.882

Table 18.2 Pearson correlation

Variables	MFIs Perf	HC1 (K)	HC2 (S)	CC	SC
MFIs performance	1.000	0.513	0.556	0.519	0.562
Human capital (K)		1.000	0.631	0.572	0.680
Human capital (S)			1.000	0.485	0.804
Customer capital				1.000	0.591
Structural capital					1.000

Table 18.3 Collinearity statistics

Variables	Collinearity statistics	
	Tolerance	VIF
Human capital (K)	0.474	2.108
Human capital (S)	0.339	2.949
Customer capital	0.596	1.679
Structural capital	0.280	3.576

18.4.3 Collinearity Statistics

In supporting the correlation result, Table 18.3 demonstrates that the tolerance statistics for all variables are above 0.2, suggesting that there is no collinearity within the data. This is also supported by the VIF value for all the variables, which are less than 10. Tolerance below 0.2 indicates a potential problem, and if the values of VIF in the model are greater than 10, then there is a cause for concern (Field 2009).

18.4.4 Multiple Regression Analysis

The model explains the relationship between components of IC towards performance of MFIs. The model is significant [F (4, 148) = 25.204, $p < 0.01$] with the predictors explaining 38.9% of the variation in MFIs performance.

The findings as shown in Table 18.4 revealed that intellectual capital components, which are human capital (skills) and customer capital, have positive significant effect on the performance of MFIs. In terms of importance, human capital (skills) has the largest unique contribution to the model followed by customer

Table 18.4 Multiple regression analysis

Dependent variable	MFIs performance		
Adjusted R^2	38.9%		
F statistics	25.204		
Sig level	0.000		
Independent variables	**Unstd Coeff Beta**	**Sig. level**	**Std Coeff Beta**
Constant	2.150		
HC knowledge	0.125	0.182	0.124
HC skills	0.179	0.019**	0.257
CC	0.274	0.003**	0.250
SC	0.092	0.306	0.123

*p < 0.10, **p < 0.05, ***p < 0.01

capital. However, human capital (knowledge) and structural capital have the lowest contribution. Among the four predictors entered into the model, two made statistically significant contributions with human capital (skills) and customer capital having a positive relationship with MFIs performance. The relationship between these variables is at 95% level of significance. Thus, it was found that relationship between human capital (knowledge) and structural capital towards MFIs is insignificant.

18.5 Conclusion

Ensuing from the foregoing results of the study, in the microfinance services business context, the development of human capital resources is one of the most significant intellectual capital elements of economic success (Kamukama 2013a). To boost the wealth of MFIs, managers should use a suitable intellectual capital blend that increases firm value. Since the results of this study clearly show that human capital is the most important intellectual resource, microfinance institutions (MFIs) should take the initiative to source for competent people or build the capacity of the employees who play key roles in the industry. In effect, the microfinance institutions staff selection system should place greater emphasis on social competences, employee motivation, employee agility and leadership abilities of staff, instead of their professional competences. It is not the quality of the people whom a firm hires that will promote business success but rather the ability of the hired people to network well among themselves and their agility in addressing sensitive matters in a firm (Welbourne 2009).

In addition, to provide an enduring customer service excellence, microfinance institutions need to have strong internal structures and processes in place to facilitate employees to succeed in carrying out the tasks. In this case, MFIs should endeavour to have the best quality of stock of knowledge (information systems, procedures, distribution networks, and policies). Building strong information systems, sustainable internal processes, social capital, and all-inclusive organizational culture can accomplish this. Thus, integration of internal processes, strong corporate purpose, and compelling values in the MFIs infrastructure are vital for exceptional services (Kamukama 2013b). Furthermore, MFIs which possess all the intellectual capital components are endowed with more strength to compete in the business as compared to those which possess only a single intellectual capital resource (Amrizah and Rashidah 2013). MFIs, which are balanced in human, relational and structural capital, perform better in terms of financial and market performance. Therefore, MFIs should possess a balance intellectual capital model, which consists of world-class infrastructure, highly educated, and skilled workforce couple with local and global contacts.

The result reflects that there exist significant relationships with human capital skills and customer capital towards MFIs performance. The findings are in line with the essential role of human beings in enhancing the skills and expertise to positively contribute to the development and productivity of MFIs (Kamaluddin and Kasim 2013). The paper highlights the relevance of the research to be expanded to the microfinance providers, as the characteristics owned by the employees should make them more dynamic and productive. This is in tandem with the development of today's scenario whereby huge investments are allocated in training and education to nurture the human capital development in order to improve productivity, which eventually will improve the well being of the society as a whole.

Results have indicated that positive and significant relationship exists between human capital skills and customer capital on the performance of microfinance institutions. This signifies that an improvement in intellectual capital elements boosts their association with institutions' performance. These findings are consistent with conclusions made by F-Jardón and Martos (2009), Stovel and Nick (2002), Youndt and Snell (2004), Kamukama (2013b) and Khalique et al. (2013). In a nutshell, it is thus proven and confirmed that positive association between human capital, structural capital, customer capital and financial performance exists in microfinance industry (Kamukama et al. 2010). Overall, the research results indicate that two intellectual capital elements (HC and CC) significantly impact on the performance of microfinance institutions. This finding corroborates Wang and Chang's (2005) observations; they argued that customer capital can influence institutions' performance if complemented by human capital. Other scholars like Welbourne (2009) remarked that human and customer capital are intrinsically linked because it is people within the firm that create, maintain and nurture the relationship that contribute to firm performance every day. Similarly, Pfeffer (1994) and Uzzi (1996) recognized that human capital and customer capital play a very important role in enterprise performance and survival of the business.

References

Acha Ikechukwu, A. (2012). Microfinance banking in Nigeria: Problems and prospects. *International Journal of Finance and Accounting, 1*(5), 106–111.

Adejoke, A. U. G. (2010). Sustainable microfinance institutions for poverty reduction: Malaysian experience. *OIDA International Journal of Sustainable Development, 2*(4), 47–56.

Adnan, N. S., Kamaluddin, A., & Kasim, N. (2014). Intellectual capital in religious organisations: Malaysian Zakat Institutions perspective. *Accounting Research Institute, 16*(June), 2013–2014. doi:10.5829/idosi.mejsr.2013.16.03.11092.

Adongo, J., & Stork, C. (2005). *Factors influencing the financial sustainability of selected microfinance institutions in Namibia*. The Namibian Economic Policy Research Unit.

Akpinar, A. T., & Akdemir, A. (1999). Intellectual capital. In *Third European Conference* (pp. 332–340).

Al-Shami, S. S. A., Majid, I. B. A., Rashid, N. A., & Hamid, M. S. R. B. A. (2013). Conceptual framework: The role of microfinance on the wellbeing of poor people cases studies from Malaysia and Yemen. *Asian Social Science, 10*(1), 230–242.

Amrizah, K., & Rashidah, A. R. (2013). Intellectual capital profiles: Empirical evidence of Malaysian companies Kamaluddin & Rahman. *International Review of Business Research Papers, 9*(6), 83–101.

Kamaluddin, Amrizah, & Kasim, Nawal. (2013). The relationship between human resource management and islamic microfinance providers' performance: The mediating role of human capital. *International Journal of Business and Social Science, 4*(16), 52–57.

Babandi, G. G. (2011). Micro finance institutions in Nigeria Outreach and sustainability: Questionnaire survey findings. *International Journal of Business and Social Science, 2*(9), 126–130.

Baron, A. (2011). Measuring human capital. *Strategic HR Review, 10*(2), 30–35.

Bontis, N., Keow, W. C. C., & Richardson, S. (2000). Intellectual capital and business performance in Malaysian industries. *Journal of Intellectual Capital, 1*(1), 85–100.

Bryman, A. (1989). *Research methods and organization studies. Organization studies* (Vol. 20).

Chen, M.-C., Cheng, S.-J., & Hwang, Y. (2005). An empirical investigation of the relationship between intellectual capital and firms' market value and financial performance. *Journal of Intellectual Capital, 6*(2), 159–176.

F-Jardón, C. M., & Martos, M. S. (2009). Intellectual capital and performance in wood industries of Argentina. *Journal of Intellectual Capital, 10*(4), 600–616.

Field, A. (2009). *Discovering Statistics using SPSS.*

Kahaso, T. N. (2012). *the key success factors for microfinance industry In MOMBASA.*

Kamukama, N. (2013a). Intellectual capital: Company's invisible source of competitive advantage. *Competitiveness Review: An International Business Journal, 23*(3), 260–283.

Kamukama, N. (2013b). Intellectual capital: Firms' hidden source of service quality in the microfinance industry in Uganda. *Journal of African Business, 14,* 150–161.

Kamukama, N., Ahiauzu, A., & Ntayi, J. M. (2010). Intellectual capital and performance: testing interaction effects. *Journal of Intellectual Capital, 11*(4), 554–574.

Khalique, M., Shaari, N., Abdul, J., Isa, A. H. B. M., & Ageel, A. (2011). Relationship of intellectual capital with the organizational performance of pharmaceutical companies in Pakistan. *Australian Journal of Basic & Applied Sciences, 5*(12), 1964–1969.

Khalique, M., Shaari, N., Abdul, J., Isa, A. H. B. M., & Samad, N. B. (2013). Impact of intellectual capital on the organizational performance of Islamic banking sector in Malaysia. *Asian Journal of Finance & Accounting, 5*(2), 75.

Khan, B., Farooq, A., & Hussain, Z. (2010). Human resource management: An Islamic perspective. *Asia-Pacific Journal of Business Administration, 2*(1), 17–34.

Pallant, J. (2011). *SPSS survival manual.* Retrieved from www.allenandunwin.com/spss.

Pfeffer, J. (1994). Competitive advantage through people. *Calfornia Management Review, 36*(2), 9–28.

Prawiranata, I. R. (2013). *Sustainable microfinance in Indonesia : A sociocultural approach.* Victoria University.

Stovel, M., & Nick, B. (2002). Voluntary turnover: Knowledge management—friend or foe? *Journal of Intellectual Capital, 3*(3), 303.

Tabachnik, B. G., & Fidell, L. S. (1996). Multivariate normality. In *Using multivariate statistics* (p. 381).

Tofael Hossain, M. (2012). Human resource management practices and employees' satisfaction towards private banking sector in Bangladesh. *International Review of Management and Marketing, 2*(1), 52–58.

Tuyon, J., Ali, R., & Mohammad, S. J. S. (2011). The role of microfinance in development of micro enterprises in Malaysia. *Business & Management Quarterly Review*, 2(3), 47–57.

Uzzi, B. (1996). The sources and consequences of embeddedness for the economic performance of organizations: The network effect. *American Sociological Review, 61,* 674–698.

Wang, W.-Y., & Chang, C. (2005). Intellectual capital and performance in causal models: Evidence from the information technology industry in Taiwan. *Journal of Intellectual Capital, 6*(2), 222–236.

Welbourne, P. (2009). Social work: The idea of a profession and the professional project. *Locus SOCI@L, 3,* 19–35.

Youndt, M. A., & Snell, S. A. (2004). Human resource configurations, intellectual capital, and organizational performance. *Journal of Managerial Issues, 16*(3), 337–360.

Chapter 19
An Analysis of House Price Index as the Alternative Pricing Benchmark for Islamic Home Financing

Nur Harena Redzuan and Salina Kassim

Abstract Currently, major interest rates, such as the Base Lending Rate (BLR) and Kuala Lumpur Interbank Offered Rate (KLIBOR), are widely used as reference rates by the Islamic financial institutions to benchmark a broad range of financial products and contracts. This study aims to compare the viability of alternative pricing mechanisms for the Islamic home financing products. By comparing the interest-based benchmark with the non-interest benchmark, this study attempts to highlight the sensitivity and fragility of the Islamic home financing product to financial market volatility. The study focuses on Malaysia as the case study and uses quarterly data frequency covering the period from 2001 to 2015. Specifically, the study compares the lending rate and Housing Price Index (HPI) with the economic growth as the indicator of economic activities. Through the correlation analysis, the study found that the non-interest benchmark shows better relationships with macroeconomic variable compared to the interest-based benchmark. It shows that these alternative benchmarks have the connection to the economic movements that lead to the stability of the non-interest financing instruments. The findings of this study would provide important insights on the viability of House Price Index as the alternative to the benchmark of the equity financing home financing product. This study contributes to the empirical evidence for the feasibility of adopting interest-free benchmark to price Islamic home financing product.

Keywords House Price Index · Pricing benchmark · Equity financing · Islamic finance

N.H. Redzuan (✉) · S. Kassim
IIUM Institute of Islamic Banking and Finance (IIiBF),
International Islamic University, Kuala Lumpur, Malaysia
e-mail: nurharenaredzuan@yahoo.com

S. Kassim
e-mail: ksalina@iium.edu.my

F. Noordin et al. (eds.), *Proceedings of the 2nd Advances in Business Research International Conference*, https://doi.org/10.1007/978-981-10-6053-3_19

19.1 Introduction

In the current socio-economic context, home ownership is considered as a form of a basic need for the human being to enable them to lead a decent life. However, due to the high cost of housing, not everybody can realise the dream of owning a house. The process of home ownership can be relatively more challenging for the observing Muslims who are refrained from the conventional banking arrangement which is based on the prohibited element of interest rate. Despite this, the conventional banking home financing product has been adopted for so long in many countries since the money lending model of conventional finance is simple. In facilitating home ownership, the conventional banks play the role as an intermediary, collecting funds from the surplus units, and then allocate the money to those who wish to purchase a home. The bank generates revenue by requiring payment of the principal with a certain amount of interest, and as a precautionary measure, the bank obtains collateral as the assurance for the repayment of money.

In providing loans for purchase of houses, conventional banks lend out the stipulated amount of money needed to pay for the house, charge interest on the amount loaned out, and require the customer to pay the principal and interest over an agreed loan tenure. The bank generates revenue by requiring payment of the principal with a certain amount of interest, and as a precautionary measure, the bank keeps the house as the collateral until the loan is fully paid by the customer. For the Muslim customers, this credit arrangement is prohibited since interest on the money-based loan is not permissible as clearly highlighted in the Holy Quran.

The Muslims home purchasers who adhere to the principles of *Shariah* want to fully comply with the faith of Islamic law, which prohibits the payment and collection of *riba*. In the contemporary system, *riba* is commonly interpreted as interest. The *Shariah* also prohibits *gharar*, generally interpreted as excessive uncertainty. In response to these prohibitions and to assist the Muslim home purchasers to avoid the use of interest and *gharar*, the Islamic financial institutions developed several concepts of contracts for carrying out interest-free home financing transactions. Consequently, there is a need for the Islamic financial institutions to be creative and innovative in providing a home financing product that is both appealing (in terms of pricing) to the Muslim customers as well as able to fit into the requirements (in terms of free from the prohibited elements, or *Shariah* compliant) of the observing Muslims.

The Islamic banks offer their home financing products based on several contracts such as *murabahah* (cost-plus) and *musyarakah* (joint-venture) so as to be *Shariah* compliant. However, in the absence of a benchmark which is free from the interest rate, the current practice of relying on the conventional interest rate as a pricing benchmark for the home financing products by the Islamic banks has been a subject of criticism by many. Even though this practice is allowable, it is highly discouraged (Usmani 2008). Continuous practice of benchmarking on the interest rate for the Islamic banking product would result in several consequences and negative implications of the Islamic banking industry.

It is argued that one of the consequences of the heavy reliance on debt-based financing is due to the wide practice of benchmarking against the conventional interest rate. The reliance on the interest rate to price the Islamic banking products would also have wide socio-economic implications as the objective of an equitable society as envisioned in the *maqasid al-shariah* (objective of the *Shariah*) will not be able to be achieved. The fundamental reason for introducing a new benchmark as an alternative to interest-based borrowing and lending benchmark is the prohibition of *riba* itself. According to a prominent Muslim scholar, Sheikh Muhammad Taqi Usmani (2008), Islamic banks and financial institutions should get rid of the conventional practice as soon as possible. He argues that using interest rate as a benchmark for halal business is permissible, but not desirable. He further argued that interest rate does not advance the basic philosophy of promoting Islamic economy, as it makes no impact on the distribution system.

Thus, there is an urgent need to model the alternative benchmarking for pricing the Islamic home financing. The alternative benchmark should be free from the prohibited elements highlighted by the shariah and truly reflective of the real market situations. Omar et al. (2010) further argued that the alternative pricing benchmark should be based on the risk profiles of the real economic ventures. It must be tied to the movement of the real economy and based on productivity and profitability of assets. More importantly, the alternative benchmark should also help the Islamic banks to be an agent to facilitate the achievement of the *maqasid al-Shariah.*

19.2 The Islamic Home Financing

19.2.1 An Overview of the Industry

The Islamic banking industry has grown across various financial segments. This sector continues to dominate the global portfolio of Islamic financial assets accounting for an estimated 79.8% share as at the first half of 2014. Globally, Islamic finance is now a USD2.1 trillion industry with Islamic banking and *sukuk* market accounting for 95% of the industry' asset (MIFC Report 2015). Malaysia is the largest Islamic finance market with Islamic assets amounted to USD365 billion as at 1H2014. The Islamic home financing has been particularly increased. Over the years, Islamic home financing contributes to 24.5% to Islamic banking's total financing (BNM, November 2014).

The development of home financing was due to the high demand for houses in the residential sector market. There are more than fifteen home financing products offered in the Malaysian market. Most of the Islamic banks exercise sales-based concept, particularly offered by the local Islamic banks. Meanwhile, some of the Islamic banks exercise share equity financing and very few exercise AITAB financings. Figure 19.1 shows the list of Islamic home financing products provided by Islamic banks in Malaysia. The majority of the Islamic banks offer sales-based

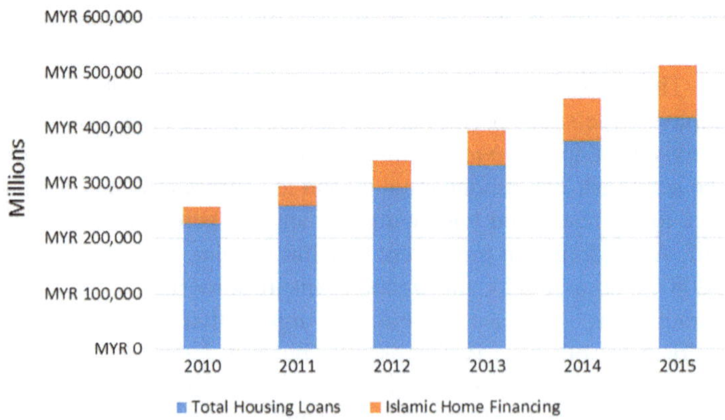

Fig. 19.1 Market share of Islamic home financing in Malaysia. *Source* Bank Negara Malaysia, monthly statistical bulletin, publication 2010–2015

Islamic home financing products, Malaysia has been well known for offering *murabahah* of home financing over the years. This concept, however, has been accused to merely replicate the conventional home loan by replacing interest rate with profit rate. Critics have labelled this replication as a sort of manipulation carried out by Islamic banks (Khan and Mirakhor 1989).

In the Islamic banking industry, Islamic home financing continues to expand and make strong presence in the mortgage market Over a span of a 5-year period, total Islamic financing soars from 12% (or RM29.5 billion) of the total mortgage market in 2010 to 22% (RM96 billion) in 2015, recording an encouraging growth of 27%. Also, the financing portfolio of the Islamic banks is still dominated by home financing. In 2014, Islamic home financing contributes to 24.5% to Islamic banking's total financing (BNM, November 2014). The development of home financing was due to the high demand for houses in the residential sector market. Currently, there are more than fifteen home financing products offered by the Islamic banks in the Malaysian mortgage market. A wide range of contracts have been applied such as *murabahah* and *bay' bithaman ajil* financing applied cost-plus or debt-based financing. Meanwhile, some of the Islamic banks offer share equity financing or *musharakah mutanaqisah* (diminishing partnership) home financing. In addition, other contracts may also be adopted such as *ijarah* and *istisna* financing. While there are more than fifteen Islamic home financing products offered in the Malaysian market, the majority of the Islamic banks offer sale-based Islamic home financing products and in fact, over the years, Malaysia has been well known for offering the *murabahah* home financing. Among these contracts, *musharakah* is the only contract of home financing having the characteristics of profit-loss sharing.

19.2.2 Musharakah Mutanaqisah *Home Financing Model*

The *musharakah mutanaqisah* (diminishing partnership in ownership) contract has enabled the Islamic banks to offer a *Shariah*-compliant home financing product through a combination of three contractual principles, namely *musharakah* (partnership), *ijarah* (leasing), and *al-bay* (sale). This product was gradually developed to meet the increasing demand for Shariah-compliant products and to alleviate concerns that industry players were being complacent in offering debt-based *murabahah* home financing. Meera and Abdul Razak stated that *musharakah mutanaqisah* is a preferred alternative to *murabahah* home financing, particularly in the context of compliance with the *Shariah* (Meera et al. 2005). Despite this, Mydin Meera and Abdul Razak (2009) acknowledged several practical difficulties in the implementation of the *musharakah mutanaqisah* as a home financing product in the context of Islamic banking today.

There have been intense discussions among *Shariah* scholars regarding the fundamental characteristics of the *musharakah mutanaqisah* contract, its permissibility in the context of *Shariah,* the conditions for its validity, and other *Shariah* issues related to this contract. Compared to the more dominant *murabahah* home financing, this product is clearly superior as a contract of partnership. Its permissibility by way of *Shariah* ruling is widely discussed and well-accepted in the classical book of *fiqh* (Osmani and Abdullah 2010). In Malaysia, the *Shariah* Advisory Council (SAC) of the Central Bank of Malaysia had, in its 56th meeting, issued a fatwa ruling that Islamic financing products which are structured based on *musharakah mutanaqisah* are permissible, given that *musharakah mutanaqisah* is a recognised contract in Islamic *mu'amalat.* The following illustration shows the basic structure of the *musharakah mutanaqisah* home financing in Fig. 19.2.

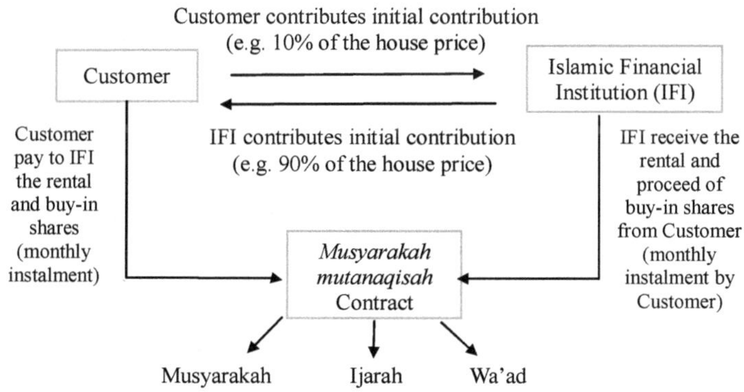

Fig. 19.2 Structure of *musharakah mutanaqisah* home financing

Basic steps involved in the *musyarakah mutanaqisah* home financing structure are:

1. A customer intends to purchase a house and applies for the financing from the Islamic financial institution. The Islamic financial institution processes the application and once approved, both parties enter a *musyarakah* agreement;
2. The Islamic financial institution and the customer will jointly purchase the real property based on a determined share (for example 90:10) depending on the amount of financing requested. Now the customer and the Islamic financial institution are joint-owner of the house;
3. The initial contribution paid by the customer is deemed as his initial share of ownership;
4. The Islamic financial institution's share of ownership will be leased based on *ijarah* (rental) to the customer; and
5. The monthly instalment paid by the customer will be used to gradually purchase the share of the Islamic financial institution until the entire share of the Islamic financial institution is fully purchased by the customer.

The Islamic financial institutions operate in Malaysia offers Shared Equity Home Financing, as the product name is *musharakah mutanaqisah* Home Financing-i. This facility offers for new and existing corporate and commercial customers for asset acquisitions and refinancing such as landed properties, plant and machinery, vessels and commercial vehicles. The customer can apply for this facility for the purpose of financing purchases of asset/property such as landed properties, plant and machinery, vessels and commercial vehicles. Normally, the Islamic financial institutions offer this product for tenure up to 20 years. The pricing is competitive as per the conventional loan which could be offered under fixed rate, floating rate or a combination of fixed rate and floating rate. Customer's monthly instalments for the financing paid to the bank will increase customer's ownership of the asset/property. The ownership of the asset/property will progressively move towards the customer and the financing ends when the customer owns 100% of the asset/property.

There is a normal procedure for purchasing a house by applying for a mortgage in conventional banks. A buyer approaches a bank and asks for the intention of home loan. The bank assesses the credit history of the customer and agrees to lend money for the purpose of customer purchasing the house. The customer and the bank sign a mortgage contract that will require monthly payments over a period of years. The bank, of course, charges interest rate based on the amount of the principal, whose rate depends on prevailing market conditions and the time period of the loan. The bank asks for the house as the collateral to secure the loan over the period of time.

19.2.3 Justification of Adoption House Price Index as the Pricing Benchmark

The HPI reflected in the pricing benchmark of *musharakah mutanaqisah* home financing is consistent with the spirit of Islamic finance, as it is based on the real value of the property (Rosly 2005). Amin et al. (2013) advocated the importance of using the real value of property in determining the pricing of Islamic home financing products, based on the *musharakah mutanaqisah* concept. Currently, interest rate is being used as the pricing benchmark, which is based on the value of money. In fact, the use of rental price or house price would be more stable given that those are based upon the real value of property.

The pricing benchmark should be disclosed to all contracting parties to avoid any conflict of interest. For financing activities, the benchmarks may vary depending on concerns in relation to the real sectors and products. The alternative pricing benchmark should be made transparent to be in line with *maqasid Shariah*. A benchmark derived from a real sector of the economy may prevent disputes on the pricing of financial products among the parties involved. In addition, transparency of the pricing benchmark used will bring honesty into the banking business, in turn boosting society's level of trust and confidence in the Islamic financial system. By doing away with interest rate benchmark, the banks can be assured of halal transactions and income.

Islamic finance promotes mutual co-operation as the solution to deal with calamities. The related parties engage in mutually beneficial financial arrangements intended to alleviate hardship. In the case of Malaysia, the setting of Overnight Policy Rate (OPR) will translate into Base Financing Rate (BFR) or Base Rate (BR). The current practice is to benchmark the cost of fund and rely on interest rate in deciding the price of home financing products. This study proposes the adoption of HPI and rental rate instead, which are based on the movement of market value of the property. These alternative benchmarks could be used in determining the rate of return for *musharakah mutanaqisah* home financing.

19.3 Data and Method

19.3.1 Data Specification

The study compared the Base Lending Rate (BLR) for mortgage and alternative rates; Base Financing Rate (BFR), House Price Index (HPI) and KL-PBR RI. The study chose HPI as the index has been established in Malaysia by National Property Information Centre under the portfolio of Valuation and Property Services Department, Ministry of Finance Malaysia. The data were taken from Annual Property Report of Malaysia. The Gross Domestic Product (GDP) was selected as the macroeconomic variables in this analysis. The data are gathered from Bank Negara Malaysia's Quarterly Bulletin of various issues. The sampled data ranged from 2001 to 2015 of a quarterly basis.

19.3.2 Method

This study examines the relationship between the Base Lending Rate (BLR), an alternative benchmark rate, and Housing Price Index (HPI) with selected macroeconomic variables that could have related to the economic activities. The study adopts a Pearson Correlation Analysis which enables the direction of the relationship and the strength of relationship between variables to be understood. Hence, this study is expected to explain the relationship between these variables.

In general statistical usage, correlation or co-relation refers to the departure of two variables from independence. It also indicates the strength and direction of a liner relationship between two random variables. A number of different coefficients are used for different situations. The best known is the Pearson product-moment correlation coefficient, which is obtained by dividing the covariance of the variables by the product of their standard deviations.

A series of "n" measurement of X and Y written as xi and yi where i = 1, 2, 3, …, n, then the Pearson product-moment correlation coefficient can be used to estimate the correlation of X and Y. The Pearson coefficient is also known as the "sample correlation coefficient". The Pearson correlation coefficient is then the best estimate of the correlation of X and Y. The Pearson correlation coefficient is written as below:

$$\mathrm{p}x, y = \frac{cov(X, Y)}{\sigma_x \sigma_y}$$

where:

cov is the covariance
σ_x is the standard deviation of X

$$cov(X, Y) = E[(X - \mu_x)(Y - \mu_y)]$$

Then the formula for ρ can also be written as:

$$\mathrm{p}x, y = \frac{E[(X - \mu_x)(Y - \mu_y)]}{\mu_x \mu_y}$$

where:

cov and σ_x are defined as above

μ_x is the mean of X
E is the expectation.

And the correlation coefficient formula for sample is defined as:

$$\text{p}x, y = \frac{E(XY) - E(X)E(Y)}{\sqrt{E(X^2) - E(X)^2}\sqrt{E(Y^2) - E(Y)^2}}$$

19.4 Finding and Analysis

Table 19.1 shows the mean and standard deviation between Base Lending Rate, House Price Index and Gross Domestic Product as below.

Table 19.2 shows correlation analysis between base lending rate (BLR), Housing Price Index (HPI) and Gross Domestic Product (GDP).

The above result finds that non-interest benchmark, namely House Price Index, has a better significant relationship with selected macroeconomic variable compared to the interest-based benchmark. Specifically, the House Price Index has a better correlation as compared to base lending rate. The correlation of HPI to GDP is 0.3384, while the correlation of BLR to GDP is 0.2663.

As shown in table, the House Price Index has a positive and significant correlation with the macroeconomic variable that leads to the stability of the non-interest financing instruments. The findings of this study would provide important insights on the viability of House Price Index as the alternative to benchmark the equity financing home financing product. This study contributes to the empirical evidence for the feasibility of adopting interest-free benchmark to price Islamic home financing product. It shows that this alternative benchmark has the connection to the economic activities in Malaysia. Alternatively, it can also be stated that the non-interest benchmarks are truly reflective of the macroeconomic conditions of the country.

The Fig. 19.3 shows the trend of Base Lending Rate, House Price Index, and Gross Domestic Product. The plotted graph shows the similarity of a trend from the year 2001 to 2015 for House Price Index and Gross Domestic Product. In the year 2008, the Gross Domestic Product experienced a downward shift with similar to

Table 19.1 Mean and standard deviation

Variable	Mean	Standard deviation
BLR	6.3808	0.3655
HPI	5.6067	3.4357
GDP	4.8749	2.7923

Table 19.2 Result of correlation analysis

	BLR	HPI	GDP
BLR	1		
HPI	0.3026	1	
GDP	0.2663	0.3384	1

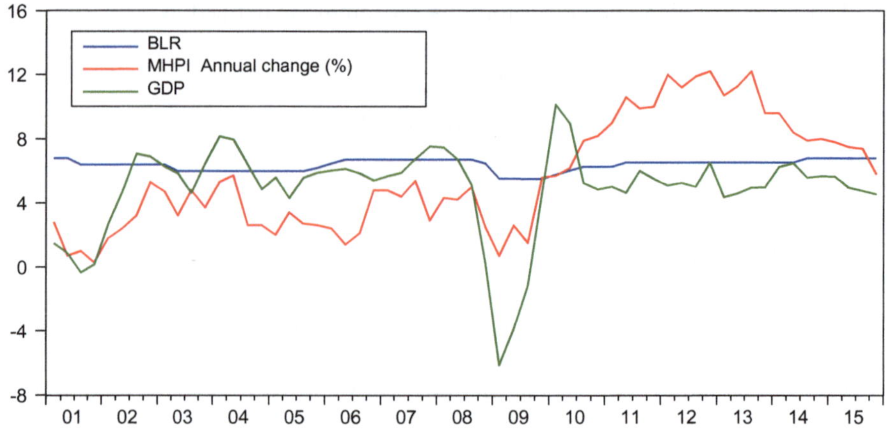

Fig. 19.3 Plotting graph of BLR, HPI and GDP

House Price Index in the same year. As at 2009, the Gross Domestic Product moved upward from the previous year. The House Price Index also moves upward from 2008 to 2009. In contrary, the conventional Base Lending Rate trend from 2001 to 2015 moved at its own trend and did not follow the macroeconomic indicator.

19.5 Conclusion

There is enormous demand for Islamic banking and financial services. This translates into a potential increasing demand for financing services for homes, automobiles, and businesses. In order to succeed in reaching this huge demand for Islamic banking and finance, much work should be done to educate the industry players and customers regarding both the need and the demand for such services. The key to reaching the desired level of *maqasid shariah* is moving away from benchmarking interest or lending rate to alternative benchmark which this paper empirically tested the correlation among these variables. Although benchmarking against the conventional interest rate is permissible, but it is a need to model an alternative benchmarking for the Islamic home financing based on the Malaysian case.

The main significance of carrying out this research is that it addresses important gaps in current knowledge and existing literature on the alternative benchmark of home financing product, which is opposed to the current practice of benchmark. For instance, the most fundamental level, there are few little studies at present on the viability of benchmark to a real economic condition in relation to the movement of trends in real economic activities. Therefore, this study applies the index for guidance in measuring the rate of return that relates to real transactions that are permissible in *Shariah*.

The study looks into the benchmark pricing which was used as a guide and indicator to calculate the rate of return of the financing. In the Malaysia case, it is not known whether residential property rents have significantly grown with the economy generally, and it is viable to benchmark the property rental index against the home financing. Therefore, the analysis from this study should help to shed light in these areas. This study would recommend on future studies to adopt more enriching statistical and econometric analysis to arrive at more robust findings of the alternative benchmark for pricing mechanism of Islamic home financing.

References

Amin, H., Abdul-Rahman, A.-R., & Abdul-Razak, D. (2013). An integrative approach for understanding Islamic home financing adoption in Malaysia. *International Journal of Bank Marketing, 31*(7), 544–573. doi:10.1108/IJBM-02-2013-0008.

Khan, M. S., & Mirakhor, A. (1989). The financial system and monetary policy in an Islamic economy. *JKAU: Islamic Economics, 1*(2), 39–57. doi:10.4197/islec.3-1.5.

Meera, M., Kameel, A., & Abdul Razak, D. (2005). Islamic home financing through Musharakah Mutanaqisah and Al-Bay'Bithaman Ajil contracts: A comparative analysis. *Review of Islamic Economics, 9*(2), 5–30.

Mydin Meera, A. K., & Abdul Razak, D. (2009). Home financing through the musharakah mutanaqisah contracts: Some practical issues. *JKAU: Islamic Economics, 22*(1), 3–27.

Omar, M. A., Md Noor, A., & Mydin Meera, A. K. (2010). *Islamic pricing benchmark.* International Shariah Research Academy for Islamic Finance (ISRA).

Osmani, N. M., & Abdullah, F. (2010). Musharakah Mutanaqisah home financing : A review of literatures and practices of Islamic Banks in Malaysia. *International Review of Business Research Papers, 6*(2), 272–282. Retrieved from http://www.bizresearchpapers.com/21.Osmani.pdf.

Rosly, S. A. (2005). *Critical issues on Islamic banking and financial markets: Islamic economics, banking and finance, investments, Takaful and financial planning*. Dinimas Publishing.

Usmani, M. T. (2008). *An introduction to Islamic finance*. Adam Publishers and Distributors.

Chapter 20
Global Digital Divide: Inter-regional Study on the Impact of ICT Diffusion on Economic Growth

Debbra Toria Nipo, Imbarine Bujang and Hamizah Hassan

Abstract This paper investigates the impact of ICT on economic growth as measured by GDP growth, on 149 countries divided into 5 regions—Africa, America, Arab, Asia and Europe, over a 9-year period from 2006 to 2014. Using pooled OLS and generalized method of moments (GMM) estimation methods, findings from dynamic panel data models revealed that ICT has significant impact on economic growth particularly in regions such as America, Asia and Europe. It is still unclear whether or not regions such as Africa and Arab would benefit from diffusion of ICT; nevertheless, fixed broadband appears promising for Africa's future economic progress, whereas significance of fixed telephone reflects the importance of telecommunication networks in the Arab region.

Keywords ICT · Digital divide · GMM

20.1 Introduction

The spread of advanced information and communications technology (ICT) in businesses has positively impacted efficiency and innovative capacity, thus leading to a profound transformation of an economy's production system (Di Carlo and Santarelli 2010). As ICT goods and services improve and become cheaper over time, growth of demand in the ICT sector would in turn stimulate the growth of all

D.T. Nipo (✉) · I. Bujang
Faculty of Business Management, Universiti Teknologi MARA (UiTM), Sabah, Malaysia
e-mail: dtoria@live.com

I. Bujang
e-mail: imbar074@sabah.uitm.edu.my

H. Hassan
Faculty of Business Management, Universiti Teknologi MARA (UiTM), Shah Alam, Malaysia
e-mail: hamiza013@salam.uitm.edu.my

F. Noordin et al. (eds.), *Proceedings of the 2nd Advances in Business Research International Conference*, https://doi.org/10.1007/978-981-10-6053-3_20

other sectors of the economy. Primary or intermediate inputs from non-ICT sectors are required to produce and deliver ICT goods and services. Therefore, innovation leads to new ICT goods and services, which consequently create new demands, new markets and new sectors of production. This degree of concentration and distribution of ICT throughout the economy is what commonly referred to as ICT diffusion, where adoption of new technologies leads to further spread of ICT through learning from experience (Bakay et al. 2010).

Closer look at the data in International Telecommunication Union (ITU) report in 2014, however, revealed that digital divide continues to exist and that some parts of the global population still have limited access to and usage of ICT. Regions such as Asia, America and Europe are made up of countries that extensively embrace ICT in their economies, but this is an opposite case for regions such as Africa and Arab. This could be due to the clear distinctions between countries across the globe, be it in terms of population share, size of economy or geographic location, which altogether reflects their level of ICT development (ITU 2014). Despite falling behind their more developed counterparts, ICT is no less important for the economic growth of the developing countries or regions. Taking into consideration other underlying determinants of economic growth, this paper attempts to empirically assess the impact of ICT on GDP growth across these different regions. The remaining sections of this paper are organized as follows: Sect. 20.2 explains the theoretical review relating to diffusion of ICT, Sect. 20.3 lays out the data and methodology adopted to carry out the study, while Sect. 20.4 discusses data analysis and interpretation of statistical findings obtained from the empirical analysis. Last but not least, Sect. 20.5 summarizes the entire study with relevant conclusions and appropriate recommendations.

20.2 Roger's Diffusion of Innovation Theory

Originated by Everett M. Rogers, the diffusion of innovation theory that describes the process of adopting new innovations remains a central theoretical model in investigating technology diffusion and adoption. Roger's theory involves categorizing members of social system based on their degree of innovation: innovators, early adopters, early majority, late majority and laggards, where each of their distribution follows a normal, bell-shaped pattern (Fig. 20.1).

Adopters within the same category are deemed to possess similar innovativeness, whose rate of adoption depends on 5 different attributes namely, relative advantage, compatibility, complexity, trialability and observability. For instance, innovators and early adopters are not only perceived to have higher relative advantage and lower complexity in understanding and using new technologies, but they also assume typical socioeconomic profiles such as being more educated, wealthier and having higher social prestige. Looking at the global scale, regions that are home to more digitized countries such as Europe and Asia are expected to fall among the innovators and early adopters categories, while countries that are mainly

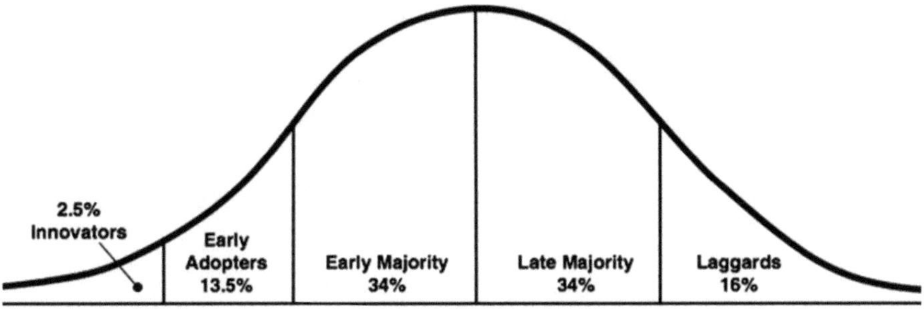

Fig. 20.1 *Source* Rogers, E.M. (2003), Diffusion of Innovation, 3rd ed.

made up of ICT end consumers such as Africa fall within the late majority and laggards categories. When there is widespread diffusion and proper usage of the new technology, only then its contribution to economic growth can be realized (Hall and Khan 2003; Sabu and Shaijumon 2014).

20.3 Data and Methodology

Solely sourced from World Development Indicators database (World Bank 2014), a panel dataset consisting of 149 countries on a 9-year period (2006 to 2014) is used, whereby the sample countries are further divided into five regions: Africa, America, Arab, Asia and Europe. The dependent variable is GDP growth (%) while the independent variables used to analyze the impact of ICT on GDP comprise of several ICT variables, namely fixed broadband subscriptions (per 100 people), fixed telephone subscriptions (per 100 people), mobile cellular subscriptions (per 100 people) and Internet users (per 100 people), as well as a set of control variables consisting of foreign direct investment (FDI) and population share.

20.3.1 Regression Model

To investigate the relationship between ICT and GDP, this study improvises the dynamic panel data model of Shiu and Lam (2008) by including a set of control variables, X_{it}.

$$GDP_{it} = \alpha_i + \sum_{m=1}^{M} \beta_m ICT_{i,t-m} + \sum_{m=1}^{M} \gamma_m GDP_{i,t-m} + \sum_{m=1}^{M} \delta_m X_{i,t-m} + \varphi_t + \mu_{it} \quad (20.1)$$

where *GDP* is GDP growth; *ICT* represents ICT variables as measured by fixed broadband subscriptions (FBB), fixed telephone subscriptions (FTEL), mobile cellular subscriptions (MOB) and Internet users (INTR); and X refers to control variables consisting of foreign direct investment (FDI) and population share (POP). This study employs the Arellano–Bond (AB) GMM estimator whereby model (1.0) will be estimated in its first-difference form as follows:

$$GDP_{it} - GDP_{i,t-1} = \alpha_i + \sum_{m=1}^{M} \beta_m \left(ICT_{i,t-m} - ICT_{i,t-m-1}\right) + \sum_{m=1}^{M} \gamma_m \left(GDP_{i,t-m} - GDP_{i,t-m-1}\right) + \sum_{m=1}^{M} \delta_m \left(X_{i,t-m} - X_{i,t-m-1}\right) + \left(\mu_{it} - \mu_{i,t-1}\right) \quad (20.2)$$

The regression model is estimated separately using both first-difference GMM and system GMM estimators. If, however, any of the regression models turn out to be unfit to GMM estimation, the pooled ordinary least squares (POLS) estimator will be employed instead. More specifically, the Newey–West method developed by Newey and West (1987) will be used to correct standard errors in the OLS estimator to make them robust and heteroscedasticity and autocorrelation consistent.

20.4 Empirical Findings

In the case of the African region as shown in Table 20.1, POLS was selected as the estimation method as the dataset for this region did not seem to fit GMM estimators. Lagged dependent variable in this case appears positive and highly significant in all model specifications. This indicates that sustaining high level of GDP growth can result in higher level of GDP growth in the following period. As far as the ICT variables are concerned, all of them appear insignificant in all model specifications. This result may suggest that the low technological diffusion and adoption in the region have yet to yield an impact on Africa's economic growth. Consistent with Roger's diffusion of innovation theory, Africa is made up of countries whose populations are mainly end consumers of technology and fall among the late majority and laggards categories (Kabanda 2011). FDI meanwhile, although positive, is not significant. POP on the other hand, entered with significant and positive values, implying that greater number of population leads to higher GDP growth in the region.

Unlike findings for the African region, ICT variables in the case of American region as revealed in Table 20.1 emerge significant in all model specifications. All ICT variables have significant relationship with GDP; however, only mobile cellular has negative coefficient.

The significance of fixed broadband in this context is also consistent with studies by Czernich et al. (2011) covering 25 OECD countries and by Zaballos and López-Rivas (2012) covering 26 Latin America and Caribbean countries. Fixed

Table 20.1 Estimation results for region Africa and America

Independent variable	Region							
	Africa				America			
	(1) POLS	(2) POLS	(3) POLS	(4) POLS	(1) GMM	(2) GMM	(3) GMM	(4) GMM
GDP_1	0.3052*** (0.0001)	0.3018*** (0.0001)	0.2968*** (0.0001)	0.3032*** (0.0001)	−0.2130*** (0.0170)	−0.4926*** (0.0001)	−0.4992*** (0.0001)	−0.3833*** (0.0001)
FBB	0.0111 (0.9750)				0.3308*** (0.0060)			
FTEL		−0.0339 (0.1590)				0.5659* (0.0700)		
MOB			−0.0061 (0.1700)				−0.0483** (0.0340)	
INTR				−0.0674 (0.2180)				0.2094* (0.0590)
FDI	0.0301 (0.1750)	0.0323 (0.1320)	0.0295 (0.1730)	0.0294 (0.1750)	−0.0746 (0.6020)	0.0308 (0.7720)	0.0854 (0.3200)	1.2850 (0.3160)
POP	7.04e-07*** (0.0040)	6.49e-07*** (0.0070)	6.71e-07*** (0.0040)	7.34e-07*** (0.0020)	8.58e-08 (0.7910)	−4.63e-07*** (0.041)	-1.86e-07 (0.5900)	4.16e-09 (0.8490)
Constant	2.6424*** (0.0001)	2.8305*** (0.0001)	3.0865*** (0.0001)	2.7604*** (0.0001)	14.4321 (0.1260)	32.3592*** (0.0010)	12.8092 (0.2000)	14.0735*** (0.0001)
No. of groups	40	40	40	40	31	31	31	31
BP LM test	34.62*** (0.0001)	32.15*** (0.0001)	33.43*** (0.0001)	33.54*** (0.0001)	48.14*** (0.0001)	33.11*** (0.0001)	61.82*** (0.0001)	48.31*** (0.0001)
Hausman test	2.62 (0.2698)	2.20 (0.3332)	1.98 (0.3709)	4.58 (0.1011)	16.24*** (0.0003)	22.56*** (0.0001)	22.40*** (0.0001)	18.02*** (0.0001)
AR(1)					−0.7403 [0.4591]	0.7999 [0.4238]	−1.5082 [0.1315]	−0.9342 [0.3502]

(continued)

Table 20.1 (continued)

Independent variable	Region							
	Africa				America			
	(1) POLS	(2) POLS	(3) POLS	(4) POLS	(1) GMM	(2) GMM	(3) GMM	(4) GMM
AR(2)					−1.3651 [0.1722]	−1.4436 [0.1489]	−0.7022 [0.4825]	−0.8167 [0.4141]
Sargan test					10.3871 (0.7334)	7.9500 (0.8919)	11.3868 (0.6554)	11.9879 (0.4467)

Notes Columns denoted by POLS and GMM represent pooled OLS estimator and first-difference GMM estimator or system GMM estimator, respectively. Values in parentheses are p-values, whereby ***, ** and * are significance at 1%, 5% and 10% level, respectively. T-statistics for first- and second-order correlation are indicated by AR(1) and AR(2), with their corresponding p-values presented in brackets

telephone meanwhile appears to record the highest coefficient value, which means that fixed telephone line yields the coefficient of the Internet is also consistent with study in Nordic countries by Amiri and Reif (2013), whose findings support the claim that the Internet directly drives economic growth in the region where these ICT powerhouses are.

Table 20.2 reports empirical results for the Arab region. Fixed telephone is the only ICT variable that appears significant out of the four ICT variables used in the regression. This evidence indicates the capability of this form of telecommunication technology in making great contributions to GDP growth, as compared to the other forms of ICT. The significance of fixed telephone in this study is consistent with study covering Arab Gulf countries by Nour (2011), whose findings also revealed that telecommunication variables have positive and more significant relationship with income (as measured by GDP per capita) as compared to the Internet. This result could be partly due to the fact that the Internet requires good literacy skills to be well used, considering that there is still a substantial amount of illiterates that make up the Arab population. Meanwhile, FDI also emerges significant and positive in all model specifications, thus rendering it as the only control variable to have substantial impact on GDP.

Estimation results for the Asian region as shown in Table 20.2 reveal a rather interesting set of evidence. All four ICT variables are significantly and positively correlated with GDP, except mobile cellular that surprisingly entered with a negative coefficient. The significance of all ICT variables in this study is consistent with study on South Asian Association for Regional Cooperation (SAARC) countries by Tripathi and Inani (2015), whose primary findings show positive and significant impact of teledensity (fixed telephone and mobile phones) on economic growth. This evidence is expected, since the region is made up of countries that are home to a number of ICT powerhouses such as Japan and Taiwan. Although POP is insignificant in most model specifications, FDI appears to have positive relationship and high significance in this case. These results not only imply that fixed broadband, fixed telephone, mobile cellular and the Internet play major roles in influencing the level of GDP in the Asia region, but also suggest that greater FDI positively promotes GDP growth in the region.

Table 20.3 meanwhile presents empirical findings for European region. Almost similar to results for the Asian region, most of the ICT variables have significant relationship with GDP growth, although fixed telephone and mobile cellular enter with unexpected negative values. The positive and significant effect of fixed broadband is also consistent with study by Koutroumpis (2009) whose results reveal a significant causal positive link between broadband penetration and economic growth. The high coefficient value of the Internet also implies that it is the most influential form of ICT in positively affecting GDP growth in the region.

Table 20.2 Estimation results for region Arab and Asia

Independent variable	Region							
	Arab				Asia			
	(1) POLS	(2) POLS	(3) POLS	(4) GMM	(1) GMM	(2) GMM	(3) POLS	(4) GMM
GDP_1	0.4362*** (0.0001)	0.4028*** (0.0010)	0.4359*** (0.0001)	−0.0724 (0.3950)	−0.2610*** (0.0001)	−0.3641*** (0.0001)	0.3554*** (0.0001)	−0.3068*** (0.0001)
FBB	0.0681 (0.1890)				0.2657** (0.0340)			
FTEL		0.0948* (0.0660)				0.4546*** (0.0001)		
MOB			0.0079 (0.1660)				−0.0136*** (0.0140)	
INTR				−0.0577 (0.6170)				0.1253*** (0.0001)
FDI	0.1567*** (0.0080)	0.1657*** (0.0030)	0.1623*** (0.0110)	0.1924*** (0.0030)	0.3629*** (0.0001)	0.3788*** (0.0001)	0.1787*** (0.0001)	0.2480*** (0.0001)
POP	−8.31e-08 (0.8490)	−1.94e-07 (0.6510)	−2.75e-07 (0.5230)	−7.35e-08 (0.8490)	3.04e-08 (0.1680)	4.61e-08 (0.1190)	1.62e-09*** (0.0001)	3.43e-08 (0.1580)
Constant	1.1787** (0.0250)	0.6481 (0.2920)	0.7733 (0.2790)	6.2863 (0.2910)	2.9396 (0.1510)	−15.4771*** (0.0001)	3.4470*** (0.0001)	4.2693* (0.0800)
No. of groups	16	16	16	16	41	41	41	41
BP LM test	35.13*** (0.0001)	30.48*** (0.0001)	33.71*** (0.0001)	30.12*** (0.0001)	66.38*** (0.0001)	50.08*** (0.0001)	83.76*** (0.0001)	74.12*** (0.0001)
Hausman test	1.96 (0.3744)	0.65 (0.7242)	3.77 (0.1517)	7.50** (0.0235)	5.36* (0.0686)	9.13*** (0.0104)	2.75 (0.2532)	4.74* (0.0936)
AR(1)				−2.2015** [0.0277]	−3.0095*** [0.0026]	−2.5004*** [0.0124]		−3.085*** [0.0020]

(continued)

Table 20.2 (continued)

Independent variable	Region							
	Arab				Asia			
	(1) POLS	(2) POLS	(3) POLS	(4) GMM	(1) GMM	(2) GMM	(3) POLS	(4) GMM
AR(2)				−0.6498 [0.5158]	−1.1431 [0.2530]	−0.1663 [0.8680]		−0.6039 [0.5459]
Sargan test				8.7355 (0.9989)	28.9837 (0.5701)	32.1561 (0.4092)		33.2830 (0.3567)

Notes Columns denoted by POLS and GMM represent pooled OLS estimator and first-difference GMM estimator or system GMM estimator, respectively. Values in parentheses are p-values, whereby ***, ** and * are significance at 1%, 5% and 10% level, respectively. T-statistics for first- and second-order correlation are indicated by AR(1) and AR(2), with their corresponding p-values presented in brackets

Table 20.3 Estimation results for region Europe

Independent variable	Region			
	Europe			
	(1) GMM	(2) POLS	(3) POLS	(4) GMM
GDP_1	−0.2240*** (0.0001)	0.3325*** (0.0001)	0.3402*** (0.0001)	−0.2535*** (0.0001)
FBB	0.2304*** (0.0070)			
FTEL		−0.0397*** (0.0010)		
MOB			−0.0153 (0.1170)	
INTR				0.2580*** (0.0001)
FDI	−0.0172*** (0.0001)	0.0189** (0.0490)	0.0126 (0.1310)	−0.0084** (0.0510)
POP	−5.86e-07** (0.0290)	2.18e-09 (0.7000)	1.44e-09 (0.8000)	−3.86e-08 (0.1890)
Constant	17.6234*** (0.0010)	2.1017*** (0.0001)	2.5138** (0.0310)	4.7793** (0.0500)
No. of groups	44	44	44	44
BP LM test	7.79*** (0.0053)	3.51* (0.0611)	15.45*** (0.0001)	11.16*** (0.0008)
Hausman test	15.44*** (0.0004)	2.65 (0.2662)	4.50 (0.1054)	16.92*** (0.0002)
AR(1)	−0.7944 [0.4270]			−1.4739 [0.1405]
AR(2)	0.5416 [0.5881]			1.1035 [0.2698]
Sargan test	40.1060 (0.1538)			23.0178 (0.4007)

Notes Columns denoted by POLS and GMM represent pooled OLS estimator and first-difference GMM estimator or system GMM estimator, respectively. Values in parentheses are p-values, whereby ***, ** and * are significance at 1%, 5% and 10% level, respectively. T-statistics for first- and second-order correlation are indicated by AR(1) and AR(2), with their corresponding p-values presented in brackets

20.5 Conclusion and Recommendation

This paper examines the contribution of ICT on economic growth for 149 countries in 5 different regions: Africa, America, Arab, Asia and Europe during the 2006–2014 period. Using pooled OLS and GMM estimation methods, empirical findings reveal that ICT brings significant contributions to economic growth, although each region shows varying degree of importance. The reason behind insignificance of fixed broadband in certain regions may be attributable to the relatively weak competition in the market and also the fact that mobile broadband scores better in terms of price and flexibility. There is limited evidence on whether or not the African region would benefit from diffusion of ICT; nevertheless, fixed broadband appears promising for its future economic progress. Likewise, the positive values of fixed telephone and mobile cellular in the Arab region reflects the importance of telecommunication networks in the region despite fixed telephone being the only significant ICT variable. America, Asia and Europe show strong link between all forms of ICT and their regional economic growths, with mobile cellular possibly reaching market saturation as reflected by its small coefficient values.

All in all, this study found that significant impacts of ICT are more evident for the highly ICT-intensive regions such as America, Asia and Europe, but remains unclear for regions with low levels of ICT diffusion and adoption such as Africa and Arab. Corresponding well with Roger's diffusion of innovation theory as well as studies by Hall and Khan (2003) and Sabu and Shaijumon (2014), this finding implies that regions such as Africa and Arab may have yet to adopt a holistic approach to access and use ICT to its fullest extent possible, unlike their more developed counterparts such as America, Asia and Europe. This could be due to the fact that there are still a number of supply- and demand-side barriers that inhibit ICT adoption in the less privileged regions. Maximizing the impact of ICT heavily relies on ICT skills; therefore, it is recommended that future researchers should also look at the effect of literacy or educational attainment on ICT. This will help to uncover the link between ICT and education as well as to find out whether education plays any significant role in channeling the impact of ICT to economic growth.

References

Amiri, S., & Reif, B. (2013). Internet penetration and its correlation to gross domestic product: An analysis of the Nordic Countries. *International Journal of Business, Humanities and Technology, 3*(2), 50–60.

Bakay, A., Okafor, C. E., & Ujah, N. U. (2010). Factors explaining ICT diffusion: Case study of selected Latin American Countries. *The International Journal on Advances in ICT for Emerging Regions, 3*(2), 25–33.

Czernich, N., Falck, O., Kretschmer, T., & Woessman, L. (2011). Broadband infrastructure and economic growth. *The Economic Journal, 121,* 505–532.

Di Carlo, C., & Santarelli, E. (2010). Contribution of ICT to economic growth in Italy: Input Output analysis. *Mondo Digitale, 1,* 3–8.

Hall, B. H., & Khan, B. (2003). Adoption of new technology. *NBER Working Paper* 9730, NBER, Cambridge, MA.

International Telecommunication Union. (2014). Measuring the Information Society Report. Place des Nations CH-1211 Geneva, Switzerland.

Kabanda, G. (2011). Impact of information and communication technologies (ICTs) on millennium development goals (MDGs): Context for diffusion and adoption of ICT innovations in East and Southern Africa. *Journal of African Studies and Development, 3*(8), 154–170.

Koutrompis, P. (2009). The economic impact of broadband on growth: A simultaneous approach. *Telecommunications Policy, 33*(9), 471–485.

Newey, W. K., & West, K. D. (1987). A simple, positive semi-definite, heteroskedasticity and autocorrelation consistent covariance matrix. *Econometrica, 55,* 703–708.
Nour, S. (2011). The use and economic impacts of ICT at the macro–micro levels in the Arab Gulf countries. MERIT Working Papers Maastricht Economic and Social Research Institute on Innovation and Technology, UNU, 2011–059.
Rogers, E. M. (2003). *Diffusion of innovations*. New York: Free Press.
Sabu, M., & Shaijumon, C. S. (2014). Socio-economic impact of information and communication technology: A case study of Kerala marine fisheries sector. *International Journal of Information Dissemination and Technology, 4*(2), 124–129.
Shiu, A., & Lam, P. L. (2008). Causal relationship between telecommunications and economic growth: A study of 105 countries. *Paper presented at the 17th Biennial Conference of the International Telecommunications Society*. Montreal.
Tripathi, M., & Inani, S. K. (2015). Impact of Information Communication Technology on Economic Growth: Empirical Evidence from SAARC Countries.
World Bank. (2014). *World Development Indicators*. Washington, D.C.: World Bank.
Zaballos, A. G., & López-Rivas, R. (2012). Socioeconomic Impact of Broadband in Latin American and Caribbean Countries. Inter-American Development Bank.

Chapter 21
The Mediating Role of Emotional Exhaustion on the Relationship Between Job Factors and Turnover Intention Among Service Employees

Abdul Kadir Othman, Mohd Zulkifli Abdullah, Mutiiah Mohamad, Farahannida Ahmad, Sulaiha Awang Rozalli and Nursyahida Ashikin Nor Izlanin

Abstract Service employees are expected to portray a positive image in dealing with their day-to-day job. This image will be the first impression of customers or clients towards the services offered. A positive image can only be shown if the employees are happy with their job. In delivering services required by the customers, emotional exhaustion experienced by service employees is not inevitable and if it is not properly managed, it will lead to turnover intention. The objective of the study is to investigate the mediating role of emotional exhaustion on the relationship between job factors and turnover intention among service employees. Analysing 108 data collected from employees using a mediated regression analysis reveals that the emotional exhaustion did not have any mediation effect on the relationship between job factors (work balance, role conflict, role clarity and emotional labour) and turnover intention. The results indicate that employees will leave the organisation if there is low work life balance, high role conflict, low role clarity and low emotional labour. The implications of the study are further discussed in the paper.

Keywords Emotional exhaustion · Job factors · Turnover intention

A.K. Othman · M.Z. Abdullah (✉)
Faculty of Business and Management, Universiti Teknologi MARA Puncak Alam, 42300 Puncak Alam, Selangor, Malaysia
e-mail: mohdzulkifli_aq@yahoo.com

M. Mohamad · F. Ahmad · S.A. Rozalli · N.A.N. Izlanin
Faculty of Business and Management, Universiti Teknologi MARA Dungun, Dungun, Terengganu, Malaysia

F. Noordin et al. (eds.), *Proceedings of the 2nd Advances in Business Research International Conference*, https://doi.org/10.1007/978-981-10-6053-3_21

21.1 Introduction

Turnover intention is a serious issue currently faced by the organisations in which employees leave the organisation or organisation fired them. Employee turnover intention or employee intention to stay is crucial because employees who feel fulfilled and are happy with their job tend to perform significantly better than those who are not in ensuring customer satisfaction and customer loyal. In order to minimise the turnover intention among the front liners, the organisation needs to be clear on the employees' perception through emotional display and their job dimensions.

Alexander-Hamwi et al. (2011) in investigating the relationship between emotional exhaustion and perceived organisational support found that emotional exhaustion has been identified as one of the factors that lead to employee turnover intention. Brand (2007) stated, an emotionally exhausted person is characterised by a depletion of emotional energy and a feeling that one's emotional resources are inadequate to deal with the situation at hand. Previous study by Saeed et al. (2014) showed the effects of these five variables on turnover intention: job satisfaction, organisational commitment, leader membership exchange (LMX), emotional intelligence and job performance. Some researchers mentioned that the effect of surface acting on organisational and employee criteria indicates a wide range of negative outcomes, such as lower job satisfaction, higher levels of emotional exhaustion, reduced motivation and increased turnover intention (Bono and Vey 2005; Grandey 2003; Scott and Barnes 2011; Wang and Groth 2014). A different study conducted by Jyoti et al. (2015) examined the mediating effect of emotional exhaustion (EE) on the relationship between high-performance human resource practices (HPHRPs) and intention to leave (ITL) in the education sector. The study revealed that high-performance human resource practices have negative effect on intention to leave; it is partially mediated by emotional exhaustion. It means that when the organisation practices high performing HR, teachers feel less exhausted and they will remain with the organisation. In line with these findings, Long and Perumal (2014) and Zimmerman revealed that there is a negative relationship between employees' job performance management and their intention to quit. According to study conducted by Karatepe (2013), it shows that emotional exhaustion reduces job embeddedness and impedes high-quality performance in service delivery process.

Although several studies have been conducted on the influence of emotional exhaustion on turnover intention, most of the common highlighted variables were job satisfaction, job performance, organisational commitment, leader membership exchange (LMX) and emotional intelligence. However, a study conducted by Kraemer and Gouthier (2014) stated that organisational pride significantly decreases employee turnover and emotional exhaustion.

In order to generalise the findings, this research was conducted involving service personnel from various sectors instead of focusing on one function or perspective only. The main objective of the study was to investigate the relationship between emotional exhaustion and turnover intention among employees. The study was also conducted to verify the mediation role of emotional exhaustion on the relationship between job factors such as work life balance, role conflict, role clarity and emotional labour on the turnover intention among respondents.

The following hypotheses for this study are highlighted:

H_1 Emotional exhaustion mediates the relationship between work life balance and turnover intention among service employees.

H_2 Emotional exhaustion mediates the relationship between role conflict and turnover intention among service employees.

H_3 Emotional exhaustion mediates the relationship between role clarity and turnover intention among service employees.

H_4 Emotional exhaustion mediates the relationship between emotional labour and turnover intention among service employees.

21.2 Methodology

The study adopted a correlational research design in describing the relationship between the studied variables. The sampling frame is based on a list of service employees working in a few business companies, namely banking, telecommunications, health care and others (oil and gas, property and maintenance services and IT services companies) in Terengganu and Kelantan, Malaysia. A total of 156 sets of questionnaire were distributed to the respective respondents. A total of 108 sets of the questionnaire were returned, recording the return rate of 66.7%. The questionnaire was adapted from the established questionnaire, and the items were modified in order to get the required responses to the research questions (Alexander-Hamwi et al. 2011; Hur et al. 2015). The questionnaire utilised closed-ended questions with a fixed range of possible answers using a five-point Likert scale with the following values; 1 = strongly disagree, 2 = disagree, 3 = uncertain, 4 = agree and 5 = strongly agree.

The collected data were analysed using the statistical software, i.e. SPSS Version 21. The study used both descriptive statistics (mean and standard deviation) and inferential statistics (a multiple regression analysis). Besides, the hierarchical multiple regression (also known as sequential regression) analysis was used to test the mediating roles of emotional exhaustion on the relationship between job factors and turnover intention among the respondents.

21.3 Findings

21.3.1 *Profile of Respondents*

Describing the participants involved in the study, 71 respondents or 64.5% are male and 39 respondents' or 35.5% are female. Their age is categorised into three groups with 20 of them or 18.2% aged below 25 years old, 69 respondents or 62.7% aged between 25 and 39 years old and 21 of them or 19.1% aged between 40 and 55 years old.

Regarding the participants' working experience, majority of them (31 respondents or 28.2%) had been working with the company for 2 to 5 years. A total of 28 respondents or 25.5% had more than 10 years of working experience, and 26 respondents or 23.6% had 6 to 10 years of experience. The remaining respondents (25 of them or 22.7%) had less than 2 years of working experience. The respondents participating in this study came from various sectors. A total of 70 respondents or 63.6% did not disclose in which sector they were working, 23 respondents or 20.9% were from health care sector, 13 respondents or 11.8% came from telecommunication sector. The remaining respondents (4 respondents or 3.6%) are from banking sector. There is a fair representation of respondents according to their backgrounds.

21.3.2 *Correlation Analysis, Reliability Analysis, Mean and Standard Deviation*

The results of correlation analysis reveal that the independent variables, which consist of work life balance, role conflict, role clarity and emotional labour, are highly correlated with each other with r values ranging from −0.383 ($p < 0.01$) to 0.287 ($p < 0.01$), indicating that the independent variables are interrelated with each other (convergent validity). The moderating variable or emotional exhaustion is highly correlated with almost all independent variables with r values between −0.244 ($p < 0.01$) and −0.556 ($p < 0.01$), signifying concurrent validity of the constructs. Emotional exhaustion is not significantly correlated with emotional labour ($r = 0.073$, $p > 0.05$). Besides, emotional exhaustion is also moderately correlated with the dependent variable or turnover intention with r value of 0.531 ($p < 0.01$), indicating concurrent validity. Furthermore, all independent variables and the mediating variable are significantly correlated with the dependent variable with r values ranging from −0.465 ($p < 0.01$) to 0.601($p < 0.01$). These correlation values indicate potential mediating effect of emotional exhaustion on the relationship between the independent variables and the dependent variable (Table 21.1).

Table 21.1 Results of correlation analysis, reliability analysis and mean and standard deviation

No	Variables	Mean	SD	1	2	3	4	5	6
1	work life balance	3.27	1.13	(0.951)					
2	Role conflict	2.85	0.68	−0.370**	(0.904)				
3	Role clarity	3.61	0.65	0.032	−0.364**	(0.895)			
4	Emotional labour	2.91	1.03	−0.383**	0.287**	−0.098	(0.961)		
5	Emotional exhaustion	2.50	0.76	−0.244**	0.505**	−0.556**	0.073	(0.861)	
6	Turnover intention	2.42	0.87	−0.356**	0.601**	−0.465**	0.482**	0.531**	(0.877)

Notes ** Correlation is significant at the 0.01 level (1-tailed); Cronbach's alphas are along the diagonal in the parentheses; N = 110

Table 21.2 Results of regression analysis (emotional exhaustion as the dependent variable)

Variables	Standardised beta values
work life balance	−0.183*
Role conflict	0.357**
Role clarity	−0.459**
Emotional labour	−0.174*
R	0.701
R^2	0.492
Adjusted R^2	0.472
F values	25.184
Sig. F values	0.000
Durbin-Watson	1.970

21.3.3 Results of Regression Analysis

A multiple regression analysis was conducted with employee emotional exhaustion serving as the dependent variable. The R squared of 0.492 indicates that 49.2% of the variance in the model is explained by the independent variables. The regression model is significant ($F(4, 104) = 25.184$, $p = 0.000$). Durbin-Watson of 1.970 signifies that there is no problem of autocorrelation in the model. Looking at the contribution of each independent variable to explaining the dependent variable or employee emotional exhaustion, all four factors are significant to predict emotional exhaustion: work life balance ($\beta = -0.183$, $p < 0.01$), role conflict ($\beta = 0.357$, $p < 0.01$), role clarity ($\beta = -0.459$, $p < 0.01$) and emotional labour ($\beta = -0.174$, $p > 0.05$) (Table 21.2).

21.3.4 Results of Hierarchical Regression Analysis

A hierarchical regression analysis was conducted to assess the mediating role of emotional exhaustion on the relationship between job factors and turnover intention among front-line employees. The first step of the regression model was to run the analysis without emotional exhaustion, and in the next step, the regression analysis was conducted with the inclusion of emotional exhaustion in the model. The results of the first model show the R squared of 0.581 denoting 58.1% of the variance explained. The model is significant ($F(4, 104) = 36.102$, $p = 0.000$) with Durbin-Watson value of 2.034 indicating the absence of autocorrelation problem. The second model of regression analysis with the inclusion of emotional exhaustion presents an increase in R squared to be 0.593 indicating 59.3% of variance explained. The model is also significant ($F(4, 104) = 29.990$, $p = 0.000$). Pertaining to the relationship between the mediator and the dependent variable, emotional exhaustion is not significant to predict turnover intention ($\beta = 0.150$, $p < 0.01$) (Table 21.3).

From the first model, three of independent variables are significant to influence turnover intention among front-line employees: role conflict ($\beta = 0.407$, $p < 0.01$), role clarity ($\beta = -0.308$, $p < 0.01$) and emotional labour ($\beta = 0.271$, $p < 0.01$). The remaining factor, work life balance ($\beta = -0.112$, $p > 0.05$), is not significant.

Table 21.3 Results of hierarchical regression analysis (turnover intention as the dependent variable and emotional exhaustion as the mediating variable)

Variables	Standardised beta values without mediator	Standardised beta values with mediator	Remarks
work life balance	−0.112	−0.084	No mediation effect
Role conflict	0.407**	0.354**	No mediation effect
Role clarity	−0.308**	−0.239**	No mediation effect
Emotional labour	0.271**	0.297**	No mediation effect
Emotional exhaustion		0.150	Mediator is not significant
R	0.762	0.770	
R^2	0.581	0.593	
Adjusted R^2	0.565	0.573	
F value	36.102	29.990	
Sig. F value	0.000	0.000	
Durbin-Watson	2.034	2.034	

With the inclusion of emotional exhaustion in the regression model, there is a no significant reduction in β values as a result; there is no mediation effect of emotional exhaustion on the relationship between job factors and turnover intention.

21.4 Discussion

The findings of the present study indicate that turnover intention among service employees is directly influenced by the job factors of work life balance, emotional labour, role conflict and role clarity. The findings also indicate that emotional exhaustion does not mediate the relationship between all of the independent variables (work life balance, role conflict, role clarity and emotional labour) and turnover intention.

Moreover, the findings are different from those discovered by Baba et al. (2009) where individuals who experience high emotional exhaustion are more likely to see their individual performance weakens and their motivation to respond to job demands decreases, thereby provoking higher levels of emotional exhaustion and consequently affecting performance. Employees experiencing emotional exhaustion may evoke a turnover reaction to cope with the status (Yavas et al. 2008). Thus, employees experiencing high level of emotional exhaustion should be more likely to leave their organisation.

The positive relationship between work–family conflict and emotional exhaustion was expected due to their significant relationship in previous research. However, the result achieved in this research is different compared to them. The previous researchers came up with the exertion that if a salesperson cannot satisfy the needs of his/her job without sacrificing family needs or vice versa, it is likely to create an emotionally charged situation that can be stressful and exhausting. Often, a salesperson may fail to meet the needs of both their family and their job, likely due to a lack of resources to adequately handle both situations creating a tense and possibly deteriorating the situation on both ends (Greenhaus and Beutell 1985). The problem with meeting demands of work might affect performance at work, causing the salesperson to become detached, less driven and less concerned for customers and their needs. This will be reflected in decreased productivity. Decreased productivity on the job will create an entirely different category of stressors. The salesperson already lacks the adequate cognitive and physical resources to deal with their existing stress. Additional stress can begin to influence his/her family life.

Based on the research done by Alexander-Hamwi et al. (2011), their finding shows that work–family conflict and role conflict both significantly affect emotional exhaustion. Work–family conflict was also found to influence the relationship between perceived organisational support and emotional exhaustion. According to the research done by Goussinsky (2011), it shows that emotional dissonance is significantly associated with a decreased sense of well-being, even after controlling for negative disposition. The results also confirm that customer aggression relates to job-induced tension through its influence on emotional dissonance, and that emotional dissonance is less likely to increase job-induced tension and emotional exhaustion when the level of job autonomy is high.

Furthermore, previous research has examined the emotional exhaustion, one of the three dimensions of burnout that is considered the core driver of the burnout construct (Maslach and Jackson 1981). Excessive psychological and emotional demands on salespeople lead to emotional exhaustion (Jackson et al. 1986). In the sales profession, emotional exhaustion is a frequent occurrence (Singh et al. 1994). Salespeople who experience emotional exhaustion tend to blame it on their firm (Maslach and Jackson 1981). They become less open-minded, less driven and more apathetic (Alexander-Hamwi et al. 2011). Their orientation towards customer satisfaction and long-term relationship building suffers. This ultimately leads to the salesperson becoming more dissatisfied with their job, and eventually he/she will leave his/her position (Singh et al. 1994). A great deal of research has examined the effect that role conflict has on emotional exhaustion (Singh et al. 1994). Boles et al. (1997) found that a direct, positive relationship exists between role conflict and emotional exhaustion. Elloy et al. (2001) found the same result in their investigation of self-managed work teams. The relationship was also found in nurses (Gil-Monte et al. 1993) and lawyers (Jackson et al. 2006).

For the final findings, it clearly indicates that emotional exhaustion is not having mediation effects on the relationship between job factors and turnover intention among service employees. There are numbers of reasons contributed to the findings. Based on the demographic information of this study, it is noted that the percentage of service employees who have more than 2 years of experience is 77 and 82% are above 25 years old. At this stage, the employees are expected to be well versed in managing the service operations and matured in delivering their responsibility. Based on the communication with the respondents, they are well prepared with the challenges in managing their work because their employers' involvement and support to them. This is supported by a study done by Karatepe (2015) on service employees, who receive sufficient support from the organisation high in positive affectivity, intrinsically motivated and self-efficacious at elevated levels. These employees experience low levels of emotional exhaustion and turnover intentions and display high levels of extra-role customer service behaviours. The researcher found out that these employees are also able to handle problems arising from emotional exhaustion. There is also the possibility to create a good record of treatment by the organisation through support provided to employees.

21.5 Conclusion

Every service organisation is determined to deliver the best services to their customers. The service people in these organisations are the face of their employers. Based on the findings of the present study, it clearly indicates that the mediating role of emotional exhaustion does not have mediation effects on the relationship between job factors and turnover intention among the service employees. This finding provides insights of different result compared to previous research done and provides dissimilar perspectives of turnover intention among service employees.

21.5.1 Managerial Implications

The findings indicate that emotional exhaustion is not having mediation effects on the relationship between job factors and turnover intention among service employees. Although it is not a significant mediator, it is still important for service organisations to be proactive in reducing the consequences of emotional exhaustion. The nature of the service employees and their working environment inherently lead to a great deal of emotional exhaustion. The firm should foster an environment of open communication among sales managers and between sales managers and salespeople so that cohesiveness and synergy can be created among themselves. The introduction of effective employee retention policies and practices may prevent employees from leaving their jobs. The service organisations can also practice a subtle measure to enhance employees' feelings of control and readiness to face any situation whenever they deal with customers through training and intervention programmes for self-development. The employees should also be given clear job description so that they are able to perform their job effectively. With these measures in place, the service organisations are likely to mitigate the turnover rates of service employees in today's challenging service sector.

21.5.2 Suggestions for Future Research

This study was conducted in several service organisations, i.e. banking, telecommunications, health care and others (oil and gas, property and maintenance services and IT services companies). However, the questionnaire was done in English without the Malay translation. Based on the researchers' observation, the service employees are more interested or favour to answer the questionnaire in Malay. Future studies should consider bilingual questionnaire to gauge or attract service employees to provide genuine answers. This will eventually increase the number of feedback to be shared. Future studies are also recommended to get bigger data so that structural equation modelling (SEM) can be applied in analysing the mediating effect of employee engagement. SEM is the most practical analysis when testing the mediating effect of a variable on certain relationships.

References

Alexander-Hamwi, G., Rutherford, B. N., & Boles, J. S. (2011). Reducing emotional exhaustion and increasing organizational support. *Journal of Business and Industrial Marketing, 26*(1), 4–13.

Baba, V. V., Tourigny, L., Wang, X., & Liu, W. (2009). Proactive personality and work performance in China: The moderating effects of emotional exhaustion and perceived safety climate. *Canadian Journal of Administrative Sciences/Revue Canadienne des Sciences de l'Administration, 26*(1), 23–37.

Boles, J. S., Johnston, M. W., & Hair Jr, J. F. (1997). Role stress, workfamily conflict and emotional exhaustion: Inter-relationships and effects on some work-related consequences. *Journal of Personal Selling and Sales Management, 17*(1), 17–28.

Bono, J. E., & Vey, M. A. (2005). Toward understanding emotional management at work: A quantitative review of emotional labor research.

Brand, T. (2007). *An exploration of the relationship between burnout, occupational stress and emotional intelligence in the nursing industry.* Unpublished master‘s thesis, Stellenbosch University.

Elloy, D. F., Terpening, W., & Kohls, J. (2001). A causal model of burnout among self-managed work team members. *The Journal of Psychology, 135*(3), 321–334.

Gil-Monte, P. R., Valcaárcel, P., & Zornoza, A. (1993). Role stress: Burnout antecedent in nursing professionals. *The European Work and Organizational Psychologist, 3*(3), 217–227.

Goussinsky, R. (2011). Customer aggression, emotional dissonance and employees' well-being. *International Journal of Quality and Service Sciences, 3*(3), 248–266.

Grandey, A. A. (2003). When "the show must go on": Surface acting and deep acting as determinants of emotional exhaustion and peer-rated service delivery. *Academy of Management Journal, 46*(1), 86–96.

Greenhaus, J. H., & Beutell, N. J. (1985). Sources of conflict between work and family roles. *Academy of Management Review, 10*(1), 76–88.

Hur, W. M., Moon, T. W., & Han, S. J. (2015). The effect of customer incivility on service employees' customer orientation through double-mediation of surface acting and emotional exhaustion. *Journal of Service Theory and Practice, 25*(4), 394–413.

Jackson, S. E., Schwab, R. L., & Schuler, R. S. (1986). Toward an understanding of the burnout phenomenon. *Journal of Applied Psychology, 71*(4), 630.

Jackson, D. W., Jr., Hollmann, T., & Gallan, A. S. (2006). Examining career development programs for the sales force. *Journal of Business & Industrial Marketing, 21*(5), 291–299.

Jyoti, J., Rani, R., & Gandotra, R. (2015). The impact of bundled high performance human resource practices on intention to leave: Mediating role of emotional exhaustion. *International Journal of Educational Management, 29*(4), 431–460.

Karatepe, O. M. (2013). High-performance work practices and hotel employee performance: The mediation of work engagement. *International Journal of Hospitality Management, 32*, 132–140.

Karatepe, O. M. (2015). Do personal resources mediate the effect of perceived organizational support on emotional exhaustion and job outcomes? *International Journal of Contemporary Hospitality Management, 27*(1), 4–26.

Kraemer, T., & HJ Gouthier, M. (2014). How organizational pride and emotional exhaustion explain turnover intentions in call centers: A multi-group analysis with gender and organizational tenure. *Journal of Service Management, 25*(1), 125–148.

Long, C. S., & Perumal, P. (2014). Examining the impact of human resource management practices on employees turnover intention. *International Journal of Business and society, 15*(1), 111.

Maslach, C., & Jackson, S. E. (1981). The measurement of experienced burnout. *Journal of organizational behavior, 2*(2), 99–113.

Saeed, I., Waseem, M., Sikander, S., & Rizwan, M. (2014). The relationship of Turnover intention with job satisfaction, job performance, Leader member exchange, Emotional intelligence and organizational commitment. *International Journal of Learning and Development, 4*(2), 242–256.

Scott, B. A., & Barnes, C. M. (2011). A multilevel field investigation of emotional labor, affect, work withdrawal, and gender. *Academy of Management Journal, 54*(1), 116–136.

Singh, J., Goolsby, J. R., & Rhoads, G. K. (1994). Behavioral and psychological consequences of boundary spanning burnout for customer service representatives. *Journal of Marketing Research,* 558–569.

Wang, K. L., & Groth, M. (2014). Buffering the negative effects of employee surface acting: The moderating role of employee–customer relationship strength and personalized services. *Journal of Applied Psychology, 99*(2), 341.

Yavas, U., Babakus, E., & Karatepe, O. M. (2008). Attitudinal and behavioral consequences of work-family conflict and family-work conflict: does gender matter? *International Journal of Service Industry Management, 19*(1), 7–31.

Chapter 22
Factors Influencing the Loyalty of Employee in Relation to Organizational Climate from an Islamic Perspective

Zurina Abd Ghani, Junaidah Hashim and Rozailin Abdul Rahman

Abstract The main purpose of this paper is to understand the determinants of loyalty in relation to organizational climate from an Islamic perspective. The data were collected among the 172 Muslim managers and 509 Muslim employees in various industries, public and private sectors. The respondents of 172 Muslim managers are HR managers in particular. The study used measurement adopted from previous study. The implications of the study are discussed. Findings of this study could be used by HR practitioners and scholars in building management concerns and strategic plan for a better HRD systems and practices from the Islamic point of views.

Keywords Human resource development · Organizational climate · Loyalty Islamic perspective

22.1 Introduction

You have to be loved by your employee, to become the best employer or the employer of choice. The late Steve Jobs said "*The only way to do great work is to love what you do*". Question is how you want to achieve that kind of self-fulfilling motivational factor in your employee in a holistic environment and/or organization, which eventually lead to their loyalty. Their loyalty which translated in their length of service or their hard work to ensure assignments was accomplished successfully and loyalty that reflects in the way their face lightened up to the mentioned of their organization's name. HR development commitment is one of the most important

Z. Abd Ghani (✉) · J. Hashim · R. Abdul Rahman
Faculty of Economics and Management Sciences, IIUM, Gombak, Malaysia
e-mail: zag@iium.edu.my

J. Hashim
e-mail: junaidahh@iium.edu.my

R. Abdul Rahman
e-mail: rozailin@iium.edu.my

F. Noordin et al. (eds.), *Proceedings of the 2nd Advances in Business Research International Conference*, https://doi.org/10.1007/978-981-10-6053-3_22

elements to ensure employees' satisfaction. Most, if not all, organizations strive hard and invested huge amount of capital to ensure its long-term sustainability. People from all levels are the most important asset in any organization. The term "human resource development" was first used by Harbison and Myers (1964) in the context of human capital theory. Both were economists and believed that HRD was important for national development. Schultz's (1961) human capital theory suggested that organizations receive economic value from their employees' knowledge, skills, competencies and experience and that human capital can be increased by training and education (Carbery and Cross 2015). Hashim (2010) believed that since Islam considers work as an essential element of man's success in his life; thus, Islam does not only encourage individuals to work, but also motivate them to seek perfection and excellence in all that they do. In this regard, workers should work with full capacity and commitment to achieve excellence and success for themselves as well as for the society, and more importantly for the life in the Hereafter (Yousef et al. 2001).

It is undeniable that the importance of investing for a proper human resource (HR) department and managers has yet to become one of the major priorities of many organizations. This is supported by Sikula (2001), which emphasized that unfortunately, large majority of organizations have yet to recognize the strategic importance of HR and HR people have yet to be recognized as partners in the strategic planning process. While in the new economy, human capital is the foundation of values creation, this most important asset is poorly understood and poorly managed (Norton 2001). Hence, this paper attempts to provide more information and adding to the inventory of studies conducted on issues regarding HR and particularly HRD and how it is related to organizational climate and its effects on Muslim employees' loyalty. In addition to that, this study included the Islamic perspectives on how HRD factors, for example, trainings, employers' *Ehsan*, can improve individual not only for the betterment of the organizations but the most vital part was for the employee themselves in the long run.

22.2 HRD and Organizational Climate

HRD practices from multiples researches conducted previously showed a positive relation with organizational climate and work environment. Central to most, if not all, models of organizational behavior are perceptions of the work environment, referred to generally as "organizational climate" (Rousseau 1988). Primarily understood as an intervening variable between the context of an organization and the behavior of its members, and attempting to understand how employees experience their organizations, the concept has inspired many descriptions and operationalization (Patterson et al. 2005). The dominant approach conceptualizes organizational climate as employees' shared perceptions of organizational events, practices, and procedures. These perceptions are assumed to be primarily descriptive rather than affective or evaluative (Schneider and Reichers 1983).

However, more recent work contradicts this view, suggesting strong evaluative or affective components (Patterson et al. 2004). At the individual level of analysis, referred to as "psychological climate," these perceptions represent how work environments are cognitively appraised and represented in terms of their meaning and significance for individual employees in organizations (James and Jones 1974). Organizational climate has been linked to various outcomes affecting both the employees and management in an organization which includes employees' job satisfaction, especially in terms of loyalty toward the organization which is the main focus of the current research. Research has suggested that climate perceptions are associated with a variety of outcomes at the individual, group, and organizational levels. These include leader behavior, turnover intentions (Rosseau 1988; Rentsch 1990), job satisfaction (Mathieu et al. 1993), individual job performance (Brown and Leigh 1996), and organizational performance (Patterson et al. 2004).

A study by Hassan et al. (2006) examined the contribution of HRD systems and practices on HRD climate, and quality orientation. The results indicated that employees' satisfaction with human resource development climate was predicted by learning and training system, employee development system (such as mentoring and coaching), action research, reward and recognition system, and information system (related to internal changes within the organization, technology, company policy, etc.). Therefore, it is obvious that the climate of an organization to some extent is dependent on the type HRD practices applied in order to determine the organizational values, norms and overall climate. The significance between the relation of HRD practices and organizational climate is explained after further examination in which HRD climate involving work values such as openness, trust, delegation and decentralization, quality orientation, etc., system of reward and recognition, quality of organizational communication, and empowerment of employees amply demonstrate that successful organizations have gone a long way to bring revolutionary changes in their HR systems and practices (Zairi 1998). Thus, it can be seen that a successful and productive organizational climate could be ensured through a proper HRD planning with a strong commitment from the top management.

22.3 Employees' Loyalty

Employees' loyalty or organizational commitment in particular as discussed by Salem and Syed Agil (2012), refers organizational commitment as the relative strength of an employee's attachment or involvement with the organization where he or she is employed, and also organizational commitment is important because committed employees are less likely to leave for another job and are more likely to perform at higher levels. In short, the incorporation of HRD from the Islamic practices into organizational climate and its effect and influence on loyalty is the main focus of this particular study. The outcomes would provide explanation on the relationship and connection of how organizational climates with Islamic influence

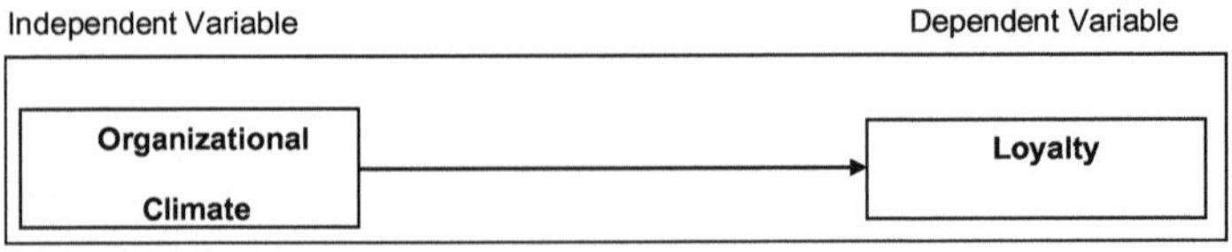

Fig. 22.1 Research framework

affecting commitment and loyalty among employees and retention of staff for organizations in general.

This study is significant in order to provide new perspectives and additional knowledge on HR and Islamic practices impact on organizational climate which contribute to loyalty and organizational commitment among employees. This will benefit the organization financially in the long run by reducing cost from investing on new recruitment and basic trainings. Instead, organization could invest more on other important organizational functions such as employees benefits and welfare, research and development, advance training modules based on relevant competencies needed, employees' development system to enhance and boost current employees' skills of whom from intermediate and advance level, and hence increased productivity as the ultimate goal.

Theoretical Framework

See (Fig. 22.1).

22.4 Methodology

22.4.1 Sample and Data Collection

The population of this study constitutes the different industries in Malaysia where Muslim managers and employees were attached. These industries include Advertising, Biotechnology/Biomedical, Contractors/Construction, Consumer, products/retail/wholesale, Consulting, Education, Engineering/Architecture, Entertainment, Finance/Banking/Accounting, Food and Beverages, Government, Insurance, Industrial Technology, Manufacturing Medical/Health Services, Military, Real Estate, Information and Communication Technology (ICT), Training, Transportation, Travel/Hotel/Hospitality, Utilities/Oil and Gas/Electricity/Water and others which we might have not indicated earlier in the survey form. These different industries were chosen to measure different practices and conduct of HRD and by the population and different stages of organizational climate. Furthermore, they have their own vision, mission, and objectives in running their organizations, especially for the betterment of Muslim people in Malaysia. In addition to that, they can be categorized further into the public and private sectors and nonprofit or non-government organizations (NGOs).

The total respondents were 172 Muslim managers and 509 Muslim employees in various industries who vary in positions and were purposely selected to represent each of the industries. To ensure the managers to be respondents, they must understand and are familiar with their organizations' HR practices. The respondents selected were those in charge of HR and performing in any of the HR functions and they carry the duties as supervisors. The enumerators were requested to approach the human resource manager of the organizations and acquire permission to collect the data. The questionnaires were left with the respondents to enable them to read and understand the items. Subsequently, questionnaires were collected by the enumerators within three to five days. In each industry, 10 organizations were selected based on the number of potential respondents, and about 40 questionnaires were distributed for each industry, 10 for the Muslim managers and 30 for the employees. However, some companies failed to return all of them.

22.4.2 Instrumentation and Data Analysis

Descriptive statistics and factor analysis were used to analyze the information gathered from the questionnaires. The respondents' profiles were also collected (Table 22.1). Based on the survey, 341 respondents are male, while 340 are female. About 43% of the respondents are up to 30 years of age. Majority of them are bachelor degree holders which in total of 285 persons.

Table 22.1 Respondent demographic

Characteristics	Total number
Position	172
Managers	509
Employees	
Gender	
Male	341
Female	340
Age	
Up to 30	293
31–40	261
41–50	110
51–60	16
60 and above	1
Education level	
Secondary (high) school	152
Diploma	216
Bachelor's degree	285
Master's degree	28

Table 22.2 Summary of factor analysis results on the loyalty of employee in relation to the organizational climate from an Islamic perspective

Items	Factor loading			
	F1	F2	F3	F4
Innovation and flexibility				
This company is quick to respond when changes need to be made	0.716			
New ideas are readily accepted here	0.716			
Management here is quick to spot the need to do things differently	0.706			
Assistance in developing new ideas is readily available	0.705			
This organization is very flexible it can quickly change procedures to meet new conditions and solve problems as they arise	0.701			
People in this organization are always searching for new ways of looking at problems	0.691			
Welfare of employees				
This company tries to be fair in its actions toward employees		0.726		
This company cares about its employees		0.722		
This company tries to look after its employees		0.720		
This company pays attention to the interests of employees		0.678		
Employees are strongly encouraged to develop their skills		0.677		
Supervisors' support				
Supervisors here are really good at understanding peoples' problems			0.809	
Supervisors show that they have confidence in those they manage			0.751	
Supervisors can be relied upon to give good guidance to people			0.639	
Supervisors here are friendly and easy to approach			0.608	
Supervisors show an understanding of the people who work for them			0.607	
Employees training				
People are properly trained when there is a new machine or bit of equipment				0.850
People receive enough training when it comes to using new equipment				0.829
The company gives people the minimum amount of training they need to do their job				0.542
Total % of variance				61.412

A Likert scale of 1–5 (1 representing strongly disagree and 5 representing strongly agree) was used to measure the loyalty of employee in relation to organizational climate from an Islamic perspective. Eighty-two statements were constructed to the loyalty of employee in relation to organizational climate from an Islamic perspective. For the explanatory factor analysis, the reliability of each factor was tested using Cronbach's alpha to measure the internal reliability consistency. The principal component method was used to extract the latent factors influencing the loyalty of employee in relation to organizational climate from an Islamic perspective. The factor loading from the principal component factor analysis was obtained after the varimax rotation was performed on the responses of the employees to the 61 statements related to their loyalty of their organization. From the results of the rotated factor matrix, only items with a factor loading of at least 0.50 and above are considered significance items. The factors are then named based on the sub-variables that fall within each factor. Table 22.2 shows factors that influence the loyalty of employee in relation to organizational climate from an Islamic perspective.

22.5 Discussion and Conclusion

This study examines mainly the determinants that influence the loyalty of employee in relation to organizational climate from an Islamic perspective in Malaysia. A factor analysis of the data generated four factors as the determinants. From the analysis, the study found determinants like innovation and flexibility, welfare of employees, supervisors' support, training and development are positively and significantly influencing the employees' loyalty. Hence, organizations should emphasize these four factors in order to obtain high commitment from Muslim employees to enhance loyalty and boost organizational performance. Higher organizational performance is vital in order to sustain their competitive advantage in the long run. Innovation and flexibility is related to the adoption of new ideas such as flexi working hours in the office, readiness to accept changes, and adopt new policy to meet the needs of employees or solving problems. In addition to that, innovation and flexibility presently is very much relevant due to the high technology availability, the lifestyle, and different new generations in the workforce.

Another factor is the welfare of employees such as their remuneration and benefits. It is undeniable that Islam promotes brotherhood, good tidings and love between mankind for the sake of Allah. Thus, policies and guidelines for employees' welfare should address the most that the organization can offer. It also includes how serious is the organization in providing opportunities to their Muslim employees to develop themselves. In order to materialize this, supervisors' supports are needed to coach those they manage as on-job training. Supervisors should understand the different background and functions of employees. They have to know how to think out of the box, to be creative to assist the employees in time they are in need without breaking any procedures of the organization. They should not be too rigid in executing their job. Last factor that was generated from the finding is training. Training and development are one of the HR development items that contributed to employees' loyalty. This finding is in line with the study conducted by Hassan et al. (2006) mentioned earlier, which indicated that employees' satisfaction with human resource development climate was predicted by learning and training system, employee development system (such as mentoring and coaching). Muslim employees perceived learning and developing themselves are extremely important as propagated by the Prophet Muhammad SAW. It is regard as vital for their benefit in this world and hereafter. Excellence in the Hereafter is the most blessed as it is indefinite, since you are attempting to seek Allah's pleasure, i.e., *al-falah*. Please note that this finding could only be generalized to the Muslim employees in this context.

Future research should be conducted in Muslim organizations in Malaysia. It is proposed to use other types of sampling techniques in order to gain in-depth findings in relation to this study. The findings of the study reinforce the assumption that investment in human capital brings competitive advantage to the company (Prahald and Hamel 1990; Winterton and Winterton 1996) resulted from employees' loyalty. Results as highlighted above reflect the importance of adequate HR practices, to promote employees' trust and satisfaction which eventually lead to loyalty. It is also in line with the findings of previous studies showing the contribution of HRD on employees' performance (Sandberg 2000), organizational commitment (Iles et al. 1990), and organizational retention (Robertson et al. 1991).

References

Akdere, M., Russ-eft, D., & Eft, N. (2006). The Islamic worldview of adult learning in the workplace; surrendering to god. *Advances in Developing Human Resources, 8*(3), 355–363.

Branine, M., & Pollard, D. (2006). Human resource management with Islamic management principles: A dialectic for a reverse diffusion in management. *Personnel Review, 39*(6), 712–727.

Carbery, R., & Cross, C. (2015). *Human resource development: A concise introduction* (pp. 2–10). Palgrave Publishing.

Halstead, J. M. (2004). An Islamic concept of education. *Comparative Education, 40*(4), 517–529.

Hashim, J. (2010). Human resource management practices on organizational commitment: The Islamic perspective. *Personnel Review, 39*(6), 785–799.

Hassan, A., Hashim, J., & Zaki, A. (2006). Human resource development practices as determinant of HRD climate and quality orientation. *Journal of European Industrial Training, 30*(1), 4–18. doi:10.1108/03090590610643842.

Hassi, A. (2012). Islamic perspectives on training and professional development. *Journal of Management Development, 31*(10), 1035. doi:10.1108/02621711211281816.

Hilgendorf, E. (2003). Islamic education: History and tendency. *Peabody Journal of Education, 78*(3), 63–75.

Husain, S. S., & Ashraf, S. A. (1979). *Crisis in Muslim education.* London: Hodder and Stoughton.

James, L. R., & Jones, A. P. (1974). Organizational climate: A review of theory and research. *Psychological Bulletin, 81,* 1096–1112.

Lawler, E. E. III & Morhman, S. A. (1996). Unions and new management. In G. R. Ferris, & M. R. Buckley (Eds.), *Human Resource Management: Perspectives, Context, Functions and Outcomes*, Prentice-Hall, Englewood Cliffs, NJ.

Norton, D. (2001). Foreword. In B. E. Becker, M. A. Huslid, & D. Ulrich (Eds.), *The HR Scorecard*. Boston, MA: Harvard Business School Press.

Patterson, M. G., Warr, P. B., & West, M. A. (2004). Organizational climate and company performance: The role of employee affect and employee level. *Journal of Occupational and Organizational Psychology, 77,* 193–216.

Patterson, M. G., West, M. A., Shackleton, V. J., Dawson, J. F., Lawthom, R., Maitlis, S., Robinson, D. L. & Wallace, A. M. (2005). Validating the organizational climate measure: Links to managerial practices, productivity and innovation. *Journal of Organizational Behavior, 6*. doi:10.1002/job.312.

Prahald, L. K. & Hamel, G. (May–June, 1990). The core competencies of the corporation. Harvard Business Review.

Rousseau, D. M. (1988). The construction of climate in organizational research. In C. L. Cooper, & I. T. Robertson (Eds.), *International Review of Industrial and Organizational, Psychology* (vol. 3, pp 139–158), Wiley, New York.

Salem, Z. O., & Syed Agil, S. O. (2012). The effects of Islamic management ethics on organizational commitment of employees in Libyan public banks. *Australian Journal of Basic and Applied Sciences, 6*(7), 260–270.

Sandberg, J. (2000). Understanding human competence at work: An interpretive approach. *Academy of Management Journal, 43*(1), 9–17.

Schneider, B. (1990). The climate for service: An application of the climate construct. In B. Schneider (Ed.), *Organizational Climate and Culture* (pp. 383–412). Sans Francisco, CA: Jossey-Bass.

Schneider, B., & Reichers, A. E. (1983). On the etiology of climates. *Personnel Psychology, 36,* 19–39.

Schultz, T. W. (1961). Investment in human capital. *The American Economic Review, 51*(1), 1–17. Retrieved from http://www.jstor.org/pss/1818907.

Sikula, S. A. (2001). The five biggest HRM lies. *Public Personnel Management, 30*(3), 419–429.

Tolbize, A. (2008). *Generational differences in the workplace*. Research and Training Center on Community Living. University of Minnesota (pp. 9).

Zairi, M. (1998). Managing human resources in healthcare: Learning from world class practices—part 1. *Health Manpower Management, 24*(2), 48–57.

https://www.google.com/search?q=steve+jobs+quotes+on+work.

[illegible] (2000). Unions and new management. In G. R. Ferris & M. R. Buckley (Eds.), *Human Resource Management: Perspectives, Context, Functions, and Outcomes*. Prentice Hall, Englewood Cliffs, NJ.

[illegible] Boston, MA: Harvard Business School Press.

[illegible] (2016). Organizational [illegible] employee [illegible]

[illegible]

Chapter 23
Determinants of Generation Y Engagement in Electronic Word of Mouth

Mohamad Niza Md Nor, Zulaiha Ahmad, Ahmad Nizan Mat Noor, Nurwahida Fuad and Noor Amirah Binti Kamaruddin

Abstract Evolution of Internet has become an important phenomenon in the marketing activities since social network sites such as Twitter, Facebook and MySpace dramatically give a huge impact towards online marketing among Generation Y. The emergence of social network sites has profoundly changed the way the information is transmitted to the customer. Thus, electronic word of mouth plays an increasingly important role in consumer's purchase decisions. Specifically, the study identifies innovativeness, trust, social capital and opinion leader as important antecedent of electronic word of mouth. A total of 230 students of School of Computer Science responded to a questionnaire. The results indicate that innovativeness, trust and opinion leader have a significant relationship with electronic word of mouth. The implications of this study are important for marketers to improve their business through media social.

Keywords Generation Y · Electronic word of mouth · Students · SNSs

M.N. Md Nor (✉) · Z. Ahmad · A.N.M. Noor · N. Fuad · N.A.B. Kamaruddin
Faculty of Business Management, Universiti Teknologi MARA, Arau, Perlis, Malaysia
e-mail: mohdniza@perlis.uitm.edu.my

Z. Ahmad
e-mail: zulaiha895@perlis.uitm.edu.my

A.N.M. Noor
e-mail: ahmadnizan@perlis.uitm.edu.my

N. Fuad
e-mail: wahida.fuad@perlis.uitm.edu.my

N.A.B. Kamaruddin
e-mail: amirah.kamaruddin@gmail.com

F. Noordin et al. (eds.), *Proceedings of the 2nd Advances in Business Research International Conference*, https://doi.org/10.1007/978-981-10-6053-3_23

23.1 Introduction

Electronic word of mouth (e-WOM) has recently received a great deal of attention among practitioners as an alternative to traditional marketing communication tools. According to Nail (2005), ineffectiveness of traditional forms of communication makes e-WOM more viable among marketers. Furthermore, empirical evidence also explained that e-WOM is predominantly prominent feature of the Internet (Trusov et al. 2009). From another perspective, e-WOM also has become a phenomenal in social networking sites among Generation Y. Majority of people, especially Generation Y reviewed products, frequently posted up opinions and participated in online networking activities through email communication, blogs, message boards, chat room and instant messaging (Valenzuela et al. 2012). Empirical study also reported that people nowadays have a freedom to communicate with others in the distance and sometimes they will share their common interests to one another in online communities (Zhu and Chang 2014). E-WOM also is reported to play vital role in customer's purchase decision, especially the young generation who are active in today's digital environment and marketing strategies (Adjei et al. 2010; Parmelee and Perkins 2012; Wang et al. 2012). However, Generation Y certainly is not afraid about discussing the brands online and the comment can either be positive or negative.

According to Chang and Wu (2014), fake information which is spread by the consumers may affect the negative electronic word of mouth adoption. In addition, Generation Y is using social media because it is affecting peoples' behaviour in many domains such as Facebook in which they can express their feelings or opinions truly from their heart. If they felt unhappy about the products they may complain and boycott the products, but if the products are good they would automatically share the information of the products within their circle (Berry et al. 2010). Previous findings showed that e-WOM could spread information widely through online networking sites. Moreover, Generation Y was able to influence others to purchase products because of their attitude, knowledge and high level of education. They also like to read or to discover certain products that they themselves are interested in.

Generation Y is a unique and influential consumer group. They are easily being motivated to purchase new products in the market and directly impacted the e-WOM. The most important factor that the marketers need to look is on how to make Generation Y trust their products and services, whether or not they are reliable and innovative to be used in the current era. For that reason, the current study focuses on seeking information about the factors that influence the electronic word of mouth towards purchase decision among Generation Y. The four objectives of this study are: (1) to identify the influence of innovativeness on e-WOM towards purchase decision (2) to identify the influence of trust on e-WOM towards purchase decision (3) to identify the influence of social capital on e-WOM towards purchase decision and (4) to identify the influence of opinion leader on e-WOM towards purchase decision.

23.2 Past Literature

23.2.1 Electronic Word of Mouth

E-WOM has received great attention among marketing practitioners recently as an alternative tool for traditional marketing. E-WOM is person-to-person communication regarding any positive or negative statement made by potential, actual or former customers about a product or company which is made available to multi-people and institutions via Internet (Hennig-Thurau et al. 2004). All the data in e-WOM can be stored for future references. Due to ineffectiveness of traditional forms of communication in marketing, therefore, marketers are particularly interested in better understanding regarding e-WOM (Nail 2005).

Internet has become the main platform of WOM which enables the consumers to share their views, experiences and preferences with others easily. E-WOM become important and relevant communication channel among customers. Business firms also get the advantages of e-WOM marketing to catch the attention of global marketing at the lowest cost and fastest, through blogging campaign (Whitman 2006). Social networking sites (SNSs) as one of the fastest growing arenas of World Wide Web have become a driving force for building business networking. For instance, SNS is typically initiated by a small group of founders who send out invitations to join the site to the members of their own personal networks. In turn, the new members send invitations to their networks, and so on (Trusov et al. 2009).

23.2.2 Innovativeness and Electronic Word of Mouth

Innovation continues to be an important topic of study for a number of different disciplines, including economics, business, engineering, science and sociology. Kotler and Keller (2006) agreed that innovation has been one of the vital factors in area of business as well as marketing. Therefore, innovation is not a new phenomenon anymore in today's business due the rapidly changing in technology. The fact is that, innovation has made radical changes in business lifetime and significant transformation for economy (Fagerberg 2003). Schumpeter (1954) stated that innovation is classified into five different types, namely new products, new methods of production, new sources of supply, exploitation of new markets and new ways to organize business. However, the first two types have become the most preferable by economies (Fagerberg 1996).

Innovation is the backbone of business organization to sustain as a competitive advantage and leader of the market share. Therefore, innovative ideas in product development are crucial to meet the business challenges as well as the customer's satisfaction. Thus, since e-WOM has become great platform in sharing views, knowledge and preference among customers, as well as business firms, the opportunity may emerge for the firms to create innovative products. For instance, from the data of consumer's and firm's conversation stored in e-WOM, business firm perhaps can have better understanding of consumer's needs and wants, business global issues and latest technology available for the product development.

23.2.3 Trust and Electronic Word of Mouth

Trust towards e-WOM can be defined as the belief in e-WOM content, of which is characterized by dignity and plausibility of product- or service-related comments (Cheung et al. 2009). Awad and Ragowsky (2008) defined e-WOM as the system on the Web site that is believed to be relevant and useful. His study also discussed e-WOM on trust differs across genders because genders communicate and evaluate communications differently. Thus, previous studies found that 15 men and women have different buying attitudes, women are more emotional, while men are more realistic.

In other words, trust towards e-WOM is the tendency that determines the internalization of online customer feedbacks. Influence by e-WOM can be referred as the changes in the attitudes, behaviour or thoughts of an individual towards a product or service, and that change happens afterwards that meets with e-WOM comments (Litvin et al. 2008).

Trust and online word of mouth is crucial in the business transaction; hence, the previous study discussed that social networks have changed from consumer to consumer communication, and these social networks have become an important marketing tool (Chu and Kim 2011). According to Hennig-Thurau et al. (2010), information in the SNS has become an important information for the consumers who are seeking for the opinions of the products. E-WOM is much greater than traditional WOM because people nowadays are busy with their lifestyles and have limited time to express their opinions online. Thus, they will scroll the reviews from the previous post of the products.

23.2.4 Social Capital and Electronic Word of Mouth

The contribution of social capital in enhancing the quality and quantity of knowledge transfer among society is undeniable. Social capital refers to the resources accumulated through the relationships among people (Coleman 1988). Furthermore, social capital is developed through interactions when the parties in the relationship facilitate those interactions (Huang et al. 2010). In general, social capital has positive influence on interaction among participants (Putnam 2000).

Furthermore, individuals, companies and vendors are selling their products through SNSs nowadays. Customers are having freedom in making purchasing decision, while business firms have broad view in gaining information. It is undoubted that, the SNSs have made customer's life borderless and business globally. Consequently, any kind of information is worldwide and available just at the fingertips. E-WOM becomes one of the sources of social capital in encouraging people to share their knowledge that enables innovating organization to achieve sustainable competitive advantage (Adler and Kwon 2002; Hung and Li 2007).

23.2.5 Opinion Leader and Electronic Word of Mouth

Opinion leaders have a critical importance in the buying decision and diffusion of innovative products by the word of mouth in the marketing communication method (Yusuf and Ahmet 2014). An opinion leader is a well-known individual or organization that has the ability to influence public opinion on the subject matter for which the opinion leader is known. Opinion leaders can be politicians, business leaders, community leaders, journalists, educators, celebrities and sports stars, (Grimsley 2015).

From the previous study, consumers can influence other consumers in different ways and those consumers with a greater influence on others constitute opinion leaders (Anil et al. 2014). Opinion leadership is the individual's behavioural tendency and ability to spread information and influence others' purchase decisions (Ruvio and Shoham 2007). According to Jeong and Jang (2011), opinion leaders shared their opinions and experiences related to products not only to their family but also to others. It influenced Generation Y to buy the products due to the exposure of someone that they look up to and like such as their favourite singers, actresses, actors, businesswomen and others. Opinion leaders became an important source of information to the Generation Y. Opinion leaders play an important role because they may influence many people due to their status and background. Opinion leader is a person who is being recognized based on his popularity and leadership position (Valente and Pumpuang 2007).

23.3 Methodology

23.3.1 Respondents

This study employs quantitative approach and cross-sectional in nature. The respondents are Generation Y who was born in between 1980s–2000s. Respondents of the study (N = 230) included 82 (35.7%) and 148 (64.3%) students in School of Computer Science located at northern region of Peninsular Malaysia. The majority of respondents identified themselves as Malay (57.8%), Chinese (22.6%), the second highest population, Indian (11.3%) and others (8.3%) the least population. Ages ranged from 18 to 35 years with the majority of respondents are from 18 to 22 years old (63.9%).

23.3.2 Measures

For the purpose of this study, all measurement items mainly in 5-point Likert Scale from 1 (strongly disagree) to 5 (strongly agree). Respondents were asked to voluntarily complete a survey that measured the following demographics, e-WOM, innovativeness, trust, social capital and opinion leader.

E-WOM was measured using 9 items adopted from Kucukemiroglu and Kara (2015). Sample items from this measure include the following: "I tend to forward my friend's positive reviews on products", "I like forwarding interesting emails about products to my friends", "Share this post to my friend" when I find interesting products" and "I like to share with others my favourite products". Internal consistency reliability (coefficient alpha) for the measure used in this study was 0.92.

Sample items from the 6 items of innovativeness scale include "Try new products if I heard that some new products were available online, I would be interested to obtain it", "I like to buy new products before other people do" and "I rarely purchase the latest fashion styles until I am sure my friends approve of them". The internal consistency reliability (coefficient alpha) of this innovativeness scale used in this study was 0.84. The level of trust among respondents was measured using 7 items Likert-type scale. Internal consistency reliability (coefficient alpha) for the measure used in this study was 0.90.

Among the items include the following: "I feel confident about having discussions with the contacts on my friends list on the social media", the contacts on my friends list in social media will do everything within their capacity to help others" and "My contacts on friends list on social media offer honest opinion". Similarly, social capital and opinion leader were measured on 6 item scale. The internal consistency reliability of social capital scale used was 0.85. Sample items include "Interacting with people on the social media makes me want to try new things", "Interacting with people on the social media makes me feel like a part of the larger community" and "Interacting with people on the social media reminds me that everyone in the world is connected".

Finally, internal consistency reliability for opinion leader was 0.82. Sample items include "On the social media site, I often influence my contacts opinions about products", "My contacts on the social media pick their products based on what have told them" and "My contacts on the social media rarely come to me for advice about choosing products". Overall, measurement of innovativeness, trust, social capital and opinion leader adopted from Kucukemiroglu and Kara (2015) ranging from 5 (strongly agree) to 1 (strongly disagree).

23.4 Data Analysis

Table 23.1 shows the descriptive statistics and intercorrelations for all relevant study variables. Significant relationships were expected between e-WOM and the following four variables: Innovativeness, thrust, social capital and opinion leader. The predicted relationships were all significant ($p < 0.01$), providing initial support for the previously stated hypotheses.

From Table 23.1, it can be seen that all means for variables constructed ranging from 3.16 to 3.89. The results revealed that the Cronbach's alpha values of all variables were considered good and excellent with the range of 0.82–0.92 (Sekaran 2003).

The results showed that a significant positive correlation coefficients between trust and e-WOM ($r = 0.57$, $p < 0.01$). Rules of thumb have been suggested to characterize the strength of association between variables (Hair et al. 2007). A significant moderate and positive correlation coefficients showed between innovativeness and e-WOM with the value of 0.61 ($p < 0.01$). Result also revealed that both social capital ($r = 0.48$, $p < 0.01$) and opinion leader ($r = 0.68$, $p < 0.01$) have a moderate and positive correlation with e-WOM.

To test the hypotheses, a multiple regression analysis was done. The R square for model in Table 23.2 was able to explained 56.2% of the variance in electronic word

Table 23.1 Descriptive, internal consistency reliabilities and intercorrelations

Variables	M	SD	1	2	3	4	5
Trust	3.16	0.77	(0.90)				
Innovativeness	2.89	0.85	0.48**	(0.84)			
Social capital	3.64	0.70	0.45**	0.49**	(0.85)		
Opinion leader	3.17	0.73	0.56**	0.57**	0.48**	(0.82)	
E-WOM	3.22	0.87	0.57**	0.61**	0.46**	0.68**	(0.92)

** $p < 0.01$

Table 23.2 Regression results

Variables	*β*	*t*	*Sig.*
Trust	0.194	3.48	0.001
Innovativeness	0.279	4.88	0.000
Social capital	0.048	0.89	0.374
Opinion leader	0.384	6.45	0.000
R	0.75		
R Square	0.562		
Adjusted R square	0.554		
F value	72.127		

Dependent Variable: Electronic word of mouth

of mouth. Among all, only trust, innovativeness and opinion leader were significant with e-WOM which trust (t = 3.48), innovativeness (t = 4.88) and opinion leader (t = 6.45) and it was statistically significant at $p < 0.01$. Therefore, trust, innovativeness and opinion leader can be used to explain electronic word of mouth.

23.5 Discussion and Conclusion

Current study focuses on the factors that influence the e-WOM towards purchase decision among Generation Y. The objectives of this study are: (1) to identify the influence of innovativeness on e-WOM towards purchase decision (2) to identify the influence of trust on e-WOM towards purchase decision (3) to identify the influence of social capital on e-WOM towards purchase decision and (4) to identify the influence of opinion leader on e-WOM towards purchase decision. This study found three factors, namely trust, innovativeness and opinion leader were significantly and positively related to e-WOM. The result implies that trust, innovativeness and opinion leader can be used to explain e-WOM or had influenced the Generation Y in their purchased decision through electronic word of mouth. This finding is tandem with previous researchers (Berry et al. 2010), who also reported that Generation Y had influenced by the design of the products and interactive services such as brand loyalty, purchase behaviour and lifetime value added factors of the products or services. Furthermore, Jones and Leonard (2008) also reported that trust is one of the factors that would make people choose to buy product.

The finding on opinion leader in this study is also in tandem with previous study by Smith (2015) who stated that opinion of a well-known person in the organization is important in changing people behaviour. From practical perspectives, the results of this study offer several suggestions to practitioners. Specifically, marketers can raise the understanding of the effects of online WOM by transmitting their marketing messages via electronic word of mouth and the importance of e-WOM by exploring on how to stimulate positive thinking among consumers. Several limitations of the studied were identified. First, the predictors investigated in this study were limited in scope. Only trust, innovativeness, social capital and opinion leader were examined. Other predictors such as customer lifetime value and social contagion may play a role in explaining e-WOM towards purchase decision among Generation Y. Future researchers may need to widen the scope of the investigation by incorporating these predictors. Second, this study is limited to one of public universities in a particular region of the country. The results obtained may not be generalized to other sample across different regions or industries. The same research could be replicated with a larger sample of Generation Y from different regions within the same industry or across different industries. The use of larger sample within the same industry or from other industries would expand the generalization of the findings.

References

Adjei, M. T., Noble, S. M., & Noble, C. H. (2010). The influence of C2C communications in online brand communities on customer purchase behavior. *Journal of the Academy Marketing Science, 38*(5), 634–653.

Adler, P. S., & Kwon, S.-W. (2002). Social capital: Prospects for a new concept. *Academy of Management Review, 27*(1), 17–40.

Anil, B., Cheng, P., & Jay, K. (2014). Generation Y's dining information seeking and sharing behavior on social networking sites: An exploratory study. *International Journal of Contemporary Hospitality Management, 26,* 349–366.

Awad, N. F., & Ragowsky, A. (2008). Establishing thrust in electronic commerce through online word-of-mouth: An examination across genders. *Journal of Management Information Systems, 24,* 102–103.

Berry, L., Wall, E., & Carbone, L. (2010). Service clues and customer assessment of the service experience: Lessons from marketing. *Academy of Management Perspectives, 20*(2), 43–57.

Chang, H. H., & Wu, L. H. (2014). An examination of negative e-WOM adoption: Brand commitment as a moderator. *Decision Support Systems, 59,* 206–218. doi:10.1016/j.dss.2013.11.008.

Cheung, M., Luo, C., Sia, C., & Chen, H. (2009). Credibility of electronic word-of-mouth: Informational and normative determinants of on-line consumer recommendations. *International Journal of Electronic Commerce, 13*(4), 9.

Chu, S. C., & Kim, Y. (2011). Determinants of consumer engagement in electronic word-of-mouth (e-WOM) in social networking sites. *International Journal of Advertising, 30*(1), 47–75.

Coleman, J. S. (1988). Social capital in the creation of human capital. *American Journal of Sociology, 94*(1), 95–120.

Fagerberg, J. (1996). Technology and competitiveness. *Oxford Review of Economic Policy, 12,* 39–51.

Fagerberg, J. (2003). Schumpeter and revival of evolutionary economics: An appraisal of the literature. *Journal of Evolutionary Economic, 13*(2), 125–159.

Grimsley, S. (2015). Opinion leader in marketing: Definition and explanation. Retrieved from http://study.com/academy/lesson/opinion-leader-in-marketingdefinition-lesson-quiz.html.

Hair, J. F., Money, A. H, Samouel, P., & Page, M. (2007). *Research methods for business.*(5th ed.). West Sussex: Wiley.

Hennig-Thurau, T., Gwinner, K. P., Walsh, G., & Gremler, D. D. (2004). Electronic word-of-mouth via consumer-opinion platforms: What motivates consumers to articulate themselves on the internet? *Journal of Interactive Marketing, 18,* 38–52.

Hennig-Thurau, T., Malthouse, E. C., Friege, C., Gensler, S., Lobschat, L., Rangaswamy, A., et al. (2010). The impact of new media on customer relationships. *Journal of Service Research, 13* (3), 311–330.

Huang, K., Choi, N., & Horowitz, L. (2010). Web 2.0 use and organizational innovation: A knowledge transfer enabling perspective. In *Proceedings of the 16th Americas Conference on Information Systems, Lima* (pp. 1–14).

Hung, K. H., & Li, S. Y. (2007). The influence of e-WOM on virtual consumer communities: Social capital, consumer learning, and behavioral outcomes. *Journal of Advertising Research, 47*(4), 485–495.

Jeong, E., & Jang, S. (2011). Restaurant experience triggering positive electronic word of mouth motivations. *International Journal of Hospitality Management, 30,* 356–366.

Jones, K., & Leonard, L. N. K. (2008). Trust in consumer-to-consumer electronic commerce. *Information and Management, 45*(2), 88–95. doi:10.1016/j.im.2007.12.002.

Kotler, P., & Keller, K. L. (2006). *Marketing Management* (12th ed.). Upper Saddle River, NJ: Prentice-Hall.

Kucukemiroglu, S., & Kara, A. (2015). Online word of mouth communication on social networking sites. *International Journal of Commerce and Management, 25*(1).

Litvin, S. W., Goldsmith, R. E., & Pan, B. (2008). Electronic word-of-mouth in hospitality and tourism management. *Tourism Management, 29,* 458–468.

Nail, J. (May 2005). What's the buzz on word of mouth marketing? Social computing and consumer control put momentum into viral marketing. *Forrester Research.* Retrieved from May 31, 2016.

Parmelee, J. H., & Perkins, S. C. (2012). Exploring social and psychological factors that influence the gathering of political information online. *Telematics and Informatics, 29,* 90–98.

Putnam, R. D. (2000). Bowling alone: America's declining social capital. In *Culture and Politics.* New York, NY: Simon and Schuster.

Ruvio, A., & Shoham, A. (2007). Innovativeness, exploratory behavior, market mavenship, and opinion leadership: An empirical examination in the Asian context. *Journal of Psychology and Marketing, 24*(8), 703–722.

Schumpeter, J. (1954). *History of economic analysis.* New York: Allen & Unwin.

Sekaran, U. (2003). *Research methods for business. A skill building approach.* New York: Wiley.

Smith, B. (2015). Engaging health: Health research and policymaking in the social media sphere. *Academy Health.*

Trusov, M., Bucklin, E. R., & Pauwels, K. (2009). Effects of word-of-mouth versus traditional marketing: Findings from an internet social networking site. *Journal of Marketing, 73,* 90–102.

Valente, Thomas W., & Pumpuang, P. (2007). Identifying opinion leaders to promote behavior change. *Health Education and Behavior, 34*(6), 881–896.

Valenzuela, S., Arriagada, A., & Scherman, A. (2012). The social media basis of youth protest behavior: The case of Chile. *Journal of Communication, 62,* 299–314. doi:10.1111/j.1460-2466.2012.01635.

Wang, X., Yu, C., & Wei, Y. (2012). Social media peer communication and impacts on purchase intentions: A consumer socialization framework. *Journal of Interactive Marketing, 26*(4), 198–208.

Whitman, J. (2006). Lessons learned: New dot-coms seek attention cheaply. *The Wall Street Journal.*

Yusuf, K., & Ahmet, U. (2014). Influence of opinion leaders on the diffusion of innovative products: A study on smartphone users. *Journal of Business, Economics and Finance, 3*(2), ISSN: 2146-7943, Press Academia.

Zhu, D. H., & Chang, Y. P. (2014). Understanding motivations for continuance intention of online communities in china: A comparison of active users of social networking sites and virtual communities. *Information Development, 30*(2), 172–180.

Chapter 24
Empowering Knowledge Sharing in Business

Norfadzilah Abdul Razak, Rozilah Abdul Aziz, Zulkefli Abdul Rahman and Sharifah Ali

Abstract In business, the activity of organizational learning, competitiveness and innovation is a platform to prepare and develop human capital. These platforms usually practice of knowledge sharing that believe will empower the business to high performance work practices (HPWPs). This study highlights a comprehensive literature review on how practices of the knowledge sharing embedded the activities. The discussion lead by understanding nature of knowledge sharing, process and continued with the practices of knowledge sharing. Finally, this study contributes to the strategy on how to improve the practices of knowledge sharing and perform well in business.

Keywords Knowledge sharing · Innovation · Organizational learning Competitiveness

24.1 Introduction

Knowledge sharing has widely been recognized as an initiative to be innovative and competitive in business (Hayati et al. 2013; Susanne et al. 2007). It plays an important role in organizational learning (Alavi et al. 2010), competitive advantages (Shih and Chiang 2005) and innovation in business (Moustaghfir and Schiuma, 2013; Pai and Chang 2013). From the perspective of organizational learning,

N.A. Razak (✉) · R.A. Aziz · Z.A. Rahman · S. Ali
Faculty of Business and Management, Universiti Teknologi MARA, Puncak Alam, Selangor, Malaysia
e-mail: norfadzilah0438@gmail.com

R.A. Aziz
e-mail: rozilah@puncakalam.uitm.edu.my

Z.A. Rahman
e-mail: zulke796@puncakalam.uitm.edu.my

S. Ali
e-mail: sharifahali@salam.uitm.edu.my

F. Noordin et al. (eds.), *Proceedings of the 2nd Advances in Business Research International Conference*, https://doi.org/10.1007/978-981-10-6053-3_24

numerous previous studies found that knowledge sharing is a platform for effective learning in the organization (Shang et al. 2009). The employers or employees share and exchange their knowledge, ideas, expertise and skills with others who need their assistant. Besides organizational learning, knowledge sharing view as a competitive advantages for organization to survive in the business (Grandy and Wicks 2008). It is a value added by individual and organization to be differ from others. I In additional to organizational learning and competitive advantages, knowledge sharing has contributed to innovation in business. Marsh and Stock (2003) mentioned that knowledge sharing is a root of innovation to create a new product or platform for problem-solving. Many scholars have investigated comprehensively the roles and importance of knowledge sharing in business. However, the discussion needs to further discuss on how knowledge sharing can practice well in a business. There is a lack of discussion in terms of strategy, practices, and tools of knowledge sharing and how it works in a business. Hence, this paper objectively to enhance the understanding of how knowledge sharing practice particularly to activities of organizational learning, competitive advantages and innovation. A comprehensive study from literature review analysis proposes comparable knowledge sharing practices into these three activities.

24.2 Overview of Knowledge Sharing

The definition of knowledge sharing has widely been discussed in studies of knowledge management. Knowledge sharing is defined as an activity to exchange knowledge (Cummings and Teng 2003; Pai and Chang 2013). It involves the process of creation, dissemination, use and storing knowledge (Sanjaghi et al. 2013). Other definition, knowledge sharing is a set of an individual behavior that refers to willingness (Chang and Chuang 2011) or a set of incorporating behavioral to exchange, diffuses or acquire the knowledge (Connelly and Kelloway 2003). From this point of view, this study defined knowledge sharing as readiness to share and learn knowledge from others. It is a process that requires consistency of an individual behavior to share knowledge (Lee and Choi 2003; Wasko and Faraj 2005).

The process of knowledge sharing involves communication between two persons known as knowledge creator and knowledge recipient. A knowledge creator known as a source is needed to communicate and interact with knowledge recipient (Gagne 2009). Knowledge creator shares his or her ideas, information, knowledge, experiences and skills with knowledge recipient (Lin et al. 2012). On the other hand, knowledge recipient will react by utilizing and applying knowledge into a work context (Eckl, 2012). Thus, the basis of knowledge sharing is communication and interaction between two or more people. In a business context, everyday people meet and it is routine to communicate and interact with others. Further discussion reviews the two types of knowledge and how it is delivered to the knowledge recipient.

24.3 Nature of Knowledge

Knowledge is defined as a fluid mix of experience, values, contextual information, and expert (Wulff and Suomi 2007). Knowledge begin from a raw data, fact and process into an information. When information has been transformed into an individual mind, it can form as knowledge. When information has been transforming in the mind of an individual the information convert as knowledge (Alavi and Leidner 2001). Knowledge can present in two forms: tacit and explicit knowledge. Tacit knowledge is defined as a subjective form of knowledge such as ideas, experience and skills (Reychav and Weisberg 2009). It lives and places intensely in the mind of the individual (Janson and Mcqueen 2007). Not only that, tacit knowledge is based on a mental model, values, belief, perceptions, insights and assumptions (Smith 2005). Tacit knowledge is described as knowledge that is unable to express through the words (Smith 2005). In practice, tacit knowledge is shared through observation, experiment, job training or demonstration by the expert. From that, knowledge delivers to recipient by visualize how and what knowledge is all about.

Explicit knowledge is different from tacit knowledge. According to Hansen et al. (1999), explicit knowledge is document oriented. Document is defined as database, written paper, notes, case studies, manual and practices of documents. All documents mentioned usable for other to access and reuse when they need (Smith 2005). Given this point, explicit knowledge describes knowledge which can be expressed in words, sentences, numbers or formulas. It is highly codified and transmittable ways such as formal structure, organize, systematic, manuals, or into form of databases (Lam 2000). Eventhough there are differences between tacit and explicit, but the roles of knowledge, perceive as intangible assets of human intellectual. It will be meaningful as the knowledge created only by individual and encourage and promote to share their knowledge with others (Kumaraswamy and Chitale 2012) (Nonaka and Takeuchi 1995). In practice, explicit knowledge is shared through a written manual or book that will be used as references in future. People may easily access and retrieve knowledge from the written form. They can be used many times and be copied by others. Consistent with the discussion, this study highlights the roles of tacit and explicit knowledge and contributes to deciding the tool and strategy to share and transfer the knowledge.

24.4 Knowledge Sharing and Organizational Learning

Organizational learning is a platform where knowledge can create, modify, share and apply to a work context (Connelly and Kelloway 2003). It is a learning process by a learner and requires learner's ability to create, share and apply the knowledge that they have obtained (Kontoghiorghes et al. 2005). There are three types of organizational learning such as individual learning, interpersonal learning, and learning by the organization (Massey and Weiss 2006). Individual learning is defined as independent learning (Walsh and Ungson 1991). A person will be learning from organizational climate, norms and values (March 1991; Miller et al. 2006). They learn by observe and understand the culture, norms and interpersonal interaction (Levinthal and March 1993). Finally, learning from the organization code refers to learning from a manual, a handbook or written instructions provided by the organization (March 1991). Thus, knowledge sharing practices apply by provide a continuous learning, inquiry, dialogue session and team learning for people to share and learn from others (Jo and Joo 2011). This well justifies that people learn on the job. Continues practices of knowledge sharing provides an opportunity to learn from others. They learn by inquiry and dialogue with other employee by expressing their views, active listening and giving feedback opinion, views, support questioning, and participating in experiment. In addition, as team learning, it develops people to think innovative, creative and expects to learn and work together. For example, organization learning assists in developing employee self-efficacy, self-interest, the trust to share and receive knowledge from others (Bock et al. 2005). An organizational learning exposes them to know-what and know-how to perform of their work context (Nonako and Takeuchi 1995). Thus, in previous discussion knowledge sharing agreed to provide a platform for individual learning, interpersonal learning, and learning by the organization. The practices of knowledge sharing can be done by continuous learning, inquiry, dialogue session, and team learning. In other words, knowledge sharing provides the learning environment and facilitates the process of learning in a business.

24.5 Knowledge Sharing and Innovation

In business nature, innovation is viewed as a mechanism to sustain a highly competitive business in market (Salaman and Storey 2002). Innovation potentially improve the efficiency and value of developing new intangible asset in business. Empirical studies show that the innovation effect increases business by eliminating costs, differentiation and producing high-quality product and services (Utami 2013). Integration of business and innovation able to increase consumer satisfaction, need and create new opportunity for a business (Calantone et al. 2002). Essentially innovation relies on individual knowledge, skill and experience to create a new idea, solution, decision and suggestion (Wang and Wang 2012). Innovation requires dynamic capability of an individual because the knowledge that resides in an individual is needed to be shared with the other employees. This will create a collaboration and encourage innovation behavior practices in business. It can happen when employee shared a new information, and resources with others, indirectly will enhance an individual critical thinking of the idea, creative in problem-solving, provide suggestion and new ideas for product and service improvement. Pertaining to practice of knowledge sharing and innovation, this study found that innovation facilitates the dynamic capabilities to survive in the business (Chandran 2004; Zollo and Winter 2002). From the discussion above, knowledge sharing has been supported as a positive force for innovation by share the experience with others, encouragement of the free flow of ideas, nurture innovative work behavior, generates new ideas, and help in solving a problem by giving ideal suggestion (De Marchi and Grandinetti 2013; Pai and Chang 2013; Nonako and Takeuchi 1995; Wang and Neo 2010). There is no doubt that practices of knowledge sharing and innovation are necessary for business. As a business, it cannot escape from the innovation and knowledge sharing. Lack of innovation in business initial identifies as there is less participation of the employee to share knowledge. Thus, knowledge sharing must be nurtured and educate employee to actively share knowledge with others.

24.6 Knowledge Sharing and Competitiveness

Competitiveness is defined as being different from others in the organization (Zonooz et al. 2011). A competitive is an ability to attract customers to choose their offering over all the alternative provided. However, this study defined competitive is a strategy to sustain, act and react within a competitive environment. Essentially, business practices are highly concentrate to the strategy, operations, resource-based view and economics to survive and sustain longer in a business (Argote and Ingram 2000). According to Spender and Grant (1996), the principal source of competitive advantage is all about human capital. Hayati et al. (2013) and Hislop (2003) supported human capital is a valuable resources as knowledge that belongs to employee such as specific roles, skills and cognitive abilities is unique and different from others. According to Aldisent (2002), human capital is a pool of values capabilities, knowledge, skill, life experiences and motivation of the workforce. While Kaplan and Norton (2004) added human capital is about intellectual capital which reflects the thinking, knowledge, creativity and decision-making capability. From the discussion, human capital is a valuable resource that belongs to business. It is an intellectual asset that is unreplaced and difficult to develop. Therefore, it is important to practice knowledge sharing in business to manage knowledge, human skill, competency, and directly prepare for being competitive in business. One of the issues highlighted by previous studies is the need to retain the knowledge from retired workers or expert persons by practices of knowledge sharing (Calo 2008). A retired employee may leave the organization without sharing their experience and knowledge with others who remain in the organization (Paton 2008). There is a possibility to recruit a new employee for replacing who leave the organization, however, it does not guarantee the knowledge will continue by the new employee or transfer through training and development. This implies loss of competitive advantages as the business losses the knowledge and competence of employees. Pertaining to this discussion, practice of knowledge sharing may allow better managing the flow of organizational knowledge, that belongs to an individual. Throughout knowledge sharing the business may create a potential to develop their own competitive advantages by minimizing dependency on individual and out-sourcing resources.

24.7 Conclusion

As conclusion, knowledge sharing plays a significant role in a business context in organizational learning, being innovative and managing competitive advantages. The role of knowledge sharing contributes to a positive and large effect to the business. An increase in the awareness of practicing knowledge sharing may encourage and promote all the employees including the employer and top management to practice knowledge sharing for a better benefit for the business. Therefore, this study proposed a framework which links knowledge sharing with organizational learning, innovation and competitiveness. This framework explains that knowledge sharing has played a significant role in the organizational learning, innovation and competitiveness at the organizational level. In a future study, this review recommends exploring with data analysis of knowledge sharing and the three contexts as organizational learning, innovation and competitiveness. Second, studies are needed to concentrate on the process of knowledge sharing which influences the process of learning in the organization, developing innovative work behavior and managing high competition.

Acknowledgements This paper has been supported by Faculty of Business of Universiti Teknologi MARA.

References

Alavi, M., & Leidner, D. E. (2001). Review: Knowledge management and knowledge management systems: Conceptual foundations and research issues. *MIS Quarterly*, 107–136.

Alavi, S., Wahab, D. A., & Muhamad, N. (2010). Exploring the relation between organizational learning and knowledge management for improving performance. In *Information Retrieval & Knowledge Management (CAMP), 2010 International Conference on* (pp. 297–302). IEEE.

Aldisent, L. (2002). Valuing People! How Human Capital Can Be Your Strongest Asset.

Argote, L., & Ingram, P. (2000). Knowledge transfer: A basis for competitive advantage in firms. *Organizational Behavior and Human Decision Processes, 82*(1), 150–169.

Bock, G., Zmud, R., Kim, Y. & Lee, J. (2005). Behavioral intention formation in knowledge sharing: Examining the roles of extrinsic motivators, social-psychological forces, and organizational climate (pp. 87–111). Mis Quarterly.

Calantone, R. J., Cavusgil, T. S., & Zhao, Y. (2002). Learning orientation, firm innovation, and firm performance. *Industrial Marketing Management, 31*(6), 515–524.

Calo, T. (2008). Talent management in the era of the aging workforce: The critical role of knowledge transfer. *Public Personnel Management*, (Vol. 37, 4, pp. 403–416). Retrieved November 6, 2009, from ProQuest Business database.

Chandran, J. P. (2004). Managing new industry creation: Global knowledge formation and entrepreneurship in high technology. *The Academy of Management Review, 29*(2), 303–306.

Chang, H. H., & Chuang, S. S. (2011). Social capital and individual motivations on knowledge sharing: Participant involvement as a moderator. *Information & management, 48*(1), 9–18. Chicago, IL: Dearborn Trade Publishing.

Connelly, C. E., & Kevin Kelloway, E. (2003). Predictors of employees' perceptions of knowledge sharing cultures. *Leadership & Organization Development Journal, 24*(5), 294–301.

Cummings, J. L., & Teng, B.-S. (2003). Transferring R&D knowledge: The key factors affecting knowledge transfer success. *Journal of Engineering and Technology Management, 20,* 39–68.

De Marchi, V., & Grandinetti, R. (2013). Knowledge strategies for environmental innovations: the case of Italian manufacturing firms. *Journal of Knowledge Management, 17*(4), 569–582.

Eckl, V. C. (2012). *Creating an Interactive-Recursive Model of Knowledge Transfer*. Copenhagen, Denmark: CBS.

Gagné, M. (2009). A model of knowledge-sharing motivation. *Human Resource Management, 48* (4), 571–589.

Grandy, G., & Wicks, D. (2008). Competitive advantage as a legitimacy-creating process. *Qualitative Research in Organizations and Management: An International Journal, 3*(1), 21–41.

Hansen, M. T., Nohria, N., & Tierney, T. (1999). What's your strategy for managing knowledge? *The knowledge management yearbook, 2000–2001,* 55–69.

Hayati, A. J., Toulson, P., & Tweed, D. (2013). Knowledge Sharing Success for Sustaining Organizational Competitive Advantage. *Procedia Economic and Finance, 7,* 150–157.

Hislop, D. (2003). Linking human resource management and knowledge management via commitment: A review and research agenda. *Employee Relations, 25,* 182–202.

Janson, A., & McQueen, R. J. (2007). Capturing leadership tacit knowledge in conversations with leaders. *Leadership & Organization Development Journal, 28*(7), 646–663.

Jo, S. J., & Joo, B. K. (2011). Knowledge sharing: The influences of learning organization culture, organizational commitment, and organizational citizenship behaviors. *Journal of Leadership & Organizational Studies,* 1548051811405208.

Kaplan, R., & Norton, D. (2004). *Measuring the Strategic Readiness of Intangible Assets* (pp. 52–60). Harvard Business Review, Boston: MA, Harvard Business School Press.

Kontoghiorghes, C., Awbre, S. M., & Feurig, P. L. (2005). Examining the relationship between learning organization characteristics and change adaptation, innovation, and organizational performance. *Human Resource Development Quarterly, 16*(2), 185–212.

Kumaraswamy, K. S. N., & Chitale, C. M. (2012). Collaborative knowledge sharing strategy to enhance organizational learning. *The Journal of Management Development, 31*(3), 308–322.

Lam, A. (2000). Tacit knowledge, organizational learning and societal institutions: An integrated framework. *Organization studies, 21*(3), 487–513.

Lee, H., & Choi, B. (2003). Knowledge management enablers, processes, and organizational performance: An integrative view and empirical examination. *Journal of Management Information Systems, 20*(1), 179–228.

Levinthal, D.A. & March, J.G. (1993), The myopia of learning. *Strategic Management Journal,* 14, (Special Issue), 95–112.

Lin, T. C., Wu, S., & Lu, C. T. (2012). Exploring the affect factors of knowledge sharing behavior: The relations model theory perspective. *Expert Systems with Applications, 39*(1), 751–764.

March, J. G. (1991). Exploration and exploitation in organizational learning. *Organization Science, 2*(1), 71–87.

Marsh, S. J., & Stock, G. N. (2003). Building dynamic capabilities in new product development through intertemporal integration. *Journal of Product Innovation Management, 20*(2), 136–148.

Massey, A. P., & Montoya-Weiss, M. M. (2006). Unraveling the temporal fabric of knowledge conversion: A model of media selection and use. *MIS Quarterly, 30*(1), 99–114.

Miller, K. D., Zhao, M., & Calantone, R. J. (2006). Adding interpersonal learning and tacit knowledge to march's exploration-exploitation model. *Academy of Management Journal, 49*(4), 709–722.

Moustaghfir, K., & Schiuma, G. (2013). Knowledge, learning, and innovation: Research and perspectives. *Journal of Knowledge Management, 17*(4), 495–510.

Nonaka, I., & Takeuchi, H. (1995). *The Knowledge-Creating Company*. New York, NY: Oxford University Press.

Pai, F. Y., & Chang, H. F. (2013). The Effects of Knowledge Sharing and Absorption on Organizational Innovation Performance–A Dynamic Capabilities Perspective. IJIKM, 8.

Paton, N. (2008). Manager at work: Organizations ignore the transfer of knowledge. The Edge Singapore. Retrieved September 9, 2009, from www.lexisnexis.com.

Reychav, I., & Weisberg, J. (2009). Going beyond technology: Knowledge sharing as a tool for enhancing customer-oriented attitudes. *International Journal of Information Management, 29*(5), 353–361.

Salaman, J. G., & Storey, J. (2002). Managers' theories about the process of innovation'. *Journal of Management Studies, 39*(2), 147–165.

Sanjaghi, M., Akhavan, P., & Najafi, S. (2013). Fostering knowledge sharing behavior: The role of organizational culture and trust. *Sanjaghi, ME, Akhavan, Peyman, and Sobhan Najafi (2013), Fostering knowledge sharing behavior: The role of organizational culture and trust, International journal of the academy of Organizational behavior management*, 2(5), 9–33.

Shih, H. A., & Chiang, Y. H. (2005). Strategy alignment between HRM, KM, and corporate development. *International Journal of Manpower*, *26*(6), 582–603.

Shang, S. S. C., Lin, S. F. & Wu Y. L.,(2009). Service innovation through dynamic knowledge management, *Industrial Management & Data Systems, 109*(2009), 322–337.

Smith, P. A. (2005). Knowledge sharing and strategic capital: The importance and identification of opinion leaders. *The Learning Organization, 12*(6), 563–574.

Spender, J.-C., & Grant, R. M. (1996). Knowledge and the firm: Overview. *Strategic Management Journal, 17,* 5–9.

Susanne, S., Kerr, M., & Clegg, C. (2007). Sharing knowledge: Contextualising socio-technical thinking and practices. *The Learning Organization, 14*(5), 423–435.

Utami, M. M. (2013). How intellectual stimulation effects knowledge sharing, innovation and firm performance. *International Journal of Social Science and Humanity, 3*(4), 420.

Walsh, J. P., & Ungson, G. R. (1991). Organisational Memory. *Academy of Management Review, 16*(1), 57–91.

Wang, S., & Noe, R. A. (2010). Knowledge sharing: A review and directions for future research. *Human Resource Management Review, 20*(2), 115–131.

Wang, Z., & Wang, N. (2012). Knowledge sharing, innovation and firm performance. *Expert Systems with Applications, 39*(10), 8899–8908.

Wasko, M. M., & Faraj, S. (2005). Why should I share? Examining social capital and knowledge contribution in electronic networks of practice. *MIS Quarterly*, 35–57.

Widén-Wulff, G., & Suomi, R. (2007). Utilization of information resources for business success: The knowledge sharing model. *Information Resources Management Journal (IRMJ), 20*(1), 46–67.

Zollo, M., & Winter, S. G. (2002). Deliberate learning and the evolution of dynamic capabilities. *Organization Science, 13*(3), 339–351.

Zonooz, B. H., Farzam, V., Satarifar, M., & Bakhshi, L. (2011). The relationship between knowledge transfer and competitiveness in "SMES" with emphasis on absorptive capacity and combinative capabilities. *International Business and Management, 2*(1), 59–85.

Chapter 25
The Relationship Between Job Stress and Quality of Life Among Working Adults

Mumtaz Ahmad, Siti Noorsuriani Maon and Nor Intan Shamimi Abdul Aziz

Abstract Job stress is a serious threat to the working people's quality of life (QoL). Stress at workplace gives a big impact on a person's health. The purpose of this study was to investigate the relationships between job stress and the QoL of working people. A total of 400 validated sets of questionnaire were distributed to respondents in the selected areas of Meru, Klang and the acquired data were analysed using IBM SPSS 22.0. The findings revealed that there was a significant relationship between job stress and the quality of life among employees. The most influential factor on the QoL was job-related stress, followed by organisational, interpersonal, perceived stress and work environment related stress. The lack of reward and recognition was highly related to the causes of stress and influence the employees' concentration and confidence. In conclusion, the measurement of stress in the QoL is important because it will also reflect on people's life evaluation, expectancy and standard of living.

Keywords Stress · Stressor · Job stress · Quality of life

25.1 Introduction

A high quality of life (QoL) is important for organisations to attract and retain qualified, committed and motivated employees. Every people have experienced stress, and some of them can manage it effectively, while the rest are not. However, stress can help people to perform better under pressure and motivate them to

M. Ahmad (✉) · S.N. Maon · N.I.S.A. Aziz
Faculty of Business and Management, Universiti Teknologi MARA, Kampus Selangor, Selangor, Malaysia
e-mail: mumtaz2627@salam.uitm.edu.my

S.N. Maon
e-mail: sitinoor123@puncakalam.uitm.edu.my

N.I.S.A. Aziz
e-mail: shamimi4576@puncakalam.uitm.edu.my

F. Noordin et al. (eds.), *Proceedings of the 2nd Advances in Business Research International Conference*, https://doi.org/10.1007/978-981-10-6053-3_25

achieve the best. Thus, stress can be either positive or otherwise. Yet stress is often not a handful and can do worse if it is not effectively managed. For most people, stress is negative and unpleasant. People who experienced self-conflict, such as feeling of fear and frustration, occasionally and sometimes cannot be controlled. People nowadays need to tackle their workloads, social relationships, and self-responsibilities. When experiencing stress, individuals may not display symptoms of stress while some may realise and be aware of it. Today, there is a lot of diseases related stress and it is important to investigate the stress experienced by people as this may assisting finding the best alternative to cope with stress. The entire situation can lead to stress toward an individual. If this is not being resolved, it may lead to the worst condition which can affect one's health. One of the health conditions resulting from stress is heart attack in which could lead to death.

Qualities of life in Malaysia are being observed and measured frequently by the Economic Planning Unit (EPU) for future development and references. In 2010, the EPU stated that Malaysia's quality of life in the sector of working condition recorded to be the lowest sub-index shared placed with family compared to another subject such as environment, education, transport and housing. However, there was a slight increase in 2011 which indicated more conducive working environment and less number of industrial accidents (EPU 2011).

Work stress appears to be a more pervasive problem in recent years. It arises when demand exceed abilities, while job-related strains are reactions or outcome resulting from the experiences of stress. Some of the examples are excessive workload, being forced to work overtime and unsatisfying job performances. According to Haider and Supriya (2007), stress is now becoming a global issue affecting all countries, all categories of employees and societies.

Moreover, World Health Organisation (2015) stated that occupational stress is the stress related to the workload burden that is usually experienced by most of the working individuals which happens in both the government and private sectors. If an individual has a job that is challenging, he or she will feel some pressure at work. However, when that pressure is excessive and one deems it as a burden, then it becomes stress. Consequently, people usually experience anxiety, mood changes and will have many health problems when stress become excessive, contributing to physical and psychological impairment.

Therefore, the aim of this research is to investigate the relationship between job stress and quality of life among employees working at selected areas, particularly in Meru, Klang. This study will show which type of stress could either positively or negatively affect the quality of life among working people. The study was conducted due to the growing empirical evidence suggesting workplace stress adversely affects task performance, physical health and well-being of employees. This evidence of negative effects of workplace stress is a unilateral cause for concern and makes a strong case for understanding this issue in greater detail.

25.2 Literature Review

25.2.1 Overview of Quality of Life

Quality of life is a broad concept that incorporates all aspects of life and has been used in a variety of subjects and disciplines such as geography, philosophy, medical, advertising, as well as in the working life. According to Barcaccia (2013), quality of life can be described as the multidimensional factors that include everything from physical health, psychological state, the level of independence, family, education, wealth, religious beliefs, a sense of optimism, local services and transport, employment, social relationships, housing and the environment. However, World Health Organization Quality of Life assessment instrument (WHOQOL-100) had identified four domains of quality of life, which are physical, psychological, social relationship and environment (WHO 1986). Quality of life covers all aspects of people life that would affect the health of the persons and relationship of the persons with the environment and other people.

The quality of life is an elusive concept approachable at varying levels of generality from the assessment of societal or community wellbeing to the specific evaluation of the situations of individuals or groups (Felce and Perry 1995). Dorfinan, as cited in Bronson (1999), defined quality of life as "satisfaction, a sense of well-being indicating how the individual perceives his or her quality of life." This was supported by Revicki et al. as cited by Nagy et al. (2011), indicating that the quality of life is a broad range of human experiences related to one's overall well-being, in which minimally includes the broadly-defined assessments of the physical, psychological and social domains of functioning.

25.2.2 Job Stressor

Stress can be defined as a normal physical response to events that caused people feel threatened or upset in some way (Smith et al. 2015). Stress is the psychological and physical state that results when an individual's resources are not sufficient to cope with the demands and pressures of the situation (Michie as cited in Mosadeghrad et al. 2011). Stress often occurs when individuals' physical and emotional states do not match or cannot handle their job demands, constraints and/or opportunities (Ismail et al. 2009). Causes of stress are also known as a stressor. Lack of exposure incomprehension of stress in their interpersonal, intrapersonal, relationship and environmental surrounding become the major causes of stress among individuals. The relationships at work with superiors, colleagues, and subordinates have also been identified as potential stressors (Oke and Dawson 2008). Additionally, the variety of job-related, interpersonal, organisational and environmental factors could influence a person's level of job stress (Mosadeghrad et al. 2011).

According to Wight et al. (2011), a sick environment can threaten health through biological and psychological pathways. Stress not only influences mental health and quality of life but also increases chronic diseases such as heart disease. Mazumdar et al. (2011) contended that work stress due to unusual posture or improper postural adjustment to the work results in back pain, headaches, nervousness, aching muscles, excessive perspiration and depressions. Hussain et al. (2013) also indicated that stress is very harmful to the human body because it increases blood pressure, sugar, and suppresses the immune system, decreases digestive system activity and reduces urine output. Stress experienced by workers at work is called job stress.

25.2.3 The Relationship Between Job Stress and Quality of Life

The quality of life encompasses the fulfilment of human needs such as a satisfactory material life, health, education, security, living in a clean environment and also the enjoyment of the aesthetic and spiritual need (Narehan et al. 2014). The ability of employees to manage their physiological and psychological stresses may have a significant impact on their job satisfaction (Fairbrother and Warn 2003). Quality of life can be defined as individuals' perception of their position in life in the context of the culture and value systems in relation to their goals, expectations, standards, and concerns (Chadha et al. 2012).

Saxena and Orley (1997) defined quality of life as the individuals' perception of their position in life in the context of culture and value systems in which they live and in relation to their goals, expectations, standards and concerns. Meanwhile Borthwick-Duffy, as cited by Felce and Perry (1995), presented three perspectives on quality of life: quality of one's life conditions, one's satisfaction with life conditions, and the combination of both life conditions and satisfaction. This was supported by Revicki et al. as cited by Nagy et al. (2011) by asserting that quality of life is a broad range of human experiences related to one's overall well-being that minimally includes the broadly-defined assessments of the physical, psychological and social domains of functioning. Besides that, Mosadeghrad et al. (2011) stated that quality of life refers to an employee's satisfaction with working life, which depends on the employee's feeling about various dimensions. Physiological stress is often viewed as a physiological reaction of the body such as headache, migraine, abdominal pain, backache and also sleep disturbance (Ismail et al. 2009). Figure 25.1 illustrates a framework of stress related to quality of life which is adopted from Mosadeghrad et al. (2011).

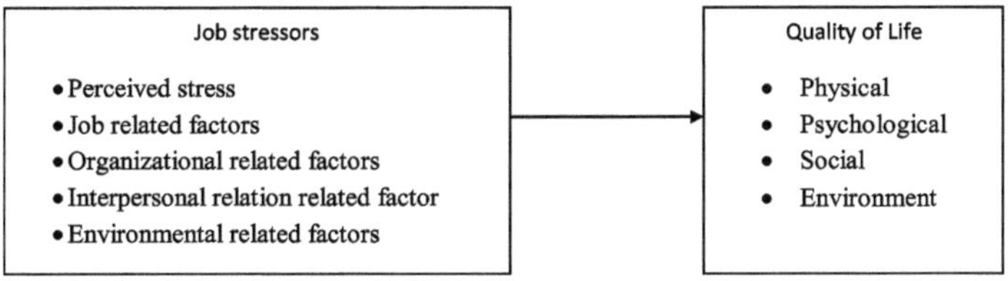

Fig. 25.1 Stress related to quality of life framework

25.3 Methodology

This study employed a cross-sectional method. Data collection using questionnaire was carried out at Meru, Klang, Selangor. Convenience sampling technique was chosen due to the unavailability of the sampling frame. The questionnaires were personally distributed and accompanied with a cover letter in order to avoid any difficulties in understanding the questions among the respondents. It was also to convince the respondents that the information used was only for academic purpose and would be kept confidential. Respondents were given 20 min to complete the questionnaires. After 20 min, the researchers personally collected the questionnaires from the respondents. A total of 400 respondents volunteered to participate in this research study. However, the number of valid questionnaires for data analysis were 377 which represented 99.73% of the response rate.

25.4 Results and Discussions

Assumptions of normality and linearity of the obtained data were examined and found acceptable. The reliability testing was considered as acceptable with Cronbach alpha value of 0.902 for 46 items in the questionnaire. A descriptive analysis was conducted to examine the demographic profile. The demographic profile of the respondents includes gender, age, marital status, employment status and highest educational background. Findings of the demographic profile are described in Table 25.1. Female respondents were the majority (74.5%; n = 281) whereas male employees made up the other 25.5% (n = 96). There were 72.4% (n = 273) respondents within the age range of 18–27 years old and 18.3% (n = 69) of the respondents were aged 28–37 years old. Only 6.9% (n = 26) of the respondents were between the age group of 38 and 47 years old, followed by 1.6% (n = 6) in the age range of 48–57 years old. Only 1% (n = 3) of respondents were 58 years old and above. In terms of academic background, it was found that 52.3% (n = 197) of the respondents were undergraduate, followed by 38.7% (n = 146) of the respondents who were school leavers and 4.8% (n = 18) of the respondents were postgraduate. Meanwhile, 4.2% (n = 16) of the respondents had other qualifications.

Table 25.1 Demographic profile (n = 377)

Items	Frequency	Percentage
Gender		
Male	96	25.5
Female	281	74.5
Age		
18–27	273	72.4
28–37	69	18.3
38–47	26	6.9
48–57	6	1.6
58 and above	3	0.8
Marital status		
Single	245	65
Married	122	32.4
Others	10	2.7
Employment status		
Permanent	216	57.3
Contract	92	24.4
Others	69	18.3
Education level		
School leavers	146	38.7
Undergraduate	197	52.3
Postgraduate	18	4.8
Others	16	4.2

More than 65% of the respondents were single (n = 245) while 32.4% (n = 122) of the respondents were married and 2.7% (n = 10) stated others. Nearly 60% (n = 216) of the respondents were permanent employees and 24.4% (n = 92) of the respondents were on contract basis. On the other hand, 18.3% (n = 69) of respondents were identified as in other employment status.

A bivariate correlation analysis was carried out to investigate the relationship between job stress and quality of life. Table 25.2 shows the descriptive and correlation analysis of the variables. Based on the mean analysis, figures indicated that the varying degree of respondents' score on the studied variable. Pertaining to the independent variables, the highest mean value was Organizational Related Stress [M = 3.53, SD = 0.799] while the lowest was Working Environment Related Stress [M = 2.87, SD = 0.635].

The correlation coefficient result was interpreted using "Eyeball method" which the correlation between 0.8–1.0 was said to be very strong, 0.6–0.8 was said to be strong, 0.4–0.6 was moderate relationship, 0.2–0.4 was interpreted as weak and 0.0–0.2 was very weak. The results indicated that there was a weak positive relationship between Quality of Life and Perceive Stress, Working Environment Stress, and Interpersonal Stress. From the findings, the output indicated a marked degree of

Table 25.2 Descriptive and correlational analysis of job stress constructs and quality of life

No	Variables	1	2	3	4	5	6
1	Perceive Stress	–	0.87*	0.281**	0.152**	.015	0.362
2	Job Related Stress	–	–	0.030	0.569**	0.632**	0.460**
3	Working Environment Stress	–	–	–	–0.14	–0.20	0.112**
4	Organizational Stress	–	–	–	–	0.582**	0.437**
5	Interpersonal Stress	–	–	–	–	–	0.399**
6	Quality of Life	–	–	–	–	–	1
	Mean	3.03	3.26	2.87	3.53	3.45	3.45
	SD	0.800	0.932	0.635	0.800	0.908	0.520

** *Correlation is significant at the 0.01 level (1-tailed)*

correlation $r = 0.362$, $r = 0.112$ and $r = 0.399$ respectively with $p < 0.05$. Therefore, the hypothesis was accepted.

The other two variables were verified to have a significant moderate positive relationship with quality of life. From the findings, the output confirmed that there was a significant positive relationship for the Organization Stress and Job Stress with employees' Quality of Life. The results of the finding of the correlation were $r = 437$ and $r = 0.460$ respectively with $p < 0.05$. Therefore, the hypothesis was accepted.

25.5 Discussion

Based on the findings, the perceived stress had a weak correlation with quality of life among working adults in Meru, Klang. It was revealed that the feelings or thoughts of an individual had about how much stress they are under at or over a given point in time did not really influence their quality of life. The presence of perceived stress could lead a person to fail in controlling important things in their lives due to failure of making decisions, and will affect the way of their lives (Duxbury 1994). This happens because the person was afraid of making a wrong decision and what people may think of him or her. This was consistent with a study conducted by Eswi et al. (2013), in which they stated that stress started within self-perception and he or she will express it through behaviour. Since most of the respondents were still young, the probability of making decision is low.

A weak relationship between job-related stress and quality of life among employees in Meru was also discovered. Employees who have the authority or have the opportunity to make a decision on how they should finish their tasks will have the lowest stress at work and become healthy (Pediwal et al. 2011). According to Hussain et al. (2013), job-related stress is an unpleasant emotional situation that an individual experiences when the requirements of the job are not counter balanced with his ability to cope with the situation. Most of the cases, the lack of reward and recognition were the causes of stress and affect the concentration and confidence of employees. Meanwhile, according to Pediwal (2011), job stress is a phenomenon where the employees or employers face at the job and handles it differently according to their own way. Basically, a job stress is a mismatch between the individual capabilities and organisational demand and can lead to poor health condition due to worry about discomfort and difficulties in sleeping.

However, the work environment related stress has a moderate positive relationship with the quality of life. The factors that influence stress at working environment are the physical demands of work and the distress caused by environmental factors, such as, noise, vibration, extremes of temperature, workload, work hours (including shift work), the effects of technological changes, and exposure to risks and hazards (Oke and Dawson 2008). This was supported by Ulleberg and Rundmo (1997) by stating that the environment is the main factor of stress including noise, lighting, air and safeties. All of these will affect the moodiness of the workers and it will directly affect their life. Besides that, it also disrupts their working performance such as losing concentration on their work. Mostly the employees or workers become distracted and unable to concentrate on their job due to a lot of noise in the workplace. Cooper et al. (1997) stated that most employees are getting stress by disturbance due to noisy environment. Consequently, it affects their concentration to complete their tasks and indirectly causing them to go back home late. Due to this problem, the employees will experience lack of sleep and cannot perform excellently at work. Besides that, it was stated that a healthy working environment is free from noise which was ranked first in environment stress (Neelamegam and Asrafi 2010). Stress among employees depends on smooth work routine and conducive workplace. Employees who are satisfied with their working environment will be more motivated to accomplish their tasks satisfactorily and at the same time influence their relationship with family members and colleagues.

There was a significant relationship between organisational stress and quality of life ($r = 0.39$, $p < 0.05$). To maintain safety at the workplace the organisation need to prepare a work environment which is efficient and effective especially with adequate equipment and facilities. Hayes et al. (1998) verified this fact by stating that employees who are satisfied with their job safety will stay longer at the organisation compared with those who feel insecure with the organisation at which they are working for. Moreover, employees who think that the organisation will take care of them will make them stay longer in the organisation and will make them happy with their work.

The findings also revealed that there is a relationship between interpersonal related stress and quality of life among employees. According to Dixon and Robinson (2005), if parties involved in a dispute cannot reach to an understanding of solving the problem, this will lead to dissatisfaction. This condition can contributenegatively to an individual's psychology. As stated by the National Institute for Occupational Safety and Health (2006), the interpersonal relationships that influence the stressor are the poor social environment and lack of support or help from co-workers, supervisors and inadequate equipment provided. This was supported by Oke and Dawson (2008) who stated that relationships at work with superiors, colleagues, and subordinates have been identified as potential stressors. Furthermore, Danna and Griffin (1999) found that mistrust of co-workers is related to high role ambiguity, poor communication, low job satisfaction, and poor psychological well-being.

Masterson et al. (2000) stipulated that when the management and employees are working together to make sure the safety of the workplace is maintained, employees feel more motivated to finish the job. An employee's stress level depends on how a person is treated by his supervisor, interaction with the supervisor and nature of the work, such as being involved in decision-making process. A good relationship with the supervisor will reduce stress among employees and can contribute to high job performance. When the relationship between employees and supervisor is fair in anything which involves work, such as getting information, empowerment and receiving sufficient equipment, their job will be simplified and stress at the workplace will be avoided (Konovsky and Pugh 1994).

25.6 Conclusion

The result shows that the mean score for organisational related stress is the highest among all of the job stressors. It can be concluded that the employees, particularly who work in Meru, Klang, perceived that organisational related stress is the main factor which contributes to their quality of life (QoL). Understanding the causes of job stress by measuring it accurately, subsequently enabling to identify problem areas, implementing interventions and re-evaluating the situation could prove useful. Therefore, focus should be given to the five factors of stress which are perceived stress, job-related stress, work environment related stress, organisational stress and interpersonal related stress in order to improve the present situation, as well as to rectify the problems.

References

Barcaccia, B., Esposito, G., Matarese, M., Bertolaso, M., Elvira, M., & De Marinis, M. G. (2013). Defining Quality of Life: A Wild-Goose Chase?. *Europe's Journal of Psychology*, *9*(1), 185–203. doi:10.5964/ejop.v9i1.484

Bronson, T. (1999). Quality of Life of the Hemodialysis Patient. Masters Theses. 531.http://scholarworks.gvsu.edu/theses/531

Chadha, M., Sood, K., & Malhotra, S. (2012). Effects of organizational stress on quality of life of primary and secondary school teachers. *Delhi Psychiatry Journal, 15*(2), 342–346.

Cooper, R. P., Abraham, J., Berman, S., & Staska, M. (1997). The development of infants' preference for motherese. *Infant Behavior & Development*, *20*, 477–488.

Danna, K., & Griffin, R. W. (1999). Health and well-being in the workplace: A review and synthesis of the literature. *Journal of Management, 25*(3), 357–384.

Dixon, S, K. & Robinson, E. (2005). Depression and college stress among university undergraduates. *Journal of College Student Development*, *49*(5), 412–424.

Duxbury, L., Higgins, C., & Lee, C. (1994). Work-Family Conflict: A Comparison by Gender, Family Type, and Perceived Control. *Journal of Family Issues, 15*(3), 449–466. doi:10.1177/019251394015003006

Eswi, A. S., Radi, S., & Youssri, H. (2013). Stress/ stressors as perceived by baccalaureate Saudi nursing students. *Middle East Journal of Scientific Research, 14*(2), 193–202.

Fairbrother, K., & Warn, J. (2003). Workplace dimensions, stress and job satisfaction. *Journal Managerial Psychology, 18*(1), 8–21.

Felce, D., & Perry, J. (1995). Quality of Life: Its definition and measurement. *Research in Developmental Disabilities, 16,* 51–74.

Haider, Y., & Supriya, M. V. (2007). Career management: A view through stress window. *International Review of Business Research Papers, 3*(5), 182–192.

Hayes, B. E., Perander, J., Smecko, T., & Trask, J. (1998). Measuring perceptions of workplace safety: development and validation of the work safety scale. *Journal Safety Research, 29,* 145–161.

Hussain, N. S. M., Khan, M. A., Kant, A. Q., & Khan, S. N. (2013). Job stress and employees' productivity: Case of Azad Kashmir public health sector. *Interdisciplinary Journal of Contemporary Research in Business, 5*(3), 525–542.

Ismail. A, Yao. A & Yunus. N. (2009). Relationship between Occupational Stress and Job Satisfaction: An Empirical Study in Malaysia. *The Romanian Economic Journal, 8*(34), 3–29.

Konovsky, M. A., & Pugh, S. D. (1994). Citizenship behavior and social exchange. *Academy of Management Journal, 37*(3), 656–669.

Masterson, S. S., Lewis, K., Goldman, B. M., & Taylor, M. S. (2000). Integrating justice and social exchange: The differing effects of fair procedures and treatment on work relationships. *Academy of Management Journal, 43*(4), 738–748.

Mazumdar, H., Haloi, N., and Mazumdar, M.(2011). Impact of job stress on urban and rural employees in Kamrup district, Assam (India). *A physiological and psychological study, 3*(6), 377–382.

Mosadeghrad, A. M., Ferlie, E., and Rosenberg, D. (2011). Health Services Management Research. A study of relationship between job stress, quality of working life and turnover intention among hospital employees. *Health Services Management Research, 24*(4),170–181. doi:10.1258/hsmr.2011.011009.

Nagy, J., Pifko, J., & Nagy, K. (2011). Quality of life of H&E cancer patient after prosthetic rehabilitation. *Journal Dentist Research, 90*(3), 773.

Narehan, H., Hairunnisa, M., Norfadzillah, R., & Freziamella, L. (2014). The effect of Quality of Work Life (QWL) programs on quality of life (QOL) among employees at multinational companies in Malaysia. *Social and Behavioral Sciences, 112,* 24–34.

Neelamegam, R., & Asrafi, S. (2010). Work stress among employees of Dindigul district central cooperative bank, Tamil Nadu: A study. *The IUP Journal of Management Research, 5*(2), 57–69.

Oke, A. & Dawson, P. (2008). Contextualizing workplace stress: The experience of bank employees in Nigeria. Research Online. Retrieved June 16, 2011 from http://ro.uow.edu.au/compapers/503.

Pediwal, G. L. (2011). Excessive stress and its impact on employee behavior. *Journal of Global Economy, 1*(1), 13–40.

Saxena, S., & Orley, J. (1997). Quality of life assessment: The world health organization perspective. *European Psychiatry, 12*(3), 263-266. doi: 10.1016/S0924-9338(97)89095-5

Smith, M., Segal, R., & Segal, J. (2015). Stress Symptoms, Signs, and Causes. The Effects of Stress Overload and What You Can Do About It. Retrieved from http://www.helpguide.org/articles/stress/stress-symptoms-causes-andeffects.htm

Sutherland, V.J. (1995). Stress and the new contract for general practitioners. *Journal of Managerial Psychology,10*(3), 17–28. doi: 10.1108/02683949510081347

Ulleberg, P. & Rundmo, T. (1997). Job stress, social support, job satisfaction and absenteeism among offshore oil personnel. *An International Journal of Work, Health & Organisations, 11* (3), 215–228. doi:10.1080/02678379708256836

Wight, E., Chen, W., Dodd, V., & Weiler, R. (2011). Healthy Workplaces: The Effects of Nature Contact at Work on Employee Stress and Health. *Public Health Reports, 126*(1), 124–130.

Chapter 26
The Influence of Team Characteristics on Team Performance Among Employees at Selected Telecommunication Companies

Abdul Kadir Othman, Muhammad Iskandar Hamzah and Arina Mohd Nor

Abstract To survive in today's competitive business environment, organizations are implementing various strategies to optimize the use of existing resources. One of the strategies is to focus on teamwork. The outcome of using this strategy is that the organizations can experience the synergistic performance. However, some organizations are unable to gain this outcome as they are unable to identify and leverage the factors that are associated with team performance. The objective of this study is to investigate the factors that are important to team and their contribution to team performance. Analyzing 356 data collected from two major telecommunication companies in Malaysia, the results of regression analysis indicate that leadership support, trust and knowledge sharing significantly contribute to team performance. The managerial and research implications of the study are discussed in detail in the paper.

Keywords Team characteristics · Team performance · Telecommunication companies · Leadership support · Trust · Knowledge sharing

26.1 Introduction

Realizing the benefits of having high-performing team, a lot of organizations have embarked on initiatives to organize their workforce based on a team structure. However, not all teams are successful. Some failed due to, among others, the team structure itself, and most team organizations are implementing matrix organization. Members of the team come from different units, and they have to report to two

A.K. Othman (✉) · M.I. Hamzah
Faculty of Business and Management, Universiti Teknologi MARA Puncak Alam, 42300 Puncak Alam, Selangor, Malaysia
e-mail: abdkadir@salam.uitm.edu.my

A.M. Nor
Faculty of Business and Management, Center for Postgraduate and Professional Studies, Universiti Teknologi MARA, 40450 Shah Alam, Selangor, Malaysia

F. Noordin et al. (eds.), *Proceedings of the 2nd Advances in Business Research International Conference*, https://doi.org/10.1007/978-981-10-6053-3_26

bosses and this might create conflicting interests. So, to be successful, leadership plays a significant role to support this establishment. Another reason for the study is that although there are a lot of studies that have been conducted around the world regarding team performance or team effectiveness, studies specific to the Malaysian setting are still insufficient to confirm the relevant predictors of team performance. Therefore, this study is highly required.

Team performance is defined as the aggregate outcome of the effort of every member in a team to achieve the established goals. The popular understanding regarding team is that one plus one is more than two due to synergistic effect of a team establishment. By adding value to existing knowledge rather than telling team members what they already know, each member contributes to the success of the whole (Wing 2005). Relying on this understanding, a lot of companies have concentrated their effort in organizing their human resources around team establishment and the results are mixed. Some are successful at achieving the targeted outcomes, but others failed due to various reasons. Most of them are related to the structure or leadership, lack of trust among team members, communication failure, knowledge sharing capability of team members, team composition, and levels of motivation among members.

Team performance has a critical role in the overall performance of an organization, which can be realized through gainsharing plans and team-based incentives (Welbourne et al. 1998). Teamwork brings wide benefits in either frontline services or operations settings. In the service setting, a cohesive group is positioned to deliver seamless service to customers and they take ownership and responsibility of customer issues (Macaulay and Cook 1995). Meanwhile, teamwork is highly valued in production lines as it highly relates to lean manufacturing practices (Inamizu et al. 2014). Nevertheless, teamwork may be harder to be implemented in non-routine white-collar work as compared to routine blue-collar work in manufacturing (Richards et al. 2012). In certain cases, scholars have criticized that actual teamwork practice may not exist inside a team due to its existence as a form of management control to coordinate spatially distant workforce (Ryan 2012; van den Broek et al. 2004). As such, this study looks at team performance in the white-collar service sector in which the academic debate on teamwork often dominates within the manufacturing setting.

26.1.1 Leadership Support

"Great minds think alike" is an evergreen adage that possibly emphasizes the potential benefits of recruiting team members with similar traits or visions. However, having ambitious people within a team does not necessarily produce the intended results should every member insist on heading toward his or her own direction. The leader acts as a team steward that spearheads the direction and provides task- and relationship-based support to its members. Transformational leadership is recognized as one of the seminal leadership concepts that are commonly discussed or cited in the literature. It involves the leader establishing higher motive, and arousing followers' motivation and positive emotions by creating and representing an inspiring vision of the future (Avolio and Yammarino 2013). Recent findings by Chou et al. (2013) indicate that transformational leadership has indirect positive effect on team performance through trust and collective efficacy among team members. In another study, team building is found to partially mediate the relationship between transformational leadership and project success (Aga et al. 2016). A transformational leadership climate also leads to intention to share knowledge and strengthens team identity among team members (Liu and Phillips 2011). Besides transformational leadership, servant leadership also positively affects team performance via affect-based trust and psychological safety (Schaubroeck et al. 2011). Servant leadership is concerned on the leader's altruistic attitude in serving others, building a sense of community, emphasizing teamwork, and sharing power (Walumbwa et al. 2010).

26.1.2 Trust

Interdependency of members in a team is indispensable for it to provide mutual benefits. By having trust on other team members, an employee is expected to have a comfortable sense of belief and reliance toward their words and actions. Trust acts as a vital ingredient for developing and protecting team spirit that is built through cooperation and solidarity among team members (Erdem and Ozen 2003). Deeper trust among teammates is shown to lead to higher levels of team performance (Mach et al. 2010; Bijlsma-Frankema et al. 2008). In most circumstances, team members may find it difficult to achieve coherent conclusion and mutual understanding due to doubts and differing prejudices each member probably has toward each other. Therefore, the inculcation of trust within a team should be initiated and observed by the leaders. According to a study by Lee et al. (2010) in a large automotive firm, team leaders who engender trust among team members are most likely to contribute to team performance. Other than gaining trust from their leaders, employees also take inspiration of the firm's past success stories that serve to motivate the spirit of togetherness especially in difficult and challenging times. Thus, the existence of trust is also argued as the precedent and outcome of performance. In his study of American college basketball players, Dirks (2000) theorized that trust in leadership mediates the relationship between past performance and future performance. Paradoxically, his findings indicate that trust among members has nonsignificant ties with team performance though the proposition was earlier theorized to be an equally important predictor alongside trust in leadership.

26.1.3 Communication

Teamwork requires a lot of input and output from each team member as any action is made based on collective decision making process. Thus, communication plays an integral part prior to executing tasks via teamwork. Communication is defined by O'Reilly and Pondy (1979, p. 212) as "the exchange of information between a sender and a receiver and the inference of meaning between organizational participants." Ineffective communication may bring issues such as misinterpretations, communication errors, inadequate feedbacks, and lack of information quality. If these problems are not appropriately addressed, it may hamper a team from progressing forward. Besides, team members' perception toward the conduct of communication within and across teams in an organization may influence the overall team's performance. In a study by Carlson (2011) among athletes, teams that are more successful have athletes that are more satisfied with the communication that is taking place than the less successful teams. Other than perceived satisfaction, communication frequency is another predictor of team performance that has received considerable level of interest within the academia. Communication frequency has positive effect on convergent information (inference of meaning from information transmitted by others), which in turn is significantly related to higher task quality (Espinosa et al. 2015). Effective team member to leader communication is also predicted to influence team success in innovative decision making (Gajendran and Joshi 2012). Nevertheless, it is discovered that either too little or too much communication among team members may impede team performance (Patrashkova-Volzdoska et al. 2003).

26.1.4 Knowledge Sharing

The term knowledge sharing within the context of teamwork represents the exchange of explicit and tacit knowledge that are relevant to the team task (Lee et al. 2010). While communication is an important proposed predictor of performance, it brings no added value if information is not properly disseminated to the intended recipient. This can be attributed to lack of knowledge culture in the organization (Al-Alawi et al. 2007), unidirectional "top-down" only sharing, and lack of team-based sharing incentives (Zhang et al. 2010; Welbourne et al. 1998). Past literature has yielded solid evidence on the positive effect of knowledge sharing among team members on team performance (Liu et al. 2011; Srivastava et al. 2006). Meanwhile, others have established innovation outcomes as the results of knowledge sharing. As observed by Liu and Phillips (2011), team knowledge sharing intention is positively related to team innovativeness. In some other instances, knowledge sharing is found to have indirect effect on team performance. Specifically, knowledge application is inferred as the by-product of knowledge sharing and at the same time is also the predictor of team performance (Choi et al. 2010).

26.1.5 Team Composition or Membership

Team composition is described as "a cause that shapes various teamwork processes and outcomes of interest" (Bell 2007, p. 595). In this case, highly composed teams are those that are made of team members with diverse cultural origins, functional tasks, and seniority. Moreland et al. (2013) classified team composition according to three main dimensions: (1) team characteristics such as the number of team members, demographic profiles, abilities, and personal traits, (2) the characteristics of group members can be measured in numerous ways, such as central tendency (proportion, mean level) and variability (heterogeneous or homogeneous), and (3) analytical perspectives (either as cause, outcome, or context). Teams ought to benefit from having diversity of members in terms of inputs received, such as discovery of new problem solving methods and discovering mistakes that are otherwise ignored. Team performance of a highly diverse team may be contingent upon the complexity of tasks. A highly diverse team performs well when tasks are becoming more complex, while lesser complex tasks actually weaken the team's performance (Higgs 2005). Nevertheless, Ten Haaf et al. (2002) asserted that there is a relationship between team composition and performance, although there is criticism on the uncertainty of the actual criteria that determine the ideal and "balanced" degree of team composition (van de Water et al. 2008). Diversity of team composition can be something that is either preferred or not preferred by team members. According to Meyer (2012), pro-diversity team is performing well when its team composition is diverse, and a similar result also occurs for the team with lesser diversity beliefs when the group is consisted of highly homogeneous team members. Apart from diversity, team size is also a relevant phenomenon that is often related to team performance. Recently, scholars have argued that a higher number of team members do not necessarily translate into higher level of team performance (Kozlowski and Bell 2013; Zarzu et al. 2013) despite Belbin's (2010) earlier contention that six is the ideal number of people for a particular team to become effective.

26.1.6 Team Motivation

People frequently establish their own identity in relation to their surrounding social groups. Therefore, in understanding team motivation in the workplace, it is hard to neglect the social identity theory. The theory highlights a process termed as social identification, which reflects a persons' sense of which they relate to a group of persons that stems from the distinct identity of that group (Ashforth and Mael 1989). When an employee perceived social identity as a salient aspiration, the person may engage in developing the team-based self-esteem by emphasizing on team-oriented values such as fostering good relationships, earning respect and peer recognition, and attaining team goals (Latham 2012). In essence, Latham (2012,

p. 130) asserted that "people are motivated to attain those goals that are compatible with their self-identity." In tandem with such statement, recent studies offer inferential linkages between team motivation and team performance. For instance, in a team that exhibits pro-diversity beliefs, fault line strength (defined as the lack of diversity in groups and the presence of homogeneity of subgroups) positively affects team's performance when motivation is high as compared to an inverse relationship outcome when motivation is low (Meyer and Schermuly 2012). Moreover, team effort-directing actions and performance pressure are found to be motivational predictors that directly influence team performance (Gardner 2012). Furthermore, work engagement (a type of positive affective-motivational state) is found to be positively and significantly related to team performance (Torrente et al. 2012).

26.2 Methodology

The present study utilized correlational research design involving respondents from two telecommunication companies in Klang Valley. Quota sampling was used to distribute the questionnaire to 356 respondents with equal number of respondents for each company (178 respondents for each company). The questionnaire was developed based on the existing questions on the intended variables. There are six independent variables which are motivation, communication, strategic leadership, trust, team composition, and knowledge sharing and one dependent variable, which is team performance. There are 8 items to measure motivation, 6 items to assess communication, 9 items to evaluate strategic leadership, 8 items to measure trust, 9 items to appraise team composition, 7 items to gauge knowledge sharing, and 9 items to assess team performance. Items for assessing motivation were adapted from Enciso (2000).

An example of motivation item is, "I feel sense of pride in the team's work." Items for measuring communication were from Graebner (2012). An example of communication items is, "Team members feel free to voice any comments during the meeting." Items to gauge strategic leadership were adapted from Moore (2007) and Basim et al. (2007). An example of question for this variable is, "Leader generally supports requests for learning opportunities and training." For trust, all items were adapted from Erdem and Ozen (2003). An example of this item is, "I can trust the expertise of team members." The items for team composition were adapted from Enciso (2000). An example of the items is, "Team members have different but necessary skills for their roles in certain projects." The items for knowledge sharing were adapted from Al-Alawi et al. (2007). An example of the items is, "The team provides various tools and technologies to facilitate knowledge sharing and exchange (for example, email and intranet)." The last variable is team performance, and the items to measure this variable were adapted from Piercy (2007). An example of the items is, "Average productivity per team member is greater than last year." The Cronbach's alphas for the items measuring each variable during the pilot test are as follows: leadership support (0.938), trust (0.912), communication (0.620), knowledge sharing (0.841), team membership (0.839), team motivation (0.735), and team performance (0.885).

26.3 Findings and Discussion

With regard to the respondents' profile, a total of 356 respondents came from two major telecommunication companies with equal representatives (Table 26.1). A total of 133 respondents or 37.4% were male, and 223 respondents or 62.6% were female. Pertaining to the age distribution of the respondents, 37 individuals or 10.4% aged below 25 years old, 133 participants or 37.4% were in the age group of between 25 and 35 years old, 153 respondents or 43% were aged between 36 and 45 years old, and 33 respondents or 9.3% were in the age category of more than 45 years old. Looking at the education level, majority of respondents had bachelor degree with 176 respondents or 49.4%, followed by those who had diploma with 130 respondents or 30.5%, those with SPM with 3 respondents or 8.7% and lastly those with STPM qualification with 19 respondents or 5.3%. Majority of respondents were married, with 264 individuals or 74.2%, and the rest were still single, with 92 respondents or 25.8%. Pertaining to job position, majority of respondents were officers (235 respondents or 66%) and the remaining were clerks (70 respondents or 19.7%). In terms of tenure, most respondents had been working with the company between 6 and 10 years with the number of individuals of 130 or 36.5% of the total respondents. 107 respondents or 30.1% had been with the company for less than 6 years, 62 respondents or 17.4% had been working with the company between 11 and 15 years, and 57 respondents or 16% had been with the company for more than 15 years. Looking at respondents' distribution according to salary, 119 respondents or 33.4% received between RM3001 and RM4000 monthly salary, 107 respondents or 30.1% received more than RM4000 salary, 95 respondents or 26.7% got between RM2000 and RM3000 monthly income, and 35 respondents or 9.8% received less than RM2000 as their monthly income (Table 26.2).

The results of a principle component factor analysis with varimax rotation indicate the existence of six factors; first factor with nine items explaining 18.20% of variance, second factor with eight items explaining 14.86% of variance, third factor with six items explaining 11.20% of the variance, fourth factor with five items explaining 8.985% of the variance, fifth factor with three items explaining 6.36% of the variance, and sixth factor with two items explaining 6.19% of the total variance. The total variance explained in the model is 65.792%, which is considered good. KMO value of 0.919 indicates that the samples are adequate for factor analysis to be conducted. Bartlett's test of sphericity of 7749.075 denotes the adequacy of correlation matrix for factor analysis. MSA values in the range of 0.815 and 0.958 indicate the adequacy of sampling for each factor. The first factor comprised items pertaining to leadership support with factor loadings in the range

Table 26.1 Respondents' profile

Variable	Descriptive	Frequency	Percentage
Company	Celcom	178	50.0
	Digi	178	50.0
Gender	Male	133	37.4
	Female	223	62.6
Age	<25 years old	37	10.4
	25–35 years old	133	37.4
	36–45 years old	153	43.0
	>45 years old	33	9.3
Education level	SPM	31	8.7
	STPM	19	5.3
	Diploma	130	36.5
	Bachelor degree	176	49.4
Marital status	Single	92	25.8
	Married	264	74.2
Job position	Clerk	70	19.7
	Officer	235	66.0
	Others	51	14.3
Tenure	<6 years	107	30.1
	6–10 years	130	36.5
	11–15 years	62	17.4
	>15 years	57	16.0
Salary	<RM2,000	35	9.8
	RM2,001–RM3,000	95	26.7
	RM3,001–RM4,000	119	33.4
	>RM4,000	107	30.1

between 0.647 and 0.812; therefore, the name was retained. The second factor contained items that reflect trust with the items loadings in the range between 0.628 and 0.760. The name of the factor was maintained as trust. The third factor consisted of items concerning communication with loadings ranged from 0.622 to 0.780. The factor was known as communication. The fourth factor contained items measuring knowledge sharing with the loadings in the range between 0.554 and 0.813, and the name was retained. The fifth factor reflects team membership with loadings ranged from 0.681 to 0.795; thus, the name of team membership was used. Lastly, the sixth factor contained items assessing team motivation with the loadings between 0.711 and 0.774; thus, the name remained (Table 26.3).

A principle component factor analysis with varimax rotation was also performed on items measuring team performance. The results show that the sampling is

Table 26.2 Results of factor analysis for team characteristics

	Component					
	1	2	3	4	5	6
Leaders take an interest in understanding the technical accomplishments of individual team members	0.812					
Leaders continually look for opportunities to learn	0.781					
Leaders ensure that the team's actions are consistent with its values	0.780					
Leaders recognize individual team member accomplishments (for example, make public announcements or rewards team members	0.775					
Leaders recognize team accomplishment (for example, celebrates accomplishments or rewards the team)	0.767					
Leaders are approachable and are friendly toward team members	0.761					
Leaders discuss problem solving methods and techniques with team members	0.759					
Leaders generally support requests for learning opportunities and training	0.704					
Leaders empower others to help carry out the team's vision	0.647					
I can trust the expertise of team members		0.760				
Team members every time share all sources with other members		0.760				
Team members encourage each other to introduce different ideas and suggestions		0.759				
Team members strive to be honest to each other		0.742				
Team members' actions are congruent with their words		0.707				
Team members respect each other's emotions and ideas		0.678				

(continued)

Table 26.2 (continued)

	Component					
	1	2	3	4	5	6
Team members can ask for help from each other with their personal problems		0.675				
Team members fulfil their undertaking successfully		0.628				
Team members have the freedom to participate in the meeting			0.780			
Other members appear to feel free to make positive and negative comments			0.739			
Team members seem to participate actively			0.722			
Team members respond to the comments made by others			0.671			
Everyone has a chance to express his or her opinion			0.645			
Team members feel free to voice any comments during the meeting			0.622			
The technological tools available in the team for sharing knowledge are effective				0.813		
Members feel comfortable using the knowledge sharing technologies available				0.801		
The team provides various tools and technologies to facilitate knowledge sharing and exchange (for example, email and intranet)				0.759		
Members are rewarded for sharing their knowledge and experience with their team members				0.559		
The knowledge sharing rewards available are effective in motivating members to spread their knowledge				0.554		
Team members actively participate in initiatives, small or big, that promote understanding among members of diverse group					0.795	

(continued)

Table 26.2 (continued)

		Component					
		1	2	3	4	5	6
Team member use a variety of relationship building skills to create connections with people who are different from them						0.701	
Team members are evaluated fairly at work, based on their performance, regardless on their background (nationality, gender and race)						0.681	
It is important for our team to work together							0.774
I feel a sense of pride in the team's work							0.711
There is a high level of cooperation on the team							0.678
% variance explained (65.792)		18.20	14.86	11.20	8.99	6.36	6.19
MSA							0.815–0.958
KMO							0.919
Bartlett's test of sphericity	Approx. Chi-square						7749.075
	Df						561
	Sig.						0.000

sufficient with KMO value of 0.815. The Bartlett's test of sphericity of 1016.768 indicates the sufficient correlation matrix to proceed with factor analysis. The MSA values ranged from 0.741 to 0.898 and indicate the samples are adequate for each item. The variance explained of 58.802 is adequate for the model. Based on the results, one factor was produced indicates the unidimensionality of the model. The items loadings ranged from 0.728 to 0.828. The factor was named as team performance (Table 26.4).

Looking at the values of means and standard deviations of variables, all values are considered high exceeding the threshold value of 2.5. The lowest mean value is 3.81 for trust and team performance, and the highest mean value is 4.16 for team motivation. All variables have Cronbach's alpha values exceeding 0.7, denoting that all items measuring the intended variables are highly reliable. Pertaining to the correlation between the independent variables, the lowest value is between team membership and team motivation ($r = 0.255$; $p < 0.001$) and the highest correlation is between trust and team membership ($r = 0.561$; $p < 0.001$), indicating convergent validity of the measure. With regard to the relationship between the independent variables and the dependent variable, the lowest correlation value is between team motivation and team performance ($r = 0.348$; $p < 0.001$) and the

Table 26.3 Results of factor analysis for team performance

		Component
		1
Average productivity per team member is greater than last year		0.732
Response time for customer complaints is better than last year		0.729
The percentage of skilled workers compared to the total workforce is greater than last year		0.728
The team uses an effective short and long-term planning process		0.783
The team meets its (internal and external) customer requirements		0.795
The team is productive		0.828
% variance explained		58.802
MSA		0.741–0.898
KMO		0.815
Bartlett's test of sphericity	Approx. Chi-square	1016.768
	Df	15
	Sig.	0.000

highest correlation is between knowledge sharing and team performance ($r = 0.509$; $p < 0.001$), signifying concurrent validity. The results of correlation analysis indicate the potential influence of the predictor variables on the outcome variable, which is team performance (Table 26.5).

A multiple regression analysis was performed to identify factors that contribute to team effectiveness. R^2 value of 0.398 indicates that 39.8% of the variance in the model was explained by the independent variables and the model is significant (F $(344,5) = 37.039$; $p < 0.001$). Durbin Watson value of 2.01 shows no problem of autocorrelation in the model. The results of a multiple regression analysis show that three variables are significant to influence team performance; leadership support ($\beta = 0.195$; $p < 0.001$), trust ($\beta = 0.177$; $p < 0.001$), and knowledge sharing ($\beta = 0.282$; $p < 0.001$).

Leadership support is significant in influencing team performance because in team organization this factor is required to ensure that employees receive the necessary resources to perform. They are given enough guidance and direction to stay on the right track. Most importantly, with leadership support, employees feel that what they do in the team is backed up by those with the authority. Besides, leaders provide the required inspiration for the members to undertake challenging tasks; as a result, team performance increases. This result is consistent with the previous findings of Aga et al. (2016) and Schaubroeck et al. (2011).

Another important factor is trust because for team to be effective, each member must trust other members' ability to execute their roles and responsibilities. Those who feel trusted will ensure that the trust given to them is not retracted. The

Table 26.4 Results of correlation analysis

No	Variables	Mean	SD	1	2	3	4	5	6	7
1	Leadership support	3.84	0.59	(0.934)						
2	Trust	3.81	0.48	0.471**	(0.903)					
3	Communication	3.83	0.53	0.560**	0.483**	(0.875)				
4	Knowledge sharing	3.89	0.52	0.488**	0.461**	0.490**	(0.844)			
5	Team membership	3.80	0.60	0.446**	0.561**	0.439**	0.474**	(0.812)		
6	Team motivation	4.16	0.54	0.351**	0.360**	0.402**	0.427**	0.255**	(0.727)	
7	Team performance	3.81	0.47	0.454**	0.473**	0.379**	0.509**	0.442**	0.348**	(0.857)

Notes ** Correlation is significant at the 0.01 level (one-tailed); Cronbach's alphas are shown in the parentheses along the diagonal; N = 356

Table 26.5 Results of regression analysis

Variables	Standardized beta coefficients
Leadership support	0.195**
Trust	0.177**
Communication	0.024
Knowledge sharing	0.282**
Team membership	0.097
Team motivation	0.038
R	0.626
R^2	0.392
F value	37.039
Sig. F value	0.000
Durbin Watson	2.010

employees will exert extra effort in most cases beyond normal requirement and as a result will favorably contribute to team performance. The result is similar with previous studies on trust and team performance (Mach et al. 2010; Bijlsma-Frankema et al. 2008) as for the team to perform, trust among team members is critical.

Another factor that contributes to team performance is knowledge sharing. In team, members normally have different background, experience, and expertise. They complement each other in executing their responsibilities, one of the ways, through knowledge sharing. That is why in team organization, one of the prerequisites for team effectiveness is the capability of members to share knowledge that they have with other members. Consistently, past studies have acknowledged the significant relationship between knowledge sharing and team performance (Liu et al. 2011; Srivastava et al. 2006).

Three hypothesized predictors are not significant in influencing team performance in the telecommunication companies. First, communication is found to be not significantly related to team performance ($\beta = 0.024$; $p > 0.05$). According to Gajendran and Joshi (2012), face-to-face communications between team members failed to predict team innovation rather than team communication frequency with the leader. It is considered a norm for team members to communicate with the leader and other team members. Second, team membership does not significantly affect team performance ($\beta = 0.097$; $p > 0.05$). Perhaps the result is similar with van de Water et al. (2008) who observed that there is no statistical relation between team composition and team performance as what matters the most is the complementary competencies of team members. Third, the results do not support the empirical relationship between team motivation and team performance ($\beta = 0.038$; $p > 0.05$). Van Kleef et al. (2010) highlighted that personality plays key roles in shaping motivation (and hence, team performance) based on their perception toward the leader's emotions. Individuals with lower levels of agreeableness reported higher motivation when confronted with an angry rather than a non-emotional leader, while those with higher level of agreeableness indicated the reverse pattern (Van Kleef et al. 2010). As such, the team members involved might have possessed either diverse or conflicting type of personalities that possibly impede the relationship between motivation and team performance.

26.4 Conclusion

Due to the importance of team in contributing to the performance of the organization especially telecommunication companies, this research was undertaken to identify critical factors that influence team performance. Based on the previous work on this matter, six variables were identified, namely leadership support, trust, communication, knowledge sharing, team membership, and team motivation. Based on the results of regression analysis, leadership support, trust, and knowledge sharing are the important predictors of team performance. Therefore, telecommunication companies should emphasize on these factors if they want to ensure that teams can work effectively to achieve the intended performance level.

26.4.1 Managerial Implications

Several implications of the study can be derived. First, the management should focus on providing the required support for teams to perform effectively. The support can be in the forms of the required resources such as financial allocation, tools and equipment, manpower, guidance and directions, and emotional support. This factor is critical as the employees will feel confident in executing their responsibilities when they have the back up if anything goes wrong during the execution of their tasks. Second, trust should be developed among the team members through various team building activities so that each team member knows his team mates very well and accepts him as he is, treats him as his close relative, and relies on him when in trouble. Therefore, the content of the team building activities must focus on these intended outcomes. Third, knowledge sharing must be considered as the culture of the organization. Every member is willing to share whatever he has without any condition and restriction. One of the ways to inculcate this practice, for a start, is through providing incentives and recognitions. Once it has been established or accepted by every member it becomes a culture, where everybody naturally acts the same way. Another way is through the recruitment and selection process where only those who have shown the required attitude and behavior are selected to be members of the team. These recommendations might be helpful in turning teams into high-performing teams and subsequently contributing to the performance of the organization.

26.4.2 Research Implication

The present study involved two telecommunication companies, and the findings may not represent other companies; therefore, future studies are required to confirm the results by involving other companies. Types of companies, the size of the companies, and other characteristics of companies might be used as the moderating variables that can specifically explain the outcomes of the study in detail. Otherwise, the findings might be affected by these factors. Another recommendation for future studies is that the number of the variables should be further explored to make it more comprehensive and specific to the Malaysian setting. The best way to do this is to utilize exploratory study by means of an interview approach to identify the factors specific to the country setting. This is because the study setting might have an influence on the factors critical to investigating the phenomenon of interest. Other than that, the present study looked at the variables that influence team performance from macro-perspective. It is recommended to further deeply explore the antecedents of these factors at the micro-level. For example, leadership support is found to be critical to team performance. However, it does not affirm what are the aspects of leadership that should be given high consideration in ensuring the establishment of high-performing teams. These recommendations are expected to enrich future studies in the area of team performance.

References

Aga, D. A., Noorderhaven, N., & Vallejo, B. (2016). Transformational leadership and project success: The mediating role of team-building. *International Journal of Project Management, 34*(5), 806–818.

Al-Alawi, A. I., Al-Marzooqi, N. Y., & Mohammed, Y. F. (2007). Organizational culture and knowledge sharing: Critical success factors. *Journal of knowledge management, 11*(2), 22–42.

Ashforth, B. E., & Mael, F. (1989). Social identity theory and the organization. *Academy of Management Review, 14*(1), 20–39.

Avolio, B. J., & Yammarino, F. J. (Eds.). (2013). *Transformational and charismatic leadership: The road ahead.* Emerald Group Publishing.

Belbin, R. M. (2010). *Team roles at work* (2nd ed.). New York: Routledge.

Bell, S. T. (2007). Deep-level composition variables as predictors of team performance: A meta-analysis. *Journal of Applied Psychology, 92*(3), 595.

Bijlsma-Frankema, K., de Jong, B., & van de Bunt, G. (2008). Heed, a missing link between trust, monitoring and performance in knowledge intensive teams. *The International Journal of Human Resource Management, 19*(1), 19–40.

Carlson, A. (2011). The connection between communication satisfaction and team success in college athletic teams. *Doctoral Dissertation*, University of Central Missouri.

Choi, S. Y., Lee, H., & Yoo, Y. (2010). The impact of information technology and trans-active memory systems on knowledge sharing, application, and team performance: a field study. *MIS quarterly*, pp. 855–870.

Chou, H. W., Lin, Y. H., Chang, H. H., & Chuang, W. W. (2013). Transformational leadership and team performance. *SAGE Open, 3*(3), 1–10.

Dirks, K. T. (2000). Trust in leadership and team performance: evidence from NCAA basketball. *Journal of Applied Psychology, 85*(6), 1004.

Erdem, F., & Ozen, J. (2003). Cognitive and affective dimensions of trust in developing team performance. *Team Performance Management: An International Journal, 9*(5/6), 131–135.

Espinosa, J. A., Nan, N., & Carmel, E. (2015). Temporal distance, communication patterns, and task performance in teams. *Journal of Management Information Systems, 32*(1), 151–191.

Gajendran, R. S., & Joshi, A. (2012). Innovation in globally distributed teams: The role of LMX, communication frequency, and member influence on team decisions. *Journal of Applied Psychology, 97*(6), 1252.

Gardner, H. K. (2012). Performance pressure as a double-edged sword enhancing team motivation but undermining the use of team knowledge. *Administrative Science Quarterly, 57*(1), 1–46.

Inamizu, N., Fukuzawa, M., Fujimoto, T., Shintaku, J., & Suzuki, N. (2014). Group leaders and teamwork in the over-lean production system. *Journal of Organizational Change Management, 27*(2), 188–205.

Kozlowski, S. W. J., & Bell, B. S. (2013). Work groups and teams in organizations: Review update. In N. Schmitt & S. Highhouse (Eds.), *Handbook of psychology: Industrial and organizational psychology* (2nd ed., Vol. 12, pp. 412–469). Hoboken, NJ: Wiley.

Latham, G. P. (2012). *Work motivation: History, theory, research, and practice*. Thousand Oaks: Sage.

Lee, P., Gillespie, N., Mann, L., & Wearing, A. (2010). Leadership and trust: Their effect on knowledge sharing and team performance. *Management Learning, 41*(4), 473–491.

Liu, Y., & Phillips, J. S. (2011). Examining the antecedents of knowledge sharing in facilitating team innovativeness from a multilevel perspective. *International Journal of Information Management, 31*(1), 44–52.

Liu, Y., Keller, R. T., & Shih, H. A. (2011). The impact of team-member exchange, differentiation, team commitment, and knowledge sharing on R&D project team performance. *R&D Management, 41*(3), 274–287.

Macaulay, S., & Cook, S. (1995). Practical teamwork for customer service. *Team Performance Management: An International Journal, 1*(3), 35–41.

Mach, M., Dolan, S., & Tzafrir, S. (2010). The differential effect of team members' trust on team performance: The mediation role of team cohesion. *Journal of Occupational and Organizational Psychology, 83*(3), 771–794.

Moreland, R. L., Levine, J. M., & Wingert, M. L. (2013). Creating the ideal group: Composition effects at work. In E. H. Witte & J. H. Davis (Eds.), *Understanding group behaviour* (Vol. 2, pp. 11–35). New Jersey: Lawrence Erlbaum.

O'Reilly, C., & Pondy, L. (1979). Organizational communication. *Organizational Behavior*, 119–150.

Patrashkova-Volzdoska, R. R., McComb, S. A., Green, S. G., & Compton, W. D. (2003). Examining a curvilinear relationship between communication frequency and team performance in cross-functional project teams. *IEEE Transactions on Engineering Management, 50*(3), 262–269.

Richards, J., Chillas, S., & Marks, A. (2012). "Every man for himself" teamwork and customer service in the hospitality industry. *Employee Relations, 34*(3), 235–254.

Ryan, S. (2012). When is a team a team? "Teamworking" and the reorganisation of work in commercial cleaning. *Employee relations, 34*(3), 255–270.

Schaubroeck, J., Lam, S. S., & Peng, A. C. (2011). Cognition-based and affect-based trust as mediators of leader behavior influences on team performance. *Journal of Applied Psychology, 96*(4), 863.

Srivastava, A., Bartol, K. M., & Locke, E. A. (2006). Empowering leadership in management teams: Effects on knowledge sharing, efficacy, and performance. *Academy of Management Journal, 49*(6), 1239–1251.

Ten Haaf, W., Bikker, H., & Adriaanse, D. J. (2002). *Fundamentals of business engineering and management: a systems approach to people and organizations* (pp. 486–515). Delft: DUP Science.

Torrente, P., Salanova, M., Llorens, S., & Schaufeli, W. B. (2012). Teams make it work: How team work engagement mediates between social resources and performance in teams. *Psicothema, 24*(1), 106–112.

van de Water, H., Ahaus, K., & Rozier, R. (2008). Team roles, team balance and performance. *Journal of Management Development, 27*(5), 499–512.

van den Broek, D., Callaghan, G., & Thompson, P. (2004). Teams without teamwork? Explaining the call centre paradox. *Economic and Industrial Democracy, 25*(2), 197–218.

Van Kleef, G. A., Homan, A. C., Beersma, B., & van Knippenberg, D. (2010). On angry leaders and agreeable followers how leaders' emotions and followers' personalities shape motivation and team performance. *Psychological Science, 21*(12), 1827–1834.

Walumbwa, F. O., Hartnell, C. A., & Oke, A. (2010). Servant leadership, procedural justice climate, service climate, employee attitudes, and organizational citizenship behavior: A cross-level investigation. *Journal of Applied Psychology, 95*(3), 517.

Welbourne, T., Johnson, D., & Erez, A. (1998). The role-based performance scale: Validity analysis of a theory-based measure. *Academy of Management Journal, 41*(5), 540–555.

Wing, L. S. (2005). Leadership in high-performance teams: A model for superior team performance. *Team Performance Management: An International Journal, 11*(1/2), 4–11.

Zarzu, C., Scarlat, C., & Falcioglu, P. (2013). Team composition and team performance: Achieving higher quality results in an international higher education environment. In *Proceedings of the Management, Knowledge and Learning International Conference* (pp. 1321–1328).

Zhang, X., Chen, Z., Vogel, D., Yuan, M., & Guo, C. (2010). Knowledge-sharing reward dynamics in knowledge management systems: Game theory-based empirical validation. *Human Factors and Ergonomics in Manufacturing and Service Industries, 20*(2), 103–122.

Chapter 27
Escalator Accidents: Causes and Users' Behavior Empirical Study of Kuala Lumpur Users

Faziatul Amillia Mohamad Basir, Amirah Husna Yaziz, Muhammad Hafizi Zamri and Abdul Hamid Abdul Halim

Abstract The escalator is inevitably a transportation method used by people around the world almost every day in their daily life and provides convenience. However, using the escalators does not guarantee one's safety. Escalators seem safe enough, but they can be extremely dangerous when used inappropriately or when not maintained correctly. There are a number of incidents involving escalator lately. Escalator accidents can happen due to many reasons. It can be from human fault or from the escalator itself. Escalator accidents are something that cannot be treated lightly as it could involve the fatality. Preventive actions and measures need to be done. Therefore, this research was conducted using travelers to investigate the factors that can contribute to escalator accidents. In doing so, researchers distributed 150 questionnaires randomly within Kuala Lumpur area. The result indicates that most respondents agreed escalator accidents happened mainly due to human factors.

Keywords Escalator · Human factor · Accidents · Risks

27.1 Introduction

Elevators and escalators are potential sources of serious injuries and deaths to the general public and to workers installing, repairing, and maintaining them (Staal and Quackenbush 1998).

F.A.M. Basir (✉) · A.H. Yaziz · M.H. Zamri · A.H.A. Halim
Faculty of Business and Management, UiTM, Shah Alam, Selangor, Malaysia
e-mail: faziatulamillia@salam.uitm.edu.my

A.H. Yaziz
e-mail: amirahyaziz@gmail.com

M.H. Zamri
e-mail: muhamm9811@puncakalam.uitm.edu.my

A.H.A. Halim
e-mail: abdulh2949@puncakalam.uitm.edu.my

F. Noordin et al. (eds.), *Proceedings of the 2nd Advances in Business Research International Conference*, https://doi.org/10.1007/978-981-10-6053-3_27

According to Department of Occupational Safety and Health (DOSH), they had received approximately 31 reports involving escalator accidents in Malaysia from the year 2011 until March 2015 (Haikal 2016). Furthermore, it was recorded that 97% of the victims were young children. This had been proved when there was a case involving a pitiful 6-year-old girl who found dead after being dragged by the escalator at Kenanga Wholesale City Mall in Pudu (Parry 2015). Another case related to escalator accident took place on 8th February this year at KL Central station where a 4-year-old boy lost part of his left foot (Lee 2016). In addition, the latest case involving escalator accident occurred recently where a 3-year-old boy's genital got caught in escalator at Bagan Serai on June 2016 (Suppayah 2016). Based on previous studies, it was proved that most Malaysians did not take this issue seriously as they have this typical mindset that nothing should be worried about as long as it did not happen to them (Escalator safety guidelines 2016).

27.2 Literature Review

Escalator is the most efficient interchange level conveyance available. It plays a critical role in any modern buildings, shopping malls, urban mass transit systems, and much more. As escalators are omnipresent, publics who used it whether frequently or not may face many kinds of risks while riding it. The risk is something unpredicted, and it can happen anywhere, everywhere, and at any time. Risk can be defined as uncertainty of an outcome in a given situation. It can be also defined as variations in outcome for a specific event (Basar et al. 2011). As a whole, this research will discuss escalator users' behavior followed by factors that can contribute to escalator accidents among the public. It also will elaborate in detail regarding the independent variables which are the human factor, escalator malfunction, and escalator design and also the dependent variable which is factors that can contribute to escalator accidents.

27.3 Human Factor

According to previous studies, it is reported that the cause of many escalator accidents happened was the human factor. According to Cameron Nicolson (2008), human error is the biggest contribution to escalator accidents. He stated that this can be seen through focusing on human escalator riding behavior. Many parents take children onto escalators for fun, without realizing the upcoming dangers (Nicolson 2008). This factor is supported by the previous study done by Drury and Brill's (1983). It is believed that human factor can be divided into two factors, which are individual factors and task factors. Examples of an individual factor are carelessness, drunkenness, and improper outfit. Meanwhile, task factors are playing on an escalator, not holding the handrail, carrying packages, stepping on the edges of escalator of escalator steps, and others (Drury and Brill's 1983). Many times people will lose their balance, causing them to fall. Other injuries happen when clothes get caught inside the escalator, like shoes or strings dangling off sneakers and sweatshirts. When most people hear 'escalator injury,' they probably think of crocs shoes or other entanglement-related injuries, primarily to hands and feet as the most common injury mode. Instead, over three quarters of all hospital-treated escalator injuries in the USA result from falls (McCann 2013).

27.4 Escalator Malfunction

Another factor that can contribute to escalator accidents is escalator malfunction. According to Drury and Brill's (1983), one of the main factors that can contribute to escalator accidents is derived from the escalator itself, which was classified as management factors. As stated by Drury and Brill's (1983), examples of escalator malfunctions are sudden stop caused by a shutdown of power supply, fast speed of escalator, and also passengers' movement. Al-Sharif (2006) stated that sudden stopping of the escalator is very dangerous because as a result, passengers might suffer injuries. Another tragedy was in America when *hockey fans* went flying off a malfunctioning *escalator inside* Philadelphia's Wells Fargo Centre following a Flyers game. The shocking incident shows people crashing into each other at the bottom of an escalator that suddenly sped up. Later in 2012, the incident happened at Washington D.C. metro station, an escalator also suddenly sped up, sending travelers tumbling down. In 2015, *a woman in China* who was riding an escalator with her son lost her life after a metal panel collapsed under her feet and she fell into the gap in the device. The escalator malfunction accident also happens in Malaysia. It is reported in October 2016 several metal plates of an escalator bounced up during a malfunction at a shopping mall and caused no injuries (Escalator falls apart at a shopping mall 2016).

27.5 Escalator Design

Like many other industry groups, escalator manufacturers have been very successful in their lobbying and other efforts to avoid meaningful safety-related oversight or mandatory safety standards. In fact, escalator manufacturers have managed to avoid any meaningful government regulation altogether. Escalator design is another factor that can contribute to escalator accidents. Articles from previous studies had highlighted that escalator design is one of the contributing factors of escalator accidents. Both design guidelines and crowd control measures have been found to be part of issues related to overcrowding on an escalator (Chi et al. 2005). Escalator accidents were also said to be caused solely by bad design of the escalators itself. For example, sudden stopping can lead to consumers' fall

(Al-Sharif 2006). According to Department of Occupational Safety and Health (DOSH), 2417 escalators in Kuala Lumpur and Putrajaya had failed to meet safety standards according to Factories and Machinery Act and Occupational Safety and Health Act in 2014. DOSH recorded 111 accidents related to faulty lifts and escalators since 2010, which had resulted in 11 deaths (The New Straits Time Online 2016). Escalators' steps speed and handrails need to be supervised frequently as these factors play an important role in running the escalators.

From this previous study, the theoretical framework for this research is as follows:

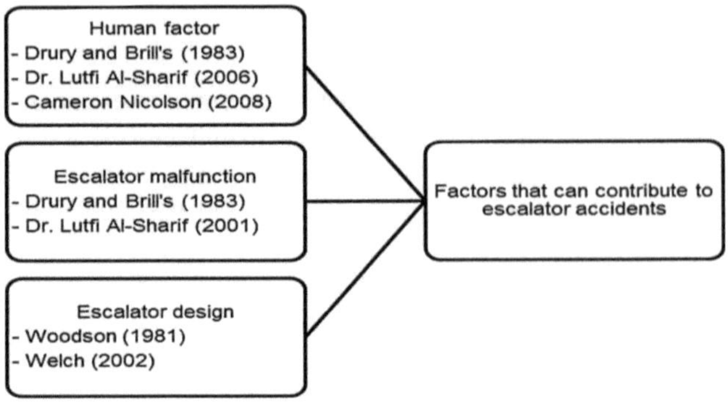

Hence, these research objectives are:

1. To identify the passengers' behavior during embarking on the escalator.
2. To investigate the main factors that contribute toward escalator accidents.

27.6 Research Methodology

The research used questionnaires as the main instrument to collect data. The questionnaires are constructed with seven-point Likert scale ranging from 'strongly disagree' to 'strongly agree' and distributed within Kuala Lumpur areas such as LRT Wangsa Maju, Kuala Lumpur Central Station, and AEON Wangsa Maju. Convenience sampling was adopted in this study.

27.7 Findings and Discussions

Demographic Profile of Respondents.

A total of 150 valid questionnaires were analyzed. Respondents who were aged 26–35 years are the majority group of age while female outnumbered which is 67.3% of the total respondents. Meanwhile, on part of race of the respondents,

Table 27.1 Demographic profile of respondents

Demographic	Frequency	Percentage (%)
Age		
1. 15–25	45	30
2. 26–35	54	36
3. 36–45	33	22
4. 46 & above	18	12
Total	150	100
Gender		
1. Male	49	32.7
2. Female	101	67.3
Total	150	100
Race		
1. Malay	93	62
2. Indian	23	15.3
3. Chinese	34	22.7
Total	150	100
Education level		
1. PMR	3	2
2. SPM	20	13.3
3. STPM	5	3.3
4. Diploma	21	14
5. Degree	91	60.7
6. Master	6	4
7. PhD	4	2.7
Total	150	100
Occupation		
1. Government servant	42	28
2. Private worker	101	67.3
3. Others	7	4.7
Total	150	100

Malay dominated the profile (62%); most of the respondents are Bachelor Degree holder and are working in private sectors (Table 27.1).

Research Objective 1: To identify the passengers' behaviors while embarking on the escalator.

To achieve the research objective, descriptive analysis of passengers' behaviors has been conducted. The highest mean (6.88) shows that the respondents agreed that parents are carrying stroller while on an escalator. The findings also found the respondents agreed that they saw parents are allowing their children's playing with the escalators (mean: 6.77). The respondents also agreed that they like to walk through the steps and not holding the escalator's handrail with the mean of 6.23 and 5.46, respectively (Table 27.2).

Table 27.2 Descriptive analysis of passenger behavior

	Mean	Std. deviation
I will stand still whenever I ride the escalator	2.91	2.436
While riding the escalator, I like to walk through the steps because it can save my time	6.23	1.489
I am not holding the escalator's handrail since I felt it is useless and dirty	5.46	2.248
There are a few times that I almost fell while riding the escalator	4.97	2.766
My outfits got caught in between the escalator's steps and shaft sometimes	5.85	1.819
I can see that most parents let their children play with the escalator	6.77	0.804
Most parents will carry their baby stroller along and ride the escalator	6.88	0.416

Research objective 2: To investigate the main factors that contribute toward escalators accidents.

This research objective can be achieved by using correlation to justify the directions of the relationship between human factors, escalator malfunction, and escalator design with the escalator accidents.

The correlations of the variables such as human factors, escalator malfunction, and escalator design are displayed in Table 27.3. Apparently, all the variables showed a positive association with the escalator accidents. Escalator malfunctions and escalator design showed moderate positive association with the escalator accidents ($r = 0.53$, $r = 0.500$), and human factors showed high positive association with the escalator accidents.

Table 27.3 Correlations among human factors, escalators malfunction, and escalator design with escalator accidents

		Human factor	Escalator malfunction	Escalator design	Escalator accidents
Human factor	Pearson correlation	1			
	Sig. (two-tailed)				
	N	150			
Escalator malfunction	Pearson correlation	0.490**	1		
	Sig. (two-tailed)	0.000			
	N	150	150		
Escalator design	Pearson correlation	0.534**	0.528**	1	
	Sig. (two-tailed)	0.000	0.000		
	N	150	150	150	
Escalator accidents	Pearson correlation	0.773**	0.530**	0.500**	1
	Sig. (two-tailed)	0.000	0.000	0.000	
	N	150	150	150	150

** Correlation is significant at the 0.01 level (two-tailed)

Table 27.4 Multiple regression analysis table

Model	Unstandardized coefficients		Standardized coefficients	t	Sig.
	B	Std. error	Beta		
(Constant)	−2.934	0.858		−3.420	0.001
Human factor	0.805	0.077	0.655	10.517	0.000
Escalator malfunction	0.460	0.159	0.180	2.899	0.004
Escalator design	0.097	0.112	0.056	0.871	0.385

a. Dependent variable: factors that can contribute to escalator accidents

Multiple regression analysis is conducted to examine the relationship between the independent and dependent variables. Based on multiple regression analysis (see Table 27.4), it is found that all variables are significant, except escalator design. The relationship between human factor ($p = 0.000$) and escalator malfunction ($p = 0.004$) is significant ($p < 0.05$) with the escalator accidents. Among the variable, it is found that human factor gives the highest beta value of 0.655 followed by escalator malfunction with the value of 0.180. Thus, it is concluded that human factor and escalator malfunctions are the main factors in contributing to the escalator accidents.

27.8 Conclusion

Escalator accidents can happen due to many reasons. The study highlighted three factors that can contribute to escalator accidents, which are a human factor, escalator malfunction, and escalator design. Findings showed that human factors and escalator malfunctions are the main factors contributing to escalator accidents. It concurs with the findings stated human factors are chosen as the major leading cause of escalator accidents (Abas 2016). Users, especially parents those with their children, are the biggest issue. Most parents took their children onto escalators for fun, without realizing potential danger (Nicolson 2008). There are also parents that let their children play with the escalator, not holding their children, and not supervising their children (Abas 2016).

A part of the human factor, besides parenting, human escalator riding behavior also plays an important part (Nicolson 2008). Playing on the escalator, not holding the handrail, carrying packages, sitting on the escalator, and many others are several bad riding behaviors done by most passengers (Drury and Brill's 1983). All of these improper activities while riding the escalator could lead to serious injury or even death if passengers are still doing it. They need to open their eyes and take previous incidents as a lesson learned so that any escalator-related accidents could be minimized in the future.

References

Abas, A. (2016). Human factor leading cause of escalator accidents. Retrieved on June 20, 2016.

Dr. Al-Sharif, L. (2006). Escalator human factors: Passenger behaviour, accidents and design. Retrieved on April 3, 2016.

Basar, A., Ang, C. H., Dahan, H., Tan, L. S., Wam Aris, Y. B., & Abdul Rahman, Z. (2011). *Risk management* (2nd ed.). Shah Alam: Mc Graw-Hill Education.

Chi, C. F., Chang, T. C., Tsou, C. L. (2005). In-depth investigation of escalator riding accidents in heavy capacity MRT Stations. Retrieved on April 3, 2016.

Drury, C. G., & Brill, M. (1983). Human factors in consumer product accident investigation. *Human Factors, 25*(3), 329–342.

Escalator falls apart at a shopping mall. (2016, October 26). Retrieved from the star online: http://www.thestar.com.my/news/nation/2016/10/26/escalator-falls-apart-at-shopping-mall-metal-plates-bounce-out-of-place-during-malfunction/.

Escalator safety guidelines. (2016, February 11). Retrieved from New Straits Times http://www.nst.com.my/news/2016/02/126893/escalator-safety-guidelines.

Jalil, H. (2016, February 11). *The Sun Daily.* Retrieved from DOSH: 97% of escalator accidents.

Lee, E. (2016). Malaysia: Boy losses foot after escalator accident. Retrieved on April 3, 2016.

McCann, M. (2013). Deaths and injuries involving elevators and escalators. Retrieved on April 3, 2016.

Nicolson, C. (2008). Risk mitigation associated with airport escalator and moving sidewalk operations. Retrieved on April 3, 2016.

Parry, H. (2015, April 7). Six-year-old girl falls five stories to her death after getting caught in the escalator and being dragged over the side at Malaysian shopping center. Retrieved from The Daily Mail UK Online: http://www.dailymail.co.uk/news/article-3028660/Six-year-old-girl-falls-five-storeys-death-getting-caught-escalator-dragged-Malaysian-shopping-centre.html.

Staal, J, Quackenbush, J. (1998). Elevators, escalators, and hoists. In J. M. Stellman (Ed.) *Encyclopaedia of occupational health and safety* (4th ed., Vol. 3, Chap. 93, pp. 40–44). Geneva: International labour office.

Suppayah, P. (2016, February 10). Toddler loses forefoot in escalator mishap. Retrieved from The Malay Mail Online: http://www.themalaymailonline.com/malaysia/article/toddler-loses-forefoot-in-escalator-mishap.

The new straits time online. (2016, February 11). Retrieved from Escalator safety guidelines: http://www.nst.com.my/news/2016/02/126893/escalator-safety-guidelines?d=1.

Chapter 28
Factors Relating to Employee Engagement: A Case Study in a Selected Bank

Maimunah Mohd Shah, Idaya Husna Mohd and Mohd Khairie Khairudin

Abstract Employees are expected to engage in the organization. They are employed based on their qualifications and experiences. To achieve the goals set by top management requires full commitment or engagement from the employees. Most organizations provide conveniences in the form of monetary reward or compensation, satisfactory working environment and work–life balance to all employees. Therefore, the aim of the study is to determine the relationship between these three conveniences being the variables for this study and the employees' engagement. A survey was conducted using a set of questionnaires to collect data and analyzed using the SPSS. The population for the study were among the executives in a selected bank. The results revealed significant moderate relationship between work–life balance and employee engagement. The results support the literature and further suggestions are addressed.

Keywords Compensation · Work environment · Work–life balance · Employee engagement

28.1 Introduction

There are many factors influencing employee engagement in a banking sector. The factors include pay and benefits (compensation), leadership, working environment, role in bank and work–life balance (Kavitha et al. 2015). The more employers pay attention to these factors, the more employees will engage with these organizations. Literature witnesses absenteeism and low productivity being the most seriously and extensively discussed issues among top management of banks. They need to be aware and sensitive on the level of loyalty and total engagement of the employees to their organization. This particular bank is no exception. This bank is a large

M.M. Shah (✉) · I.H. Mohd · M.K. Khairudin
Faculty of Business and Management, UiTM Puncak Alam Campus, Kuala, Selangor, Malaysia
e-mail: maimu697@puncakalam.uitm.edu.my

F. Noordin et al. (eds.), *Proceedings of the 2nd Advances in Business Research International Conference*, https://doi.org/10.1007/978-981-10-6053-3_28

Islamic cooperative bank in Malaysia. Its headquarters is located in Kuala Lumpur. This bank is offering good Islamic finance which has attracted millions of customers in the past years. That is why this bank needs to sustain the presence of their employees in order to retain the good services offered in the banking industry. However, there are limited studies investigating engagement issues particularly in the Islamic banking industry. Therefore, this study aims to fill the gap in the literature by examining the relationship between the three factors (compensation, work environment and work–life balance) and employee engagement.

28.2 Literature Review

There are many descriptions of employee engagement discussed by past researchers. Firstly, Susi and Jawaharrani (2011) define that engagement is the state in which individuals are passionately and intellectually committed to the organization as measured by three primary behaviors which are Say, Stay and Strive. Secondly, Tiwari (2011) defines employee engagement as the ability to influence the employees with their heads, hearts and souls to instill in them an intrinsic desire and passion to success and excel. The third definition is highlighted by Ram and Prabhakar (2011) stating that employee engagement is a strategic approach for driving improvement and boosting organizational change. Interestingly, in 2014, Schuyler states that employee engagement is the extent to which employees are motivated to contribute to business success and are willing to apply discretionary effort to accomplishing tasks important to the achievement of stated business goals.

The second variable in the study is compensation. According to Dineen and Williamson (2012), compensation is arguably one of the most critical influences (if not the most critical influence) on the quality and effectiveness of human capital. Furthermore, compensation influences the quality of the people who apply, the likelihood of job acceptance, the quality of those hired, the motivation and performance, level of the workforce and the quality of who stays with the organization. There are three categories which fall under compensation.

i. Non-monetary compensation. It is any benefit an employee receives from an employer or job that does not involve tangible value. This includes career and social rewards such as job security, flexible hours, growth opportunity, praise and recognition, task enjoyment and friendships.
ii. Direct compensation. It is an employee's base wage, which can be an annual salary or hourly wage, plus any performance-based pay an employee receives, such as profit sharing bonuses.
iii. Indirect compensation is far more varied. It includes everything from legally required public protection programs such as Social Security to health insurance, retirement programs, paid leave, child care or moving expenses. Scott (2010) confirms that the total reward programs, policies and structures do influence employee engagement. The study finds that organizations which

provide incentive and rewarding programs are likely to engage employees more than organizations which do not. Szypko (2014) believes that pay fairness is very important because it will impact the employee engagement and productivity.

Chandrasekar (2011) states that the quality of workplace environment would affect the employees' level of motivation and performance. How well they engage with their organization, especially with immediate environment, influences to great extent their error rate, level of innovation and collaboration with other employees, absenteeism and ultimately, how long they stay in the job. Many studies have revealed that most employees leave their organizations because of their relationship with the top management.

According to Roelofsen (2002), working environment is the main key causing the employees to be engaged or disengaged. By enlightening the working environment, it will increase the productivity and reduce problems like absenteeism and complaints (Wells 2000).

According to Susi and Jawaharrani (2011), work–life balance policies can assist employees achieving a balance between their work and personal commitments that is right for them. The policies need to be supported by the workplace culture, which reflects the beliefs, values and norms of the whole of the organization from the CEO to staff members. Other important factors in the success of work–life balance policies include proper communication of commitment to the policies to existing and future employees, raising awareness of the policies, education of managers about the importance of policies and training of managers on 'how to' implement these policies. Besides that, initiatives to encourage work–life balance also stimulate employee engagement. According to Gupta (2014), work–life balance influences employee engagement because it gives impact on absenteeism, productivity and work satisfaction.

Based on the review of literature above, there are three hypotheses developed in the study:

H1 There is a relationship between compensation and employee engagement.
H2 There is a relationship between work environment and employee engagement.
H3 There is a relationship between work–life balance and employee engagement.

28.3 Methodology

Department of Human Resource was the target location of the study. The total population was 45 executives. Based on the sample size table, the appropriate number of respondents to be studied would be 40. Therefore, 40 questionnaires were distributed randomly based on their presence in the office. Majority of the employees were involved in the study. The process of distributing and collecting back the questionnaires was quite easy because the employees were very supportive when responding to the survey. The questionnaire comprised of demographic profile of the respondents. The items in the questionnaire were in four-point Likert scale. The other sections included employee engagement, compensation, work environment and work–life balance. The data collection procedure took three weeks before they were further sorted and the data were keyed-in accordingly. The normality of the data, the reliability and validity of the items were checked by using SPSS for statistical analysis.

28.4 Data Analysis and Findings

Out of 40 questionnaires distributed, 34 of them were returned and analyzed leaving six questionnaires were not returned. Final analysis was based on 34 cases and the response rate was 85%. Majority of the respondents were between 28 and 32 years old. There were more male respondents (53%) as compared to female respondents (47%). Most of the respondents were with work experience between 6 and 10 years. With the number of years in service, they were paid between RM6000 and RM9000 of salary. The big bulk of respondents possesses bachelor degrees and diplomas, and most of them were married.

Reliability and validity analysis was conducted to examine the Cronbach's alpha scores of the variables. The values were all above 0.7. Therefore, the items tested in the study were reliable and valid (Nunnally 1978). This indicates that the respondents involved in the study were appropriate and reliable to respond to the questionnaires.

The results in Table 1 reveal that the mean score of work–life balance is high among these respondents. The analyses were further examining the relationship of the three factors and employee engagement. The results were then compared with the three hypotheses developed.

H1 there is a relationship between compensation and employee engagement. Correlation coefficient analysis was conducted to examine the strength of the relationship. The results show there is no relationship between the two variables. The r-value is 0.365 and the p-value is 0.34. Therefore, hypothesis 1 is rejected. These results were opposed with the study conducted by Scott (2010) who found out that total reward program had an impact on employee engagement.

H2 predicted a relationship between work environment and employee engagement. The r-value is 0.535 but the p-value is 0.110 which is more than 0.05.

Table 1 Descriptive analysis and correlation results

Variables	Mean	Standard deviation	R-value	P-value
Employee engagement	3.12	0.342	Employee engagement	
Compensation	3.10	0.309	0.365	0.34
Work environment	3.25	0.369	0.535	0.110
Work–life balance	3.39	0.366	0.482	0.004

Table 2 Multiple regression results

Variables	Standardized beta coefficients
Compensation	0.272
Work environment	−0.098
Work–life balance	0.419*
R	0.539
R^2	0.291
F value	4.102
Sig. F value	0.015
Durbin watson	1.798

*p-value = <0.05

Therefore, these results did not support hypothesis 2. This hypothesis is then rejected. The results were in contrast to a study conducted by Chandraseker (2011). He stated that working environment may give an impact on employee engagement if the top management did not alert about it.

H3 stated that there is a relationship between work–life balance and employee engagement. The r-value showed moderate significant relationship. The r-value is 0.482 and the p-value is 0.004. These results supported the hypothesis. Therefore, H3 is accepted. The relationship between work–life balance and employee engagement was significantly moderate. These results were supported by Dix and Barber (2015) where they stated that employees who had better work–life balance had more sense of responsibility and more engaged with the organization. In addition, Suzi and Jawaharrani (2011) agreed that work–life balance policies help to improve employee engagement but the policies must be supported by the workplace culture. This reflects the beliefs, values and norms of the whole members from all levels.

Multiple regression analysis was conducted to determine further results. Table 2 reveals the details of the results.

The result confirms that work–life balance does influence employee engagement in the organization. Twenty-nine percent of the variance in employee engagement is explained by work–life balance. This means that work–life balance has moderate significant impacts on employee engagement.

28.5 Conclusion

Regardless of working in small or large organizations, employees are expected to perform their duties and responsibilities accordingly. Regardless of any variable tested in the study, the results would still relate to the behavior and perception of the respondents. It is not normal to know that compensation and work environment were found not to be significantly related to employee engagement. However, work–life balance is significantly related to employee engagement. Perhaps, this is due to the number of respondents tested or the location of the study. It will be good to extend this research and test the hypotheses again. The results would reveal consistency or inconsistency.

28.6 Recommendation for Future Research

In order to improve employee engagement, organizations have to go beyond compensation to a total reward mindset and must use engagement metrics in performance criteria (McMullen et al. 2013). It is recommended future researchers to include the following variables: leadership style, nature of the job and strategic alignment. Harvard Business Review (2013) reported the importance of engagement on organization. They have identified that the top three factors do business leaders view as most critical to success are achieving a high level of customer service, effective communications and achieving a high level of employee engagement and strong executive leadership. This places employee engagement as a top three business priority. In the context of this study, the top management of this bank needs to improve further the work–life balance policy by providing flexible working hours to ensure better engagement from the employees.

References

Chandrasekar, D. K. (2011). Workplace environment and its impact on organisational performance in public sector organisations. *International Journal of Enterprise Computing and Business Systems, 1*(1), 1–19.

Dineen, B. R., & Williamson, I. O. (2012). Screening oriented recruitment messages: Antecedents and relationships with applicant pool quality. *Human Resource Management, 51*(3), 343–360.

Dix, G., & Barber, S. B. (2015). The changing face of work: Insights from Acas. *Employee Relations, 37*(6), 670–682.

Gupta, N., & Shaw, J. D. (2014). Employee compensation: The neglected area of HRM research. *Human Resource Management Review, 24*(1), 1–4.

Harvard Business Review. (2013). November issue. Harvard Business Publishing.

Kavitha, N., Bhardwaj, A., Gupta, E. D., & Ibrahim, S. (2015). Teaching and Learning in Workplace: Contemporary Perspectives. *Education in Medicine Journal, 7*(3).

McMullen, J., Edington, D. W., Marzec, M. L., Lee, S. P., Cornwell, T. B., & Burton, W. N. (2013). Predictors of behavior change intention using health risk appraisal data. *American journal of health behavior, 37*(4), 478–490.

Nunnally, J. (1978). Psychometric methods. 464–465.

Ram, P., & Prabhakar, G. V. (2011). The role of employee engagement in work-related outcomes. *Interdisciplinary Journal of Research in Business, 1*(3), 47–61.

Roelofsen, P. (2002). The impact of office environments on employee performance: The design of the workplace as a strategy for productivity enhancement. *Journal of facilities Management, 1* (3), 247–264.

Schuyler, S. S., Senne, N., & Moloney, J. (2014). CA The keys to corporate responsability employee engagement.

Scott, J. L., Crompton, R., & Lyonette, C. (Eds.). (2010). Gender inequalities in the 21st century: New barriers and continuing constraints. Edward Elgar Publishing.
Susi, S., and K. Jawaharrani. (2011). Work-Life Balance: The key driver of employee engagement. *Asian Journal of Management Research, 2*(1), 474–483.
Szypko, M. A. (2014). Pay Fairness and its Impact on Employee Engagement.
Tiwari, S. (2011). Employee engagement-the key to organizational success. *Academy for professional excellence, Kolkata*. India.
PWells, M. M. (2000). Office clutter or meaningful personal displays: The role of office personalization in employee and organizational well-being. *Journal of Environmental Psychology*, *20*(3), 239–255.

Chapter 29
The Influence of Employee Empowerment on Organizational Citizenship Behavior

Shereen Noranee, Nazlinda Abdullah, Rohani Mohd, Mohd Rahim Khamis, Rozilah Abdul Aziz, Rohana Mat Som and Erma Ammira Mohd Ammirul

Abstract Organizational citizenship behavior (OCB) makes an organization more effective over time and across employees. Employee empowerment is necessary for the success and survival of organizations. However, lack of trust toward employee and misunderstanding of the employee empowerment may decrease employee OCB. Hence, the main objective of this study is to examine the relationship between employee empowerment and the dimensions of OCB. This research is based on correlational research which to identify the association between empowerment and the dimensions of OCB. Convenience sampling technique was administered. 123 respondents were among the part-time of degree students from a local university. The findings indicate that there were positive and significant relationship between employee empowerment and all dimensions of OCB. The study concludes that in general, employee empowerment would increase employee work voluntarily, lessen complaints, abrest with latest information, and maintain honesty in equal work pay.

S. Noranee (✉) · R. Mohd · M.R. Khamis · R.A. Aziz · R.M. Som · E.A.M. Ammirul
Faculty of Business and Management, UiTM, Puncak Alam Campus, 42300 Bandar Puncak Alam, Selangor Darul Ehsan, Malaysia
e-mail: shereen@salam.uitm.edu.my

R. Mohd
e-mail: rohani191@salam.edu.uitm.my

M.R. Khamis
e-mail: rahim474@salam.uitm.edu.my

R.A. Aziz
e-mail: rozilah@puncakalam.edu.uitm.my

R.M. Som
e-mail: rohana536@puncakalam.edu.uitm.my

E.A.M. Ammirul
e-mail: ermaammira@gmail.com

N. Abdullah
Faculty of Applied Science, UiTM, Shah Alam 40000, Selangor Darul Ehsan, Malaysia
e-mail: nazli003@salam.edu.uitm.my

F. Noordin et al. (eds.), *Proceedings of the 2nd Advances in Business Research International Conference*, https://doi.org/10.1007/978-981-10-6053-3_29

Keywords Organizational citizenship behavior · Employee empowerment · Altruism · Sportsmanship · Conscientiousness · Civic virtue · Courtesy

29.1 Introduction

Organizational citizenship behavior (OCB) is an important employee behavior to maintain the growth and success of the organization. OCB is where the employees act beyond their work-related role. This kind of behavior is not compulsory to possess but it plays a major role for the success of the organization. This behavior is a substantial factor in determining the productivity, efficiency and effectiveness of the organization. Almost all organizations would want to achieve their goals and profits and maintain their business in the long run. Hence, the organization must attract the right employees, with the right goals and at the right time. This situation will ensure that the organization can compete with other organizations within their business scope or the same business line.

One of the ways for an organization to response to an increasingly complex and competitive external environment is by practicing employee empowerment. Employee empowerment is necessary for the success and survival of organizations (Huq 2015). Employee empowerment in the organizational culture has becoming a trend for organization development. Organizations prefer any ways that can contribute to the achievement toward their goals and objective. Employee empowerment resulted in higher degree of authority for the employees to function independently in their job. Employees are urged to make their own decisions without even consulted or discussed with their own superior, as such this situation will enhance a bottom-up approach (Humborstad and Perry 2011). An employee is said to be empowered when they are given the power to make their own decisions and they have their own saying in the decision-making process. The feeling of empowerment will influence an employee to be loyal, satisfied and encouraged to come to work because they are happy and the turnover rate would reduce.

OCB gives several advantages such as productivity, innovative, performance, reduced turnover and increase the intention to stay in the organization. While employee empowerment is a situation where the employees are given the right and power to influence people in the decision-making process (Amir and Amen 2014). However, managers tend to avoid empowerment practices due to lack of trust (Ambad and Bahron 2012) which may lead to low employee work performance. In addition, according to Huq (2015), the benefits of employee empowerment committed by employees is not fully understood by both employees and employers. This would decrease OCB among the employees. Hence, the main objective of this study is to examine the relationship between employee empowerment and the dimensions of OCB.

29.2 Organizational Citizenship Behavior (OCB)

OCB occurs when the employees perform a task that goes beyond their work related in accordance for the success of the organizations. This behavior will influence their performance to be better and easy to get promoted. Over the past few decades, research on OCB has been focused on the citizenship at work place (Paillé and Grima 2011). This type of employee will go extra mile in order to feel satisfied with their work or non-work-related area. An employee is said to have an OCB when he or she possesses the five dimensions of OCB, namely altruism, sportsmanship, conscientiousness, civic virtue, and courtesy. OCB has an important role for the survival of the organization. OCB will bring satisfaction, team work, customer orientation, and reduced turnover, and it will increase the productivity level among employees (Organ 1988; Najafi et al. 2011).

29.3 Empowerment

Empowerment is when the employees are given the autonomy to influence others and the right to participate in the decision-making process (Kumar and Moorthy 2015). Employees that can drive their subordinates to achieve organization's objectives, goals or targets are considered to have leadership skills. In the past two decades, psychological empowerment has become a very popular topic in management field for academic researchers and business practitioners (Kumar and Moorthy 2015). A leader is said to empower employees when he can influence others to get the job done on track. It is important for a leader to empower employees because empowerment will affect the organization as a whole. Employees need to possess critical and analytical thinking in order to be empowered. Delegation, shared decision-making, and participative management are parts of empowerment (Al-Kahtani et al. 2011).

29.4 Relationship Between Employee Empowerment and OCB

Over the past few decades, there have been a lot of researchers doing research on empowerment and OCB. Subsequently, there is a positive relationship between empowerment and OCB (Jha 2014). The employees will show a positive behavior in doing the job that needed their extra role that is not within their job description, and this will promote their leadership skills and knowledge in making decisions.

OCB and Altruism. Altruism can be considered as helping others voluntarily without being asked for help and it is directed toward a person on a face-to-face basis. Furthermore, altruism includes a various interpersonal acts that will help to maintain the interpersonal and social context within employees. Altruism has a positive relationship with empowerment because there are willingly to lend a helping hand without even being asked for help and they do not take into account whether their behavior will be rewarded or not (Jha 2014).

OCB and Sportsmanship. A good sportsmanship behavior should bring the team toward achieving the organizational goals by fostering the right plan to achieve the organizational goals. When the team can work in a systematic way, it will increase the profitability of the company and the employees will treasure the social context that they have between each other. In addition, the organization should promote sportsmanship within their organization, and this has been proved to have a positive relationship with empowerment.

OCB and Conscientiousness. When an employee follows all the rules and regulations of the organization, this will create a harmonious and peaceful environment (Priyadharshini and Mahadevan 2014). This type of behavior will give an impact toward the newbies. They will eventually follow all the rules and regulations made by the organization. When the employee obeys the rules and regulations of the work place without even being supervised by their superior (Zhong et al. 2011). According to Jha (2014), empowerment has a positive impact with conscientiousness because it is predicted by the traits, skills, ability and their awareness to condone with the rules and regulations of the organization.

OCB and Civic Virtue. Civic virtue is when an employee joins or involves with any activities for the well-being of the company and to maintain the positive image of the company. An employee with this behavior will actively participate with any activities for the betterment of the organization whether in the long or short run. Empowerment have a positive relationship with civic virtue where employees are very cost-minded and they help to ensure that the organization will not be bankrupt by giving out suggestions and opinions that might directly affect the operating efficiency.

OCB and Courtesy. An employee is considered as committing a courtesy when he or she provides any useable information or prevents any problem from arising within the work limit (Zhong et al. 2011). Employees with courtesy will consider anything such as decision-making results whether it will affect other employees. They are very concern with their co-workers. They want mutual benefits between employees and employer. They will be loyal toward the organizations, supervisors, work groups, and departments (Jha 2014). There is a positive relationship between empowerment and courtesy where the supervisor will think first whether his decisions will affect his employees in a positive or negative way (Zhong et al. 2011).

Based on the above discussion, the following hypotheses were formulated:

H_1: The employee empowerment has a relationship with altruism in OCB.
H_2: The employee empowerment has a relationship with sportsmanship in OCB.
H_3: The employee empowerment has a relationship with conscientiousness in OCB.
H_4: The employee empowerment has a relationship with civic virtue in OCB.
H_5: The employee empowerment has a relationship with courtesy in OCB.

29.5 Methodology

This research is based on correlational research which to identify the association between empowerment and the dimensions of OCB. There were 700 distance learning program (DLP) part-time students from the Bachelor of Business Administration (Hons) Human Resource Management program in UiTM Puncak Alam that were selected to be the respondents for this study. From the study conducted, majority of respondents among e-PJJ students in UiTM Puncak Alam consist of female students. Most of the respondents aged between 21 and 23 years, and majority of them was single. Moreover, most of the respondents hold a bachelor degree as their highest education qualification. More than 80% respondents are Malay because UiTM only consists of student who is Malay and Bumiputera. Lastly, majority of the respondent's length of services is more than 3 years which hold a position as an executive in government sector.

Convenience sampling technique was administered. According to Kretjcie and Morgan (1970), the minimum sample size for 700 student population is 100 respondents. In total 123 questionnaires were returned which considered as adequate and valid for statistical analysis. All data of the respondents were collected in the spreadsheet using the Google Form. The questionnaire consists of three sections which are demographic information of the respondents such as age, gender, education level, and length of service; Section B is the dimensions of OCB, and Section C consists of employee empowerment items. The questionnaire for OCB dimensions was obtained from Podsakoff et al. (1990),while the employee empowerment items were adopted from Spreitzer (1995), namely 12-item Empowerment at Work Scale.

29.6 Results and Discussion

The overall results of the correlation analysis between employee empowerment and the dimensions of OCB are indicated in Table 29.1.

From Table 29.1, it can be said that all of the factors are correlated. There was a positive correlation between employee empowerment and altruism ($r = 0.585$, $n = 123$, $p < 0.01$). Overall, there was a strong, positive correlation for both variables. This view is supported by Jha (2014) who writes that altruism has a positive relationship with empowerment because there are willingly to lend a helping hand without even being asked for help and they do not take into account whether their behavior will be rewarded or not. Altruism is a behavior that a person does without even being asked to do so (Zhong et al. 2011).

There was a positive correlation between employee empowerment and sportsmanship ($r = 0.710$, $n = 123$, $p < 0.01$). Overall, there was a strong, positive correlation for both variables. Sportsmanship has the strongest correlation with employee empowerment compared to other dimensions of OCB. In the same vein, a

Table 29.1 Correlation analysis (N = 123)

Correlations	Altruism	Sportsmanship	Conscientiousness	Civic virtue	Courtesy	Employee empowerment
Altruism	1					
Sportsmanship	0.784**	1				
Conscientiousness	0.673**	0.728**	1			
Civic virtue	0.732**	0.808**	0.765**	1		
Courtesy	0.696**	0.760**	0.710**	0.726**	1	
Employee empowerment	0.585**	0.710**	0.628**	0.698**	0.681**	1

**Correlation is significant at the 0.01 level (two tailed)

person with positive minded will accept any comments from anyone and will turn the comments into a positive one. When employees can work in a systematic way, it will increase the profitability of the company and the employees will treasure the social context that they have between each other.

There was a positive correlation between employee empowerment and conscientiousness ($r = 0.628$, $n = 123$, $p < 0.01$). Overall, there was a strong, positive correlation for both variables. In accordance with the present results, a previous study has demonstrated that empowerment has a positive correlation with conscientiousness because it is predicted by the traits, skills, ability, and their awareness to condone with the rules and regulations of the organization (Jha 2014). A discipline employee will follow all the rules and regulations anywhere they go (Zhong et al 2011).

There was a positive correlation between employee empowerment and civic virtue ($r = 0.698$, $n = 123$, $p < 0.01$). Overall, there was a strong, positive correlation for both variables. Increases in employee empowerment were correlated with increases in civic virtue. The present findings seem to be consistent with other research which found that empowerment has a positive relationship with civic virtue where employees are very cost-minded, and they help to ensure that the organization won't be bankrupt by giving out suggestions and opinions that might directly affect the operating efficiency (Talat et al. 2016). An employee with civic virtue attitude will defend any negative comments being thrown at the company and the will actively participate in any meetings for the betterment of the organization (Lin 2013).

There was a positive correlation between employee empowerment and courtesy ($r = 0.681$, $n = 123$, $p < 0.01$). Overall, there was a strong, positive correlation for both variables. Increases in employee empowerment were correlated with increases in courtesy. These results agree with the finding of a study (Zhong et al. 2011), in which there is a positive relationship between empowerment and courtesy where the supervisor will think first whether his decisions will affect his employees in a positive or negative way. An employee with courtesy behavior will be loyal toward the company, and they hate to create any quarrel between their co-workers (Jha 2014).

29.7 Conclusion and Recommendation

Employee empowerment correlated with all five dimensions of OCB which is altruism, sportsmanship, conscientiousness, civic virtue, and courtesy. The employees believed that the employee empowerment would increase their work voluntarily, less of complaints, always keep up with the latest information and maintaining honesty in equal work pay. The employees thought that with employee empowerment, they are able to solve any work-related problems, maintain a positive image by gaining extra knowledge to improve the status quo and acknowledge co-workers in every area.

All employers want employees who demonstrate an initiative by taking on and completing tasks with little guidance. Of course, the expectation is that those employees will perform OCB only in ways consistent with the organization objectives and values. Hence, employees should foster an open communication, reward for self-improvement, clearly define job description, and appreciate employee efforts.

All these variables used by researcher would help the organization to consider the important things for the leaders as well other distance learning program (DLP) students who are working or pursuing their studies in UiTM Puncak Alam. Other than that, an organization should look how the relationship of variables (employee empowerment, altruism, sportsmanship, conscientiousness, civic virtue, and courtesy) would give an impact to the organization whether in good effect or vice versa.

The following are the recommendations based on findings from this study. In term of empowerment, it is good to practices greater empowerment for everyone in the organization such as continuous learning and wide involvement (Al-Kahtani et al. 2011). The organization should make all of their employees involve in the decision-making process which will increase their level of empowerment.

Besides that, in order to give a greater impact on OCB, the researcher can provide information about goal performance (Fernandez and Moldogaziev 2013). By providing information about goal performance, it can increase the level of OCB among employees. When the employee feels that he or she needs to make sure that the organization runs smoothly, they will play the role of OCB in their daily life.

The management should provide a 360° feedback system where the entire unit in organization can evaluate each other so that the management can provide an effective ways to overcome negligence. The employees also should organize their work effectively in order to perform efficiently in their day-to-day work basis. Lastly, reward those who perform better or improve greatly in their work area such as by giving bonus on their next pay. This action will keep the employees loyal with the organization.

29.8 Recommendations for Future Research

It must be noted that the research focuses only on employee empowerment. It is recommended that future research with the same study may be conducted on the public educational institutions of other cities. In order to get better finding, researcher may conduct the same survey on other public educational institutions of other cities. This is because different universities may provide different results or findings.

It also must be noted that the research focuses on the dimensions of OCB and employee empowerment. It is recommended that future research explore the study by putting the mediator between the dimensions of OCB and employee empowerment to get the best result such as reward or mental motivation.

Comparative studies are recommended which may be held for private and public institutes and other organization. This similar study can be conducted from organization itself. This is because it will be able to give clear practices that will influence the dimensions of OCB in their organization. The findings may different from the employee perspective.

References

Al-Kahtani, A. H., Sulaiman, M., Shariff, S., & Abu Jarad, I. (2011). Employee empowerment and job satisfaction: An empirical study of Malaysian management. *World Applied Sciences Journal, 13*(5), 1269–1280.

Ambad, S. N. A., & Bahron, A. (2012). Psychological empowerment: The influence on organizational commitment among employees in the construction sector. *Journal of Global Business Management, 8*(2), 73.

Elnaga, A. A., & Imran, A. (2014). The impact of employee empowerment on job satisfaction: Theoretical study. *American Journal of Research Communication, 2*(1), 13−26. www.usa-journals.com. ISSN: 2325-4076.

Fernandez, S., & Moldogaziev, T. (2013). Employee empowerment and job satisfaction in the US federal bureaucracy: A self-determination theory perspective. *The American Review of Public Administration*, 0275074013507478

Humborstad, S. I. W., & Perry, C. (2011). Employee empowerment, job satisfaction and organizational commitment: An in-depth empirical investigation. *Chinese Management Studies, 5*(3), 325–344.

Huq, R. (2015). *The psychology of employee empowerment: Concepts*. Critical Themes and a Framework for Implementation: Gower Publishing Ltd.

Jha, S. (2014). Transformational leadership and psychological empowerment: Determinants of organizational citizenship behavior.*South Asian Journal of Global Business Research, 3*(1), 18–35.

Kumar, K. M., & Moorthy, R. (2015). An investigation of relationship between psychological empowerment and Job satisfaction. *Journal of Contemporary Research in Management, 10*(1), 1.

Lin, L. F. (2013). Effects of psychological empowerment on organizational citizenship behavior in life insurance industry. *International Journal of Organizational Innovation (Online), 6*(1), 119.

Najafi, S., Noruzy, A., Azar, H. K., Nazari-Shirkouhi, S., & Dalvand, M. R. (2011). Investigating the relationship between organizational justice, psychological empowerment, job satisfaction, organizational commitment and organizational citizenship behavior: An empirical model. *African Journal of Business Management, 5*(13), 5241.

Organ, D. W. (1988). A restatement of the satisfaction performance hypothesis. *Journal of Management, 14*(4), 547–557.

Paillé, P., & Grima, F. (2011). Citizenship and withdrawal in the workplace: Relationship between organizational citizenship behavior, intention to leave current job and intention to leave the organization. *The Journal of Social Psychology, 151*(4), 478–493.

Priyadharshini, S. L., & Mahadevan, A. (2014). Mediating role of organizational citizenship behavior on HRM Practices and Turnover intention among production engineers. *International Journal of Organizational Behaviour & Management Perspectives, 3*(2), 994.

Zhong, J. A., Lam, W., & Chen, Z. (2011). Relationship between leader–member exchange and organizational citizenship behaviors: Examining the moderating role of empowerment. *Asia Pacific Journal of Management, 28*(3), 609–626.

Chapter 30
Employee Engagement Determinants and Employee Retention: A Study Among Generation Y Employees in Malaysia

Shafiq Shahruddin and Normala Daud

Abstract In today's complex business environment, organization is facing challenges in retaining their employees especially young employees, known as Generation Y. The purpose of this paper is to investigate the relationship between determinants of employee engagement toward the retention of Generation Y employees in the banking sector. The study also seeks to provide the theory-based empirical evidence using social exchange theory (SET) to determine whether the role of employee engagement influence the retention of these young employees. A total of 200 bank employees representing a range of Malaysian banks will be selected using stratified random sampling. This study attempts to contribute toward the positive relationship of young employees' retention in the organization through employee engagements determinants. Several significant findings as well as theoretical implications would be drawn from the results of the study for building better organizational environment for Generation Y employees to be retained in the organization.

Keywords Employee engagement · Employee retention · Generation Y · Social exchange theory

30.1 Introduction

Organizations in today's world oppose challenges in managing and retaining employees as more and more organizations have rapidly grow and the competitiveness among those organizations is high in order to sustain in the business (Aida 2014). Due to the highly competitive scenario among the business, retaining tal-

S. Shahruddin (✉) · N. Daud
Centre for Postgraduate and Professional Studies, Faculty of Business and Management, Universiti Teknologi MARA, 40450 Shah Alam, Selangor, Malaysia
e-mail: shafiq_shahruddin@yahoo.com

N. Daud
e-mail: normala648@salam.uitm.edu.my

F. Noordin et al. (eds.), *Proceedings of the 2nd Advances in Business Research International Conference*, https://doi.org/10.1007/978-981-10-6053-3_30

ented and young employees become more difficult to be managed by the organizations (James and Mathew 2012; George 2015). This is totally agreeable by (Aruna and Anitha 2015), as long-term success of any organization always depends upon the retention of key employees. A report from Globoforce in 2015 Employee Recognition Report had identified that employee retention is among the challenges facing by the organization. The report had stated that 40% of human resource professionals and practitioners saying that they are facing employee retention issue in the organization.

To a great extent, employee satisfaction, organizational commitment and organizational performance, is reliant on the ability of the organization to retain the top employees (Margaret and Leo 2015; Aruna and Anitha 2015; Zhoa 2015). Zhoa (2006) also stated that in the human resource (HR) practice, recruiting and retaining the best employees are a vibrant element to organizational success. Researchers have discussed a few definition of employee retention and the concept of employee retention was defined variedly in the literature (Gurumani 2010; Christina and Qi 2015). Encouraging employees to remain in the organization for a long period of time can be defined as employee retention (Gurumani 2010) or in other word employee retention is generally a process of making employees to stay with the organization. In a recent study, James and Mathew (2012) had defined that the concept of employee retention as a voluntary process by any organization to avail an environment which encourages and motivates employee to stay with the entity for the maximum period of time.

Many studies had verified that it is a widely held understanding that hiring knowledgeable and talented employees for the job is critical for any organization; however, employee retention is even more critical than hiring, hence the need for organizations to cultivate and implement effective retention practices in order to persuade employees to stay longer in the organization (Yamamoto 2011; Ratna and Chawla 2012; Aida 2014). Retention of talented and promising employees can be an underpinning of advantage for an organization (George 2015). Despite the advantage, there are challenges in attempting to retain these employees (Aruna and Anitha 2015). Retaining Generation Y (Gen Y) employees in today's corporate setting has become a phenomenal task for the organizations to manage (Camille and Nicole 2011). Generally, Gen Y are those who were born in the 1980s and 1990s and are the latest age group to enter the business community (Aruna and Anitha 2015). They are the children of the baby boomers who have been highly attentive, child-centered and competitive parents (Weyland 2011).

In this study, employee engagement determinants will act as tool to influence the employees to remain in the organization longer. Andrew and Sofian (2012) had verified that the determinants of employee engagement are also known as the individual factors of employee engagement. Therefore, this study will identify the key variables through a thorough literature survey that describes employee engagement and distinguishes the strength of employee engagement' determinants on employee retention. This study also aims at understanding the relationship of employee engagement determinants toward the retention of Gen Y employees.

30.2 Employee Retention

Success of any organization is dependent upon the retention of key and potential employees (Aruna and Anitha 2015). In HR practice, recruiting and retaining the best employees are a vibrant element to organizational success (Zhao 2006). The aptitude to retain the best employees will be a huge success for organizations in order to be competitive in the marketplace (Aruna and Anitha 2015; George 2015). The concept of employee retention was defined differently in the literature. In general, employee retention is a process of making employees to stay with the organization and inspiring employees to remain in the organization for a long period of time (Gurumani 2010; Aruna and Anitha 2015; George 2015). In other words, employee retention can be portrayed as the determination by employer to retain desirable workers, which will meet the organization goals and mission in the future (Frank et al. 2004). Furthermore, some scholars defined the retention as the ability to hold onto preferable employees that organizations want to keep, for longer than their rivals (Johnson 2000). ALDamoe et al. (2012) and James and Mathew (2012) expressed the concept as a voluntary process by any organization to avail an environment, which encourages and motivates the employees to remain with the organization for the maximum period of time. To understand more about the meaning of employee retention, Mahal (2012) had identified that the employee retention as an approach taken by the organization to retain employees from leaving and quitting the existing job, such as rewarding them for showing promising performance, ensuring that there are effective two way communications between employees and superiors and maintaining the healthy working environment in the organization.

Earlier research study has acknowledged several aspects relating to employee retention, situated on both organizational and employee levels (Govaerts et al. 2011). Employee retention is not persuaded by a single factor, but there are a few factors that are accountable for retaining employees in the organization (Fitz-enz 1990; Aruna and Anitha 2015). In order to retain the employee, employer needs to focus on a variety of aspects such as training and developments, compensations, work environment and supervisor support culture (Fitz-enz 1990; Mahal 2012; Ghosh et al. 2013). According to Osteraker (1999), retention factor differs in three broad measurements, which are social, mental, and physical aspect. The mental dimension of retention consist of work characteristics; employees always prefer flexible work tasks where they can use their knowledge and see the results of their efforts which, in turn, helps in retaining the valuable resources. The social dimension consists of the contacts that the employees have with other people, both internal and external. The physical dimension consists of working conditions and pay (Das and Baruah 2013).

30.2.1 Employee Engagement and Its Determinants

This definition is originated from Kahn (1990) that stated how individuals could experience a sense of engagement and also disengagement from their roles at work (Harter et al. 2002). Kahn (1990), who is considered as an academic parent of the employee engagement movement, developed the concept of "personal engagement." In his work, he defines personal work engagement as the "harnessing of organization members' selves to their work roles; in engagement, people employ and express themselves physically, cognitively and emotionally, during role performances". Kahn added that three psychological engagement conditions are necessary for an employee to be rightly engaged: meaningfulness (work elements), safety (social elements, including management style, process, and organizational norms) and availability (individual distractions). Furthermore, some studies had identified that employee engagement is the state of emotional and intellectual commitment to an organization or group (Falcone 2006). An engage employee is a person who is fully involved in, and enthusiastic about, his or her work (Falcone 2006). Schaufeli and Salanova (2007) define engagement as a positive, fulfilling, work-related state of mind that is characterized by vigor, dedication, and absorption. Robinson et al. (2004) define engagement as one step ahead of commitment. They also described that employee engagement have connection to a positive employees' emotional attachment and employees' commitment in the organization (Dernovsek 2008).

From the concept by Kahn, researchers had taken the perceptions and assessments from the Kahn literature and other relevant constructive items, in order to consolidate a number of factors that contributed toward Khan's three psychological conditions of employee engagement and employee engagement in general. Bedarkar and Pandita (2014) stated that Kahn explained that the employees experience psychological safety in the presence of other members when they relate themselves to their role performances and they are provided with sufficient personal resources to dedicate themselves to such performances. Their work is sufficiently meaningful to them. As employees feel psychologically safe and their work is meaningful to them, they are psychologically available. Thus, the condition of psychological availability refers to a situation, wherein employees and draw on their whole selves in an integrated and focused manner to enhance their role performances. There are few factors that simplify these three proportions of employee engagement were identified and were empirically tested and found to be valid determinants of employee engagement (Bedarkar and Pandita 2014; Anitha 2014). Based on the study done by Anitha (2014), the determinants of employee engagement in organization are work environment, leadership, team and co-worker, training and career development, compensation, organizational policies, and lastly workplace well-being. Merry (2013) also had identified the engagement determinants into 6 categories, which are company practices (communication, talent and staffing), the basics (work environment, workplace well-being, benefits), the work (autonomy, empowerment, work tasks), performance (career opportunities, training and development, rewards), leaderships (senior leadership, supervisor, team and co-worker) and brand (reputation, corporate responsibility). Andrew and Sofian (2012) had stated that the determinants of employee engagement are also known as individual factors. They identified that employee communication, employee development, and co-employee support as the factors that have significant relationship toward the employee engagement.

30.2.2 Employee Engagement Outcomes

Along the way of the study of the driver that lead to the employee engagement, the researchers had revealed a range of outcomes that organizations were seeking from developing the engagement of their people (Richard 2007). Symptomatically, these outcomes of the employee engagement were seen as impacting directly on employee performance and employee retention (Merry 2013). Moreover, there are some studies that have discovered a few positive and promising outcomes of employee engagement in the organization (Saks 2006), such as encouraging relations with organizational outcomes, that lead to the better financial performance and profitability of the organization (Salanova et al. 2005; Saks 2006; Xanthopoulou et al. 2007; Gibbons 2008; Armir and Buckley 2009; Schaufeli et al. 2009).

Merry (2013) had stated that Aon Hewitt model discuss the outcome of the employee engagement determinants which are engagement outcomes and business outcomes. The engagement outcomes have showed that three significant results, which are 'say', 'stay' and 'strive'. Furthermore the business outcomes from the Aon Hewitt model are talent (retention, absenteeism, wellness), operational (productivity, safety), customer (satisfaction, retention) and financial (revenue, total shareholder return). Another example that showed the outcome for the employee engagement is the model develop by Andrew and Sofian (2012) which the study explained the impact of individual factors as the employee engagement determinant and the work outcomes of the employee engagements. The study had identified that employee engagement has significant relationship toward the job satisfaction, organization commitment, intention to quit and organizational citizenship behavior (Andrew and Sofian 2012). According to Saks (2006), employee engagement determinants had shown to be negatively associated to employee intentions to quit and this can explained that employee willing to prolong their service in the organization. These findings are consistent with literature as posited by Harter et al. (2002) and Schaufeli and Bakker (2004) that employee engagement determinants could be a strong element and predictors for organizational performance and their success, as it seems to have a significant potential to affect employee retention, their loyalty and productivity in the organization.

30.3 Research Framework

The focus of this research study will be on the employee engagement determinants and the study assumes that these determinants lead to employee retention. The main purpose of the study is to examine a research framework (Fig. 30.1) that can enhance the understanding of the uncertainty about employee engagement determinants (independent variables) on employee retention (dependent variables) using the measure of employee engagement as the mediating variables and the social exchange theory (SET) as the underpinning theory. In this study, SET is the most suitable framework to be used in order to relate between the employee engagement determinants and employee retention. The SET is grounded on two main literatures, which are by Homans (1961) and Blau (1964), and it has become a popular theoretical basis in organizational studies concerned with assessing social behavior and interactions (Jepsen and Rodwell 2010; Allen and Shanock 2013). This will provide researchers both in academia and in organizations with an understanding of the employee engagement determinants that influencing Generation Y employees' retention in the organization.

The research study will focus on seven specific employee engagement determinants, as these determinants are the common engagement practice in the organization. The employee engagement determinants are work environment,

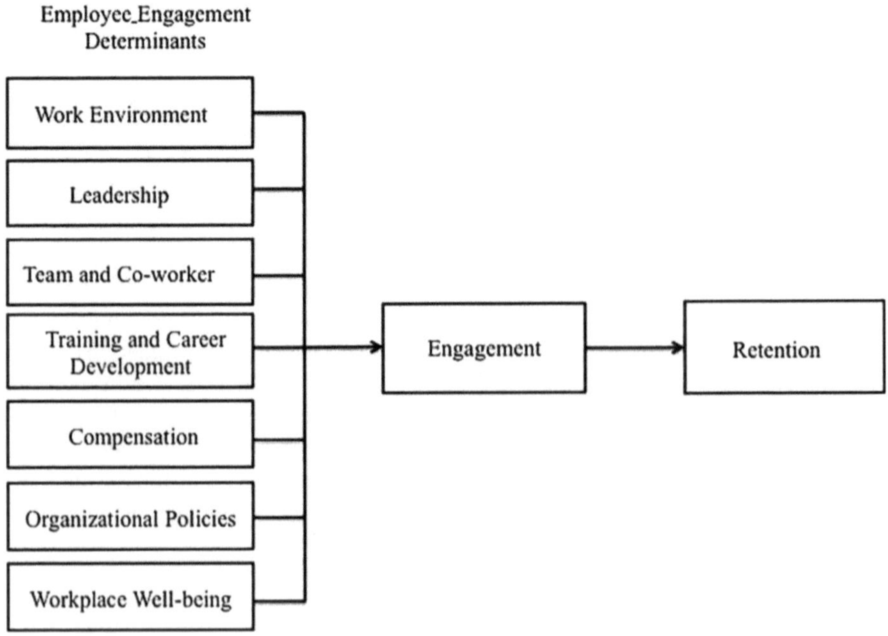

Fig. 30.1 Proposed research framework

leadership, team and co-worker, training and career development, compensation, organizational policies, and workplace well-being.

30.4 Research Methodology

The unit of analysis (sample) of this study comprised of individuals that have been categorized as Generation Y (ages between 20 and 35 years old) in local commercial bank headquarters in Malaysia. The sampling frame for this study is the headquarters of all commercial local banks in Malaysia that has been listed by Bank Negara Malaysia. Bank Negara Malaysia had listed that it will consist of eight commercial banks, which are Malayan Banking Berhad, CIMB Bank Berhad, RHB Bank Berhad, Affin Bank Berhad, Alliance Bank Berhad, Public Bank Berhad, Ambank (M) Berhad, and Hong Leong Bank. The data will be collected through probability sampling, which is proportionate stratified random sampling. The minimum sample size for this research study that had been calculated by G*power 3 is 160. However, for this study, the sample size chosen is 200 because according to Hair et al. (2010), the number is sufficient for research study, and the bigger sample size, more accurate the sample size represents the total population. Hair et al. (2010) also stated that sample size between 200 and 400 is believed to be sufficient for research study. SmartPLS 3.0 software will be used to evaluate the relationship among the constructs of the research model by conducting partial least square (PLS) analysis. The analysis will be analyzed by following the guidelines of Hair et al. (2014) in reporting the partial least square-structural equation modeling (PLS-SEM) approach.

The measurement items used for the questionnaire were already identified from previous literatures. The work environment, leadership, team and co-worker, compensation, and workplace well-being were adapted from Ghosh et al. (2013) and Anitha (2014). Next, training and career development and organizational policies were adapted from Anita (2014). The measurement items of employee engagement were adapted from Ghosh et al. (2013) and Anitha (2014) to measure the employee engagement in the organization, which might effects the retention of the employees. The items for employee retention were adapted from Ghosh et al. (2013) to measure the employee's intention to stay in the organization. The questionnaires will be measured using five-point Likert-type scale, ranging from 1 (strongly disagree) to 5 (strongly agree).

30.5 Conclusion

In conclusion, this study is to provide significant theoretical and practical contribution to the employee engagement practices in organization. The model can be used by organizations to focus on key aspects that would result in both employee and employer benefits in the future. The most important value for this study is that it will provide profile of Gen Y employees that has high retention capacity in the organization. For further investigation for this study, pre test will be done before the researcher collect the data to examine the result of this study. There is no one-size-fits-all answer to employee engagement and the determinants will surely provide significant contributions to the retention of Gen Y toward employees.

References

Aida, I. (2014). Flexible working as an employee retention strategy in developing countries. *Journal of Management Research, 14*(2), 71−86.

ALDamoe, F. M. A., Yazam, M., & Ahmid, K. (2012). The mediating effect of HRM outcomes (employee retention) on the relationship between HRM practices and organizational performance. *International Journal of Human Resource Studies, 2*(1), 75−88.

Ali, Q. A., Christina, S., & Qi, W. (2015). The vital role of employee retention in human resource management: A literature review. *IUP Journal of Organizational Behavior, 15*(3), 7–32.

Allen, D. G., & Shanock, L. R. (2013). Perceived organizational support and embeddedness as key mechanisms connecting socialisation tactics to commitment and turnover among new employees. *Journal of Organisational Behaviour, 34*(3), 350–369.

Andrew, O., & Sofian, S. (2012). Individual factors and work outcomes of employee engagement. *Procedia-Social and Behavioral Sciences, 40,* 498–508.

Anitha, J. (2014). Determinants of employee engagement and their impact on employee performance. *International Journal of Productivity and Performance Management, 63*(3), 308 −323.

Armir, A. C., & Buckley, F. (2009). Linking trust in the principle to school outcomes: The mediating role of organization identification and work engagement. *Journal of Education Management, 23*(7), 574–589.

Aruna, M., & Anitha, J. (2015). Employee retention enablers: Generation Y employees. *SCMS Journal of Indian Management,* 94−103.

Bedarkar, M. & Pandita, D. (2014). A study on the drivers of employee engagement impacting employee performance. *Procedia-Social and Behavioral Sciences, 133,* 106−115).

Blau, P. M. (1964). *Exchange and power in social life*. New York, NY: Wiley.

Camille, K., & Nicole, S. (2011). Understanding and managing generational differences in the workplace. *Worldwide Hospitality and Tourism Themes, 3*(4), 308−318.

Das, B., & Baruah, M. (2013). Employee retention: A review of literature. *OSR Journal of Business and Management (IOSR-JBM), 14*(2), 8−16.

Dernovsek, D. (2008). Creating highly engaged and committed employee starts at the top and ends at the bottom line. *Credit Union Magazine, May 2008*. Credit Union National Association, Inc.

Falcone, P. (2006). Preserving restless top performers: Keep your top performers engaged so they don't jump ship once job opportunities arise. *HR Magazine*. March.

Fitz-enz, J. (1990). Getting and keeping good employees. *personnel, 67*(8), 25–29.

Frank, F. D., Finnegan, R. P., & Taylor, C. R. (2004). The race for talent: Retaining and engaging workers in the 21st century. *Human Resource Planning, 27*(3), 12–25.

George, C. (2015). Retaining professional workers: What makes them stay? *Employee Relations, 37*(1), 102–121.

Ghosh, P., Satyawadi, R., Joshi, J. P., & Mohd. S. (2013). Who stays with you? Factors predicting employees intention to stay. *International Journal of Organizational Analysis, 21*(3), 288 −312.

Gibbons, J. (2008). Employee engagement: A review of current research and its implications, The Conference Board, New York, NY.

Govaerts, N., Kyndt, E., Dochy, F., & Baert, H. (2011). Influence of learning and working climate on the retention of talented employees. *Journal of Workplace Learning, 23*(1), 35–55.

Gurumani, V. S. (2010). Invaluable tools for talent retention. *Human Capital,* 54−55.

Hair, J. F., Sarstedt, M., Hopkins, L., & Kuppelwieser, V. G. (2014). Partial least squares structural equation modeling (PLS-SEM): An emerging tool in business research. *European Business Review, 26*(2), 106–121.

Hair, J., Black, W., Babin, B., & Anderson, R. (2010). *Multivariate data anlysis.* (7th ed.) New Jersey: Prentice-hall, Inc.

Harter, J. K., Schmidt, F. L., & Hayes, T. L. (2002). Business-unit-level relationship between employee satisfaction, employee engagement, and business outcomes: A meta-analysis. *Journal of Applied Psychology, 87*(2), 268–279.

Homans, G. L. (1961). *Social Behavior: Its Elementary Forms.* NewYork: Harcourt Brace Jovanovich.

James, L., & Mathew, L. (2012). Employee retention strategies: IT industry. *SCMS Journal of Indian Management, 19*(3), 79−87, 53.

Jepsen, D. M., & Rodwell, J. (2010). A social exchange model of the employment relationship based on keeping tally of the psychological contract. *European Relations Record, 10*(2), 20−45, 54.

Johnson, M. (2000). *Winning the people war.* Copyright Licensing Agency, London: Talent and the Battle for Human Capital.

Kahn, W. A. (1990). Psychological conditions of personal engagement and disengagement at work. *Academy of Management Journal, 33*(4), 692–724.

Mahal, P. K. (2012). HR practices as determinants of organisational commitment and employee retention. *The IUP Journal of Management Research, 11*(4), 37−53, 52.

Margaret, D., & Leo, J. (2015). Revisiting talent management, work-life balance and retention strategies. *International Journal of Contemporary Hospitality Management,* 27(3), 453−472.

Merry, J. (2013). Aon hewitt's 2013 trends in global engagement: Where do organizations need to focus attention? *Strategic HR Review, 13*(1), 24−31.

Osteraker, M. C. (1999). Measuring motivation in a learning organization. *Journal of Work Place Learning.*

Ratna, R., & Chawla, S. (2012). Key factors of retention and retention strategies in telecom sector. *Sona Global Management Review, 6*(3), 35–46.

Richard, M. B. (2007). The practice of engagement: Research into current employee engagement practice, *Strategic HR Review,* 6(6), 16−19.

Robinson, D., Perryman, S., & Hayday, S. (2004). The drivers of employee engagement, Report No. 408, Institute for Employment Studies, Brighton, April.

Saks, A. M. (2006). Antecedents and consequences of employee engagement. *Journal of Managerial Psychology, 21*(7), 600–619.

Salanova, M., Agut, S., & Peiro, J. M. (2005). Linking organizational resources and work engagement to employee performance and customer loyalty: The mediation of service climate. *Journal of Applied Psychology, 90*(6), 1217–1227.

Schaufeli, W. B., & Bakker, A. B. (2004). Job demands, job resources, and their relationship with burnout and engagement: A multi-sample study. *Journal of Organizational Behavior, 25,* 293–315.

Schaufeli, W. B., & Salanova, M. (2007). Work engagement: an emerging psychological concept and its implications for organizations. In S. W. Gilliland, D. D. Steiner, & D. P. Skarlicki (Eds.), *Research in social issues in management* (pp. 135–177). CT: Information Age Publishers, Greenwich.

Weyland, A. (2011). Engagement and talent management of Gen Y. *Industrial and Commercial Training, 43*(7), 439–445.
Xanthopoulou, D., Bakker, A. B., Demerouti, E., & Schaufeli, W. B. (2007). The role of personal resources in the job demands-resource model. *International Journal of Stress Management, 14* (2), 121–141.
Yamamoto, H. (2011). The relationship between employee benefit management and employee retention. *The International Journal of Human Resource Management, 22*(17), 3550–3564.
Zhao, H. (2006). Expectations of recruiters and applicants in large cities of China. *Journal of Managerial Psychology, 21*(5), 459–475.

Chapter 31
A Conceptual Study on the Factors Influencing Behavioural Intention to Use Mobile Health Application Among Young Women in Malaysia

Khairul Nazlin Kamaruzaman, Zuhal Hussein and Amily Fikry

Abstract Mobile health (mHealth) is now becoming an alternative medium in order for the society to have a healthy lifestyle. People may use mobile health to manage, find and deal with information related to health consciousness. In Malaysia, the mobile health application has already been introduced, but the implementation of this application is still at the preliminary stage. This concept paper will discuss elements such as perceived usefulness, perceived ease of use and the concept of mobility with regard to the behavioural intention to use the mobile health application. It is hoped that this paper will create a better understanding of mobile health application in Malaysia.

Keywords Behavioural intention · mHealth · Mobility concept · Malaysia

31.1 Background of Study

Mobile phone devices are well known around the world. The innovativeness and functions of this device are enormously updated. Currently, the most popular type of mobile phone is the smartphone. This device has been offering a lot of appli-

---

K.N. Kamaruzaman
Faculty of Business Management, Universiti Teknologi MARA, 40450 Shah Alam, Selangor, Malaysia

Z. Hussein (✉)
Faculty of Business Management, Universiti Teknologi MARA, Kota Bharu Campus, Wisma KUB, Jalan Sultan Ibrahim, 15050 Kota Bharu, Kelantan, Malaysia
e-mail: zuhal@kelantan.uitm.edu.my

A. Fikry
Centre for Professional and Postgraduate Studies, Universiti Teknologi MARA, 40450 Shah Alam, Selangor, Malaysia
e-mail: amily@salam.uitm.edu.my

F. Noordin et al. (eds.), *Proceedings of the 2nd Advances in Business Research International Conference*, https://doi.org/10.1007/978-981-10-6053-3_31

cations for education, social media, lifestyle, health, games, travel and others. Respectively, users of the iPhone Operating System (iOS) may download an application from AppStore while users of Android System (OS) may download from Google Play. In Malaysia, the local sector is very supportive of citizens using smartphones. This is an advantage to Malaysians, given that they get to own a smartphone at an affordable price.

In this new era, the technology of mobile phones is not limited to just communication through calls and messaging. There are lots of applications available. One of the applications that are being offered via download is mobile health. The mobile health (mHealth) application is an effective interaction medium, and it attracts lots of users for its medical purposes (Mcgillicuddy et al. 2013). However, others give the definition of mHealth as an electronic device that has been using mobile communication technologies which focuses on promoting health care (Aranda-Jan et al. 2014). This technology was developed to help people with achieving good health care management. It is undeniable that this device may offer several benefits such as being user-friendly, easy to access anywhere and anytime, and it may reduce the cost of setting up a medical service. The consumers only need to have a smartphone with Internet network connection which enables them to use the health care application.

Maintaining a healthy lifestyle is important to everyone. In order to be a healthy individual, we need to practice eating healthy food and get involved with exercises or activities. This may minimize the risk of getting an illness. Currently, there are lots of cases of serious illnesses which impact towards our daily activities and some have potential risks which could lead to death. Therefore, this technology also offers healthy lifestyle software and application. The innovativeness of mobile technology enables the expert to create applications suitable for health care.

In many other countries, mHealth has already been introduced to their respective citizens. World Health Organization (WHO) and Global Observatory for eHealth (GOe) did a research related to mHealth in 2009. They found out that the majority or 83% of members of WHO reached at least one type of mHealth services offered. According to the global survey by WHO in 2015 (World Health Organization 2015), mHealth programmes in Malaysia were already established at the nation's intermediate and local levels, in addition, a study by Frost and Sullivan (2015) stated that there will be a high increase in Malaysia's percentage of health expenditures. They identified that the cost of health will increase up to $20 billion in 2025 which is almost a 50% increase from the current market.

It was discovered that smartphone users gradually increased from 14% in the year 2010 to 53.4% in 2014 (Malaysian Communications and Multimedia Commission 2015a, b). This was supported by Vishwanath et al. (2012). Malaysia is one of the developing countries that reached the 100% milestone of mobile market penetration. In addition, statistics of Internet users showed that out of 3607 despondences in 2014, there are 66.6% of Internet users versus 33.4% non-Internet users in Malaysia (Malaysian Communication and Multimedia Commission 2015a, b). Besides that, based on smartphone users 63.3% are accessed the Internet via their mobile phones (Malaysian Communications and Multimedia Commission 2015a, b).

Even though there are increasing numbers of smartphone users and numbers of Internet users via smartphone, the mHealth application is not being maximally utilized. The mHealth application did not meet the consumers' expectation. The sophisticated nature of the mHealth application leads to low level of implementation among consumers. Some individuals resist adopting the use of the mHealth application (Guo et al. 2013). There are also individuals who discontinue their use of the mHealth application (Tanvir et al. 2014). The negative word-of-mouth communication may twist the feeling and behaviour of consumers (Syukrina et al. 2015). This also gives consumers a negative perspective of the application. Individuals may judge the mHealth application as something that is a burden to them.

Despite many studies that examined the advance of smartphone applications, research on the factor influencing users' intention to use mHealth application is inconclusive. As highlighted by Amily et al. (2013), gender plays no significant role in the intention to adopt health care services. These results were contradicted by the studies of Jihye and Iftekhar (2016) who considered women as highly likely to use healthcare applications. Therefore, the purpose of this study is to identify the factors that contribute to the intention to use mHealth application among young women in Malaysia. Previous research shows that women are in the majority with regard to surfing the Internet for health care purposes and they have higher perceived health risks compared to men (Ashraf et al. 2015). In addition, the Malaysian Communications and Multimedia Commission (MCMC) reported that in 2014, those who surfed the Internet most were adult users aged between 20 and 49 years old (Malaysian Communication and Multimedia Commission 2015a, b). Thus, this study is focusing on young women in Malaysia.

Prior research has claimed that consumers can be influenced to implement mHealth by understanding their perspective and behavioural intention to use it (Maarop and Win 2012; Sun et al. 2013). Hence, this study will focus on understanding consumers' perception towards mHealth, because unexpected illness is something that we cannot control, as well as the associated increasing health expenditure. The objective of this study is to examine the influence of perceived usefulness (PU), perceived ease of use (PEOU) and mobility concept (MC) towards women's behavioural intention (BI) to use the mHealth application.

31.2 Women and Mobile Phone in Health Care

In the advanced mobile technology, women may use the mobile application that gives tips, information and self-management of their personal health issues. Based on the literature review, there are many advantages on using mobile health application, but there is still some space that could be improved to fulfil the women needs today.

Smartphone ownership is increasing not only in Malaysia but also around the world. There are many reasons scholars, academicians, researchers and others still want to explore the capabilities of the smartphones. For instance, day by day there are expanding number of studies specifically in mobile health applications (Azevedo et al. 2014; Banchs et al. 2014; Castro et al. 2014; Matousek et al. 2015; Park et al. 2015; Shao et al. 2015; Sujansky and Kunz 2014; Wen and Duh 2016).

Another study in Catalonia showed that young women age 35 years and below are more frequent users of mobile phone (Vancea and Olivera 2013). There are several studies that focused on elderly women upon the mobile health (Bo et al. 2014; Lim et al. 2011; Xue et al. 2012). However, only few focused on young women as users of mobile health application. It is undeniable that the women with elder age are susceptible with the chronic disease but precaution on health management needs to be taken care of at younger age. Moreover, young women also may encounter the situations or symptoms relate to the health problems soon. Thus, this study is required in order to ensure women practice healthy lifestyle as early as possible.

31.3 Behavioural Intention to Use Mobile Health

Technology acceptance model (TAM) was created in order to examine the adoption of technology by Davis (1989). The model has been cited by many scholars for many years. Table 31.1 shows TAM previous studies which are related to health care. One of the important variables is behavioural intention, which plays an important role in many studies (Faziharudean and Li-Ly 2011; Kim et al. 2010; Bo et al. 2014).

Behavioural intention can be defined as "a measure of the strength of one's intention to perform a specified behaviour" (Deng et al. 2014). Behavioural intention also can be expressed as the strength of patients to use mobile health services (Rho et al. 2014). In many studies, behavioural intention is the dependent variable (Deng et al. 2014; Bo et al. 2014; Liu and Cheng 2015). However, Ashraf et al. (2015) perform behavioural intention as the mediating variable in their studies. Their findings show that there are slight influences of perceived health risk on the intention to use health information technology.

31.4 Factors Influencing Behavioural Intention to Use Mobile Health

In this study, the researcher uses several collections of theories and models which identify the factors influencing mobile health adoption among young women in Malaysia. The proposed conceptual framework is an emerging theory of the technology acceptance model (TAM) and mobility concept (Liu and Cheng 2015) as an

Table 31.1 Technology Acceptance Model (TAM) studies in health care

Author (s)	Subjects	Technology studied	Others variables related perceived usefulness/perceived ease of use
Hussain (2013)	Patient	Mobile tracking	User satisfaction, attribute usability
Guo et al. (2013)	Elderly consumers	Mobile health services	Technology anxiety, dispositional resistance to change, resistance to change
Okazaki et al. (2015)	Physicians	Mobile health monitoring systems	Subjective norm, overall quality, perceived value, net benefits
Bo et al. (2014)	Adult female	Smart health users	Demographic factors, self-efficacy, innovativeness, user interface, perceived enjoyment
Cho et al. (2014)	College students	Smart health application	Subjective norm, health consciousness, health information orientation, eHealth literacy, Internet health information, use efficacy
Dwivedi et al. (2015)	Consumers	Mobile health	Social influence, effort expectancy, hedonic motivation, waiting time, performance expectancy, price value, facilitating conditions, self-concept
Rho et al. (2014)	Diabetic patients	Telemedicine	Performance expectancy, effort expectancy, social influence, facilitating condition
Ashraf et al. (2015)	Women Internet users	Internet for health related	Perceived severity, perceived susceptibility, health consciousness, perceived health risk
Lee et al. (2012)	Literature review	Hospital information systems	Technological factors, human factors, organizational factors, attitude, perceived behavioural control, subjective norms
Kuo et al. (2013)	Nurses	Mobile electronic medical record systems	Optimism, innovativeness, insecurity, discomfort
Deng et al. (2014)	Middle and older people	Mobile health services	Perceived value, attitude, perceived behavioural control, subjective norm, perceived physical condition, resistance to change, technology anxiety, self-actualization need

external factor. Underpinning the proposed conceptual framework, author uses TAM model which has already proven its effectiveness on adoption technology.

31.4.1 Perceived Usefulness

Davis and Venkatesh (2004) defined the perceived usefulness as *"the degree to which a personal belief that using a particular system would enhance his or her job performance"*. For many years, the technology acceptance model (TAM) has been applied in research studies. The findings of those results showed that perceived usefulness was the most significant variable in the acceptance of technology (Mohamed et al. 2011; Poydras 2013; Vélez et al. 2014).

There is a research which is related to mobile health and integrated to the TAM. Mobile health technology acceptance model (MoHTAM) was introduced in order to explore the consumers or patients' acceptance of the smartphone for health care (Mohamed et al. 2011). Studies by researchers of MoHTAM highlighted several variables which influence the acceptance of mobile health. The variables are technology design, perceived usefulness and perceived ease of use towards the intention to use the mobile health application. As a result, they found out that the most influential factor that contributes with the intention to use mobile health is perceived usefulness. Hence, it was further proposed that:

Proposition 1: Perceived usefulness has a positive impact on behavioural intention to use mobile health application.

31.4.2 Perceived Ease of Use

Perceived ease of use can be defined as *"the extent to which an individual believes using a system will be free of effort"* (Davis and Venkatesh 2004). They pointed out that experience is needed in order to make sure the technology will be interactive to use. Davis and Venkatesh (2004) assume that perceived usefulness focused on the innovativeness of technology, while perceived ease of use has been recognized as a user's evaluation of how easy it is to use the hardware and software in devices.

In 2014, there was a study of related variables and the findings showed a different result from what was expected (Bo et al. 2014). In their study, perceived usefulness is not significant with the intention to use the technology. They discovered that the demographic characteristics of respondents influence the use of health care applications. As in their studies, women who are aged 30 years and above had given the unusual result towards the intention to use the mobile health application. Thus, from those findings, this paper posited that:

Proposition 2: Perceived ease of use has a positive impact on perceived usefulness for mobile health application.
Proposition 3: Perceived ease of use has a positive impact on behavioural intention to use mobile health application.

Many studies have been conducted to examine the relationship between perceived usefulness and perceived ease of use when utilizing the behavioural intention variable (Deng et al. 2014; Bo et al. 2014; Liu and Cheng 2015). However, due to present technology, it is necessary to examine the different external factors that influence perceived usefulness and perceived ease of use. It has been reviewed that those two variables could also be the mediator in this study. Another variable that researchers would like to propose is the mobility concept.

31.4.3 Mobility Concept

Nowadays, smartphones tend to be multifunctional devices and thus could be used for education, entertainment, health and others. Therefore, the mobility concept can also be considered as an effective medium with regard to sending and receiving the data. Faziharudean and Li-Ly (2011) have also discussed mobility in their study, but their focus is based on mobile data services. The findings show that there is a positive relationship between mobility towards behavioural intention to use mobile data. Based on their discussion, the mobility concept should consist of two elements, which are mobile entertainment and information service provided. This may have an influence on the behavioural intention to use mobile data services (Table 31.2).

Mobility concept gives a positive and negative impact to the user. The user may find that there are lots of positive impacts from the use of mobility. Based on the study, there are positive significant results between mobility and behavioural intention. But these are slightly affected by negative impact, which is a perceived threat towards the behavioural intention to use technology (Liu and Cheng 2015). In this study, the mobility concept is different from the prior research. The dimension of mobility concept in this study is focusing on mobile systems, mobile information and the mobile services of mHealth application itself. This is an adoption variable

Table 31.2 Previous studies on mobility concept

Author (s)	Technology study	Antecedence of intention to use
Faziharudean and Li-Ly (2011)	Mobile data services	Perceived usefulness, perceived ease of use, perceived enjoyment, social influence, media influence, perceived monetary value and perceived mobility
Andersson and Calvano (2015)	Globally mobile elite (GME)	None
Liu and Cheng (2015)	Mobile electronic medical record	Perceived usefulness, perceived ease of use and perceived threat
Park and Pobil (2013)	Remote pointing technology	Perceived usefulness, perceived ease of use and control

from the mobile phone-based diabetes monitoring (MDM) system of DeLone and McLean's in (2003), which are rephrased from the overall systems quality. In line with that, it is further proposed that:

Proposition 4: Mobility concept has a positive impact on perceived usefulness for mobile health application.
Proposition 5: Mobility concept has a positive impact on perceived ease of use for mobile health application.

31.5 Discussion

The technology acceptance model (TAM) is extended to another external variable which is the mobility concept. This variable is interrelated with the adoption of technology. TAM has formulated two variables which are "perceived usefulness" and "perceived ease of use". These two variables commonly have positive significant results with regard to the behavioural intention to use technology (Mohamed et al. 2011; Liu and Cheng 2015). This study aims to indicate the current level of adoption of mobile health application among young women consumers in Malaysia. In this regard, mobile phone capabilities should be expanded, especially in health care. Through this study, by understanding the consumer's behaviour, the marketers may develop an application that meets consumers' needs and preferences. Besides that, it is hoped that consumers will be encouraged and motivated to use mobile health applications to get health care information, instead of going directly to the medical consultant.

There are many studies on the innovativeness of health technology. However, it is more focused on the functions or capabilities of the devices. In this study, the researcher focuses on the perception of individuals towards mobile health. This study emphasizes women's behavioural intention to use mobile health due to their belief and trust. According to Ashraf et al. (2015), every woman is different from the other; and women are the highest users of the Internet, on a daily basis, compared to men.

31.6 Conclusion and Future Work

In conclusion, this concept paper aims to explore the extent of users' acceptance of mHealth in Malaysia. Mostly, it is important to identify the relationship between the mobility concepts as it relates to the behavioural intention to use mHealth application among young women in Malaysia. The integrated TAM model along with another variable was used to determine the behavioural intention to use mHealth application based on user expectation. The information will be helpful for developers or designers creating the mHealth application. Besides that, for future research it is suggested that the sample of respondents be broadened, with mixed characteristics and gender. In addition, future research may also consider exploring the different factors that influence behavioural intention to use mHealth application such as perceived risk, which represents the negative value that impacts on behavioural intention to use mHealth application.

Acknowledgements The researchers like to acknowledge the Ministry of Education (MOE) Malaysia for the fund received through the Fundamental Research Grant Scheme (FRGS) [Project file: 600-RMI/FRGS 5/3 122/2014)] and to the Research Management Institute (RMI), Universiti Teknologi MARA (UiTM).

References

Amily, F., Hussein, Z., & Yusob, R. (2013). The effect of demographic characteristics towards intention to adopt healthcare services of digital home. In *BEIAC 2013–2013 IEEE business engineering and industrial applications colloquium* (Vol. 3, pp. 34–37).

Andersson, L., & Calvano, L. (2015). Perceived mobility of impact: Global elites and the bono effect. *Critical Perspectives on International Business, 11*(2), 122–136.

Aranda-Jan, C. B., Mohutsiwa-Dibe, N., & Loukanova, S. (2014). Systematic review on what works, what does not work and why of implementation of mobile health (mHealth) projects in Africa. *BMC Public Health, 14*(1), 188.

Ashraf, S. A., Sharif, S. P., Ong, F. S., & Khong, K. W. (2015). Integrating health belief model and technology acceptance model: An investigation of health-related internet use. *Journal of Medical Internet Research., 17*(2), 45.

Azevedo, A. R. P., de Sousa, H. M. L., Monteiro, J. A. F., & Lima, A. R. N. P. (2014). Future perspectives of Smartphone applications for rheumatic diseases self-management. *Rheumatology International, 35*(3), 419–431. doi:10.1007/s00296-014-3117-9.

Banchs, J. E., Benvenuto, I. V., Baquero, G. A., Hess, S. L., Heron, K. E., LaPine, S., et al. (2014). High adoption rates of mobile technology by cardiology clinic patients but limited use of health applications. *Journal of the American College of Cardiology, 1,* A1426.

Bo, R. W., Ji-Yun, P., Kyungyong, C. & In, Y. C. (2014). Influential factors of smart health users according to usage experience and intention to use. *Wireless Personal Communications*, 2671–2683.

Castro, L. A., Favela, J., Quintana, E., & Perez, M. (2014). Behavioral data gathering for assessing functional status and health in older adults using mobile phones. *Personal and Ubiquitous Computing*, 379–391. 10.1007/s00779-014-0825-9.

Cho, J., Quinlan, M. M., Park, D., & Noh, G. (2014). *Determinants of adoption of smartphone health apps among college students* (pp. 860–871).

Davis, F. D. (1989). Perceived usefulness, perceived ease of use, and user acceptance of information technology. *MIS Quarterly, 13*(3), 319–340.

Davis, F. D., & Venkatesh, V. (2004). Toward preprototype user acceptance testing of new information systems: Implications for software project management. *IEEE Transactions on Engineering Management, 51*(1), 31–46.

DeLone, W. H., & McLean, E. R. (2003). The DeLone and McLean model of information systems success: A ten-year update. *Journal of Management Information Systems, 19*(4), 9–30.

Deng, Z., Mo, X., & Liu, S. (2014). Comparison of the middle-aged and older users' adoption of mobile health services in China. *International Journal of Medical Informatics, 83*(3), 210–224.

Dwivedi, Y. K., Shareef, M. A., Simintiras, A. C., Lal, B., & Weerakkody, V. (2015). A generalised adoption model for services: A cross-country comparison of mobile health (m-health). *Government Information Quarterly.*

Faziharudean, T. M., & Li-Ly, T. (2011). Consumers' behavioral intentions to use mobile data services in Malaysia. *African Journal of Business Management, 5*(5), 1811–1821.

Frost, & Sullivan. (2015). Study: Malaysia health expenditure could exceed $20B by 2025. *Enterprise innovation* (pp. 14–17).

Guo, X., Sun, Y., Wang, N., & Peng, Z. (2013). *The Dark Side of Elderly Acceptance of Preventive Mobile Health Services in China, 23*(1), 49–61.

Hussain, M. A.-D. (2013). A questionnaire approach based on the technology acceptance model for mobile tracking on patient progress applications. *Journal of Computer Science*, *9*(6), 763–770.

Jihye, H., & Iftekhar, S. N. (2016). Comparison on the use of smartphone application between international and Korean pregnant women. *International Journal of Information and Education Technology, 6*(5), 404–409.

Kim, C., Mirusmonov, M., & Lee, I. (2010). An empirical examination of factors influencing the intention to use mobile payment. *Computers in Human Behavior, 26*(3), 310–322.

Kuo, K. M., Liu, C. F., & Ma, C. C. (2013). An investigation of the effect of nurses' technology readiness on the acceptance of mobile electronic medical record systems. *BMC Medical Informatics and Decision Making, 13*(1), 88.

Lee, H. W., Ramayah, T., & Zakaria, N. (2012). External factors in hospital information system (HIS) adoption model: A case on Malaysia. *Journal of Medical Systems, 36*(4), 2129–2140.

Lim, S., et al. (2011). A study on Singaporean women's acceptance of using mobile phones to seek health information. *International Journal of Medical Informatics, 80*(12), e189–e202.

Liu, C. F., & Cheng, T. J. (2015). Exploring critical factors influencing physicians' acceptance of mobile electronic medical records based on the dual-factor model: A validation in Taiwan. *BMC Medical Informatics and Decision Making, 15*(1), 1–13.

Maarop, N., & Win, K. T. (2012). Understanding the need of health care providers for teleconsultation and technological attributes in relation to the acceptance of teleconsultation in Malaysia: A mixed methods study. *Journal of Medical Systems, 36*(5), 2881–2892.

Malaysian Communication and Multimedia Commission. (2015a). Internet Users Survey 2014.

Malaysian Communication and Multimedia Commission. (2015b). Hand phone users survey 2014.

Matousek, A., Paik, K., Winkler, E., Denike, J., Addington, S. R., Exe, C., Riviello, R. (2015). Community health workers and smartphones for the detection of surgical site infections in rural Haiti: a pilot study. *Lancet (London, England), 385 Suppl,* S47.

Mcgillicuddy, J. W., Weiland, A. K., Frenzel, R. M., Mueller, M. Jackson, B. M. B., & Taber, D. J. et al. (2013). Patient attitudes toward mobile phone-based health monitoring: Questionnaire study among kidney transplant recipients. *Journal of Medical Internet Research, 15*(1).

Mohamed, A. H. H. M., Tawfik, H., Al-Jumeily, D., & Norton, L. (2011). MoHTAM: A technology acceptance model for mobile health applications. In *2011 Developments in E-systems Engineering*, (pp. 13–18).

Okazaki, S., Blas, S. S. & Castaneda, J. A. (2015). Physicians' adoption of mobile health monitoring systems in Spain: Competing models and impact of prior experience. *Journal of Electronic Commerce Research,* pp. 194–218.

Park, E., & Pobil, A. P. D. (2013). Extending the technology acceptance model in remote pointing technology: Identifying the role of perceived mobility and control. *Sensor Review, 33,* 40–47.

Park, Y., Lee, Y., Lee, G., Lee, J., & Shin, S.-Y. (2015). Smartphone applications with sensors used in a tertiary hospital—current status and future challenges. *Sensors, 15*(5), 9854–9869.

Poydras, B. N. (2013). *Perceived usefulness of the communicate with me application: A statisfaction survey of students with Autism* (pp. 1–77).

Rho, M. J., Kim, H. S., Chung, K. & Choi, I. Y. (2014). Factors influencing the acceptance of telemedicine for diabetes management. *Cluster Computing*, 1–11.

Shao, A. F., Rambaud-Althaus, C., Swai, N., Kahama-Maro, J., Genton, B., D'Acremont, V., et al. (2015). Can smartphones and tablets improve the management of childhood illness in

Tanzania? A qualitative study from a primary health care worker's perspective. *BMC Health Services Research, 15*(1), 1–12. doi:10.1186/s12913-015-0805-4.

Sujansky, W., & Kunz, D. (2014). A standard-based model for the sharing of patient-generated health information with electronic health records. *Personal and Ubiquitous Computing*, 9–25.

Sun, Y., Wang, N., Guo, X., & Peng, Z. (2013). Understanding the acceptance of mobile health services: A comparison and integration of alternative models. *Journal of Electronic Commerce Research, 14*(2), 183–200.

Syukrina, A. M. A., Noor'ain, M. Y., & Sri, F. A. K. J. (2015). Understanding determinants of customer retention among three service providers in Malaysia. In *Advances in Business Research International Conference 2015 (ABRIC 2015)* (pp. 301–311).

Tanvir, A., Henry, L., Azfar, S. K., Rubana, I., Abbas, B., & Mohammad, I. (2014). eHealth and mHealth initiatives in Bangladesh: A scoping study. *BMC Health Services Research, 14*(1), 260.

Vancea, M., & Olivera, N. (2013). E-migrant women in Catalonia: Mobile phone use and maintenance of family relationships. *Gender, Technology and Development, 17*(2), 179–203. doi:10.1177/0971852413488715.

Vélez, O., Okyere, P. B., Kanter, A. S., & Bakken, S. (2014). A usability study of a mobile health application for rural Ghanaian midwives. *Journal of Midwifery and Women's Health, 59*(2), 184–191.

Vishwanath, S., Vaidya, K., Nawal, R., Parthasarathy, S., & Verma, S. (2012). *Touching lives through mobile health-assessment of the global market opportunity*. India: PwC Brand and Communications.

Wen, L. R., & Duh, C. M. (2016). Use of a smartphone to improve hospital discharge plan service. *International Journal of Information and Education Technology, 6*(5), 414–417.

World Health Organization. (2015). Atlas of eHealth country profiles 2015: The use of eHealth in support of universal health coverage.

Xue, L., Yen, C. C., Chang, L., Chan, H. C., Tai, B. C., Tan, S. B., et al. (2012). An exploratory study of ageing women's perception on access to health informatics via a mobile phone-based intervention. *International Journal of Medical Informatics, 81*(9), 637–648.

Chapter 32
Translation and an Adaptation of Work-Related Attitude Questionnaire in Cross-Cultural Survey Research

Nurnazirah Jamadin and Fauziah Noordin

Abstract The purpose of this paper is to briefly discuss the techniques and process of translation instrument. Several issues that were found during the translation course were also highlighted in this paper. As suggested by past studies, a combination of few techniques and approaches to translation were utilized in this study. Several qualified bilingual and bicultural experts were involved in this study. In order to assess the accuracy, suitability, and comprehensibility of the translated instrument, several lay experts were also employed. A total of 16 items of job involvement questionnaire (JIQ) were used in this study. This study suggests that as more techniques and methods were used together, the risk of items that are not equivalent could be reduced. For future research, this study would like to recommend the use of multiple techniques and procedures on translation research.

Keywords Translation techniques · Procedure · Cognitive debriefing

32.1 Introduction

Translation of measurement instrument is one of the important steps in conducting cross-cultural survey research. The translation instrument is greatly needed not only when it involves a cross-cultural comparison between two countries, but also when a research needs to adapt the instrument to a population with cultural diversity (Warnecke et al. 1997; Harkness and Glusberg 1998; Lee et al. 2008). To date, a wide number of translation studies that mainly focuses on translation instrument were reported in the literature. However, most of studies were mostly found in nursing and clinical, and health-related field (see, for example, Beck et al. 2003;

N. Jamadin (✉) · F. Noordin
Faculty of Business Management, Universiti Teknologi MARA (UiTM), Shah Alam, Malaysia
e-mail: nurnazirah293@gmail.com

F. Noordin
e-mail: fauziah716@salam.uitm.edu.my

F. Noordin et al. (eds.), *Proceedings of the 2nd Advances in Business Research International Conference*, https://doi.org/10.1007/978-981-10-6053-3_32

Cha et al. 2007; Lee et al. 2008; Sousa and Rojjansrirat 2011; Eremenco et al. 2005; Squires et al. 2013).

Studies on instrument translation with regard to social science field are very limited. Thus, the purpose of this paper is to provide some insight into translation procedures of work—related attitude measurement instrument in the social science field. Moreover, the literature on translation studies has given so much focus on the use of new instrument rather than an established instrument. Therefore, this study would like to extent the literature by using an established instrument that were translated and adapted to the cross-cultural survey research.

A review on several past studies as mention earlier indicates that there are major agreements among the academic scholars that there is no gold standard of the translation process. Therefore, different research on translation is likely to perform different translation procedure. This study employed several translation techniques and combines several translation procedures in order to have a good quality and equivalency of the translation instrument. These two aspects as emphasized by Brislin (1970) become a major concern to the researcher in order to avoid translation error that may become a threat to the validity of research outcome. A research that employed multiple techniques has been found to have a high-quality translation as compared to those researches that focus on single technique (Maneesriwongul and Dixon 2004). As more effort was invested on the translated instruments, the higher will be the quality of the translation. Moreover, the translation instrument would be meaningful if both original source and target language version are equivalent (Weidmer 1994). This study was conducted at East Malaysia. Many translation works were reported from Western countries and Asian countries like Korea and China; hence, this study would like to contribute to the translation literature in the context of Malaysia. This would lead to better understanding on how the western theory could be adopted and adapted in the Asian context.

32.2 Background

32.2.1 Translation Technique

Fundamentally, the translation involves an activity of translating original source (OC) or original language of instrument into another language which commonly term as target language (TL). In regard to this activity, Brislin (1970) has introduced several translation techniques, namely back translation, bilingual technique, committee approach, and pretesting procedures. The *back translation technique* requires more than two translators to translate the original source language to the target language, and then, second bilingual translator is blindly translated back to the source. This step can be repeated for several rounds. During the translation events, a *decentering technique* (Werner and Campbell 1970) may be required in facilitate the translation process. Certain items may need modification due to its difficulty on translation into target language. Usually, the final back-translated version is most preferred as it is most likely to be equivalent to the target language.

A *bilingual technique* requires the bilingual translator familiar in original source of language and target language. The third technique that introduced by Campbell et al. (1970) is a *Committee approach.* A number of bilingual translators translate the source to the target language. This technique would give advantage to the bilingual translator to determine any discrepancy or mistakes during the translation events. Lastly, Campbell (1970) suggests *Pretest procedures* should be undertaken once the translation has completed. The translation version should be tested to the future subject of research in order to examine whether they could comprehend the questions.

32.3 Method

32.3.1 Translator

A total of six bilingual translators were hired in this study. The selections of translators are based on the criteria that were described by Maxwell (1996). The bilingual translator must possess a good knowledge in English, an excellent knowledge of the target language, experience in both language and cultures, and familiar with the culture associated with the target language. In this study, two of the six translators are post-graduate students, while the other four translators are from higher academic education institution where the two of them are qualified with a TESL background. The bilingual experts have been involved in translation activities for more than 10 years of working experience, and the translation activities were considered as small part of their job. All of the translators are from different ethnic background and currently working in English language environment. Prior to the translation activities, the translators are provided with a general guideline (Brislin 1986; Maxwell 1996) as a kind reminder so that the objective of translation could be achieved. The guidelines are as follows:

- Identify and minimize the cultural differences
- Finding equivalent words and phrases
- Making sure that the reading level is the same in the target language (TL—Malay) as in the original English version
- Making sure the difficulty level of achievement items does not change
- Being aware of the changes in layout due to translation

32.3.2 Reviewer

A total of 6 reviewers were employed in this study. They are the lay experts which means they are potential research subjects of this study and they are responsible to assess the translated questionnaires. The criteria of selection are based on the recommendation of past studies that suggest the lay experts are the most suitable to assess the translated instruments (Rubio et al. 2003; Eremenco et al. 2005; Wild et al. 2005; Harkness et al. 2010). The rationale of employing lay experts is because they were considered as appropriate people to test the alternative wording, checking comprehensibility, interpretation, and cultural relevance of the translation (Wild et al. 2005). A potential advantage of employing lay experts is they offer better understanding on the way respondents interpret the questions (Hughes 2004). Lay experts provide insights from the respondents' context because they could understand "on the street reality" and "everyday language of respondents" (Harkness 2010).

32.3.3 Measurement Instrument

A job involvement model by Kanungo (1982) was used in the translation of this study. The model comprises two parts: job involvement questionnaire (JIQ) has 10 items and work involvement questionnaire (WIQ) consists of 6 items. This model of instrument is one of the frequently used measurements in the social science research. To date, there is a limited report on the translation of this measurement instrument in cross-cultural research.

32.3.4 Translation Procedures

Prior to content validity stage, the instrument has to undergo several stages in translation course. The classical Brislin method (1970) and also Wild et al. (2005) approach were embedded in the translation procedures of this study. There are number of reasons that could explain the utilization of these two procedures in this study. Firstly, these two procedures were selected in this study due to its popularity and widely accepted and were used in many studies worldwide. Secondly, this study decides to combine the classic and modern procedure of translation in order to achieve a good quality of translation. Translation procedure that depends on one source is insufficient and may give some limitations to the researcher. This is due to the fact that each translation procedure presents its own strengths and weaknesses. A Brislin method of translation does not give a clear picture on which steps that need to be undertaken after translation had been performed. Thus, the translation procedure of Wild et al. (2005) would fill this gap by following several steps in their

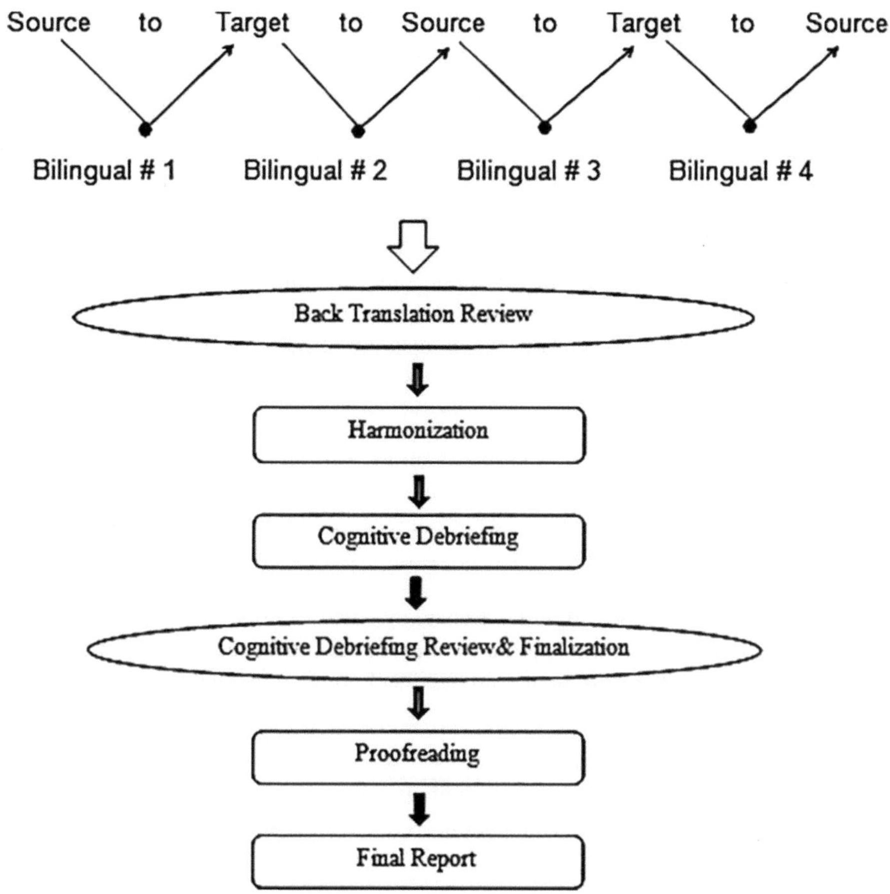

Fig. 32.1 Translation procedure of job involvement questionnaire (JIQ)

translation procedure. Furthermore, the Brislin method did not specify on how many number of bilingual translator should be involved in the translation activity (Cha et al. 2007). Hence, to overcome this limitation, the Wild et al. (2005) offers a description of key actors and their roles during the translation process. To guide the translation process of this study, a translation model was prepared as in Fig. 32.1.

Step 1—Forward and Backward Translation

In this stage, the first bilingual translator translates the English version to Malay language. Then, the second bilingual translator blindly translates the Malay language to English version. The third translator then retranslates the English version to Malay version. This step was repeated 4 rounds. During the process, the decentering approach was also used between the bilingual translators to resolve certain discrepancies existed.

Step 2—Back Translation Review
This stage was identified as one of the most important stage in cross-cultural adaptation process (Wild et al. 2005). In this stage, the researcher then needs to make comparison between the last translated versions and the original version. Certain words and items that are not fully addressed during the decentering procedure were identified. At this stage, it appears that one item that present idiom expression were identified and re-examined. While other items that consist of terms that are unclear and appear complicated were also revised. Translating idiom expression is very technical and complicated. The bilingual translators utilized idioms translation strategy by the work of Newmark (1988) to handle the idiomatic item. Other discrepancies during the translation process were highlighted, discussed, and later revised in resolving the issues.

Step 3—Harmonization
In the stage of harmonization, a comparison as well as an assessment on original source version and back translation version was performed by all bilingual translators and researcher. All versions were reviewed line by line of each item. The aim at this stage is to achieve consistency for each version as well as its meaning. At this point, the bilingual translators solved any discrepancy that may not be fully solved on the earlier stage. The bilingual translators also made important decision on suitable terms or words that would be used in translation version. The first draft was prepared based on the comment and feedback by all translators and ready for pretesting.

Step 4—Cognitive Debriefing
Cognitive debriefing is one of the qualitative approaches in gathering data from lay people in the interpretation of translation (Wild et al. 2005). The translation of job involvement translation of this study was reviewed by lay experts. Past study suggested a total of 3–10 sample size of lay people is sufficient in gathering the data. However, an average of 5 lay people would be considered as an ideal sample size (Eremenco et al. 2005). The lay experts would act as reviewers for the translated questionnaire assessment. In the context of this study, a total of 6 senior teachers who were holding the middle positions were involved in assessment of job involvement translation versions. One of the lay experts is a PhD holder. All reviewers have a working experience of 15 years and above. The process in this study was similar to the past studies that used this method. This interview took about less than 2 h in addressing each item on the research instrument. The senior teachers were given a dual set of translation versions: English back-translated version and target language (Malay) version. Firstly, the teachers were required to answer the questionnaire while at the same time evaluating the interpretation of the translations. After they had completed, the teachers were asked on item by item about the suitability and accuracy of the translation as well as cultural relevance of

the job involvement instrument. The teachers also restated the item using their own words and offer interpretation on item that was identified as problematic in translation. The aim of cognitive debriefing that was conducted in this study was to ensure that the teachers have the same or similar understanding on the meaning as what the researcher intended. In addition, this method also allows the researcher to detect "translation reversal" where the teachers understood the item but give opposite meaning on the translation.

Step 5—Cognitive Debriefing Review and Finalization

In this stage, the teachers' interpretations on the translation were compared with original version. Any discrepancies on the items were highlighted and amended on this stage. The alternative translations of teachers and bilingual experts of this study were synthesized in order to address the discrepancy in the job involvement instrument.

Step 6—Proofread

The final instrument of job involvement that was amended on the previous stage was reviewed again by the bilingual translators. This is important to ensure that the items have the same meanings as in the original version. Any minor error or mistakes that were overlooked such as typographic, grammatical error, and any other error were also highlighted and corrected before the translation version is approved and used in the pilot study and actual study. In this study, all the translators have determined that the translated version of job involvement questionnaire is equivalent with the original source.

Step 7—Final report

A final report consists of details of the translation process, and its description was documented. In this report, the changes made in the translated instruments were also recorded. A number of important aspects of job involvement translation were highlighted for future reference.

32.4 Results and Discussion

A total of 16 items of job involvement questionnaire (JIQ) were translated to Malay language and translated back to English versions. During the course of translation, a total of 8 items of JIQ have been decentred in order to resolve any discrepancy that existed on the items. The items then were re-examined by the bilingual experts at the stage of back translation review. In order to avoid the risk of "non-equivalence",

Table 32.1 Discrepant items in the original versus revised version

Item code	Original source	Revised version
1	The most important things that happen to me involve my present job	Being involved in my present job is very important to me
4	Breath my job[a]	Breath my job[a]
5	Around my job	on my job
6	String ties	Strong connection
7	I'm not feeling detached	I do not feel separated
9	Very central	Vey vital
13	Work should be only a small part	Work should only be a small part
14	Central to life	very important in life

[a]*Note* job involvement questionnaire (JIQ)

the items were translated again from original to Malay language and translated back into English. Table 32.1 depicts the original source version of JIQ and the reversed translated items.

The items in the job involvement questionnaire that have been revised are identified as items 1, 4, 5, 6, 7, 8, 9 for JIQ while 2 items in WIQ were revised, items 13 and 14. The discussions for the items are as below.

32.4.1 *Idiomatic Item*

Item 4 represents the idiom expression. The bilingual translators and reviewers decided to retain the original expression. However, the meaning of the idiom should be translated literally to the target language. A direct translation of idioms to another language may present meanings that are ridiculous, nonsense (Newmark, 1988) as well amusing (Mollanazar, 2004). Furthermore, finding the same or similar idiom(s) on the target language may not be possible. Baker (2011) also explains that the idiom expression of the source language may not be equivalent to the target language.

Even if similar idiom exists in the target language, the context and frequency of used may be different on other culture. Thus, the translators and reviewers have agreed to retain the original item. The decision was guided by the Newmark (1988, pp. 76–77) guideline which states that "the translation on idiomatic items should never be translated word by word." The literal translation is a more appropriate solution and quite useful to address the idiomatic expression in translation. Furthermore, the translation of the idiomatic items should be translated in naturally so that the translated version presents the same meaning and effect as in the original source version. It is very important to note that the global meaning on the idiomatic items has to be made clear on the translation.

32.4.2 Vocabulary, Verbs, and Grammatical Syntax

A total of 6 items were revised due to verbs and grammatical composition of the expression item. The changes made in the items are presented in Table 32.1. Minor corrections on grammatical syntax were made in items 4, 5, and 13. The terminologies of items 6, 7, 9, and 14 as well as item 1 were revised to more simple verbs so that they can be easily understood. The revision was made in the light of the translation guideline (Brislin 1970; Harkness and Glusberg 1998) where the vocabulary and syntax of translated items should be simple and the sentence length should be short. This study also revises several words and phrases based on Wild et al. (2005) guideline that greatly emphasizes item modification. They state that modifications are highly needed when the translated questionnaire consists of words or phrases are not familiar or not commonly used by the respondents. Hence, the selection and revision of words and phrases of job involvement items were addressed at harmonization stage and cognitive debriefing review, and proofreading stage.

32.4.3 Equivalency of Translation Version

The bilingual experts and reviewers have determined that the Malaysian version was comparable to the English version. All items were equivalent in conceptual, semantic, criterion, content, and technical equivalence.

32.5 Conclusion and Recommendation

This study concludes that the translation process on established instrument is possible to be conducted in cross-cultural survey research. The findings in this study reveal that there are several concerns that had surfaced during the translation course. The first concern in translating established instruments is about vocabulary, verbs, and grammatical syntax on translated version. The terminology on JIQ original source may not work well on translated version; thus, the terms need to be replaced with more simple terms that are common and frequently used by the target population. The selection of words, phrases, and sentences, grammatical and syntactical features in target language should convey intended meaning as what researcher intended (Harkness and Glusberg 1998). In addition, the translated version should use a terms that is best understood by the target population (Lee et al. 2008)

The second concern that had raised translators' and reviewers' attention during the translation process is each item presents an idiom expression. Limited study was reported on idiom translation. Consequently, when the translators reached at the idiomatic item, it took longer time to be translated as compared to other item. Translating idiom expression is the most challenging part due to a reason of equivalency. However, a comprehensive translation guideline of Newmark (1988) is very helpful in guiding the translators to reach consensus decision on translating an idiomatic item.

With regard to the quality of translation, the bilingual translators and lay experts play important roles in determining the quality of translated items. A translator and reviewer should not only be capable in the language, but it is important to recruit a translator and reviewer that are also bicultural. This is essential because language competency and cultural familiarity among the translator and reviewer are very useful when translating and reviewing the items to ensure the translated items tap into the communication and cultural context of target population. Moreover, hiring translators who have a number of experiences on translation course has made the translation procedures become easier. The experienced translators would clearly identify their own roles and task descriptions and responsibilities during the translation events. The translators of this study realized that translation events did not merely translating documents but it is their responsibility to ensure the translated document would be able to define the intended meaning of the researchers to the target population. This is in line with the guideline stated by Harkness and Glusberg (1998).

In view of multiple techniques and methods that were suggested by past studies, this study found that using multiple techniques of translation and procedures have made the translators better understand their roles and responsibilities. In addition, the issue of discrepancy and disparity of item during translation could also be resolved easily. Depending on a single technique on translation and procedure is insufficient. The issue of equivalency could be addressed effectively when several translators are involved during the translation course. This is particularly important to avoid translation bias caused by translation that is written by one person based on his or her personal speech habit and style that may lead to misinterpretation on the items (Wild et al. 2005). This study also found that the use of cognitive debriefing as a method gathering data from lay experts is very useful in improving the quality of job involvement instrument. By employing lay experts that possess similar criteria of respondents, they provide a feedback and idea on how well the respondents could understand the questions. This is in line with Squires et al. (2013) where a comprehensive translation and validation procedures would help in ensuring the relevancy of items in the context of subject of study.

Overall, the translation procedure of this study would be useful to future research as it acts as a guideline in conducting a translation course. This study has outlined in details that the activity involves on each step of translation. In the light of literature contribution, the work of this study also extents the translation literature particularly on social science field. Most studies on translation have been found mainly among medical, health and well-being, nursing field. Furthermore, this study also has discussed the appropriate solution in addressing the idiomatic expression on the item. The finding on this study also enhances the body of knowledge with regard to the idioms translation literature.

References

Baker, M. (2011). *In other words: A course book on translation*. Routledge.

Beck, C. T., Bernal, H., & Froman, R. D. (2003). Methods to document semantic equivalence of a translated scale. *Research in Nursing & Health, 26*(1), 64–73.

Brislin, R. W. (1970). Back-translation for cross-cultural research. *Journal of Cross-Cultural Psychology, 1*(3), 185–216.

Brislin, R. W. (1986). Research instruments. *Field Methods in Cross-Cultural Research: Cross-Cultural Research and Methodology Series, 8,* 137–164.

Campbell, D., Brislin, R., Stewart, V., & Werner, O. (1970). Back-translation and other translation techniques in cross-cultural research. *International Journal of Psychology, 30,* 681–692.

Cha, E. S., Kim, K. H., & Erlen, J. A. (2007). Translation of scales in cross-cultural research: issues and techniques. *Journal of Advanced Nursing, 58*(4), 386–395.

Eremenco, S. L., Cella, D., & Arnold, B. J. (2005). A comprehensive method for the translation and cross-cultural validation of health status questionnaires. *Evaluation and the Health Professions, 28*(2), 212–232.

Harkness, J. A., & Schoua-Glusberg, A. (1998). Questionnaires in translation. *ZUMA-nachrichten spezial, 3*(1), 87–127.

Harkness, J. A., Villar, A., & Edwards, B. (2010). Translation, adaptation, and design. *Survey Methods in Multinational, Multiregional, and Multicultural Contexts*, 115–140.

Hughes, K. A. (2004). Comparing pretesting methods: Cognitive interviews, respondent debriefing, and behavior coding. *Survey Methodology, 2,* 1–20.

Kanungo, R. N. (1982). Measurement of job and work involvement. *Journal of Applied Psychology, 67*(3), 341.

Lee, C. C., Li, D., Arai, S., & Puntillo, K. (2008). Ensuring cross-cultural equivalence in translation of research consents and clinical documents: A systematic process for translating English to Chinese. *Journal of Transcultural Nursing.*

Maneesriwongul, W., & Dixon, J. K. (2004). Instrument translation process: a methods review. *Journal of Advanced Nursing, 48*(2), 175–186.

Maxwell, B. (1996). Translation and cultural adaptation of the survey instruments. *Third International Mathematics and Science Study (TIMSS) Technical Report, 1*, 159–169.

Mollanazar, H. (2004). *Principles and methodology of translation*. Tehran: SAMT.

Newmark, P. (1988). *A textbook of translation* (Vol. 1, p. 988). New York: Prentice hall.

Rubio, D. M., Berg-Weger, M., Tebb, S. S., Lee, E. S., & Rauch, S. (2003). Objectifying content validity: Conducting a content validity study in social work research. *Social Work Research, 27* (2), 94–104.

Sousa, V. D., & Rojjanasrirat, W. (2011). Translation, adaptation and validation of instruments or scales for use in cross-cultural health care research: a clear and user-friendly guideline. *Journal of Evaluation in Clinical Practice, 17*(2), 268–274.

Squires, A., Aiken, L. H., van den Heede, K., Sermeus, W., Bruyneel, L., Lindqvist, R., et al. (2013). A systematic survey instrument translation process for multi-country, comparative health workforce studies. *International Journal of Nursing Studies, 50*(2), 264–273.

Wild, D., Grove, A., Martin, M., Eremenco, S., McElroy, S., Verjee-Lorenz, A., et al. (2005). Principles of good practice for the translation and cultural adaptation process for patient-reported outcomes (PRO) measures: report of the ISPOR task force for translation and cultural adaptation. *Value in Health, 8*(2), 94–104.

Werner, O., & Campbell, D. T. Translating, working through interpreters and the problem of decentering. (1970), In R. Naroll & R. Cohen (Eds.), *A handbook of cultural anthropology*. New York: American Museum of Natural History, in press.

Weidmer, B. (1994). Issues and guidelines for translation in cross-cultural research. In *Proceedings of the American Statistical Association, Section on Survey Research Methods* (Vol. 2).

Warnecke, R. B., Johnson, T. P., Chavez, N., Sudman, S., O'rourke, D. P., Lacey, L., & Horm, J. (1997). Improving question wording in surveys of culturally diverse populations. *Annals of Epidemiology*, *7*(5), 334–342.

Chapter 33
Influence of Knowledge Sharing on Job Performance: A Case Study of National Audit Department (NAD)

Kuldip Singh, Elizabeth Caroline Augustine and Zalina Mohd Desa

Abstract This study examines the influence of knowledge sharing on job performance by analyzing perceptions of 100 public employees in the National Audit Department (NAD). The instrument used to measure knowledge sharing was adopted from Chiu et al. (2006). Job performance was measured using an instrument developed by Borman and Motowidlo (Personnel selection in organizations. Jossey-Bass, San Francisco, 71, 1993). Results of the instrument's Cronbach Alpha measurement show that the score of reliability is above 0.90 which indicates an acceptable level. The results indicate that knowledge sharing is positively correlated with job performance. These results imply that job performance may be dependent on effective knowledge sharing in the public sector. This study provides insights on the relationship between knowledge sharing and job performance in the public sector. The findings of this study may help public sector to enhance its knowledge sharing and its effect on job performance. Limitations and recommendations are also discussed.

Keywords Knowledge sharing · Job performance · Public sector · Knowledge

33.1 Introduction

Knowledge has become an increasingly important assets in many organizations nowadays (Levin and Cross 2004). The concept of sharing knowledge is considered to be a crucial process in developing competitive advantage and superior perfor-

K. Singh (✉) · E.C. Augustine · Z.M. Desa
Faculty of Administrative Science and Policy Studies,
Universiti Teknologi MARA (UiTM), Shah Alam, Sarawak, Malaysia
e-mail: kuldip@sarawak.uitm.edu.my

E.C. Augustine
e-mail: elizabeth@sarawak.uitm.edu.my

Z.M. Desa
e-mail: zalina@sarawak.uitm.edu.my

F. Noordin et al. (eds.), *Proceedings of the 2nd Advances in Business Research International Conference*, https://doi.org/10.1007/978-981-10-6053-3_33

mance. Knowledge sharing provides several important advantages to both employees and organizations such as the ability to formulate strategies, good decision making and high performance level to ensure that the efficiency and effectiveness of public services will remain competitive in the respective industries. In the context of public services, the implementing of knowledge sharing is important in order to exchange and create new knowledge to achieve innovative, creative and knowledge-based public services. The success of knowledge sharing practices among the employees in the public sector organizations highly depends on the individual's willingness to share the knowledge they possessed or created with other. The process of implementing knowledge sharing will increase not only the competitive advantage of the public sector organizations but also the employees' competencies. Knowledge sharing provides better opportunity for the employees to enhance their skills by working together while improving their own performance (Gold et al. 2001). This study is motivated by the recommendations that have appeared in knowledge sharing literature (e.g., Becerra-Fernandez et al. 2004). According to Becerra-Fernandez et al. (2004), knowledge management impacts organizations on four levels: processes, products, people, and performance. However, how organizational knowledge sharing impacts job performance is still vague and ill-defined. So far, there have been no empirical studies that link knowledge sharing practices with employees learning commitments, employees' adaptability and employees' job performance. This study explores how knowledge sharing affects employee job performance in the public sector.

33.2 Literature Review

33.2.1 Knowledge Sharing

Knowledge is generally observed as the most important asset that should be carefully managed. Many organizations have realized the importance of knowledge as a strategic resource in achieving business goals. According to Bock et al. (2005), "knowledge is the foundation of a firm's competitive advantage and, ultimately, the primary driver of a firm's value. As mentioned by Sveiby (2001), knowledge is identified as an intangible asset which grows when a person uses and applies the knowledge in the organizations and tends to lose or depreciate in value when it is not used or applied. There are two types of important knowledge that needs to be possessed by an individual in the organizations which include explicit and tacit knowledge (Lam 2000). According to Davenport and Prusak (1998), knowledge sharing is identified as one of the processes in knowledge management. It is "the process of transferring knowledge from a person to another in an organization". As mentioned by Lee and Al-Hawamdeh (2002), "knowledge sharing is a deliberate act that makes knowledge reusable by other people through knowledge transfer." Knowledge sharing in broader perspective is defined as a process where individuals or group of people exchange all kinds of knowledge including explicit and tacit knowledge, hence creating and facilitating new knowledge (Van den Hooff et al. 2003). As explained by Goh (2002), knowledge sharing requires the willingness of an individual or group in an organization to display a high level of cooperative behavior by working with one another and share their knowledge for their mutual benefits. Knowledge sharing provides individual with opportunity to enhance their skills and performance by working together while improving the organizational productivity, efficiency, quality and innovation in achieving the business success. Knowledge sharing has been identified as the important capability in improving the quality and superior of service delivery in the public sector organizations (Zhang and Zhao 2006; Thomas 2005). The public sectors refer to all nonprofit organizations which include government agencies, corporations and military departments that function and perform some form of public services. For nonprofit organizations like public sectors, "knowledge sharing represents ways to increase continuous performance and is thought to improve the customers and employees satisfaction" (Pan and Scarbrough 1998). The public sector organizations can seek to maintain the practices of knowledge sharing into the activities that meet their needs and to ensure the continued participation in developing the knowledge-based environment, hence delivering quality and superior services to the customers.

33.2.2 Job Performance

In general, job performance is defined as actions or behaviors relevant to organizational goals (Campbell 1990), which includes both productive and counterproductive employee behaviors that contribute to or detract from organizational goals (Hunt 1996). Viswesvaran and Ones (2000) introduced a more recent definition of job performance as behavior and outcomes that employees undertake that are contribute to organizational goals. This means job performance refers to the effectiveness of individual behaviors that contribute to organizational objectives and should consist of task performance and contextual performance (Motowidlo 2003). Both constructs are influenced by different factors; for instance, job-related experience determines task performance while individual's personality type determines contextual performance (Motowidlo and Van Scotter 1994). Organ (1988) argues that term "job performance" may need to be redefined to essentially broaden this construct to include non-productivity or extra-role dimensions such as cooperation, helping co-workers and superiors and generalized tendencies toward compliance. Organ further proposed that job performance should be measured to the extent to which employee engages in organizational citizenship behaviors. Sarmiento et al. (2007) refer job performance as the result of two elements, which consist of the abilities and skills (natural or acquired) that an employee possesses, and his/her motivation to use them in order to perform a better job. In this study, the meaning of job performance refers to task performance or in-role job performance as defined by Motowidlo (2003) refers to the organization's total expected value on task-related proficiency of an employee, or fulfillment of tasks that are required by the formal job description. In other words, task performance is the behaviors related specifically to performing job-related matters. Therefore, from the above definitions it is clear that job performance is related to the extent to which an employee is able to accomplish the task assigned to him or her and how the accomplished task contributes to the realization of the organizational goal (Mawoli and Babandako 2011).

Schneider (2009) finds that knowledge exists in many forms and that coproduction through collaboration produces useful new ways of approaching problems, which in turn can help improve performance. Kang et al. (2008) examine the relationship between knowledge sharing and individual-level work performance in the public sector. They find that knowledge sharing significantly affects work performance, and mutual trust plays a role mediating the relationship between knowledge sharing and work performance. By testing the effect of knowledge sharing on individual performance and the interaction effect between knowledge sharing and goal-setting on individual performance, Quigley et al. (2007) find a positive impact of knowledge sharing on performance and an interaction effect between motivational mechanisms and knowledge sharing on the relationship with performance.

This study intends to test the following hypothesis:

H1: There is a significant relationship between knowledge sharing and job performance.
H1a: There is a significant difference in knowledge sharing between males and females.
H1b: There is a significant difference in knowledge sharing and educational level.
H1c: There is a significant difference in knowledge sharing and job category.
H1d: There is a significant difference in knowledge sharing and length of service.

33.3 Methodology

A survey design was used to achieve the research objectives. The specific design was the cross-sectional design, where a sample is drawn from a population at a particular point in time (Shaughnessy et al. 1997). About 100 questionnaires were distributed to employees in the National Audit Department. About 65 employees returned the questionnaire giving a response rate of 65%. Knowledge sharing was measured using a scale developed by Chiu et al. (2006). Job performance was measured using an instrument developed by Borman and Motowidlo (1993). Results of the instrument's Cronbach Alpha measurement show that the score of reliability is above 0.80 which indicates an acceptable level (Nunnally 1978). This is summarized in Table 33.1.

Majority of the respondents were male (61%) and aged between 26 to 40 years (52.3%) and mostly were married (69%). Majority of the respondents were Malay

Table 33.1 Reliability analysis, mean and standard deviation scores (N = 65)

Variables	No. of items	Cronbach's alpha	Mean	S. D.
Knowledge sharing	13	0.915	4.24	0.354
Job performance	10	0.867	4.12	0.363

(40%) followed by Bidayuh (32.3%). About 63.1% of the sample had SPM qualification. As for length of service, 46.2% had served for 3–10 years followed by 27.7% for 10–15 years. About 78.5% of the respondents were from the Support Group 2. About 73.8% of the respondents earned less than RM2,000. This is summarized in Table 33.2.

33.4 Results

Based on Table 33.1, the mean for knowledge sharing is 4.24, indicating a high level of knowledge sharing. And for job performance, the mean is 4.12 indicating a very high level of job performance. In addition, the study found a strong positive relationship between knowledge sharing and job performance ($r = 0.678$; $p < 0.01$). This is shown in Table 33.3. This indicates that knowledge sharing has a positive relationship with job performance. Table 33.4 shows no significance difference in knowledge sharing between male and female employees ($p > 0.05$). Thus, H1a is rejected. Table 33.5 shows that job category ($p = 0.003$) and educational level ($p = 0.018$) have a significant difference in the means of knowledge sharing ($p < 0.05$). Thus, H1b and H1c are accepted. However, length of service was not significant difference in the means of knowledge sharing ($p > 0.05$). Thus, H1d is rejected. This is shown in Table 33.5.

33.5 Discussion

The findings of this study confirm that knowledge sharing has a positive relationship with job performance in NAD. Majority of staff perceive the level of knowledge sharing and job performance as very high. In terms of correlation, high-level knowledge sharing is related to higher levels of job performance among the staff. This study supports previous findings by Quigley et al. (2007) who found a positive impact of knowledge sharing on performance. The study presents two major implications: theoretical contribution and practical contribution. In terms of theoretical contribution, the results of this study confirm that knowledge sharing and job performance are highly correlated and hence contribute to research on knowledge sharing and job performance in the public sector. In terms of practical contributions, the findings of this study can be used as a guideline by public

Table 33.2 Respondent's profile (N = 65)

Profile	No. of respondents	Percentages
Gender		
Male	40	61.5
Female	25	38.5
Age		
Below 25 years	12	18.5
26–30 years	15	23.1
31–40 years	19	29.2
41–50 years	15	23.0
Over 51 years	4	6.2
Race		
Malay	26	40.0
Bidayuh	21	32.3
Iban	9	13.8
Melanau	7	10.8
Chinese	2	3.1
Marital status		
Single	20	30.8
Married	45	69.2
Education's level		
SPM	41	63.1
STPM	9	13.8
Diploma	9	13.8
Degree	4	6.2
Others	2	3.1
Year of services		
< 3 years	7	10.8
3–6 years	17	26.2
6–10 years	13	20.0
10–15 years	18	27.7
15–25 years	7	10.8
More than 25 years	3	4.6
Job category		
Management and professional group	5	7.7
Support Group 1	9	13.8
Support Group 2	51	78.5
Gross salary		
Below RM2,000	48	73.6
RM2001–RM300	12	18.5
More than RM3001	5	7.7

Table 33.3 Correlation between knowledge sharing and job performance

Variables	Job Performance (r value)
Knowledge sharing	0.678**
** Correlation is significant at the 0.01 level	

Table 33.4 T test: gender and knowledge sharing

Variable	Characteristics	Mean	T value	df	Sig.
	Male	4.23	−0.420	63	0.676
	Female	4.26			

Table 33.5 One-way ANOVA: job category, educational level, length of service and knowledge sharing

Variable	Characteristics	Mean	F value	df	Sig.
Job category	Professional and management group	4.67	6.47	64	0.003
	Support Group 1	4.40			
	Support Group 2	4.17			
Educational level	SPM	4.17	3.23	64	0.018
	SPTM	4,24			
	DIPLOMA	4.27			
	DEGREE	4,66			
	MASTERS	4.75			
Length of service	1–3 years	4.17	0.300	64	0.911
	3.6 years	4.21			
	6–10 years	4.34			
	10–15 years	4.23			
	15–20 years	4.26			
	Over 21 years	4.21			

agencies to promote knowledge sharing and use it to increase its staff's level of job performance.

33.6 Conclusion

This study confirmed that knowledge sharing influences job performance. The study used valid and reliable measurement scales to measure the relationship between knowledge sharing and job performance. The correlation test revealed a positive relationship between knowledge sharing and job performance. Furthermore, the study also found significant influence of job category and educational level on knowledge sharing except for length of service. Therefore, current research and practice within knowledge sharing need to understand knowledge sharing as related to job performance. This study further suggests that a high level of knowledge sharing will strongly enhance and promote higher levels of job performance among employees in public sector. This study acknowledges several limitations. First, a cross-sectional research design was used to gather data at one point within the period of study. This may not be able to capture the developmental issues and/or causal connections between variables of interest. Second, the survey questionnaires relied heavily on the respondents' self-responses that were selected based on random sampling technique. Finally, the samples were taken from one public agency, namely National Audit Department in Kuching via survey questionnaires. These limitations may decrease the ability of generalizing the results to other public agencies in Malaysia.

References

Becerra-Fernandez, I., Gonzalez, A., & Sabherwal, R. (2004). *Knowledge management challenges, solutions, and technologies* (p. 2004). New Jersey: Pearson Education Inc.

Bock, G. W., Zmud, R. W., Kim, Y. G., & Lee, J. N. (2005). Behavioral intention formation in knowledge sharing: Examining the roles of extrinsic motivators, social-psychological forces, and organizational climate. *MIS Quarterly*, 87–111.

Borman, W. C., & Motowidlo, S. M. (1993). Expanding the criterion domain to include elements of contextual performance. *Personnel Selection in Organizations* (p. 71). San Francisco: Jossey-Bass.

Campbell, J. P., McHenry, J. J., & Wise, L. L. (1990). Modeling job performance in a population of jobs. *Personnel Psychology, 43*(2), 313–575.

Chiu, C. M., Hsu, M. H., & Wang, E. T. G. (2006). Understanding knowledge sharing in virtual communities: An integration of social capital and social cognitive theories. *Decision Support Systems, 42*(3), 1872–1888.

Davenport, T. H., & Prusak, L. (1998). *Working knowledge: How organizations manage what they know*. Harvard Business Press.

Goh, S. G. (2002). Managing effects of knowledge transfer: an integrative framework and some practical implications. *Journal of Knowledge Management, 6*(1), 22–30.

Gold, A. H., & Arvind Malhotra, A. H. S. (2001). Knowledge management: An organizational capabilities perspective. *Journal of Management Information Systems, 18*(1), 185–214.

Hunt, S. T. (1996). Generic work behavior: An investigation into the dimensions of entry-level, hourly job performance. *Personnel Psychology, 49*(1), 51–83.

Kang, Y. J., Kim, S. E., & Chang, G. W. (2008). The impact of knowledge sharing on work performance: An empirical analysis of the public employees' perceptions in South Korea. *International Journal of Public Administration, 31*(14), 1548–1568.

Lam, A. (2000). Tacit knowledge, organizational learning and societal institutions: An integrated framework. *Organization Studies, 21*(3), 487–513.

Lee, C. K., & Al-Hawamdeh, S. (2002). Factors impacting knowledge sharing. *Journal of Information & Knowledge Management, 1*(01), 49–56.

Levin, D. Z., & Cross, R. (2004). The strength of weak ties you can trust: The mediating role of trust in effective knowledge transfer. *Management Science, 50*(11), 1477–1490.

Mawoli, M. A., & Babandako, A. Y. (2011). An evaluation of staff motivation, dissatisfaction and job performance in an academic setting. *Australian Journal of Business and Management Research, 1*(9), 1.

Motowidlo, S. J. (2003). Job performance, In W. C. Borman, D. R. Ilgen, & R. J. Klimoski (Eds.), *Handbook of psychology: industrial and organizational psychology* (Vol. 12). Wiley.

Motowidlo, S. J., & Van Scotter, J. R. (1994). Evidence that task performance should be distinguished from contextual performance. *Journal of Applied Psychology, 79*(4), 475.

Nunnally, J. C. (1978). *Psychometric theory* (2nd Edn.) Hillsdale, NJ: McGraw-Hill.

Organ, D. W. (1988). *Organizational citizenship behavior: The good soldier syndrome*. Lexington Books/DC Heath and Com.

Pan, S. L., & Scarbrough, H. (1998). A socio-technical view of knowledge sharing at Buckman Laboratories. *Journal of Knowledge Management, 2*(1), 55–66.

Quigley, N. R., Tesluk, P. E., Locke, E. A., & Bartol, K. M. (2007). A multilevel investigation of the motivational mechanisms underlying knowledge sharing and performance. *Organization Science, 18*(1), 71–88.

Sarmiento, R., Beale, J., & Knowles, G. (2007). Determinants of performance amongst shop-floor employees: A preliminary investigation. *Management Research News, 30*(12), 915–927.

Schneider, K. (2009). *Experience and knowledge management in software engineering*. Springer Science & Business Media.

Shaughnessy, J. J., Zechmesiter, E. B., & Jeanne, S. (1997). *Research methods in psychology, 8th edition*. New York: McGraw-Hill.

Sveiby, K. E. (2001). A knowledge-based theory of the firm to guide in strategy formulation. *Journal of intellectual capital, 2*(4), 344–358.

Thomas, E. J. (2005). *Knowledge management in the public and private sector: a synthetic analysis the contemporary literature*. Master Thesis. School of Information Sciences and Technology, The Pennsylvania State University.

Van den Hooff, B., Elving, W. J. L., Meeuwsen, J. M., & Dumoulin, C. M. (2003) *Knowledge sharing in knowledge communities, in communities and technologies*. Deventer: Kluwer Academic Publishers.

Viswesvaran, C., & Ones, D. S. (2000). Perspectives on models of job performance. *International Journal of Selection and Assessment, 8*(4), 216–226.

Zhang, D. S., & Zhao, J. I. (2006). Knowledge management in organizations. *Journal of Database Management, 17*, No. 1.

Chapter 34
The Impact of Knowledge Management on Employee's Sense of Well-Being

Mat Khairi Siti Murni, Kamar Shah Khalisah, Muhammad Asyrul Mohd Nasir, Mohd Faizul Ibrahim, Mohd Fauzi Mohamed Noor, Akmal Irfan Sofian, Khairee Mohd Ramlee, Mohd Raphel Affendy Md. Nazar, Wan Mohd Hafizuldin Wan Hassan and Nor Azri Sharizal Abu Bakar

Abstract There have been numerous researches done on the subject of employee's sense of well-being. Among the most studied aspects of employee's sense of well-being focus on the impact of work engagement, workaholism, workplace relationships and work–family conflict on well-being. However, there have not been too many extensive researches relating knowledge management (KM) issues and employee's sense of well-being. The main purpose of this study is to investigate the impact of KM on employee's sense of well-being in the private education industry. Based on the prior literature, all the variables and dimensions are discussed in depth. On the other hand, this paper aims to develop a conceptual framework showing knowledge acquisition, knowledge sharing, knowledge creation, knowledge codification and knowledge retention as a predictor of employee's sense of well-being. It is anticipated that this study expands the scope on the importance of KM for managers to improve employee's well-being as a priority in organization.

Keywords Knowledge management · Sense of well-being

34.1 Introduction

Employees play a vital role in any organization. They are part of the stakeholders of the organization, and thus, their well-being should be taken into careful consideration to ensure that the organization is running at optimal efficiency and

M.K.S. Murni (✉) · K.S. Khalisah · M.A.M. Nasir · M.F. Ibrahim · M.F.M. Noor · A.I. Sofian · K.M. Ramlee · M.R.A.Md.Nazar · W.M.H.W. Hassan · N.A.S.A. Bakar
Arshad Ayub Graduate Business School, Faculty of Business Management, Universiti Teknologi MARA, Shah Alam, Malaysia
e-mail: murni_y3k@yahoo.com

F. Noordin et al. (eds.), *Proceedings of the 2nd Advances in Business Research International Conference*, https://doi.org/10.1007/978-981-10-6053-3_34

effectiveness. According to Grant et al. (2007), employee well-being can be defined as the overall quality of an employee's experience and functioning at work. There are three dimensions of well-being covered by this definition, and they include psychological, physical, and also social well-being.

Employee well-being is an important determinant to not only individual performance, but it also affects the organization's performance as well (Kianto et al. 2016). Poor employee well-being can manifest itself in several ways such as under-performance, absenteeism, presenteeism, sick leave, and high turnover (Baptiste 2008).

Knowledge is essential to all organizations. Knowledge is one of the keys, which affects the success of a business organization where its employees who have been equipped with the necessary and right type of information will give the organization a better competitive advantage than its competitors (Han and Anantatmula 2007).

This study contributes to the field of research in knowledge management by studying the relationship relating the impact of knowledge management practices on employee's sense of well-being. There are only a few studies that have been conducted regarding knowledge management issues and employee's sense of well-being. Previous literature discussed on the impact of work engagement, workaholism, workplace relationships and work–family conflict on well-being (Caesens et al. 2014; Brunetto et al. 2013; Shimazu et al. 2015). In addition, Chumg et al. (2015) have looked at employees' sense of well-being as a mediating effect to knowledge sharing behavior. As a result, this study is conducted since there is no other research that has studied on the impact of knowledge management practices toward employee's sense of well-being. This study aims to investigate the impact of five knowledge management (KM) practices on employee's sense of well-being in the private education industry. The five KM practices are knowledge acquisition, knowledge sharing, knowledge creation, knowledge codification and knowledge retention. Apart from that, it is hoped that this study will be able to contribute to the body of knowledge in the field of knowledge management.

34.2 Literature Review

34.2.1 Employee's Sense of Well-Being

According to a recent study by Caesens et al. (2014), indicators of well-being are job satisfaction, perceived stress and sleep problems. They studied the effects of work engagement and workaholism to the well-being of workers. From their findings, work engagement partially mediated worker's well-being as it did not create sleeping problems. Workaholism on the other hand fully mediates worker's well-being. Brunetto et al. (2013) studied the impact of workplace relationship on several factors including worker's well-being by using nurses in Australia and USA as their subjects. Worker's well-being and the other factors were then used as predictor for worker's turnover. Their findings suggested that worker's well-being was indeed a predictor for nurses' turnover.

Winefield et al. (2014) did a study on work–family conflict among academic and nonacademic university employees. In their study, work–family conflict was used as mediator relating features of work environment and worker well-being to organizational outcome. The outcome of the study suggested that work–family conflict explained substantially the affected worker's health when performing what was demanded of them from their jobs. The concept of well-being concerns with individual's perspectives of their life experience, individual's satisfaction and emotional characteristics. These showed that various instruments and concept have been studied on individual's sense of well-being. Therefore, this study adopting the concept developed by Hills and Argyle (2002) has been widely used due to its robust construct validity, the Oxford Happiness Questionnaire Short-Form (OHQ).

34.2.2 Knowledge Management and Employee's Sense of Well-Being

As studied by (Christensen 2003), it is found that knowledge management is a process that must take into account of the process and requirement that are needed to handle knowledge while, at the same time, paying regard to the processes and players influencing the knowledge one is seeking to manage.

Knowledge management required a lot of processes, and this can directly and indirectly influence the employee's well-being. Study done by Seligman et al. (2005) indicates that area of positive psychology supports the idea of purpose and positive emotion, as the key ingredients of employee well-being. This shows that there is a strong connectivity and influence between knowledge management and employee's well-being. This statement can be supported by the findings that were done by Bockerman et al. (2012). In his research, it is found that greater autonomy of knowledge management at work may lead to greater employee's well-being.

34.2.3 Knowledge Management Practices

Knowledge management can be defined as the process of identifying and influencing the collective knowledge that contributes to organizational competitive advantage which will assist the organization to compete in its operating market (Kianto et al. 2016). Previous research on concept and KM practices has been studied extensively. Dysvik et al. (2015) discussed on knowledge donating and knowledge collecting. Furthermore, Mahesh and Suresh (2009) argued that knowledge process consists of knowledge exchange and knowledge nurture and harvest. Doz (2006) identified knowledge creation and knowledge sharing as KM practices.

While there are several concept and categorization on KM practices, this paper proposes that KM can be divided into five main practices: knowledge acquisition, knowledge sharing, knowledge creation, knowledge codification and knowledge retention. Kianto et al. (2016) supported that the five main practices are important as it is proven that there is an impact of KM on 'soft' human issues which are largely unexplored in previous research. Each of these five KM practices is explained briefly as below.

Knowledge acquisition is one of the many aspects of KM. Kianto et al. (2016) defined knowledge acquisition as the collection of external sources information for an organization. This is supported by Ayala (2010) who described that knowledge acquisition is devoted to the task of transferring the knowledge from one or more sources to other users. It is similar to what has been mentioned by Liou (1992). Knowledge acquisition is the vital process of developing an expert system that involve extracting, structuring and organizing knowledge based on several knowledge resources. From the above literature, it is clear that knowledge acquisition is the process of transferring external knowledge to identify problem-solving action or any solution to the issues raised.

When focusing on the relationship of knowledge acquisition to the employee's sense of well-being, Kianto et al. (2016) concluded that from the five facets of KM, knowledge acquisition is not related to job satisfaction which influences on the employee well-being in the work place from studies conducted in Finland. On the other hand, McClenahan et al. (2007) has proven that knowledge acquisition in the workplace can promote well-being among employees in the UK. This finding is supported by Economou and Hadjidema (2011) who also found that knowledge acquisition will have impact on human resource practices which also includes employee's well-being. Furthermore, Mayo (2001) added that knowledge acquisition through which employees bring their own human capital to the organization and working together will improve the employee's well-being in the organization. Knowledge management plays an important role in the employee's sense of well-being in the organization or workplace.

Knowledge sharing. Several literatures generally specified knowledge sharing as a part of knowledge management process (Kianto et al. 2016; García-Holgado et al. 2015; Aggestaam 2015). In a detail study by Wang and Noe (2010), a knowledge sharing framework has been constructed within five areas as factors those influencing knowledge sharing, which includes: 'organizational context,' 'interpersonal and team characteristics,' 'cultural characteristics,' 'individual characteristics' and as well as 'motivational factors.' In terms of organizational context, Lee (2001) has confirmed that knowledge sharing could lead to the success of outsourcing hence proving the shared goal between inter-organization.

Individual characteristics have also strong influence to the success of knowledge sharing. Matzler et al. (2008) have proven that there is significant correlation between stable personality traits (agreeableness, conscientiousness and openness) and knowledge sharing in an engineering firm. Alternatively, Jadin et al. (2013) claimed that knowledge sharing level is different according to personality traits (pro-social value orientation, trendsetting and opinion leadership) with moderation effect of 'motivation' only affecting pro-social value orientation personality traits. Addition to that, motivational factors such as supervisory control and organizational support were proven to have positive effect on knowledge sharing (King and Mark 2008). This finding was also supported by Monica et al. (2009) who confirmed that there is significant role of support team culture in moderating the relationship of knowledge sharing and service innovation performance.

Knowledge creation. Any business that exists in today's competitive and fast-growing economy needs to have a solid knowledge management and knowledge creation setup in the organization as it is substantial in creating the competitive advantage among the players in any industry and also helps in creating opportunity in setting up one's blue ocean strategy in eliminating competition. Kianto et al. (2016) define knowledge creation as the organization's ability to encourage the development of proposing new or useful ideas and solutions. This will embrace innovation and creative culture among employees. Implementing knowledge creation will be the backbone for organizations to generate new and innovative ideas thus acknowledging the importance in embracing methods and processes that relates to knowledge creation are a much sorted requirement for today's development of any organization.

Knowledge codification can be classified as knowledge storage activities that consist of codifying the knowledge into explicit form and also at the same time provide the updated documented version of the knowledge for the organization (Filius et al. 2000). It can be said that it is the process of converting undocumented information into documented documentation. Knowledge codification will help the organization more on knowledge accessibility, visibility and also can be useable for the decision-making process.

As shown in previous study, knowledge codification is one of the factors related to employee's well-being in the organization. Knowledge codification has improved innovative behavior among employees and has positive effect on the employee's well-being (Sohrabi et al. 2015). Rocha et al. (2015) added that knowledge consolidation is one of the factors that indirectly influenced organizational changes such as employee's well-being.

Knowledge retention has been highlighted in numerous management papers as a strategy to enhance firms' knowledge management. Cepeda and Vera (2007) have elaborated in detail the four stages of knowledge evolution cycle; generative variation, internal selection, replication and retention. At the knowledge retention stage, the changes of knowledge which adapted in replication stage (through knowledge codification) theoretically turn into routines and absorbed into human behavior.

Furthermore, Riege (2005) has explained in his study how the non-retained tacit knowledge could negatively affect the organization when an employee is absent for a long period of time or resigned. Therefore, this knowledge is crucial and needs to be persistently retained in a repository of the organization as a knowledge management practices (Sánchez and Morrison-Saunders 2011).

Following to that, Martins and Martins (2012) have identified nine key factors those influencing knowledge retention which include: knowledge behavior, strategy

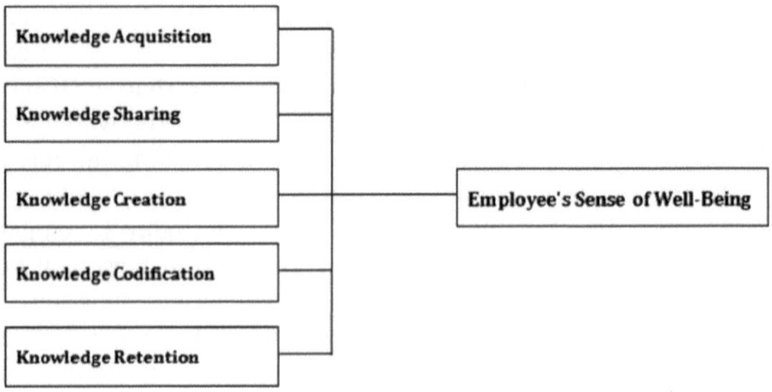

Fig. 34.1 Conceptual framework of the study

implementation and values, leadership, people knowledge loss risks, knowledge attitudes and emotions, power play, knowledge growth and development, performance management and organizational support and encouragement. This is parallel to another further research by Aggestam et al. (2014), who have proven that critical success factor of knowledge retention comprises the willingness of employees to contribute, the availability of work processes and IT systems and as well as the organizational knowledge itself.

Based on prior studies and findings in the literature, the current study developed a conceptual research framework with the purpose of examining the impact of KM practices on employee's sense of well-being. The framework between the variables is illustrated in Fig. 34.1.

34.3 Methodology

34.3.1 Research Design and Instrument

A primary data are originated for specific purpose of addressing the problem at hand. For this study, it mainly used primary data to obtain an accurate information. A set of questionnaire is used and distributed to the respondents to gather data, information and feedback from them. Questions are divided into three sections which consist of demographic information (Section A), five measures of knowledge management practices (Section B) and measurement scale for employee's sense of well-being (Section C). The five KM practices questions are adopted from Kianto et al. (2016) and in accordance with Chumg et al. (2015) employee's sense of well-being questions are adopted from Oxford Happiness Questionnaire Short-Form (OHQ) that developed by Hills and Argyle (2002). Questions which are adopted from previous study are designed using mixed positively and negatively worded statement. The construct of questionnaires is based on Category scale and

Table 34.1 Measurement of study variables

Construct	No. of items	Source
Knowledge acquisition	2	Kianto et al. (2016)
Knowledge sharing	7	Kianto et al. (2016)
Knowledge creation	8	Kianto et al. (2016)
Knowledge codification	5	Kianto et al. (2016)
Knowledge retention	3	Kianto et al. (2016)
Employee's sense of well-being	8	Chumg et al. (2015)

Likert scale (1 = strongly disagree, 5 = strongly agree). Table below illustrates the measurement of study variables (Table 34.1).

34.3.2 Sampling Design

The population of this study consists of employees from private education industry. Total of 45 private universities and university colleges located in Klang Valley are selected using the area sampling as the sampling technique. Respondents consist of employees from different departments or functional sectors of the organization.

34.3.3 Data Analysis

Data are analyzed using the Statistical Package for Social Science (SPSS) Version 24.0. The procedure used to analyze the response includes the determination of the reliability of the instrument, the descriptive statistics and correlation. Cronbach's alpha is used to test the scale of reliability. It is a reliability coefficient that indicates how well the items in a set are positively correlated with one another. The reliability of a measure is an indication of the stability and consistency with which the instrument measures the concept and helps in assessing the goodness of a measure. For this analysis, the coefficient of correlation must be determined to measure the relative strength of a linear relationship between two variables. The coefficient of correlation will have value that fits into a range from −1 which indicates perfect negative correlation to +1 which indicates a perfect positive correlation. In the case of perfect positive or perfect negative correlation, all points would be connected when plotted in a scatter plot (Levine et al. 2011). This indicates that the existence of a relationship is tested. Extra analysis to determine the cause of the strong relationship if it occurs is to be performed to add richness on the findings.

34.4 Conclusion

This study extends the research on knowledge management practices by examining the KM practices impact toward employee's sense of well-being at workplace. The presence of knowledge management practices in the organization will benefit both the employees and employers. The concept of well-being concerns with individual's perspectives of their life experience, individual's satisfaction and emotional characteristics. Thus, it is important to develop a positive sense of well-being among employees by implementing the five KM practices. Andreeva and Kianto (2012) emphasized that KM practices are an important driver of value creation, organizational success and competitiveness. Employees may gain benefits from having high positive aspects of well-being when they are engaged with effective organization's practices of KM activities. This in turn will improve the organizational productivity and performance. Overall, KM practices and employee's sense of well-being at work are crucial in any organization and managers should incorporate KM practices as a priority to improve employee's sense of well-being at work.

References

Aggestam, L., Durst, S., & Persson, A. (2014). Critical success factors in capturing knowledge for retention in IT-supported repositories. *Information, 5*(4), 558–569.

Aggestam, L. (2015). Learning organization or knowledge management—which came first, the chicken or the egg? *Information technology and control, 35*(3).

Andreeva, T., & Kianto, A. (2012). Does knowledge management really matter? Linking knowledge management practices, competitiveness and economic performance. *Journal of Knowledge Management, 16*(4), 617–636.

Ayala, A. P. (2010). Acquisition, representation and management of user knowledge. *Expert Systems with Applications, 37*(3), 2255–2264.

Baptiste, N. R. (2008). The symbiotic relationship between HRM practices and employee well-being: A corporate social responsibility perspective. *The Ashgate Research Companion to Corporate Social Responsibility*.

Bockerman, P., Bryson, A., & Ilmakunnas, P. (2012). Does high involvement management improve worker wellbeing? *Journal of Economic Behavior & Organization, 84*(2), 660–680.

Brunetto, Y., Xerri, M., Shriberg, A., Farr-Wharton, R., Shacklock, K., Newman, S., et al. (2013). The impact of workplace relationships on engagement, well-being, commitment and turnover for nurses in Australia and the USA. *Journal of Advanced Nursing, 69*(12), 2786–2799.

Caesens, G., Stinglhamber, F., & Luypaert, G. (2014). The impact of work engagement and workaholism on well-being. *Career Development International, 19*(7), 813–835.

Cepeda, G., & Vera, D. (2007). Dynamic capabilities and operational capabilities: A knowledge management perspective. *Journal of Business Research, 60*(5), 426–437.

Christensen, P. H. (2003). *Knowledge management: Perspectives and pitfalls*. [Copenhagen?]; Herndon, VA: Copenhagen Business School Press, Books International [distributor].

Chumg, H. F., Cooke, L., Fry, J., & Hung, I. H. (2015). Factors affecting knowledge sharing in the virtual organisation: Employees' sense of well-being as a mediating effect. *Computers in Human Behavior, 44,* 70–80.

Doz, Y. (2006). Knowledge creation, knowledge sharing and organizational structures and processes in MNCs: A commentary on Foss N. "Knowledge and Organization in the theory of the MNC". *Journal of Management and Governance, 10*(1), 29–33.

Dysvik, A., Buch, R., & Kuvaas, B. (2015). Knowledge donating and knowledge collecting: The moderating roles of social and economic LMX. *Leadership & Organization Development Journal, 36*(1), 35–53.

Economou V. K., & Hadjidema S. (2011). Innovative organizational forms that add value to both organizations and community: The case of knowledge management. *European Research Studies, XIV*(2).

Filius, R., De Jong, J. A., & Roelofs, E. C. (2000). Knowledge management in the HRD office: A comparison of three cases. *Journal of Workplace Learning, 12*(7), 286–295.

García-Holgado, A., García-Peñalvo, F. J., Hernández-García, Á., & Llorens-Largo, F. (2015, July). Analysis and improvement of knowledge management processes in organizations using the business process model notation. In *Annual Conference of the Global Innovation and Knowledge Academy* (pp. 93–101). Springer International Publishing.

Grant, A. M., Christianson, M. K., & Price, R. H. (2007). Happiness, health, or relationships? Managerial practices and employee well-being tradeoffs. *The Academy of Management Perspectives, 21*(3), 51–63.

Han, B. M., & Anantatmula, V. S. (2007). Knowledge sharing in large IT organizations: A case study. *VINE, 37*(4), 421–439.

Hills, P., & Argyle, M. (2002). The oxford happiness questionnaire: A compact scale for measurement of psychological well-being. *Personality and Individual Differences, 33*(7), 1073–1082.

Jadin, T., Gnambs, T., & Batinic, B. (2013). Personality traits and knowledge sharing in online communities. *Computers in Human Behavior, 29*(1), 210–216.

Kianto, A., Vanhala, M., & Heilmann, P. (2016). The impact of knowledge management on job satisfaction. *Journal of Knowledge Management, 20*(4), 621–636.

King, W. R., & Marks, P. V. (2008). Motivating knowledge sharing through a knowledge management system. *Omega, 36*(1), 131–146.

Lee, J.-N. (2001). The impact of knowledge sharing, organizational capability and partnership quality on IS outsourcing success. *Information & Management, 38*(5), 323–335.

Levine, D., Stephan, D., Krehbiel, T., & Berenson, M. (2011). *Statistics for Managers Using Microsoft Excel*. New Jersey: Pearson.

Liou, Y. I. (1992). Collaborative knowledge acquisition. *Expert Systems with Applications, 5*(1), 1–13.

Mahesh, K., & Suresh, J. K. (2009). Knowledge criteria for organization design. *Journal of Knowledge Management, 13*(4), 41–51.

Martins, E. C., & Martins, N. (2012). A Model Development Strategy to Determine Factors That Influence Knowledge Retention in Organisations. In *ECRM2012-Proceedings of the 11th European Conference on Research Methods: ECRM 2012* (p. 258). Academic Conferences Limited.

Matzler, K., Renzl, B., Müller, J., Herting, S., & Mooradian, T. A. (2008). Personality traits and knowledge sharing. *Journal of Economic Psychology, 29*(3), 301–313.

Mayo, A. (2001). *The human value of the enterprise, valuing people as assets—monitoring, measuring, managing*. London: Nicholas Brealey Publishing.

Mc Clenahan, C. A., Giles, M. L., & Mallett, J. (2007). The importance of context specificity in work stress research: A test of the Demand-Control-Support model in academics. *Work & Stress, 21,* 85–95.

Monica Hu, M.-L., Horng, J.-S., & Christine Sun, Y.-H. (2009). Hospitality teams: Knowledge sharing and service innovation performance. *Tourism Management, 30*(1), 41–50.

Riege, A. (2005). Three-dozen knowledge-sharing barriers managers must consider. *Journal of knowledge management, 9*(3), 18–35.

Rocha, C. F., Zembo, A. S., Veiga, C. P., Duclós, L. C., Quandt, C. O., & Ferrares, A. A. (2015). Knowledge processes and organizational change: A case study in a non-profit organization. *Australian Journal of Basic and Applied Sciences, 9*(23), 292–303.

Sánchez, L. E., & Morrison-Saunders, A. (2011). Learning about knowledge management for improving environmental impact assessment in a government agency: The Western Australian experience. *Journal of Environmental Management, 92*(9), 2260–2271.

Seligman, M. E. P., Steen, T. A., Park, N., & Petersen, C. (2005). Positive psychology progress: Empirical validation of interventions. *American Psychologist, 60*(5), 410–421.

Shimazu, A., Schaufeli, W. B., Kamiyama, K., & Kawakami, N. (2015). Workaholism vs. work engagement: The two different predictors of future well-being and performance. *International journal of behavioral medicine, 22*(1), 18–23.

Sohrabi, A., Tabatabaei, S. A. H., Hajifarajzadeh, H., & Aqdam, B. G. (2015). The role of knowledge management practices in developing human capital. *International Journal of Economics, Commerce and Management, 3*(5), 573–589.

Wang, S., & Noe, R. A. (2010). Knowledge sharing: A review and directions for future research. *Human Resource Management Review, 20*(2), 115–131.

Winefield, H. R., Boyd, C., & Winefield, A. H. (2014). Work-family conflict and well-being in university employees. *Journal of Psychology, 148*(6), 683–697.

Chapter 35
Leadership Styles and Employee Satisfaction Among Police Officers at Bukit Aman: A Case Study

Narehan Hassan, Izuddin Ab. Wahab, Mazuin Mat Halif, Sharrifah Ali, Rozilah Abdul Aziz and Nur Zainie Abd. Hamid

Abstract This research was conducted to investigate the relationship and the effects of leadership styles towards employee satisfaction among police officers at Bukit Aman, Kuala Lumpur. Data were gathered through questionnaires using convenience sampling. A correlational research design was used. A total of 300 questionnaires were collected and analysed. The findings revealed that there was a positive and significant relationship between leadership styles (Transformational $r = 0.733$, $p < 0.01$ and transactional $r = 0.744$, $p < 0.01$). Elements under transformational leadership styles (idealized influence, intellectual stimulation, inspirational motivation and individual consideration) were also tested using multiple regression analysis against employee satisfaction. It was found that inspirational motivation was the most influential factor towards employee satisfaction ($\beta = 0.336$, $p < 0.01$). Similarly, elements under transactional leadership (contingent reward, passive avoidant and management-by-exception) were tested against job satisfaction and it was found that contingent reward predicted employee job satisfaction ($\beta = 0.443$, $p < 0.01$). It is therefore recommended that the leaders in

N. Hassan (✉) · S. Ali · R. Abdul Aziz · N.Z. Abd. Hamid
Faculty of Business Management, Universiti Teknologi MARA,
Puncak Alam, Malaysia
e-mail: drnarehan@puncakalam.uitm.edu.my

S. Ali
e-mail: sharrifah@puncakalam.uitm.edu.my

R. Abdul Aziz
e-mail: rozilah@puncakalam.uitm.edu.my

N.Z. Abd. Hamid
e-mail: nurzainie60@puncakalam.uitm.edu.my

I. Ab. Wahab
Royal Malaysian Police, Bukit Aman, Kuala Lumpur, Malaysia
e-mail: joetiefa@gmail.com

M. Mat Halif
Faculty of Business Management, Universiti Teknologi MARA, Machang
Kelantan, Malaysia
e-mail: mazui208@kelantan.uitm.edu.my

F. Noordin et al. (eds.), *Proceedings of the 2nd Advances in Business Research International Conference*, https://doi.org/10.1007/978-981-10-6053-3_35

Royal Malaysian Police (RMP) should provide some types of inspiration and reward their subordinates the moment when the job was completed satisfactorily in order to produce a blissful workforce. The approach will minimize stressful working conditions and promote better interaction and interdependency among police officers.

Keywords Transformational leadership · Transactional leadership · Employee satisfaction · Royal Malaysian Police

35.1 Introduction

At every level of management, the role of employees and a leader are interchangeable. Researchers found that variety of styles of leadership can influence the effectiveness of an organization in terms of loyalty, satisfaction and commitment among the followers and stakeholders—internal and external to the organization (Bass 2008; Bass and Riggio 2006; Scott and Davis 2007). Bass (2008) mentioned that the success of an organization has always influenced by its leaders.

As an organization in upholding the Rule of Law, the Royal Malaysian Police has two vital conjunctions to its wide range of responsibilities. The first is to be responsible in ensuring in the implementation of rules and regulations provided by the Rule of Law in this country, and secondly, its obligation towards the expectation of the nation. The guidelines for this purpose are outlined in Section 3 (3) of the Police Act, 1967 (Act 344), which states:

The Force shall subject to this Act be employed in and throughout Malaysia (including the territorial waters thereof) for the maintenance of law and order, the preservation of the peace and security of Malaysia, the prevention and detection of crime, the apprehension and prosecution of offenders and the collection of security intelligence (p. 3)

In addition to this act, the duties and responsibilities of the police are further outlined which stated "Without prejudice to the generality of the foregoing provisions or any other law, it shall be the duty of a police officer to carry out … lawful acts necessary in connection therewith, including apprehending all persons whom he is by law authorized to apprehend, processing security intelligence, conducting prosecutions, giving assistance…" (p. 3). The long and endless duties of police officers can sometimes be very trying, stressful and dangerous. Under these circumstances, it is vital that leaders in that force provide the necessary platform for the officers to conduct their duties to the public. According to Metcalfe and Dick (2000), the police force is a unique public service entity that demands on high levels of employee dedication and commitment.

Managers and their leadership styles play an important role to achieve the organization's goals. Mosadeghrad (2003) defined leadership styles as a combination of characteristics, attitudes and skills used by a manager to deal with many situations according different people and values of the organization. Managers are adopting many types of styles in many types of situations involving many types of subordinates to motivate them to reach their full potentials in performing their tasks. Studies conducted to examine the leadership styles impact on the outcome of the organization (Kreitner and Kinicki 2008) and found that a single leadership style may not be applicable for every situation. A leader may be successful in some situation but may fail in different situations using the same leadership style (Mosad and Yarmohammadian 2006).

On the other hand, employee satisfaction is the utmost important element in keeping a workplace jubilant and plays a vital role in every aspect of organizational success. Employee satisfaction can be defined as the degree of employee's level of satisfaction beyond its fulfilment of needs at the workplace (Myskova 2011). A maximum level of employee satisfaction and engagement in an organization will result in a productive workplace (Brammer et al. 2007). Studies found that an organization will achieve as much as 2.6 times of greater customer satisfaction and profit when the level of employee satisfaction is high (Fleming and Asplund 2007).

35.1.1 Research Objectives

The objectives of the study were the following:

1.1.1 To investigate the relationship between leadership styles (transformational and transactional) and employee satisfaction among police officers.

1.1.2 To investigate the components of transformational leadership style (idealized influence, intellectual stimulation, inspirational motivation and individual consideration) and transactional leadership style (contingent reward, passive avoidant and management-by-exception) that predict employee satisfaction among police officers.

35.1.2 Research Questions

In addressing the aforementioned objective, these research questions were formulated:

1.2.1 What are the relationships between leadership styles (transformational, transactional) and employee job satisfaction?

1.2.2 Which constructs in transformational leadership style predict employee satisfaction among police officers?

1.2.3 Which constructs in transactional leadership styles predict employee satisfaction among police officers?

35.1.3 Problem Statement

In 2012, Datuk Seri Najib Tun Abdul Razak, the Prime Minister of Malaysia, announced the Government Transformation Programme (GTP)'s report card which also touched on the crime rate in the country. In the announcement, Najib tabulated on the decrease of crime rate of 27% from the period 2009–2012. However, public outcry on the functions of the police led to work dissatisfaction among the police personnel. They strived to make a more positive perception among the public (Md Izwan 2013). This finding is in line with a study conducted by Acryl (2001) on job satisfaction among police officers at Bukit Aman and found that workload has an inverse relationship with motivation among police officers. This can be interpreted that an officer's motivation decreases if he is working under stress or with heavy workload.

In developing countries such as Malaysia, the society is very responsive towards the effectiveness of government deliveries to the people. The Royal Malaysian Police (RMP) is one of the agencies, which is expected to effectively serve the public and be graciously public-interactive (Ismail Omar 2011). RMP is expected to increase the officers' work efficiency along with good relations with the public. Job satisfaction among police officers is one of the key elements that will bridge the connection with the public at large (Fosam et al. 1998). Researches in law enforcement suggested that the performance of the officers and their interaction with the public were related to job satisfaction of officers (Reiner and Zhao 1999; Judge and Larsen 2001; Lambert et al. 2002). Therefore, the Royal Malaysian Police leadership should aim to increase the employee satisfaction of police officers to fulfil expectations from the public.

Reiner and Zhao (1999) mentioned that a higher-level job satisfaction increases positive styles of officers, such as commitment and job performance, whereas the increase of negative styles such as neglecting work and absenteeism will result in the decrease of job satisfaction. However, the focus of the study was to examine the extent of leadership styles of their immediate supervisors towards job satisfaction. Other elements of employee satisfaction are employee morale/colleague's morale and perceived public view (Fosam et al. 1998). These two are very important elements and were often associated with leadership styles of their immediate superiors.

This study attempted to investigate the relationship between leadership styles and employee satisfaction in the Royal Malaysian Police because there is little or not much study conducted in that area; so it gives the researchers an opportunity to provide more insight into the organization on what leadership styles RMP can adopt to gain full commitment from the subordinates by maximizing employee satisfaction. It is also appropriate to mention that this study was carried out because employee satisfaction is largely dependent upon the leaders and their leadership styles.

35.2 Literature Review

35.2.1 Theories of Leadership Styles

Since 1940s, leadership has been one of the most researched areas in social sciences and remains as one of the most uncertain and least understood topics in that area (Humphreys 2001). In the early leadership research, the traits and qualities of those who led were assessed to determine a common set of traits that were apparent in all leaders. The focus of leadership study at this point of time was of the leaders' behaviour and how were tasks and goals of the organization completed. As the working environment of the leaders changed, the methods of studying leadership have also changed. In the current and a more globalized environment, employees are being treated more as human beings and viewed less as economic resources and the approaches to leadership have also changed with the advancement in technology (Spreitzer et al. 2005; Humphreys 2001).

The researchers decided to apply Bass and Avolio (2008) model of transformational and transactional leadership styles and for employee satisfaction using Fosam et al. (1998) model. Transformational leadership began with the Burn's (1978) formulation of the theories of charismatic and had sparked in an individual difference as the predictors of effective leadership (Bass 1985; Burns 1978; House and Shahmir 1993) as cited by Pounder (2003). In addition, Bass and Avolio (1997) established four dimensions of behaviours that constitute the transformational leadership style, which were idealized influence, intellectual stimulation, inspirational motivation and individual consideration, while three dimensions behaviour of transactional leadership consisted of contingent reward, passive avoidant and management-by-exception.

Employee satisfaction model by Fosam et al. (1998) indicated the dimensions which determined the factors of satisfaction of employees in an organization. Five dimensions were tabulated consisting of job satisfaction, employee morale/colleague morale, perceived public view, perceived service quality and the combination of communication, training, resources and career development. But for this study, the researchers only wanted to measure three dimensions which were job satisfaction, employee morale/colleague morale and perceived public view.

35.2.2 Task and Relationship-Oriented Leadership Styles

According to Mosadeghrad (2003), managers' leadership styles which comprised of managerial attitudes, behaviours and competencies would affect employees' commitment and their efficiency. Kaltreider (1997) emphasized that leaders' abilities and skills would highly affect their subordinates and that the way leaders lead and communicate with subordinates will influence the effect.

The Royal Malaysian Police leadership has to make sure that employee morale and contentment in the force are constantly at highest level to maximize organization's performance and will meet the high expectations of the public (Bass 2008; Scott and Davis 2007). The balance between being task-oriented and relationship-oriented when leading the organizations has to be recognized by the leaders (Ismail et al. 2010). According to Yuki (2010), leadership, organizational effectiveness and employee satisfaction are influenced by both task-oriented and relationship-oriented styles pertinent to the organizations.

There are varieties of theories of leadership in practice. According to Scott (2003, p. 63), leadership can be defined as "a mechanism for influencing the behaviour of individual subordinates". Kouzes and Posner (2007) stated that it is important to recognize leadership as a process of influence which can be practiced by any member of an organization and it does not always refer to the leader.

35.2.2.1 Characteristics of Leaders

Being visionary is one of the most important qualities that a leader must possess. Venugopal (2011) stated that a leader must see more than others, farther than others, before others, as well as helps others see what a leader sees. Spending a great deal of time with the vision is the only way leaders can ever make their vision clear and concise. Poor focus, little coordination and haphazard planning are the results of the lack of vision (Venugopal 2011).

A special bond created by leadership has to be earned. It is essential to clarify values, recognize the wishes of the community and employees, build an agreement, communicate shared values, stand up for beliefs and lead by example in order to build and maintain reliability. A good leader can distinguish between being the boss and bossing. Being a boss means giving employees the resources, training and coaching needed by them and making information available to them so that they can see the mission of their organization.

35.2.3 Transactional and Transformational Leadership Styles

New theories were discovered during the 1970s and 1980s based on the research of leadership as supported by Burns's (1978) pivotal work on leadership (Howell and Avolio 1993; Magliocca and Christakis 2001). Political leadership, according to Burns, can be categorized as transactional or transformational. This classification is based on the interactions between followers and their leaders. The issues of power, collective purpose and change were addressed in this classification (Burns 1978). Burns also formed a moral framework for the follower–leader interaction (Burns 1978; Magliocca and Christakis 2001). Researchers then began studying the relationship between transactional and transformational leadership with the business environment (Bass 1985; Bycio et al. 1995) and service-based industries (Chatman and Jehn 1994). The leader's interaction and activity with his or her employees is what distinguish transformational and transactional leadership styles in a business or service-based industry (Howell and Avolio 1993).

Bass' (1985) and Burns' (1978) work on transformational leadership subsequently resulted in the most literature on leadership style to focus around transactional leadership, contingent rewards, or reinforcement (Bass et al. 2003), until the terms had become interchangeable. Contingent reward is the term used to describe the process of setting job expectations and providing employee rewards for achieving their goals (Bass 1985; Bass et al. 2003). Contractual agreements were used by these leaders to exchange one thing for another (Bass 1985). In order to make certain that employees accomplish their intended duties, rewards are used to motivate and influence employee behaviour (Avolio et al. 1988; Bass 1985; Howell and Avolio 1993; Politis 2001). The transactional leader meets the needs of the employee through dispersal of rewards, believing that the employee makes an effort to fulfil his or her assigned job tasks (Bass 1985, 1997; Bass and Avolio 1993, 1994). In exchange for rewards, which may comprise of compliment, job enrichment and acknowledgement, or the avoidance of disciplinary action, the employee is likely to agree with and accept direction from the leader (Bass et al. 2003). Employees are more concerned with their individual needs than organizational goals (Bass 1985). According to Bass and Avolio (1994), contingent reward leadership is effective because the leader sets clear goals and rewards employees whenever they achieve their goals. The style that is most commonly used in the industry is the transactional style (Dubinsky et al. 1995).

35.2.3.1 General View of Transformational Leadership Styles

On the other extreme, the transformational leader encourages, arouses and inspires the employee to do more than initially expected (Bass 1997; Bass and Avolio 1994; Hater and Bass 1988; House et al. 1991). Charismatic, visionary and new leadership are the terms that have been linked to transformational leadership (Den Hartog et al. 1997). In order to encourage an employee to go beyond the exchange for rewards and make sacrifices to pursue the organization's mission (House et al. 1991), the transformational leader creates a shared vision and purpose (Den Hartog et al. 1997). While employees strive to meet the expectations of their leader, the leaders take a long-range perspective on the needs of their employees (Bass 1985, 1984; Burns 1978; Bycio et al. 1995; Dubinsky et al. 1995). The transformational style which is adopted by the leaders enables them to get their employees to surpass their own needs (Schwartz et al. 2002). Employees of leaders who adopt transformational style tend to be more satisfied with themselves and their jobs (Bass 1999) and exhibit higher performance (Hater and Bass 1988; Howell and Avolio 1993). According to Magliocca and Christakis (2001), transformational leadership facilitates and motivates real change, as opposed to transactional leadership which practiced a simplistic fix-it mentality characteristic approach. With regard to seeking ongoing enhancement in processes, organizations which are bound by tradition and long-standing rules tend to seek a status quo (Bass and Avolio 1997).

However, transformational leadership style appeals more to organizations that seek constant renewal, cultural changes and innovation and that are open to risk-taking (Bass 1985; Howell and Avolio 1993). At the opposite end of the leadership scale, transformational and transactional leadership styles establish separate leadership scopes (Burns 1978; Bycio et al. 1995; Judge and Piccolo 2004; Waldman et al. 1990). Transactional leadership factors were built by transformational leadership style (Avolio and Jung 1999; Bass and Avolio 1993; Judge and Piccolo 2004; Waldman et al. 1990). The base that the transformational leader uses to inspire an employee to employ greater effort and higher levels of performance is moulded by the transactional style (Avolio et al. 1988; Bass 1985; House et al. 1991; Howell and Avolio 1993; Judge and Piccolo 2004); Bass (1985) argued that dependability and trust between the leader and employees that were built by transactional leadership generate the opportunity for the development and use of this style. However, although the transformational leader displays characteristics of transactional leaders, the contrary is not true (Bycio et al. 1995; Den Hartog et al. 1997; Howell and Avolio 1993; Judge and Piccolo 2004). According to Judge and Piccolo (2004), transformational leadership is not attainable without transactional leadership as a base. The important consideration in this study is that traces of transactional styles present in transformational leaders but not the other way around. This may be especially accurate in areas concerning development of employee trust and dependability.

35.2.3.2 General View of Transactional Leadership Styles

As opposed to transformational leadership, transactional leadership style focuses on the communication of job rewards as a result of the successful accomplishment of a job task by an employee (Avolio and Bass 1999; Bass 1985; Burns 1978; Bycio et al. 1995; Dubinsky et al. 1995). Transactional leadership is linked to both contingent reward and active and passive management-by-exception (Avolio and Jung 1999; Bass 1985). Contingent rewards, management-by-exception and passive avoidant are the three factors of this leadership style. Contingent rewards are established when the leader explains what is expected from employee and what they will obtain if they meet the leaders expectations (Bass 1997; Dubinsky et al. 1995; Howell and Avolio 1993; Judge and Piccolo 2004; Kedia et al. 2002). Positive job dedication, satisfaction on the part of the employee (Bycio et al. 1995) and improved organizational citizenship behaviours (Bass et al. 2003) are all linked to contingent rewards. In promoting employee performance, contingent rewards leadership is proven to be effective (Bycio et al. 1995; Judge and Piccolo 2004; Waldman et al. 1990).

Observing errors as well as the level and point of the leader's intervention are the main focus of management-by-exception (Dubinsky et al. 1995; Howell and Avolio 1993). Based upon the level of the leader's monitoring and timing of his or her intervention, management-by-exception can be either active or passive, (Hater and Bass 1988; Howell and Avolio 1993; Judge and Piccolo 2004). A passive avoidant position is opted by the leader who waits for mistakes and deviations to happen before taking corrective actions (Bass 1997; Bass et al. 2003; Dubinsky et al. 1995). Active management on the other hand is an ongoing monitoring for variances and deviations and taking remedial action when necessary (Bass 1985; Bass et al. 2003; Kedia et al. 2002). Based upon the observed variant level of performance or outcome, such leader defines expectations as well as inadequate performance and gives rewards or imposes punishments towards the employee (Bass et al. 2003). Active management-by-exception is a beneficial form of leadership (Avolio et al. 1988). According to Howell and Avolio (1993), employee's satisfaction and performance are negatively related to passive management-by-exception. Evidence suggests that a leader who practices active corrective actions gets higher levels of employee performance than when using passive management-by-exception (Howell and Avolio 1993).

Passive avoidant is a form of non-leadership (Judge and Piccolo 2004). Passive avoidant is an unproductive form of leadership (Den Hartog et al. 1997) and is linked to transactional leadership; it has some connection to passive management-by-exception (Avolio and Jung 1999; Judge and Piccolo 2004). Generally, an employee is dissatisfied with passive avoidant leader because of the leader's lack of trust, communication and participation (Avolio and Jung 1999).

Employee Satisfaction

Employee satisfaction is defined as "a pleasurable or positive emotional state resulting from the appraisal of one's job or job experiences" (Locke 1976, p. 1300). The main focus is on employees' perceptions of the job and how aspects of the job influenced employee satisfaction (Locke 1976) Comm and Mathaisel (2000) stated that employees' needs should be taken into consideration when determining employee satisfaction even though employee satisfaction is difficult to determine..

Employee satisfaction has significant impact in every aspect of an organization. Herzberg et al. (1959) motivation theory highlights on what makes employees feel satisfied or dissatisfied. More productivity may have resulted from employee satisfaction, and it consequently contributes to an organization's success (Saari and Judge 2004). Jackson and Hua (2009) stated that the organization's culture is what influence employee satisfaction.

According to Moyes et al. (2008), how pleased an employee is with his or her position of employment is what makes employee satisfaction. According to Heskett et al. (1994), an improvement in company's performance is resulted from satisfied employees who stimulate a chain of positive actions.

35.2.3.3 Job Satisfaction

Contrary to employee satisfaction, job satisfaction is important for the performance of the organization (Bashir et al. 2011). According to Bodla and Nawaz (2010), attitudes towards pay, working conditions, co-workers and superiors, career prospects and the intrinsic features of the tasks performed are linked to dimensions or sources for job satisfaction.

Brief's (1998) job satisfaction definition, adopted by Whitman et al. (2010), simply described job satisfaction as "an internal state that is expressed by affectively and cognitively evaluating an experienced job with some degree of favour or disfavour" (p. 86). When actions were taken or decisions were made, followers tend to make an effort to gain inclusion and consideration (Eskildensen and Dahlgaard 2000). Organizational effectiveness and performance are the results of the exchange between leader and follower (Lawler and Porter 1967; Mardanov et al. 2008).

Job satisfaction is an emotional response workers have towards their jobs and work places, their benefits, their co-workers and their supervisors (Smith et al. 1969). Employees who devoted to know their job characteristics and produce better service are those who are happy with their jobs. Thus, organizational quality in general can be improved with the contributions of the employees. Overall, it is logical that employees will be extra productive and will involve more in the organizations they work in if they are pleased with their jobs.

35.2.3.4 Employee Morale/Colleague Morale

The first major study with regard to human relations as a critical factor influencing the interactions among employees and his/her organization was initiated and marked by the Hawthorne Studies of assembly workers in 1925. From this study, it can be concluded that the essential factors in production effectiveness and efficiency were the way workers feel about themselves, their co-workers and the organization (Roethlisberger and Dickenson 1947).

Herzberg, Mausner and Synderman conducted another classic study in 1959 relating to employee morale and job satisfaction. The study also discovered several factors that caused employees to feel dissatisfied with their workplace. Most of these dissatisfactions came from the context of which the work is performed; for example, the work environment, the physical surrounding and/or the policies which rule the organization. Holdaway conducted a study in 1978 which examined the relationship between specific components of a career with overall job satisfaction. The findings of the study indicated that achievement, career orientation, positive recognition and stimulation of the work environment were linked to the overall satisfaction.

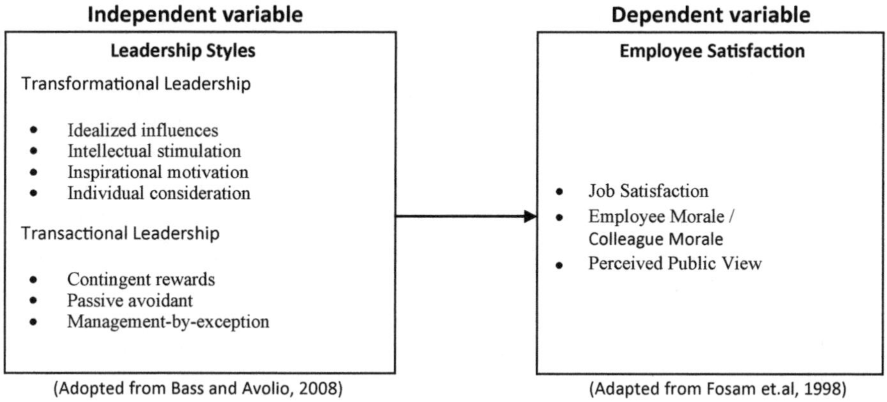

Fig. 35.1 Conceptual framework of the relationship between leadership styles and employee satisfaction

35.2.3.5 Perceived Public View

Lim et al. (2000) conducted a study to investigate the link between law enforcement officers' job satisfaction and how the officers perceived their job image in Singapore. According to Lim et al. (2000), prestige, integrity, competence and a non-routine job nature are the four elements in job image. The findings of the study indicated that job satisfaction of the officers is affected by all dimensions except the prestige dimension. Lim et al. (2000) further stated that the perceived job image of police officers is strongly related to job satisfaction.

Yim and Schafer (2009) conducted a study on how the police force believes they are perceived by the public and how the perceived image affected the officers' job satisfaction. The results revealed that police officers thought that they were perceived less positively by the community. It was also discovered that job satisfaction was significantly related to the officers' perceived image in most non-enforcement situations (Price et al. 2007).

35.2.4 Conceptual Framework

See (Fig. 35.1).

35.3 Research Design

The research design used for this research was correlational research as this study attempted to identify the relationship and effect between leadership styles and employee satisfaction among police officers at Royal Malaysian Police Headquarters, Bukit Aman, Kuala Lumpur.

35.3.1 Population, Sampling Frame and Sample Size

The sampling frame used in this study was obtained from the department of Management, Royal Malaysian Police Headquarters, Bukit Aman, Kuala Lumpur. The population was 26,000. The factors affecting decisions on sample size are the extent of precision desired the acceptable risk in predicting that level of precision, the amount of variability in the population itself, the cost and times constraints and size of the population itself. According to Sekaran and Bougie (2011), the minimum number of sample size is 30 and less than 500 was appropriate for most research. The researchers decided to distribute 320 questionnaires to police officers at the Royal Malaysian Police Headquarters in order to achieve a minimum target of 300 sample size.

35.3.2 Sampling Technique

The sampling technique used for this study was convenience sampling. According to Sekaran and Bougie (2011), convenience sampling is most often used sampling strategy during exploratory phase of a research project and is perhaps the best way of getting information quickly and efficiently.

35.3.3 Instrument

This research used a set of questionnaires as the instrument to collect the data. The questionnaire was designed based on the research questions that were prepared earlier. The questionnaire consisted of several items that were categorized into both the dependent variable and independent variable. The items of demographic background, leadership styles as well as employee satisfaction were adapted to construct the questionnaire.

The instrument designed for this research study was constructed from the combination of three studies to measure the theoretical model of this study. The leadership style instrument was adapted from Bass and Avolio (2008) and measured the elements of two leadership styles comprising of transformational leadership and transactional leadership styles. The elements of transformational leadership were based on the following areas: (1) idealized influences, (2) intellectual stimulation, (3) inspirational motivation and (4) individual consideration. Meanwhile, the elements of transactional leadership are comprised of: (1) contingent rewards (2) passive avoidant and (3) management-by-exception. All of these elements were constructed based on the conceptual framework by Bass and Avolio (2008).

Table 35.1 Cronbach's alpha scores for the leadership styles dimensions and employee satisfaction (n = 300)

Scales	No. of scale items	Reliability coefficient (Alpha) (n = 300)
Leadership Styles		
Transformational leadership		
Idealized influence	9	0.907
Intellectual stimulation	7	0.897
Inspirational motivation	5	0.910
Individual consideration	7	0.889
Transactional leadership		
Contingent rewards	4	0.881
Passive avoidant	4	0.873
Management-by-exception	4	0.845
Employee Satisfaction		
Job satisfaction	7	0.915
Employee morale/colleague morale	7	0.929
Perceived public view	7	0.961

Items of employee satisfaction were adapted from Fosam et al. (1998). It includes the following: (1) job satisfaction (2) employee morale/colleague morale and (3) perceived public view.

35.3.4 Reliability of Instrument

Table 35.1 shows the reliability statistics for both leadership styles and employee satisfaction. Cronbach's alpha for leadership styles which comprised of transformational leadership and transactional leadership was above 0.897. Meanwhile, the Cronbach's alpha for employee satisfaction that comprised of job satisfaction, employee morale/colleague morale and public perceived view was in the range of 0.929. Sekaran and Bougie (2011) reported that an alpha value above 0.8 is categorized as good for reliability measurement.

35.4 Findings

35.4.1 Research Question 1

What are the relationships between leadership styles (transformational, transactional) and employee job satisfaction?

The results of the Pearson correlation analysis indicated that there was a positive, strong and significant relationship between overall transformational leadership style and employee satisfaction ($r = 0.793$, $p < 0.01$). The finding is consistent with Hater and Bass (1988) who reported that they found a positive relationship between transformational leadership and employee job satisfaction. Further, it was also found that there was a positive, significant and strong relationship between transactional leadership style and employee satisfaction ($r = 0.744$, $p < 0.01$). The finding is in conformity with the findings of Bass (2010) who found a positive relationship between transactional leadership and employee satisfaction.

35.4.2 Research Question 2

Which constructs in transformational leadership style predict employee satisfaction among police officers?

The elements of transformational leadership style which are idealized influence, intellectual stimulation, inspirational motivation and individual consideration were found to have a significant influence on employee satisfaction. As depicted in Table 35.2, the most influential element was inspirational motivation ($\beta = 0.336$, $p < 0.01$) followed by idealized influence and individual consideration ($\beta = 0.212$, $p < 0.05$ and $\beta = 0.143$, $p < 0.05$), respectively. However, intellectual stimulation did not predict employee satisfaction among police officers ($\beta = 0.113$, $p > 0.05$). In conclusion, inspirational motivation becomes the main predictor for employee satisfaction among police officers at Royal Malaysian Police Headquarters, Bukit Aman, Kuala Lumpur.

35.4.3 Research Question 3

To what extent do the elements in transactional leadership style predict employee satisfaction among police officers at Royal Malaysian Police Headquarters, Bukit Aman, Kuala Lumpur?

Table 35.3 shows the result of multiple regression analysis between elements of transactional leadership style and employee satisfaction. Based on the table below, transactional leadership style explained 62.3% of the variance (R-square) in

Table 35.2 Correlation between leadership style and employee satisfaction (n = 300)

Variables	Mean	SD	1	2	3
Transformational leadership style	3.75	0.69	0.793**		
Transactional leadership style	3.62	0.69		0.744**	
Employee satisfaction	3.82	0.73			1

**Correlation is significant at the 0.01 level (2-tailed)

Table 35.3 Multiple regression analysis between transformational leadership style and employee satisfaction (n = 300)

Model	Standardized coefficient (Beta)	T	Sig.
Mean idealized influence	0.212	2.939	0.004
Mean intellectual stimulation	0.113	1.459	0.146
Mean inspirational motivation	0.336	4.509	0.000
Mean individual consideration	0.143	1.982	0.048
R^2	0.543		
Adjusted R^2	0.536		
R^2 change	0.543		
F change	87.462		
Significance F change	0.000		
Durbin–Watson value	1.763		

Table 35.4 Multiple regression analysis between transactional leadership style and employee loyalty (n = 300)

Model	Standardized coefficient (Beta)	T	Sig.
Mean contingent rewards	0.443	8.520	0.000
Mean passive avoidant	0.048	1.122	0.263
Mean management-by-exception	0.378	6.778	0.000
R^2	0.623		
Adjusted R^2	0.619		
R^2 change	0.623		
F change	163.059		
Significance F change	0.000		
Durbin–Watson value	1.631		

Summary of regression between leadership styles and employee satisfaction among police officers at Royal Malaysian Police Headquarters, Bukit Aman, Kuala Lumpur

employee satisfaction which was highly significant, as indicated by the F-value of 163.059 ($p < 0.05$). The Durbin–Watson value stated about 1.631 which showed there was a correlation between transformational leadership style and employee satisfaction. This indicates that elements of transactional leadership style influenced employee satisfaction.

In order to identify which transactional leadership style is most influential on employee satisfaction, beta values under Standardized Coefficients were observed and compared. As depicted in Table 35.4, it was observed that contingent rewards has the highest significant influence on employee satisfaction with $\beta = 0.443$, $p < 0.05$. In addition, management-by-exception also had a significant influence on employee satisfaction ($\beta = 0.378$, $p < 0.05$). Meanwhile, passive avoidant did not have a significant influence on employee satisfaction ($\beta = 0.048$, $p > 0.05$).

In answering research questions 2 and 3 which were to investigate which elements in the transformational leadership and transactional leadership styles predicted employee satisfaction among police officers, multiple regression analysis was used.

Based on Table 35.2, it can be concluded that inspirational motivation had the highest significant influence on employee satisfaction ($\beta = 0.336$, $p < 0.05$). In addition, idealized influence and individual consideration both had a significant influence on employee satisfaction ($\beta = 0.212$, $p < 0.05$ and $\beta = 0.143$, $p < 0.05$), respectively.

In order to identify which transactional leadership style is the most influential on employee satisfaction, it can be concluded that contingent rewards predicted employee satisfaction ($\beta = 0.443$, $p < 0.05$) as depicted in Table 35.3. In addition, management-by-exception also had a significant influence on employee satisfaction ($\beta = 0.378$, $p < 0.05$).

35.5 Conclusion and Recommendations for Royal Malaysian Police

In this research, two kinds of leadership styles were investigated: the transformational and transactional leadership styles. There are some recommendations for Royal Malaysian Police in order to enhance the organization's top leadership styles and to fulfil employee satisfaction. Based on the results of employee satisfaction among police officers at Royal Malaysian Police Headquarters, Bukit Aman, Kuala Lumpur, it was found that in transformational leadership styles, inspirational motivation has the highest significant influence on employee satisfaction. In addition, idealized influence and individual consideration also have a significant influence on employee.

Since inspirational motivation was found to be the most influential factor among police officers, the leadership at Royal Malaysian Police should concentrate in developing effective strategies to enhance the level of employee satisfaction among their officers through inspiring them. Inspirational leaders lift the officers under their supervision to attain organizational goals and raise their expectations (Bass 1984; Bass and Avolio 1994; Dubinsky et al. 1995). Emotional response from the officers is what primarily inspires this leadership (Bass 1984). The leaders should frequently and sincerely recognize and praise their officers' contribution to the achievements of the police force.

Bass and Avolio's (1994) definition of the idealized or charismatic style factor is respect, trust and admiration of the employees for their leader. As described by Bass and Avolio (1994), idealized style factor observes the nature of an employee's response to the leader and his or her manners. The Royal Malaysian Police leaders should emphasize more on what inspire their officers, making their needs met over the leaders' needs. The leader also should impart pride in their fellow officers so that they will embrace a vision, mission and the demonstration of consistent values and ethics shown by the idealized leader (Bass and Avolio 1994; Bass et al. 2003;

House et al. 1991). This type of leader is the most suitable leader to enable shifts in organizational culture, lead an organization in crisis (Bass 1985, 1998) and introduce major change (Waldman et al. 1990). According to Bass (1985), idealized leaders are most prized in innovative and flexible organizations where teamwork and a dedicated workforce are required.

The degree to which the leader cares about the needs and concerns of the employee is what defined individualized consideration (Bass 1985; Bass and Avolio 1994). Each officer's developmental needs should be considered by Royal Malaysian Police leadership. When the leader deals discretely and on one to one basis with his/her supervised officers, it will encourage a two-way dialogue; and that individualized consideration can be practiced more effectively (Bass 1985; Bass and Avolio 1994; Hater and Bass 1988). The police officers' self-image, personal fulfilment and learning capability can be improved when Royal Malaysian Police leadership develops a strong exchange with the officers.

In transactional leadership style, it was found that contingent rewards have the highest significant influence on employee satisfaction followed by management-by-exception. Contingent rewards are established when the Royal Malaysian Police leaders explain what is expected from their officers and what they will obtain if they meet the leaders expectations. Positive job dedication, satisfaction on the part of the officers and improved organizational citizenship behaviours are all linked to contingent rewards. In promoting employee performance, contingent rewards leadership is proven to be effective (Bycio et al. 1995; Judge and Piccolo 2004; Waldman et al. 1990). So the Royal Malaysian Police leaders have to monitor the key performance index by their officers and make sure all the criticisms given are not meant to be a form of punishment but more on coaching and taking remedial action.

In essence, RMP should have more leaders who inspire and reward the employees through praise, encouragement and by inviting them to make uniform or collective decisions. It is tough for an organization that places autocratic style to follow this, but, given time, inspiring followers can be achieved.

Acknowledgements The researchers wish to acknowledge Research Management Center, UiTM and the Faculty of Business Management UiTM for funding this study.

References

Avolio, B. J., & Jung, D. I. (1999). Effects of leadership style and followers' cultural orientation on performance in group and individual task conditions. *Academy of Management Journal, 42*(2), 208–219.

Avolio, B. J., Waldman, D. A., & Einstein, W. O. (1988). Transformational leadership in a management game simulation. *Group and Organizational Studies, 13*(1), 59–80.

Bashir, M., Jianquio, L., Jun, Z., Ghazanfar, F., & Khan, M. M. (2011). The role of demographic factors in the relationship between high performance work systemand job satisfaction: A multidimensional approach. *International Journal of Business and Social Science, 2*(18), 207–218.

Bass, B. M. (1984). *Leadership and performance beyond expectations*. New York: Free Press.

Bass, B. M. (1985). *Leadership and performance beyond expectations*. New York: Free Press.
Bass, B. M. (1997). Personal selling and transactional/transformational leadership. *The Journal of Personal Setting and Sales Management, 17*(3), 19–29.
Bass, B. M. (1998). *Transformational leadership: Industry, military, and educational impact*. Mahwah, NJ: Lawrence Erlbaum Associates Publishers.
Bass, B. M. (1999). Two decades of research and development in transformational leadership. *European Journal of Work and Organizational psychology, 8*(1), 9–32.
Bass, B. M. (2008). *The bass handbook of leadership: Theory, research, and managerial applications* (4th ed.). New York, NY: Free Press.
Bass, B. M. (2010). Two Decades of Research and Development in Transformational Leadership. *European Journal of Work and Organizational Psychology, 8*(1), 9–32.
Bass, B. M., & Avolio, B. J. (1993). Transformational leadership and organizational culture. *Public Administration Quarterly, 17*(1), 112–121.
Bass, B. M., & Avolio, B. J. (1994). Shatter the glass ceiling: Women may make better managers. *Human Resources Management, 33*(4), 549–561.
Bass, B. M., & Avolio, B. J. (1997). *Full range leadership development: Manual for the multifactor leadership questionnaire*. Redwood City, CA: Mind Garden.
Bass, B. M., & Avolio, B. J. (2008). *Manual for the Multifactor Leadership Questionnaire, Manual and Sampler Set* (3rd ed.). Menlo Park, CA: Mind Garden Inc.
Bass, B. M., Avolio, B. J., Jung, D. I., & Berson, Y. (2003). Predicting unit performance by assessing transformational and transactional leadership. *Journal of Applied Psychology, 88*(2), 207–218.
Bass, B. M., & Riggio, R. E. (2006). *Transformational leadership* (2nd ed.). Mahwah, NJ: Lawrence Erlbaum Associates Inc.
Bodla, M. A., & Nawaz, M. M. (2010). Transformational leadership style and its relationship with satisfaction. *Interdisciplinary Journal of Contemporary Research in Business, 2*(1), 370–381.
Brammer, S., Millington, A., & Rayton, B. (2007). The contribution of corporate social responsibility to organizational commitment. *International Journal of Human Resource Management, 18*(10), 1701–1719.
Burns, J. M. (1978). *Leadership*. New York: Harper and Row.
Brief, A. P. (1998). *Attitudes in and around organizations*. Thousand Oaks, CA: Sage.
Bycio, P., Allen, J. S., & Hackett, R. D. (1995). Further analysis of Bass's (1985) conceptualization of transactional and transformational leadership. *Journal of Applied Psychology, 80*(4), 468–478.
Chatman, J. A., & Jehn, K. A. (1994). Assessing the relationship between industry characteristics and organizational culture: How different can you be? *Academy of Management Journal, 37*(3), 522–553.
Comm, C. L., & Mathaisel, D. F. X. (2000). Assessing employee satisfaction in service firms: An example in higher education. *Journal of Business and EconomicStudies, 6*(1), 43–53.
Den Hartog, D. N., Muijen, J. J., & Koopman, P. L. (1997). Transactional versus transformational leadership: An analysis of the MLQ. *Journal of Occupational and Organizational Psychology, 70*(1), 19–35.
Dubinsky, A. J., Yammarino, F. J., Jolson, A. S., & Spangler, W. D. (1995). Transformational leadership: An initial investigation in sales. *The Journal of Personal Selling and Sales Management, 15*(2), 17–32.
Eskildsen, J. K., & Dahlgaard, J. J. (2000). A casual model for employee satisfaction. *Total Quality Management, 11*(8), 1081–1094.
Fleming, J. H. & Asplund, J. (2007). Human sigma: Managing the employee-customer encounter. *Gallup Press.*
Fosam, E. B., Grimsley, M. F. J., & Wisher, S. J. (1998). Exploring models for employee satisfaction; with particular reference to a police force. *Total Quality Management*, *9*(2, 3) 235–247.

Hater, J. J., & Bass, M. B. (1988). Supervisors evaluations and subordinates perceptions of transformational and transactional leadership. *Journal of Applied Psychology, 73*(4), 695–702.

Herzberg, F., Mausner, B., & Synderman, B. (1959). *The Motivation to Work*. New York: Wiley.

Heskett, J. L., Jones, T. O., Loveman, G. W., Sasser, W. E. Jr., & Schlesinger, L. A. (1994). Putting the service-profit chain to work. *Harvard Business Review 72*(2).

Holdaway, E. A. (1978). Facet and Overall Satisfaction of Teachers. *Educational Administration Quarterly, 14,* 30–47.

House, R. J., & Shahmir, B. (1993). Toward the integration of transformational, charismatic, and visionary theories. In M. M. Chemers & R. Ayman (Eds.), *Leadership theory and research: Perspectives and directions* (pp. 81–107). San Diego: Academic Press.

House, R. J., Spangler, W. D., & Woycke, J. (1991). Personality and charisma in the U.S. Presidency: A psychological theory of leader effectiveness. *Administrative Science Quarterly, 36*(3), 364–396.

Howell, J. M., & Avolio, B. J. (1993). Transformational leadership, transactional leadership, locus of control, and support for innovation: Key predictors of consolidated-business-unit performance. *Journal of lied Psychology, 78*(6), 891–902.

Humphreys, J. H. (2001). Transformational and transactional leader styles: The relationship with support for e-commerce and emerging technology. *Journal of Management Research, 1*(3), 149–159.

Ismail Omar (2011, April). Cabaran Kepolisan Moden. *Harian Metro Online*. Retrieve from http;// www.hmetro.com.my/myMetro/articles/Kepolisanmoden/Article/index_html.

Ismail, A., Zainuddin, N. F. A., & Ibrahim, Z. (2010). Linking participative and consultative leadership styles to organizational commitment as an antecedent of job satisfaction. *UNITAR e-Journal, 6*(1), 11–26.

Jackson, L. A., & Hua, N. (2009). Corporate social responsibility and financial performance: A snapshot from the lodging and gaming industries. *Journal of Hospitality Financial Management, 17*(1).

Judge, T. A., & Piccolo, R. F. (2004). Transformational and transactional leadership: A meta-analytic test of their relative validity. *Journal of Applied Psychology, 89*(5), 755–768.

Judge, T. A., & Larsen, R. J. (2001). Dispositional affect and job satisfaction: A review and theorical extension. *Organizational Styles and Human Decision Processes, 86,* 67–98.

Kaltreider, N. (1997). *Dilemmas of a double life: Women balancing careers and relationships*. Northvale, JN: Jason Aronson Inc.

Kedia, B. L., Nordtvedt, R., & Perez, L. M. (2002). International business strategies, decision-making theories, and leadership styles: An Integrated Framework. *Competitiveness Review, 12*(1), 28–52.

Kouzes, J. M., & Posner, B. Z. (2007). *The leadership challenge* (4th ed.). San Francisco, CA: Wiley.

Kreitner, R., & Kinicki, A. (2008). *Organizational Styles* (6th ed.) New York: McGraw-Hill.

Lambert, E., Hogan, N., & Barton, S. (2002). Satisfied correctional staff: A review of the literature on the antecedents and consequences of correctional staff job satisfaction. *Criminal Justice and Styles, 29*(2), 115–143.

Lawler, E. E., III, & Porter, L. W. (1967). The effect of performance on job satisfaction. *Industrial Relations: A Journal of Economy and Society, 7*(1), 20–28.

Lim, V. K., Teo, S. H., & See, S. K. (2000). Perceived job image among police officers in Singapore: factorial dimensions and differential effects. *Journal of Social Psychology, 140*(6), 740–750.

Locke, E. A. (1976). The nature and consequences of job satisfaction. In M. D. Dunnette (Ed.), *Handbook of industrial organizational psychology* (pp. 1297–1349). Chicago, IL: Rand McNally.

Magliocca, L. A., & Christakis, A. N. (2001). Creating transforming leadership for organizational change: The cogniscope system approach. *Systems Research and Behavioral Science, 18*(3), 259–277.

Mardanov, I. T., Heischmidt, K., & Henson, A. (2008). Leader-member exchange and job satisfaction bond and predicted employee turnover. *Journal of Leadership and Organizational Studies, 15*(2), 159–175.

Md. Izwan (2013, June) Najib: Public fear of crime needs tackling despite GTP successes. *The Malaysian Insider.* Retrieve from http://www.themalaysianinsider.com/malaysia/article/najib-public-fear-of-crime-needs-tackling-despite-gtp-successes.

Meltcalfe, B., & Dick, G. (2000). Is the force still with you? Measuring police commitment. *Journal of Managerial Psychology, 15,* 812–832.

Mosadegh, R. A., & Yarmohammadian, M. (2006). A study of relationship between managers' leadership style and employees' job satisfaction. *Journal of Leadership in Health Services, 19*(2), 11–28.

Mosadeghrad, A. M. (2003). *Principles of Health Care Administration.* Tehran: Dibagran Tehran.

Moyes, G. D., Shao, L. P., & Newsome, M. (2008). Comparative analysis of employee job satisfaction in the accounting profession. *Journal of Business and Economics Research, 6*(2), 65–81.

Myskova, R. (2011). A new measure of employee satisfaction. *Global Journal of Business Research, 5*(1), 101–110.

Police Act 1967 (Act 344) and Regulations, *International Law Book Services,* Wisma ILBS, No 10, Jalan PJU 8/5G, Perdana Business Centre, Bandar Damansara Perdana, 47820, Petaling Jaya. 3, 10–11.

Politis, J. D. (2001). The relationship of various leadership styles to knowledge management. *Leadership and Organizational Development Journal, 22*(7/8), 354–365.

Pounder, J. S. (2003). Employing transformational leadership to enhance the quality of management development instruction. *Journal of Management Development, 22*(1), 6–13.

Price, W. H., Kiekbusch, R., & Thesis, J. (2007). Causes of employee turnover in sheriff operated jails. *Public Personnel Management, 36*(1), 51–63.

Reiner, M. D., & Zhao, J. (1999). The determinants of job satisfaction among United States Air Force Security Police: A test of rival theoretical predictive models. *Review of Public Personnel Administration, 14*(3), 5–18.

Roethlisberger, F., & Dickenson, W. (1947). *Management and the Worker.* Cambridge, MA: Harvard University Press.

Saari, L. M., & Judge, T. A. (2004). Employee attitudes and job satisfaction. *Human Resource Management, 43*(4), 295–407.

Sani, A., & Sani, A. (2001). Tahap Komitmen Terhadap Organisasi: Satu Kajian Kes Di Kalangan Anggota-anggota Polis Pangkat Rendah, Kontingen Polis Kuala Lumpur. *Thesis M.Sc. (Management)*, Universiti Utara Malaysia.

Schwartz, R. W., Tumblin, T. F., & Peskin, G. W. (2002). The power of servant leadership to transform health care organizations for the 21st century economy—invited critique. *Archives of Surgery, 137*(12), 1419–1433.

Scott, W. R., & Davis, G. F. (2007). *Organizations and organizing: Rational, natural, and open system perspectives.* Upper Saddle River, NJ: Pearson Prentice Hall.

Scott, W. R. (2003). *Organizations: Rational, natural and open systems (5th ed.).* Upper Saddle River, NJ: Prentice Hall.

Sekaran, U. & Bougie, R. (2011). *Research methods of business: A skill-building approach*, 5th ed. New York: Wiley, Inc.

Smith, P. C., Kendall, L. M., & Hulin, C. L. (1969). *The measurement of satisfaction in work and retirement.* Chicago, IL: Rand-McNally.

Spreitzer, G. M., Perttula, K. H., & Xin, K. (2005). Traditionality matters: An examination of the effectiveness of transformational leadership in the United States and Taiwan. *Journal of Organizational Behavior, 26*(3), 205–227.

Venugopal, N. (2011). *The Influence of Leadership Styles/Styles and Competencies Towards the Job Satisfaction of Employees in The Royal Malaysia Police.* M.Sc thesis (Management), Universiti Utara Malaysia.

Waldman, D. A., Bass, B. M., & Yammarino, F. J. (1990). Adding to contingent-reward behavior: The augmenting effects of charismatic leadership. *Group and Organizational Studies, 15*(4), 381–394.

Whitman, D. S., Van Roddy, D. L., & Viswesvaran, C. (2010). Satisfaction, citizenship styless, and performance in work units: A meta-analysis of collective construct relations. *Personnel Psychology, 63*(1), 41–81.

Yim, Y., & Schafer, B. D. (2009). Police and their perceived image: How community influence officers' job satisfaction. *Police Practice and Research, 10*(1), 17–29.

Yuki, G. (2010). Leadership in organizations (6th ed.). Upper Saddle River, NJ: Pearson Prentice Hall.

MIX
Papier aus verantwortungsvollen Quellen
Paper from responsible sources
FSC® C105338

If you have any concerns about our products,
you can contact us on
ProductSafety@springernature.com

In case Publisher is established outside the EU,
the EU authorized representative is:
Springer Nature Customer Service Center GmbH
Europaplatz 3, 69115 Heidelberg, Germany

Printed by Libri Plureos GmbH
in Hamburg, Germany